pilgrims were people glad to take off their clothing, which was on fire

— anne carson

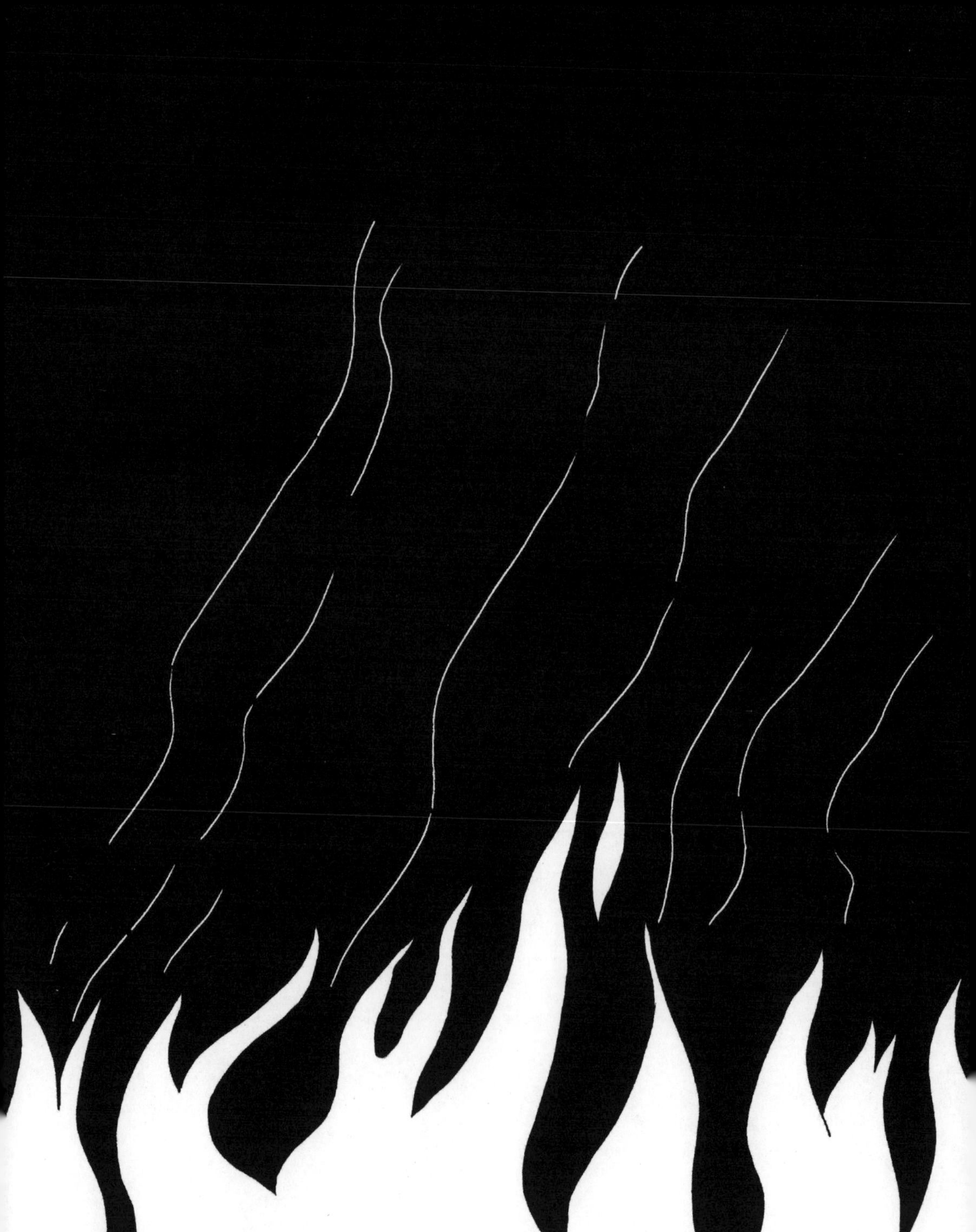

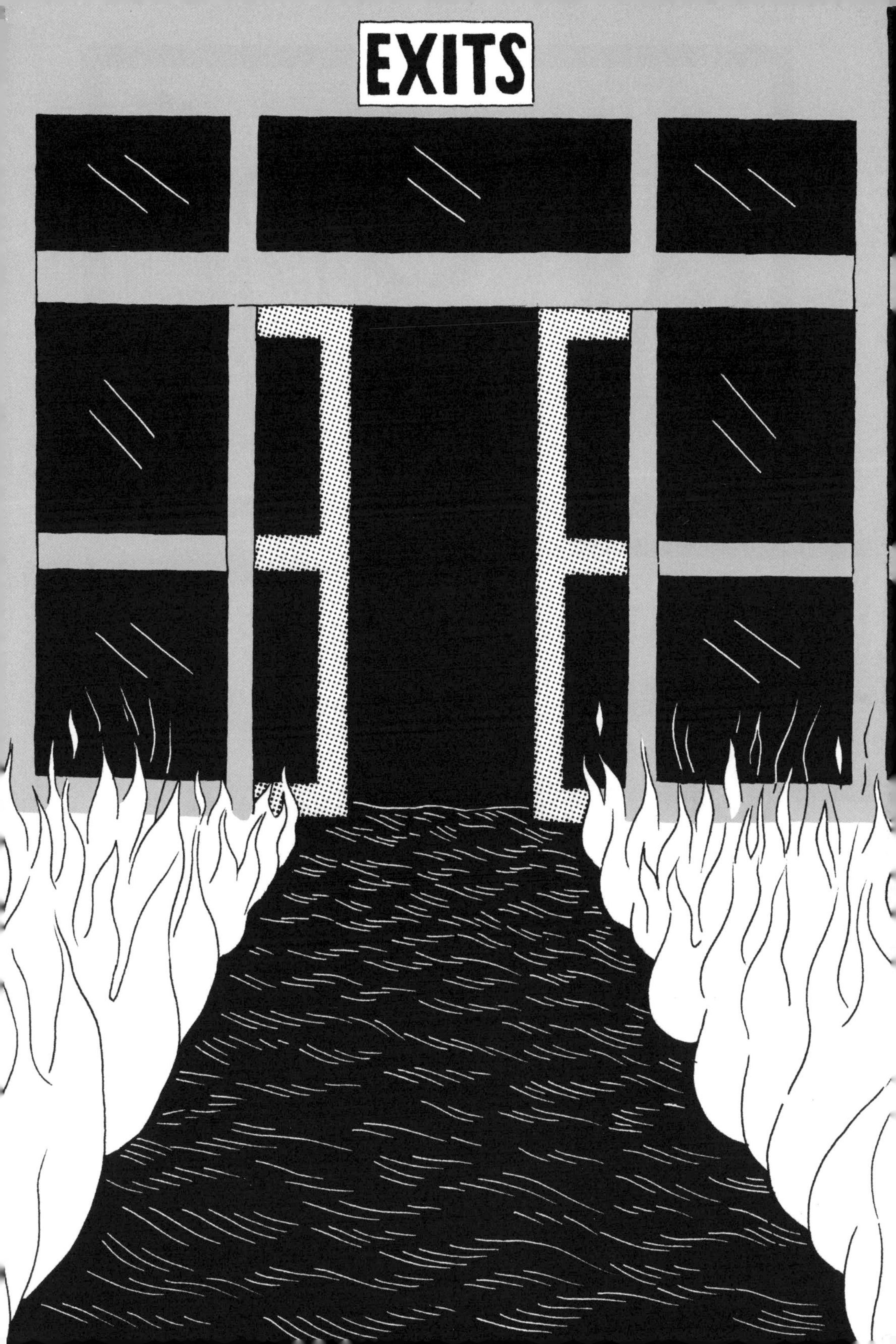
EXITS

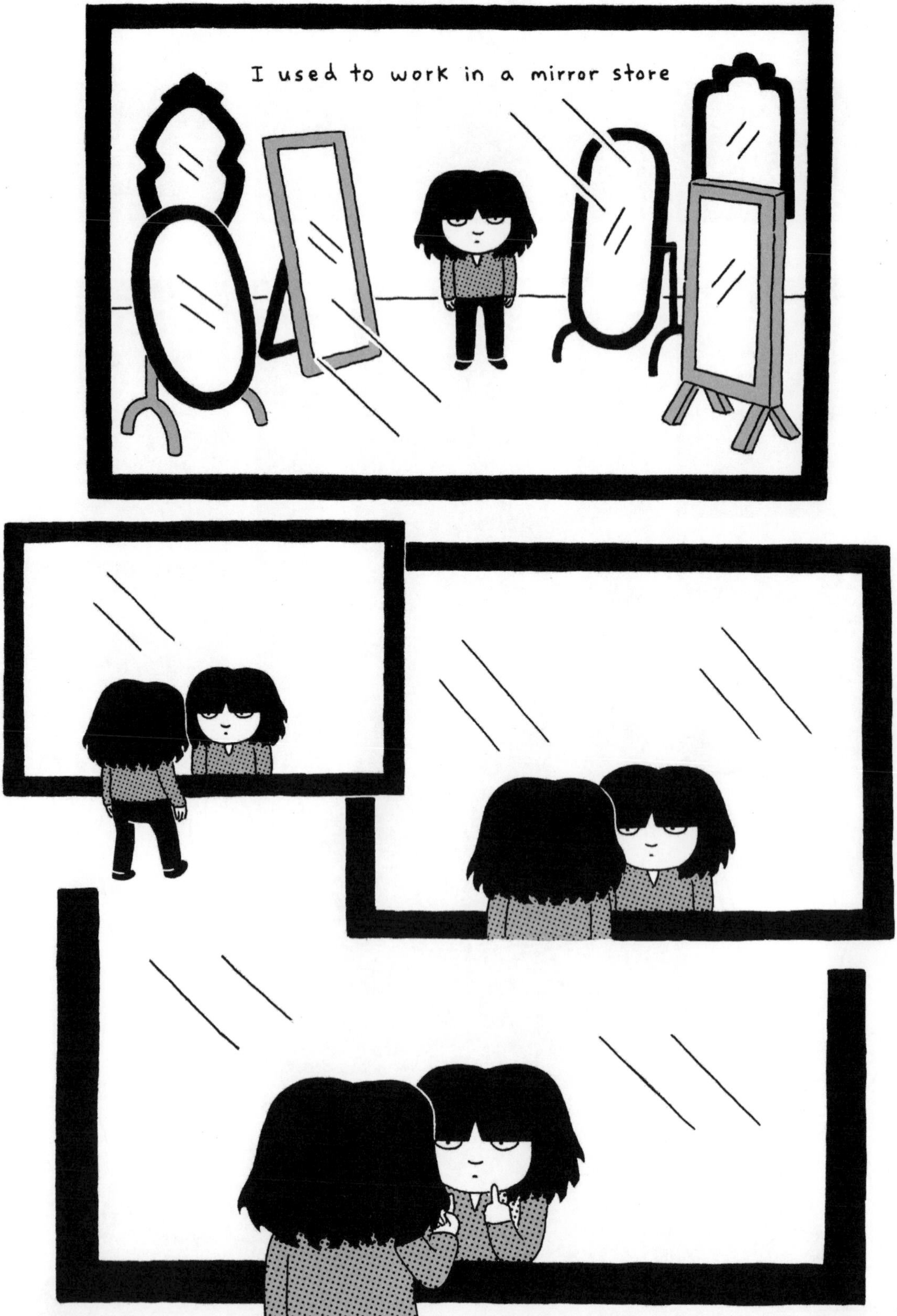
I used to work in a mirror store

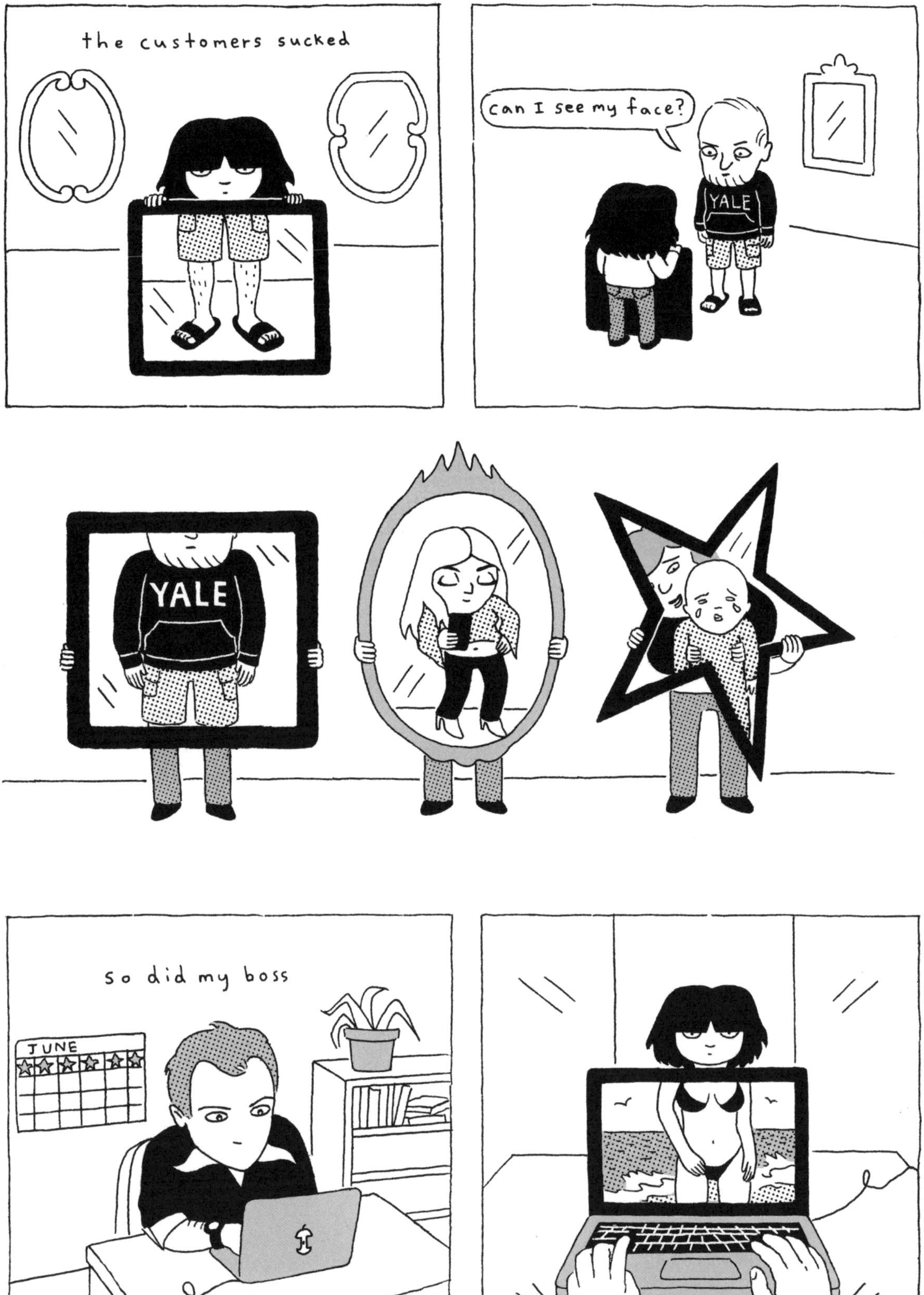

the customers sucked
can I see my face?
YALE
YALE
so did my boss
JUNE

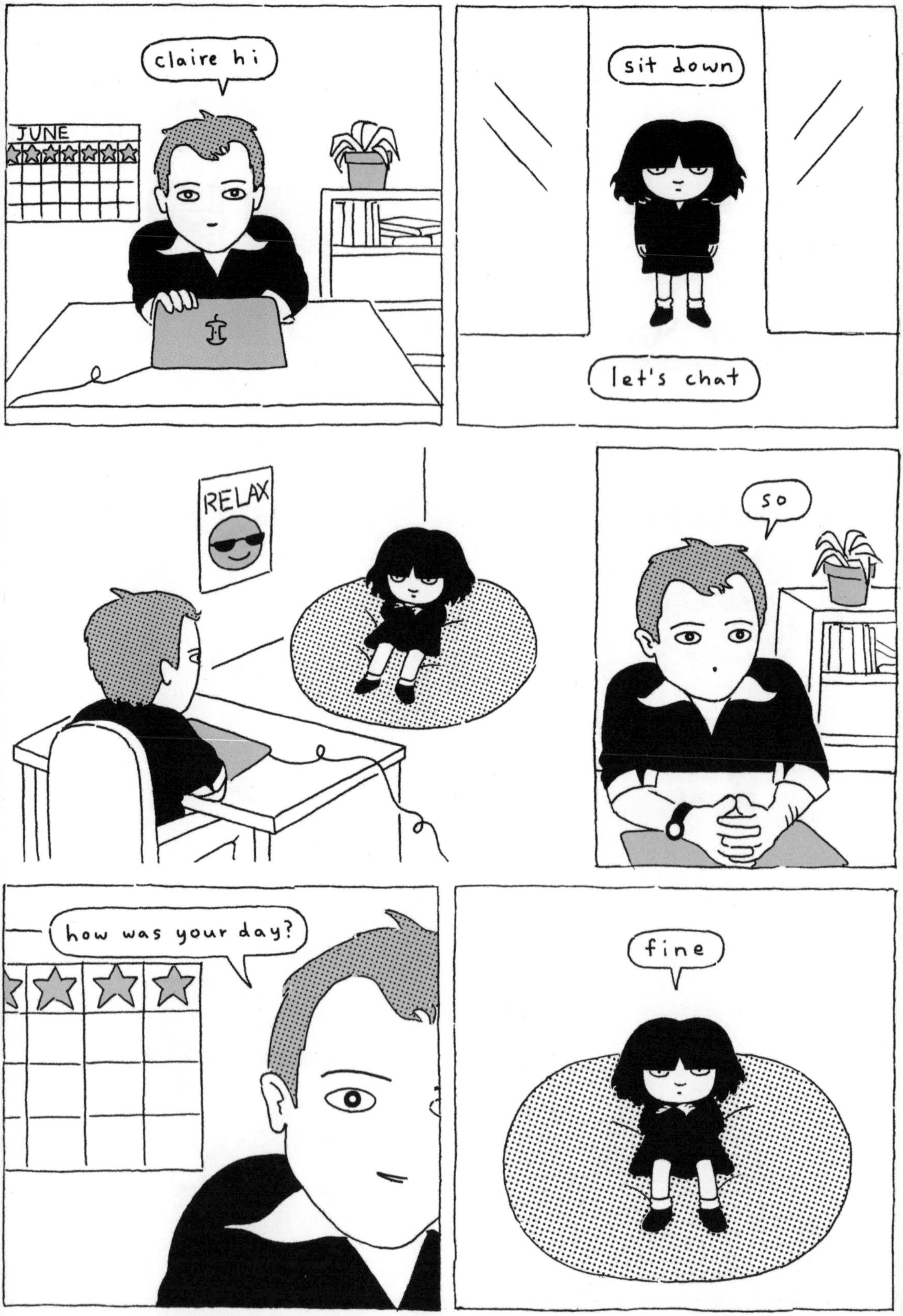
claire hi
JUNE
sit down
let's chat
RELAX
so
how was your day?
fine

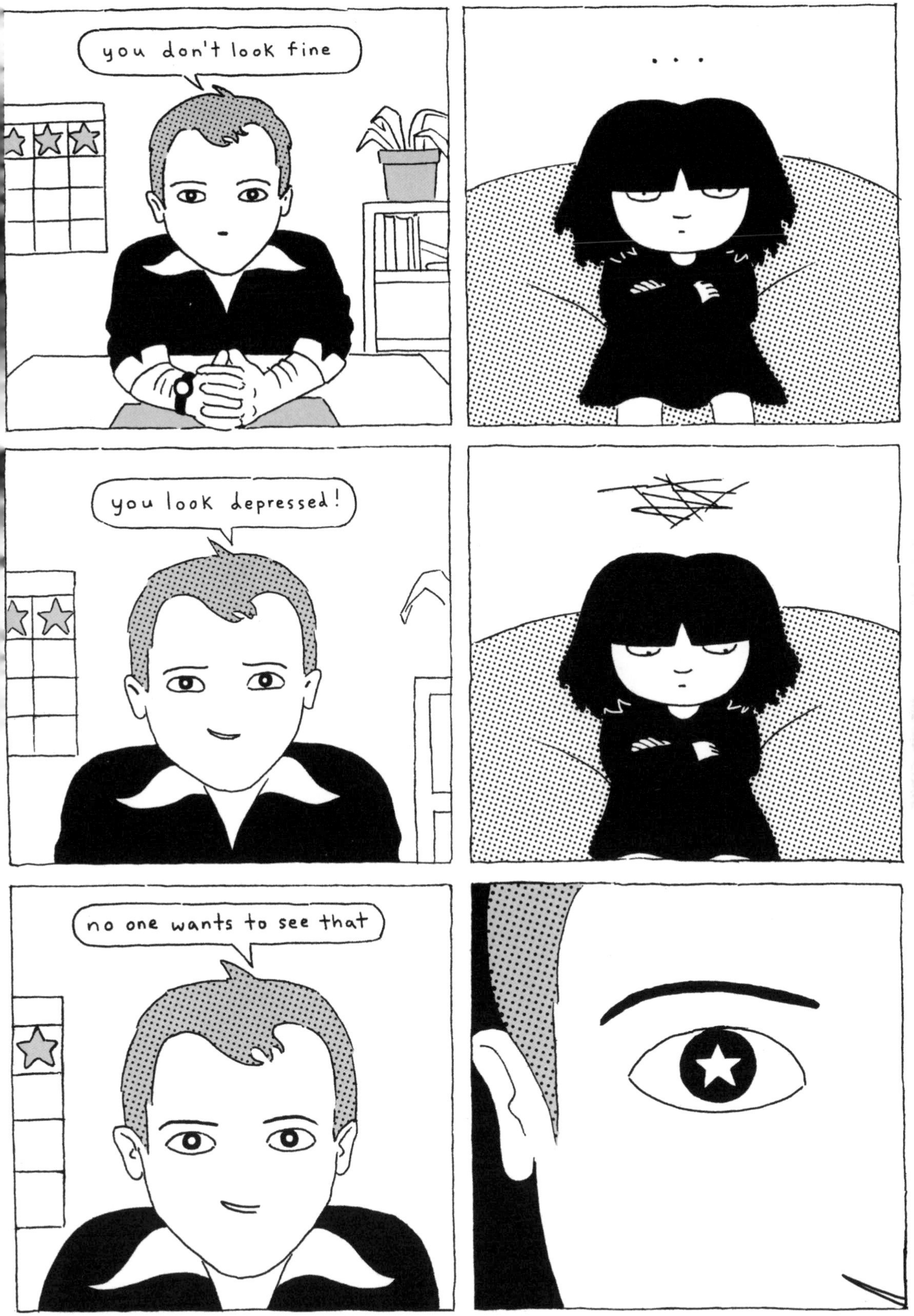
you don't look fine
. . .
you look depressed!
no one wants to see that

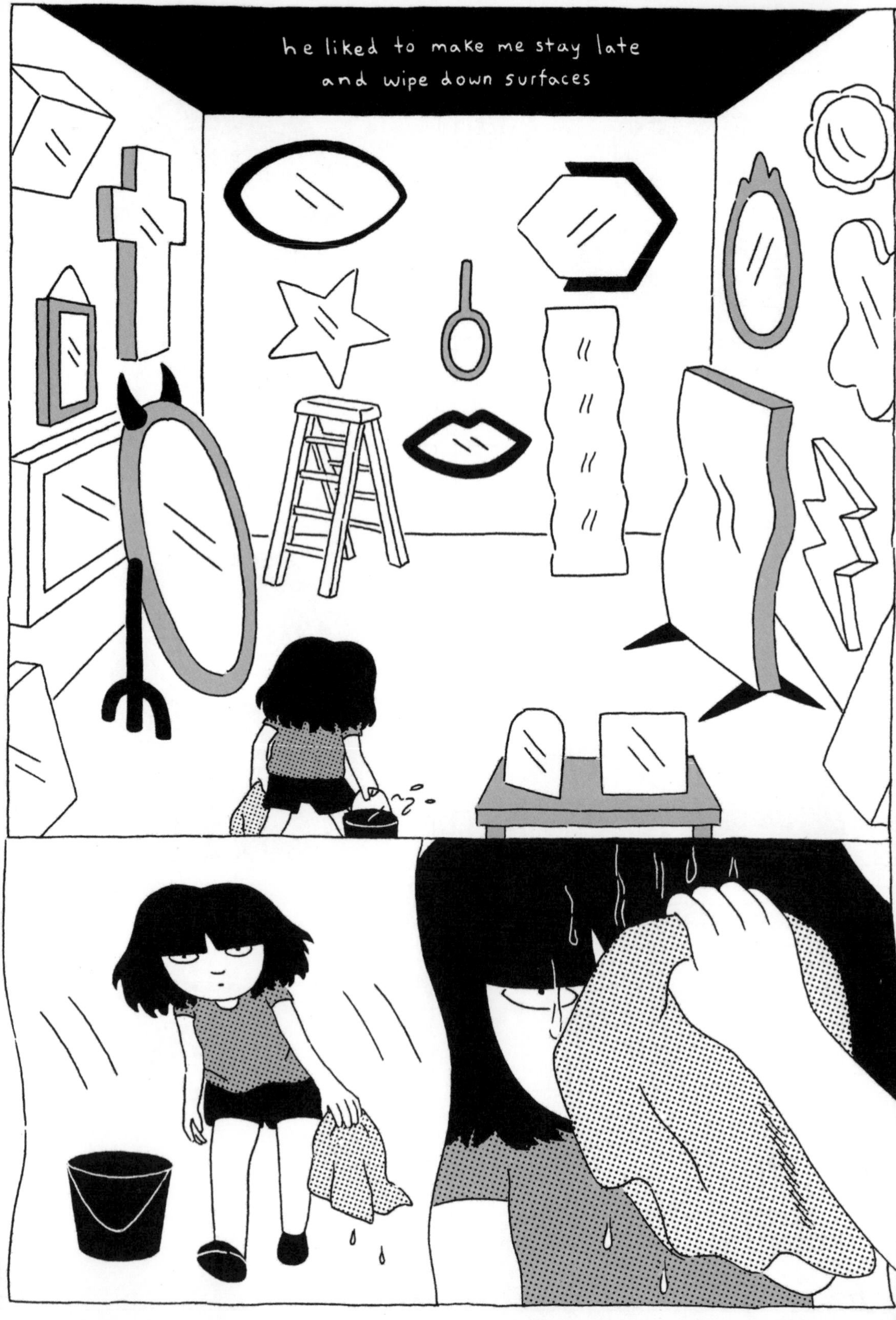
he liked to make me stay late
and wipe down surfaces

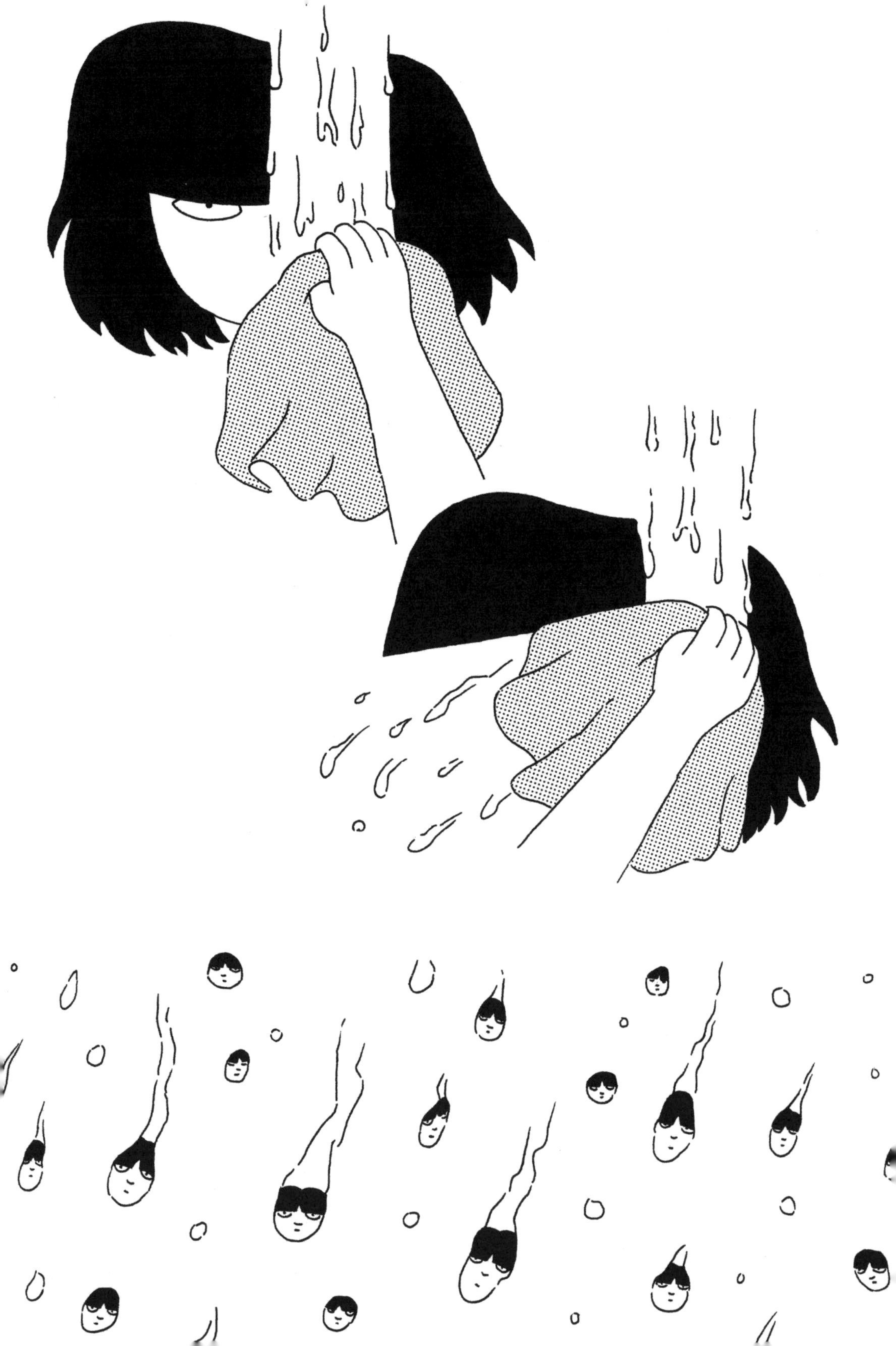

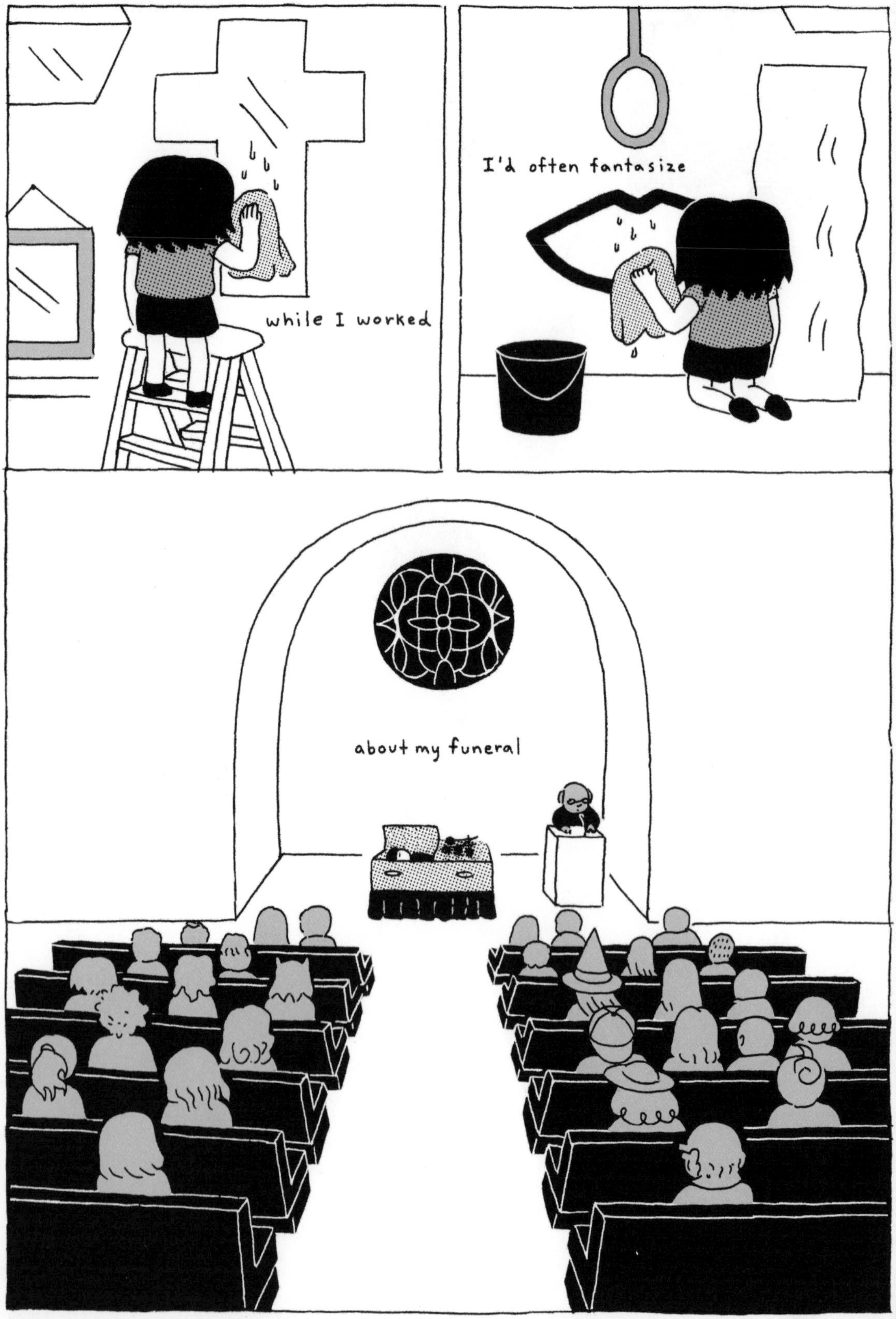
while I worked
I'd often fantasize
about my funeral

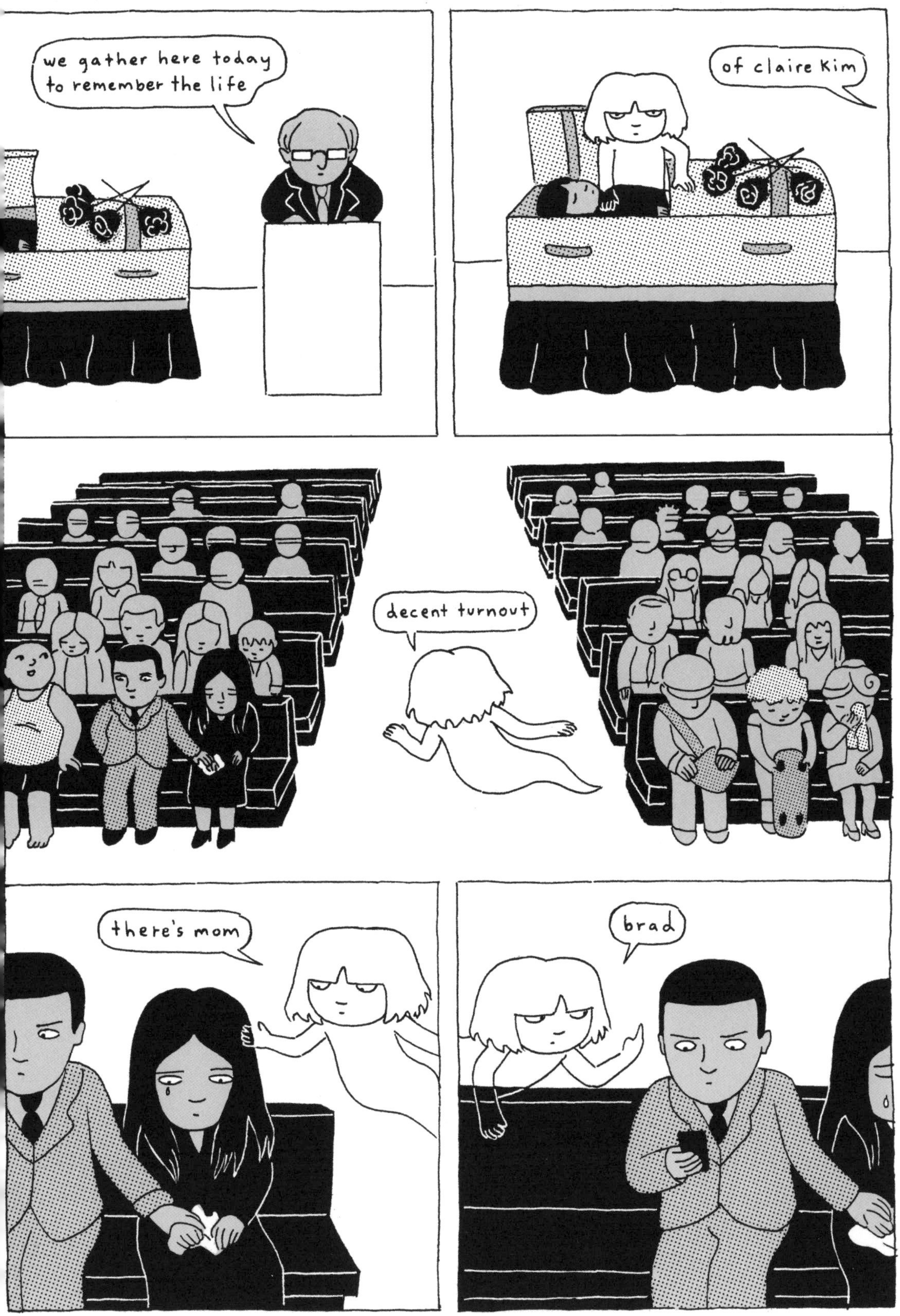
we gather here today to remember the life
of claire kim
decent turnout
there's mom
brad

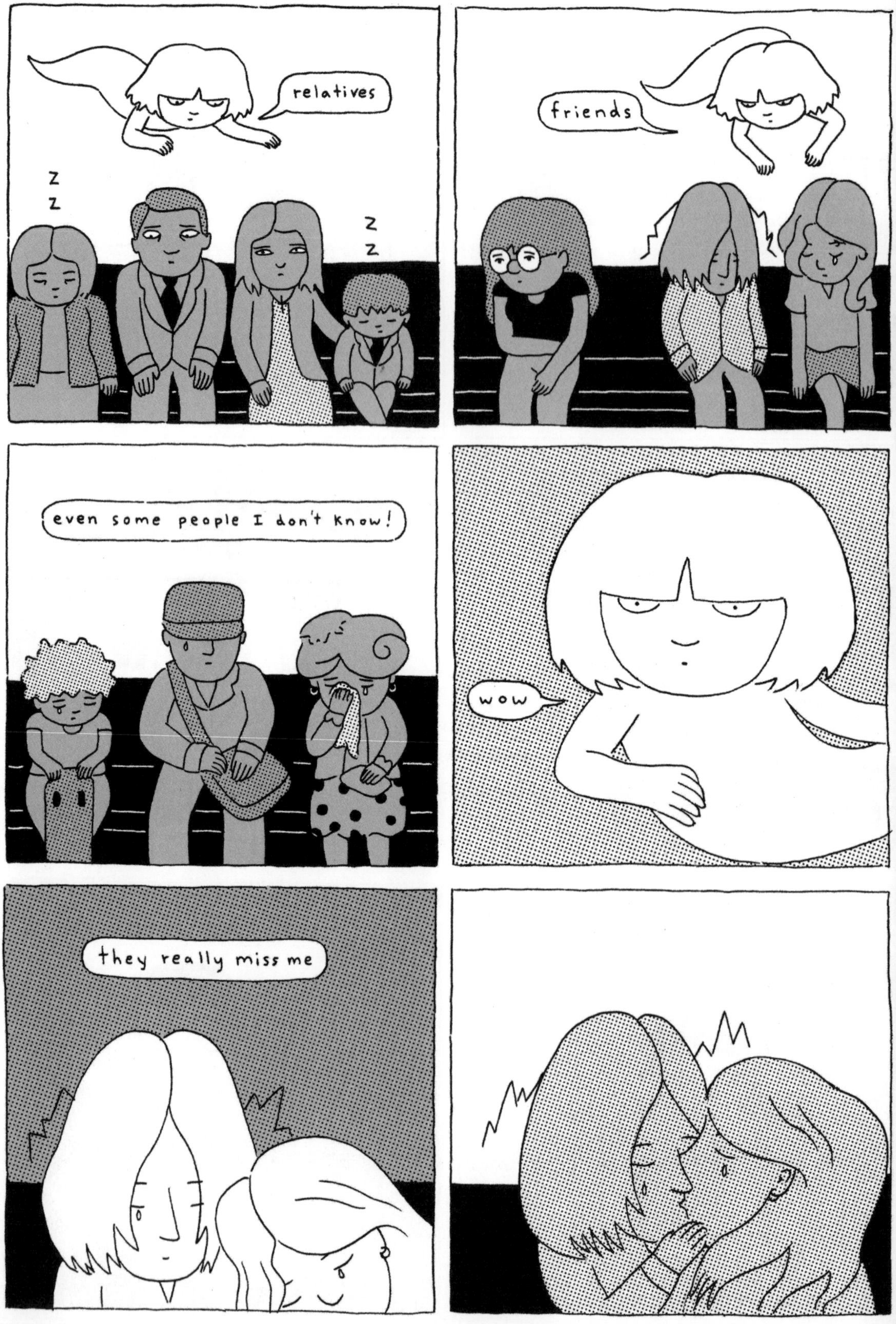
relatives
z z
z z
friends
even some people I don't know!
wow
they really miss me

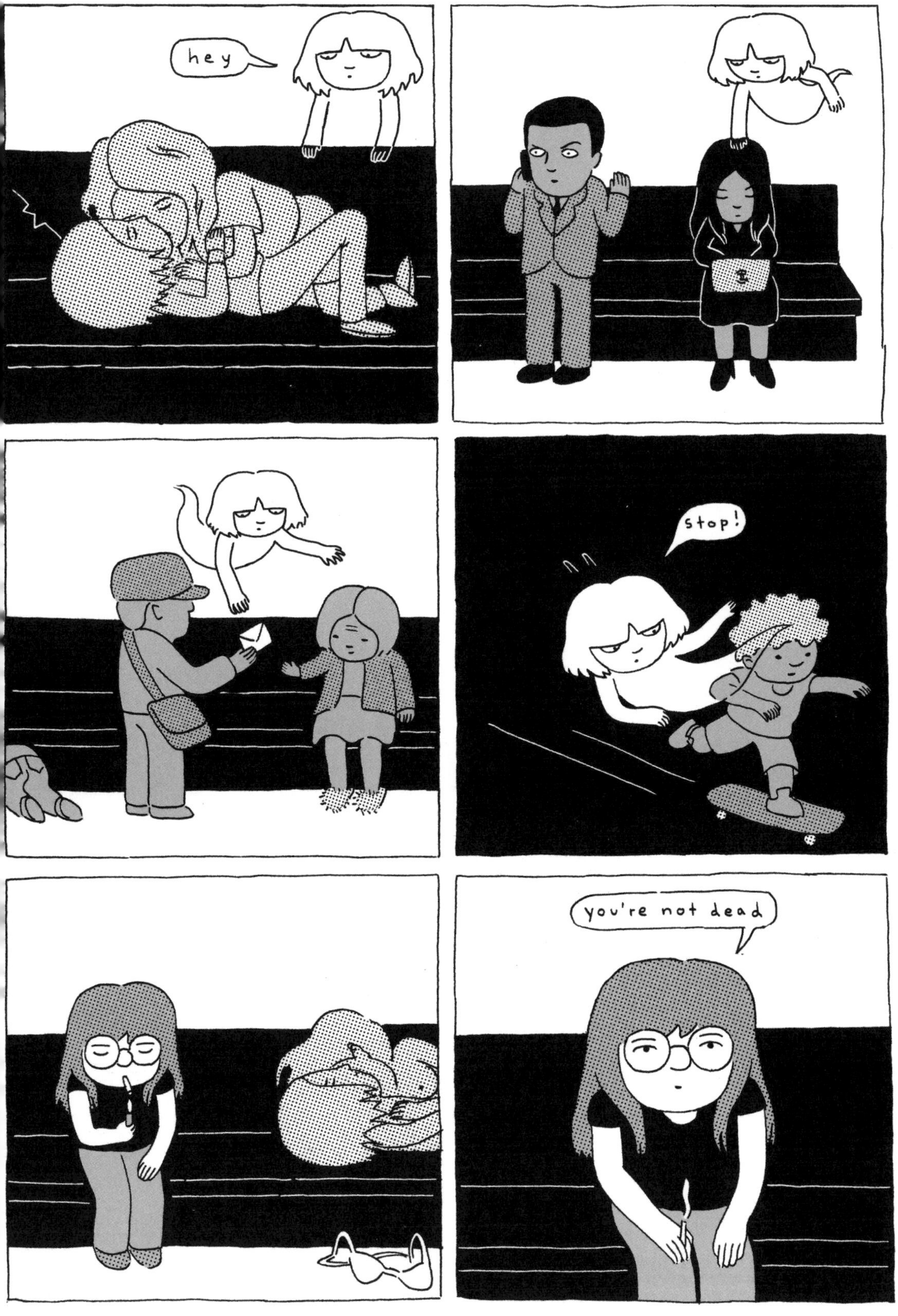
hey
stop!
you're not dead

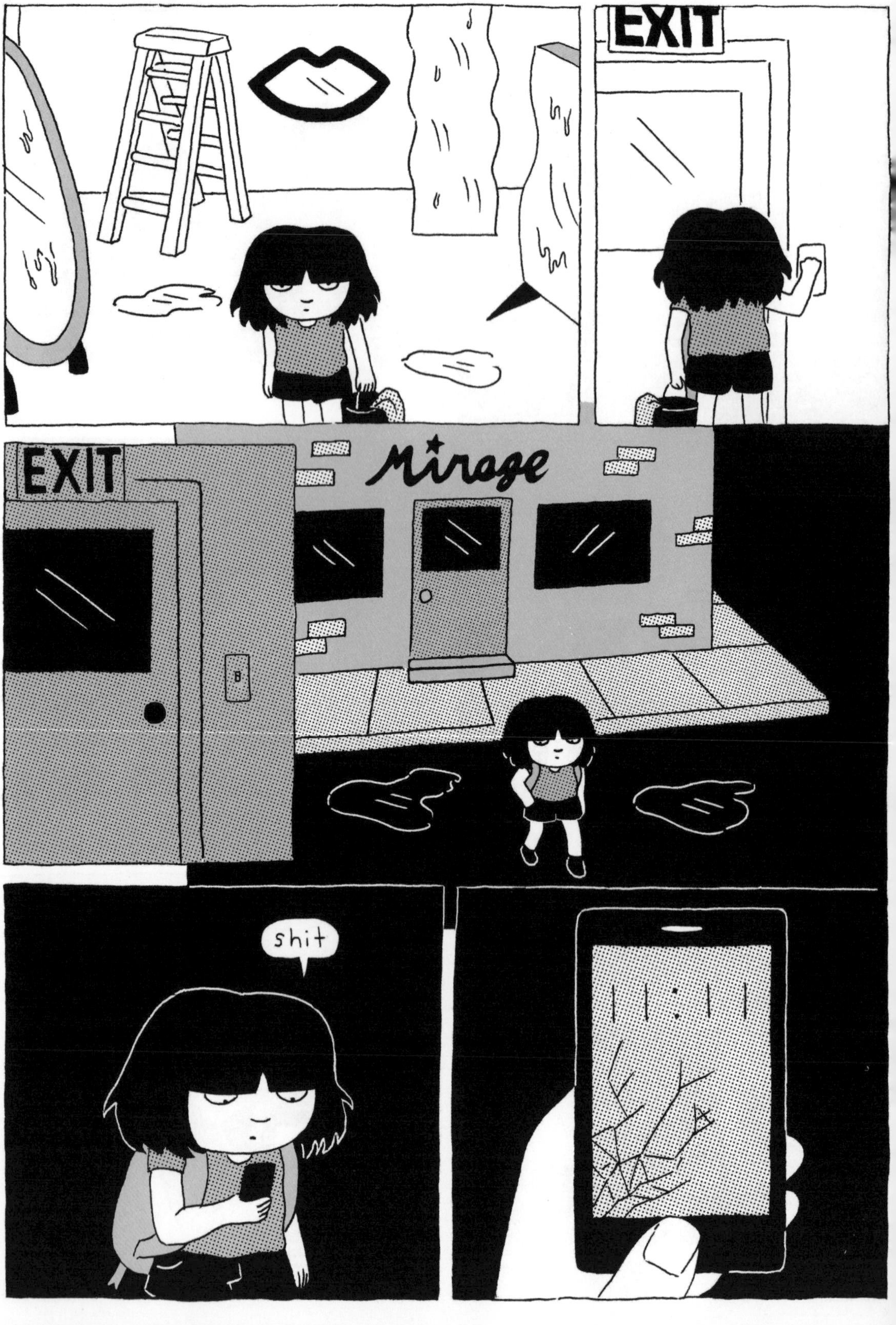
EXIT
EXIT
Mirage
shit
11:11

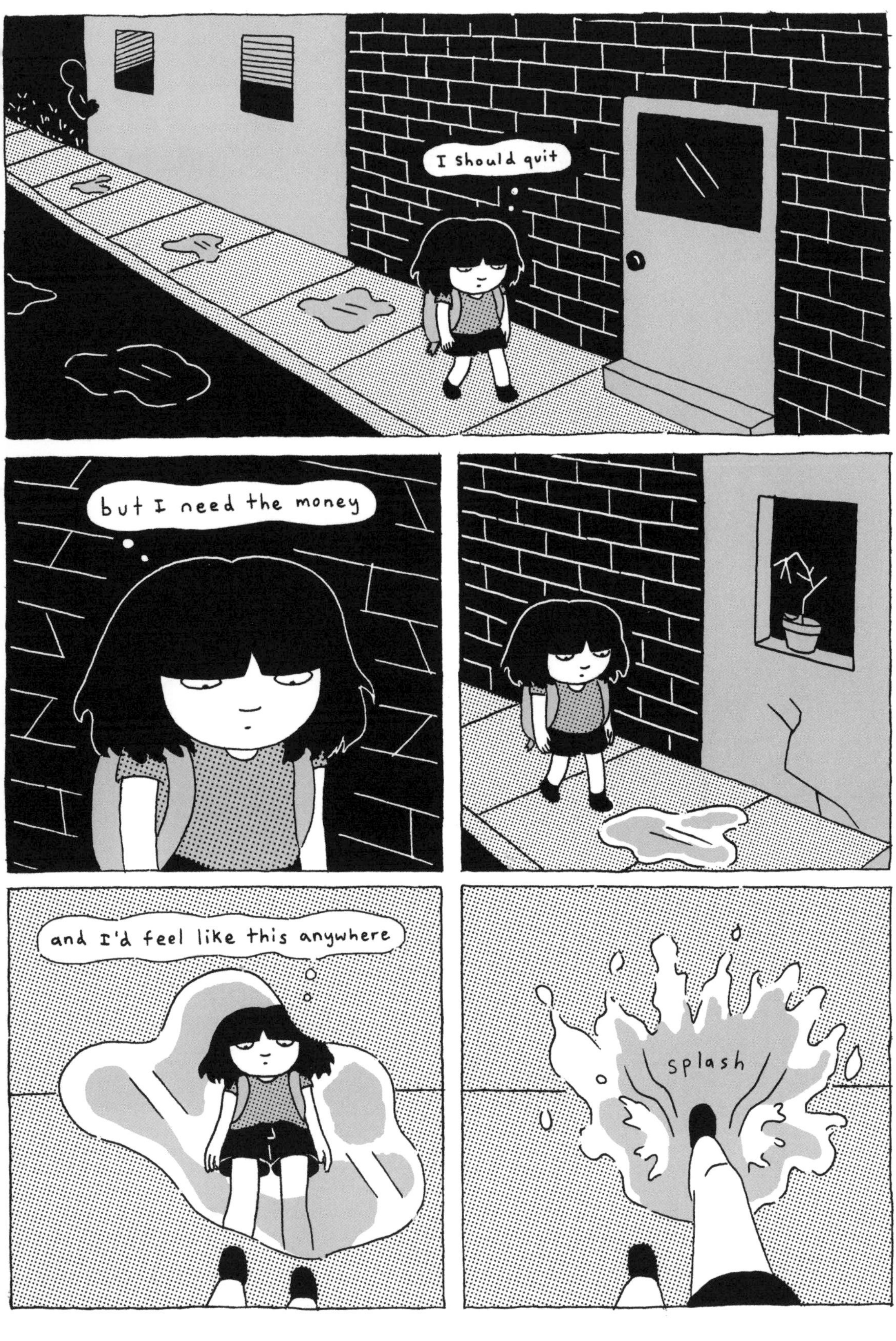
I should quit
but I need the money
and I'd feel like this anywhere
splash

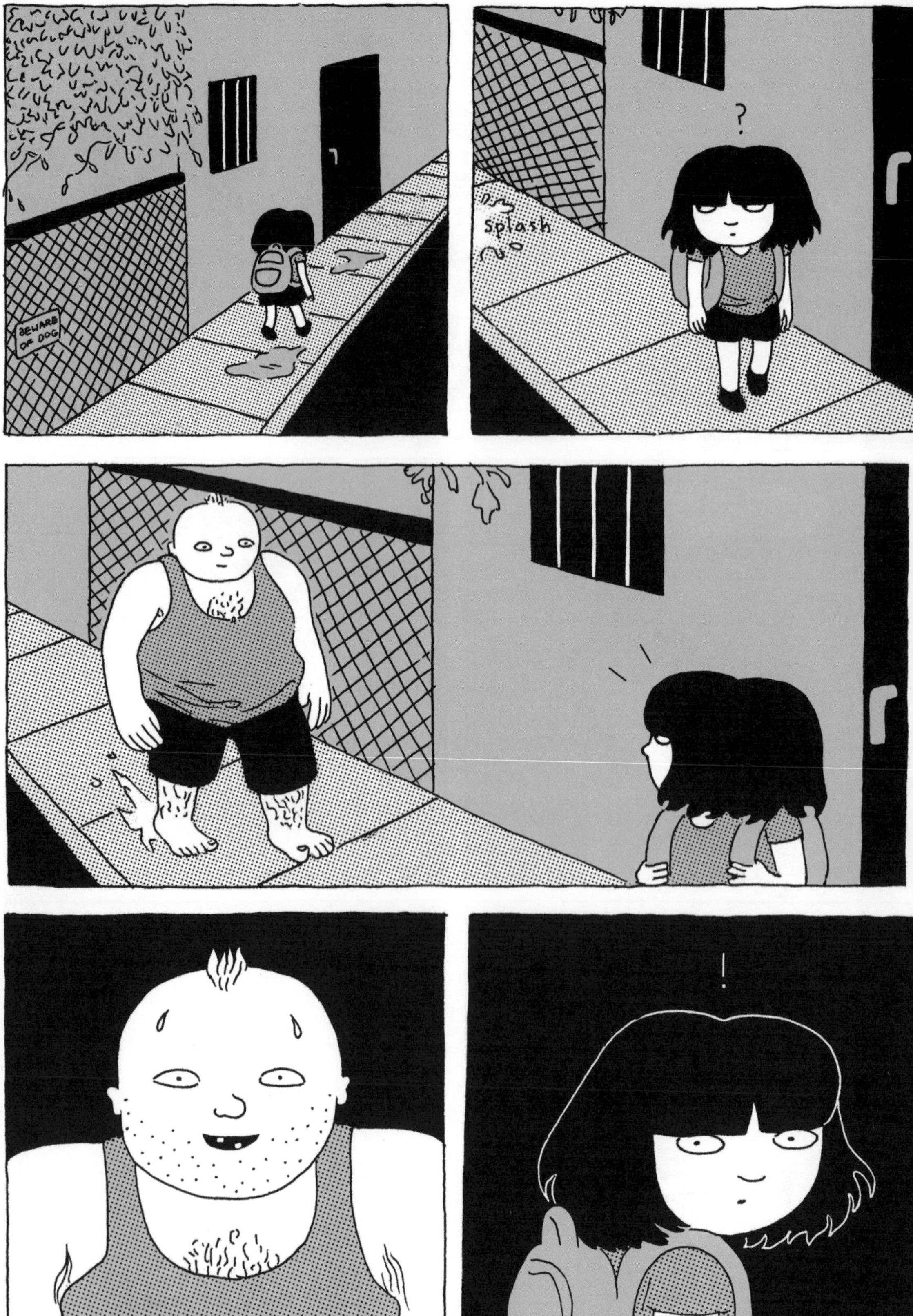
BEWARE OF DOG
splash
?
!

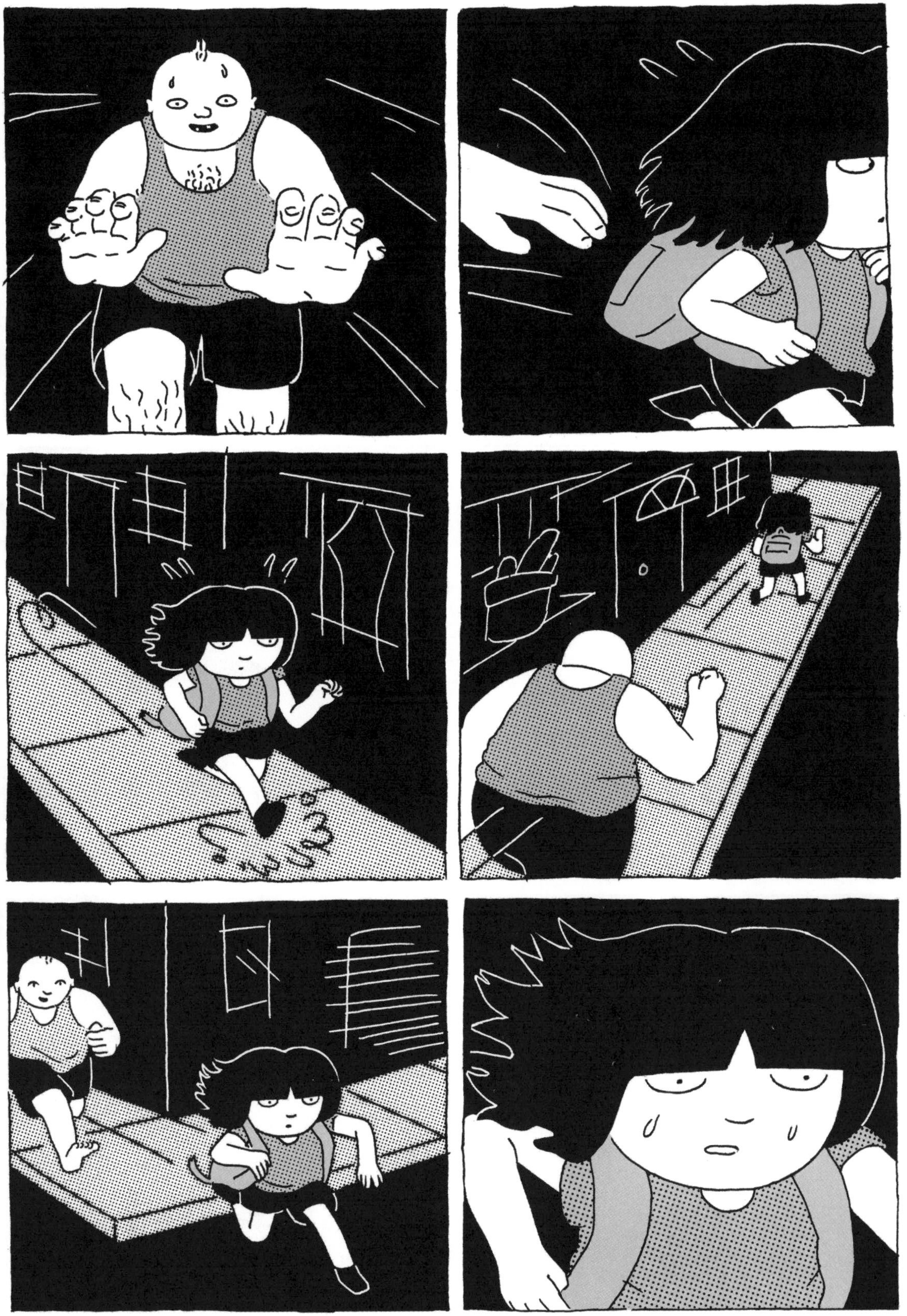

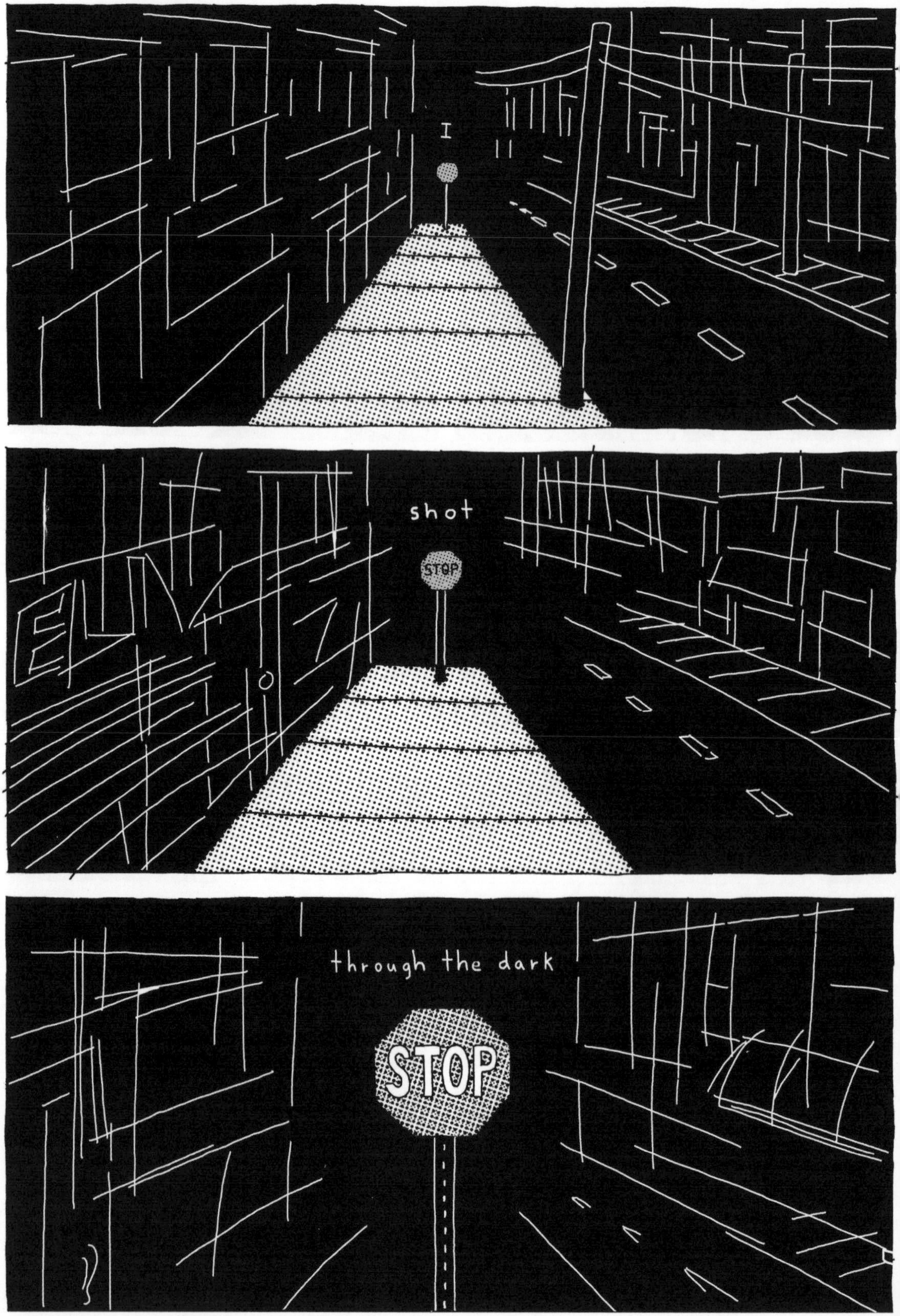
I
shot
STOP
through the dark
STOP

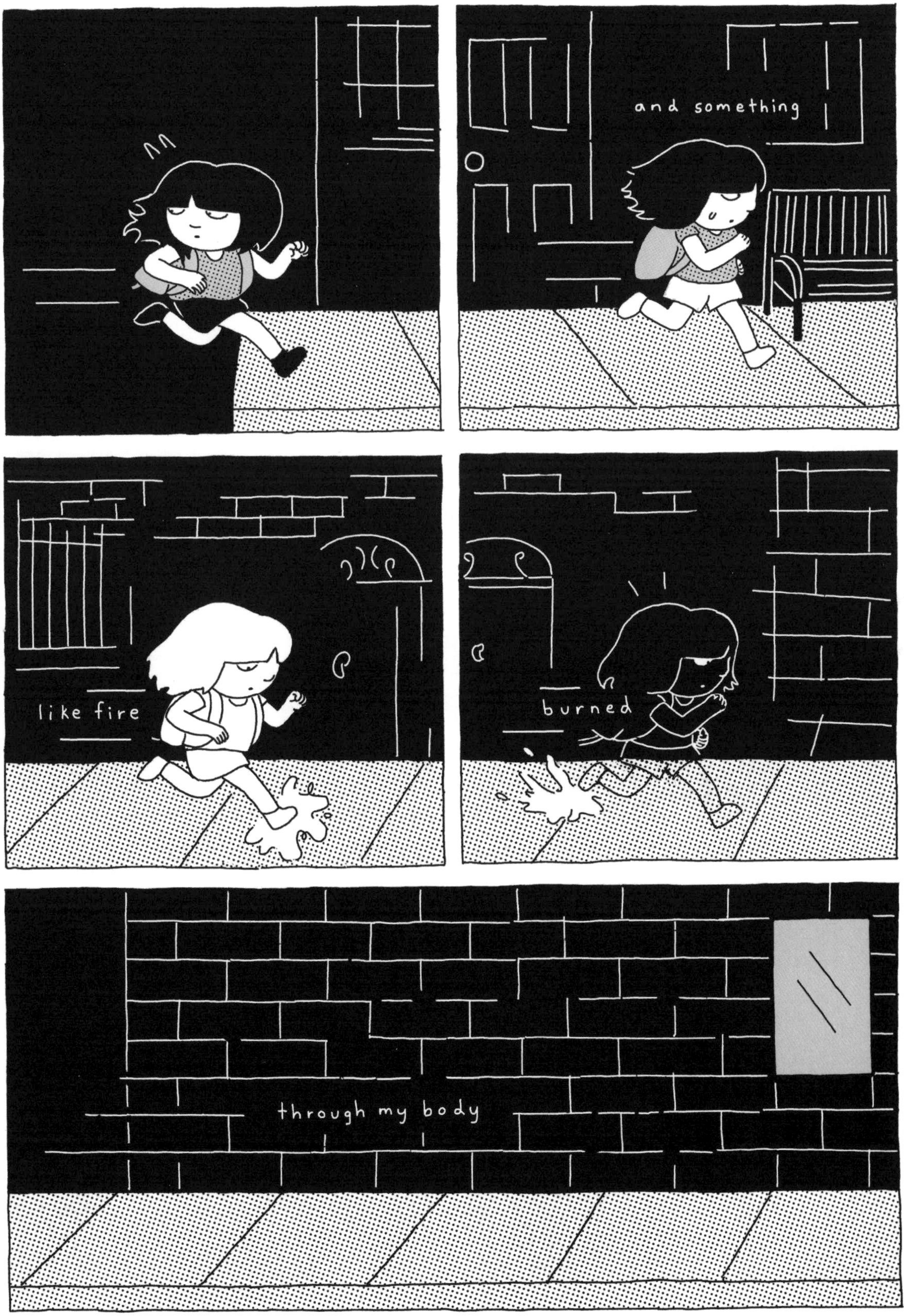
and something
like fire
burned
through my body

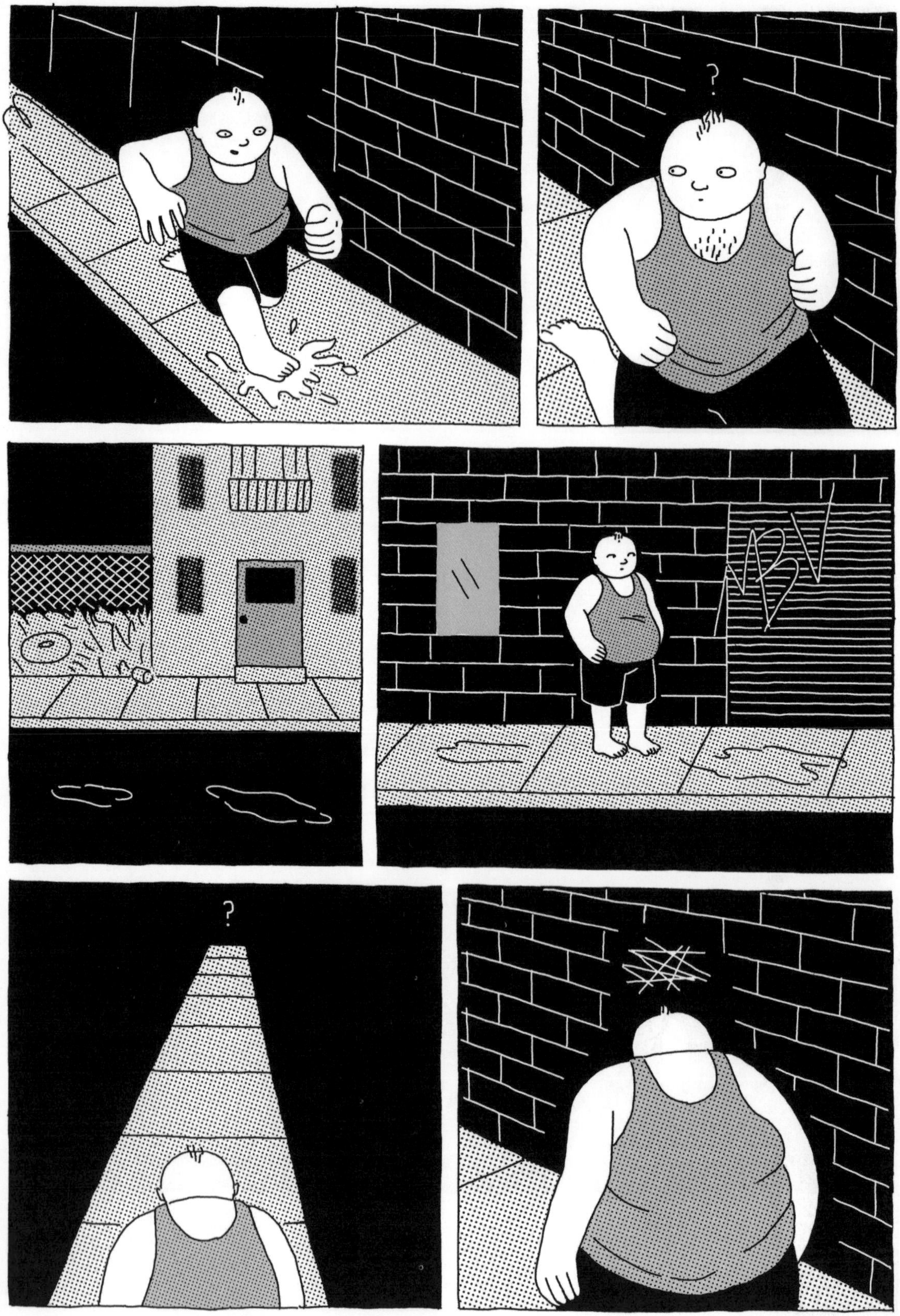
?
?

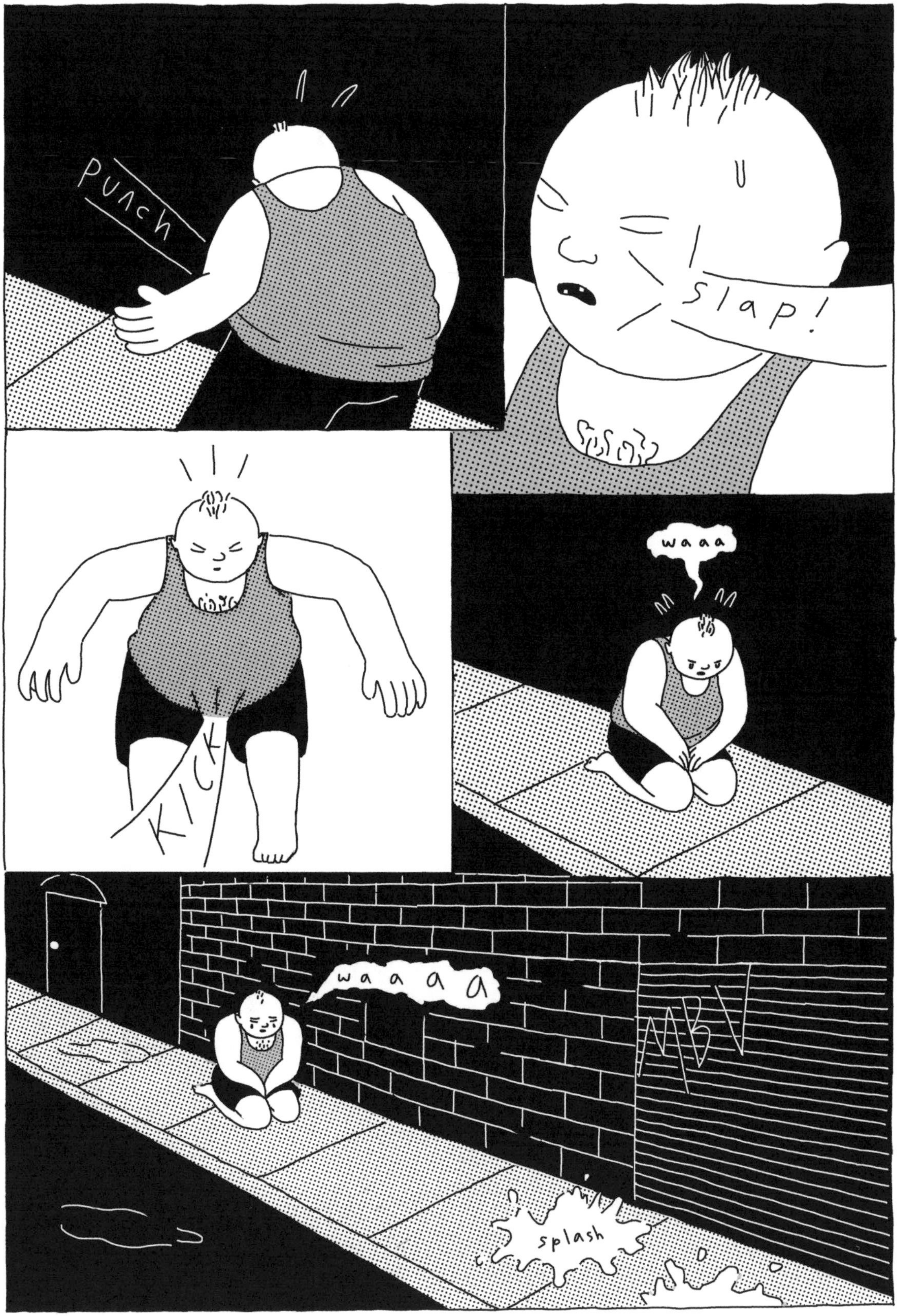
Punch
slap!
KICK
waaa
waaaa
MBV
splash

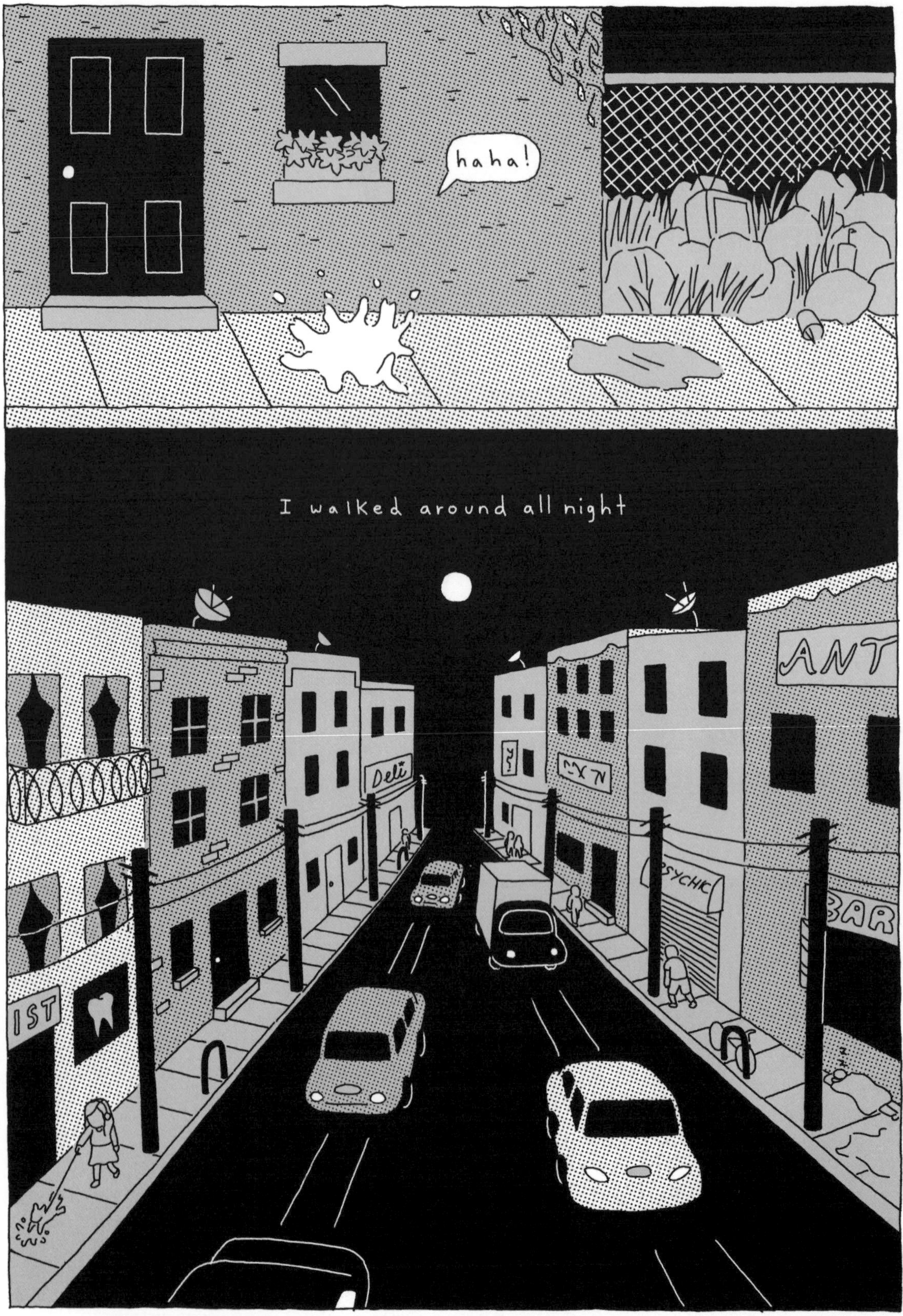
haha!
I walked around all night
ANT
Deli
PSYCHIC
BAR
IST

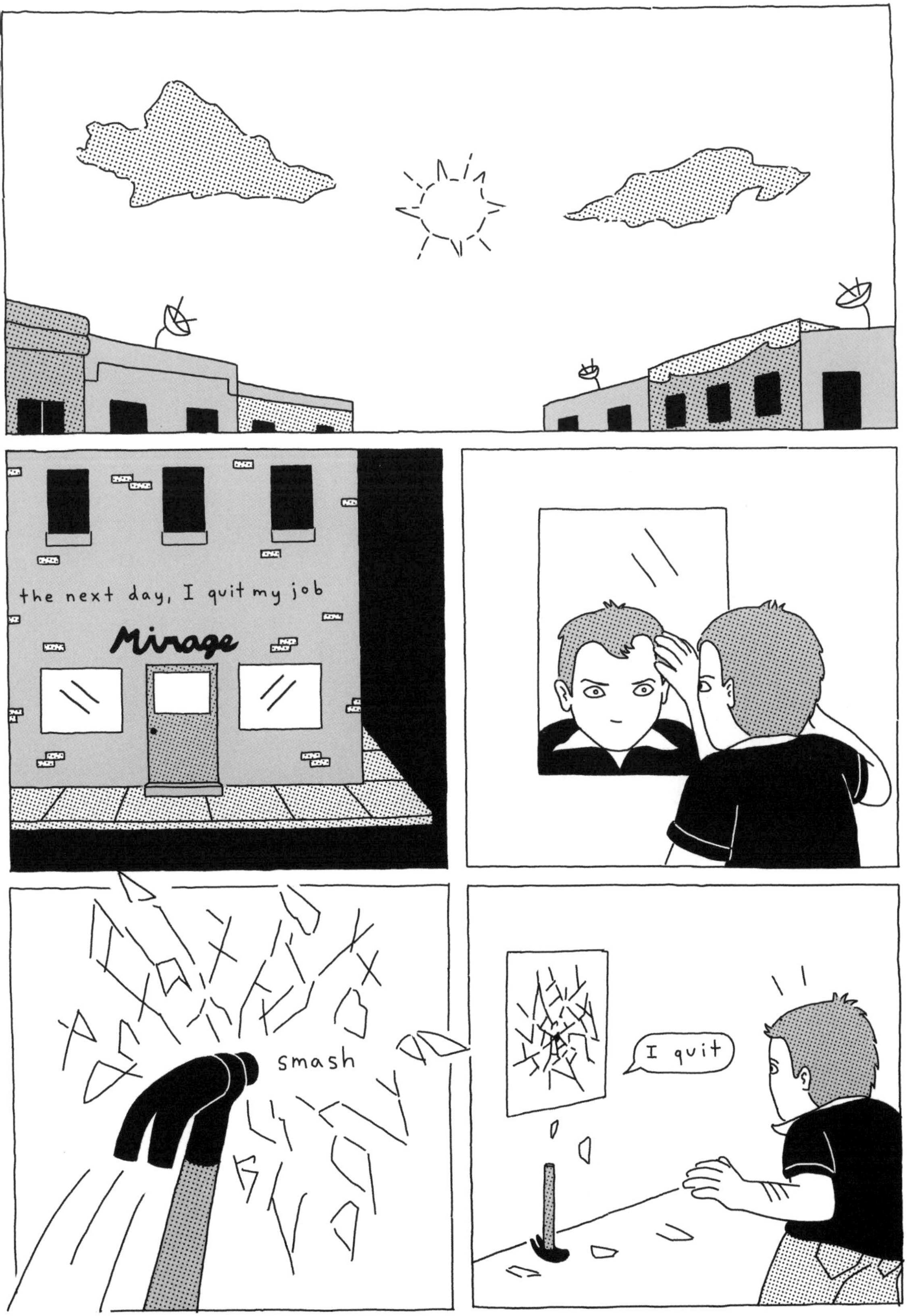
the next day, I quit my job
Mirage
smash
I quit

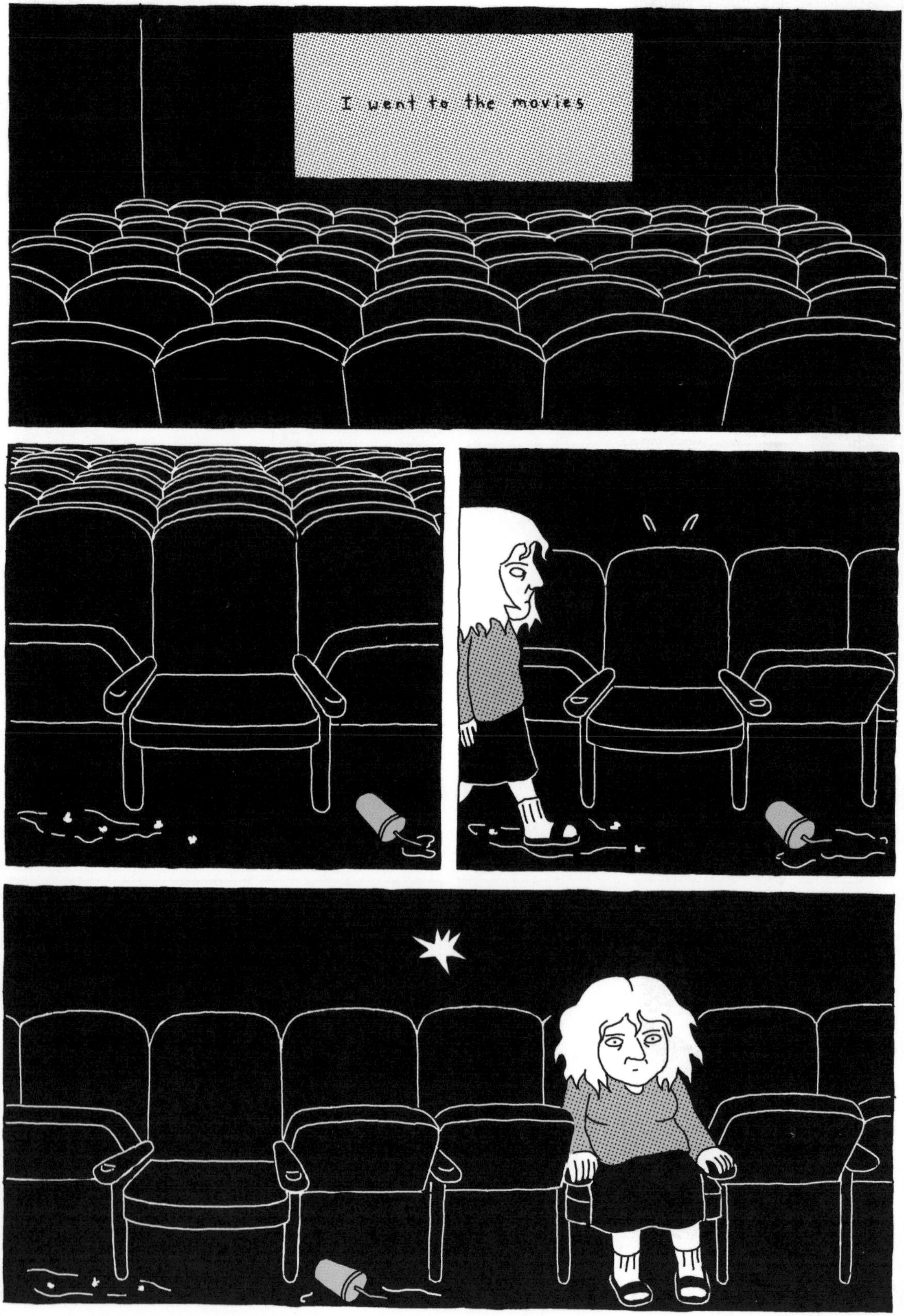
I went to the movies

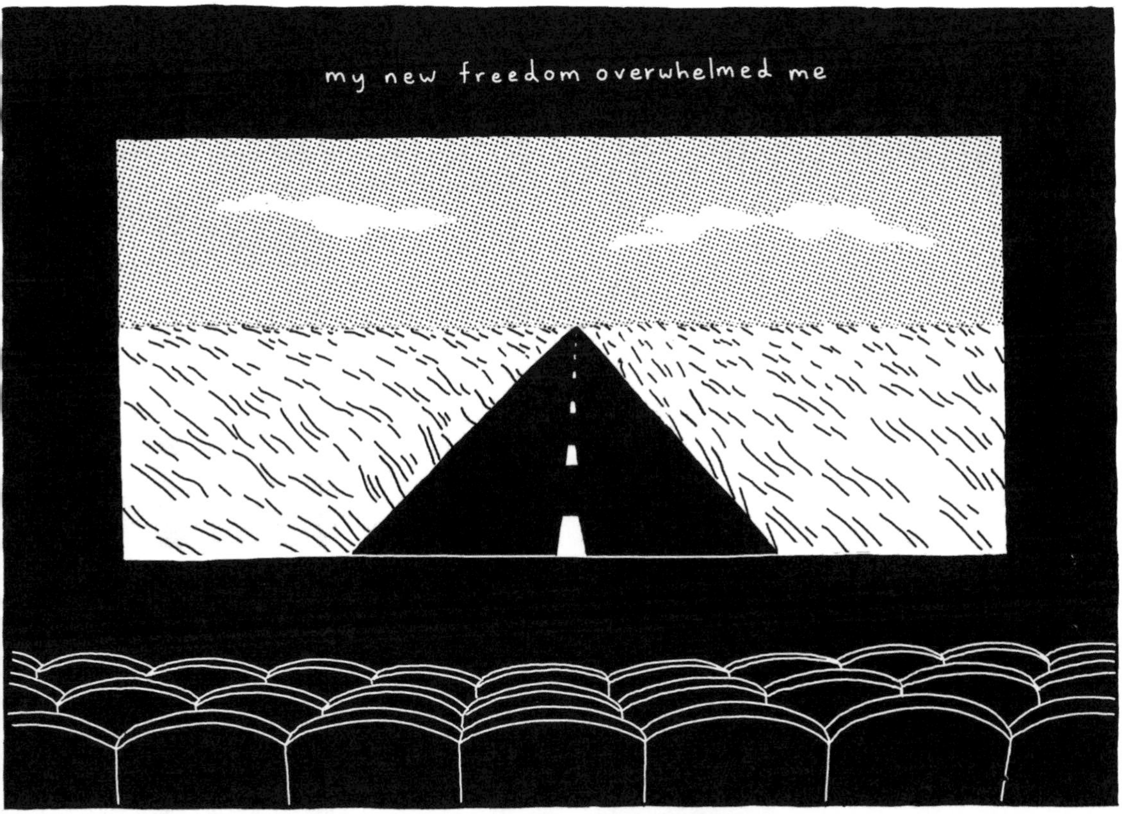
my new freedom overwhelmed me

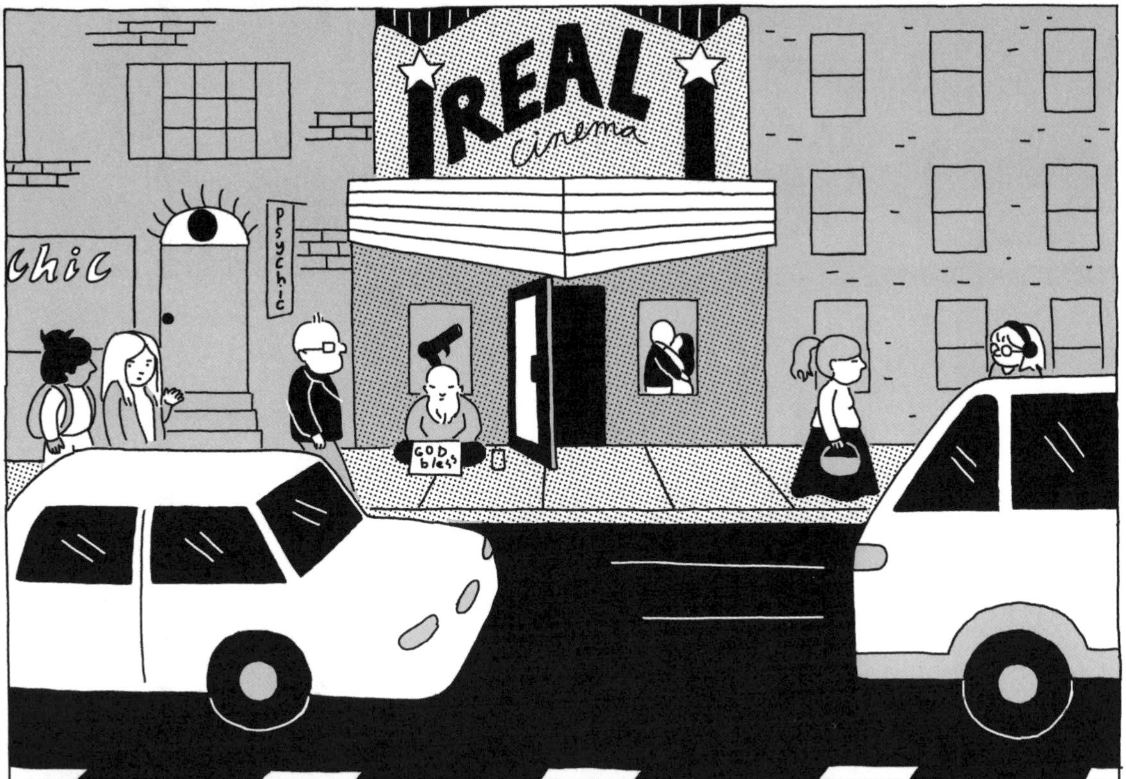
REAL
cinema
psychic
chic
GOD bless

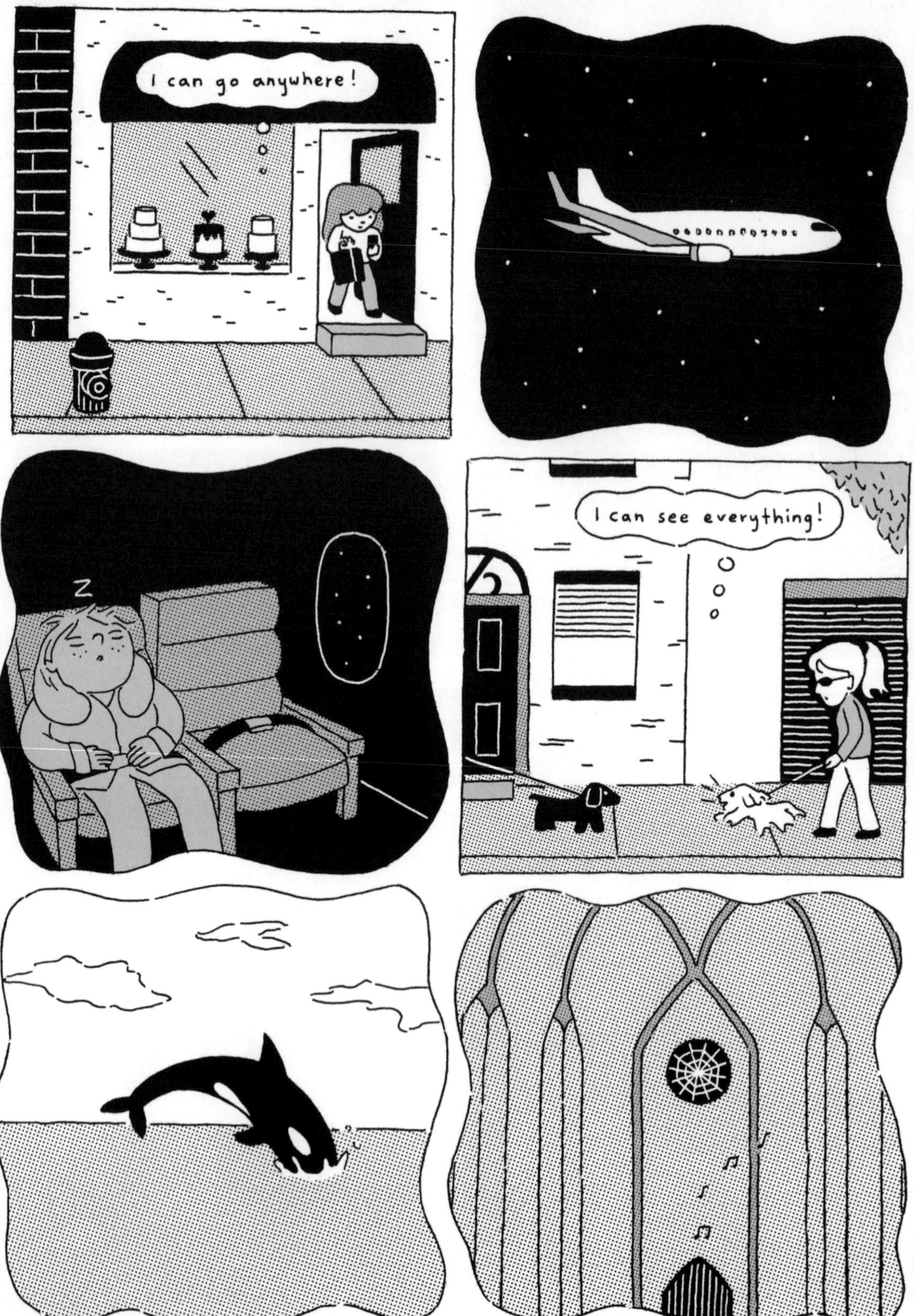
I can go anywhere!
I can see everything!

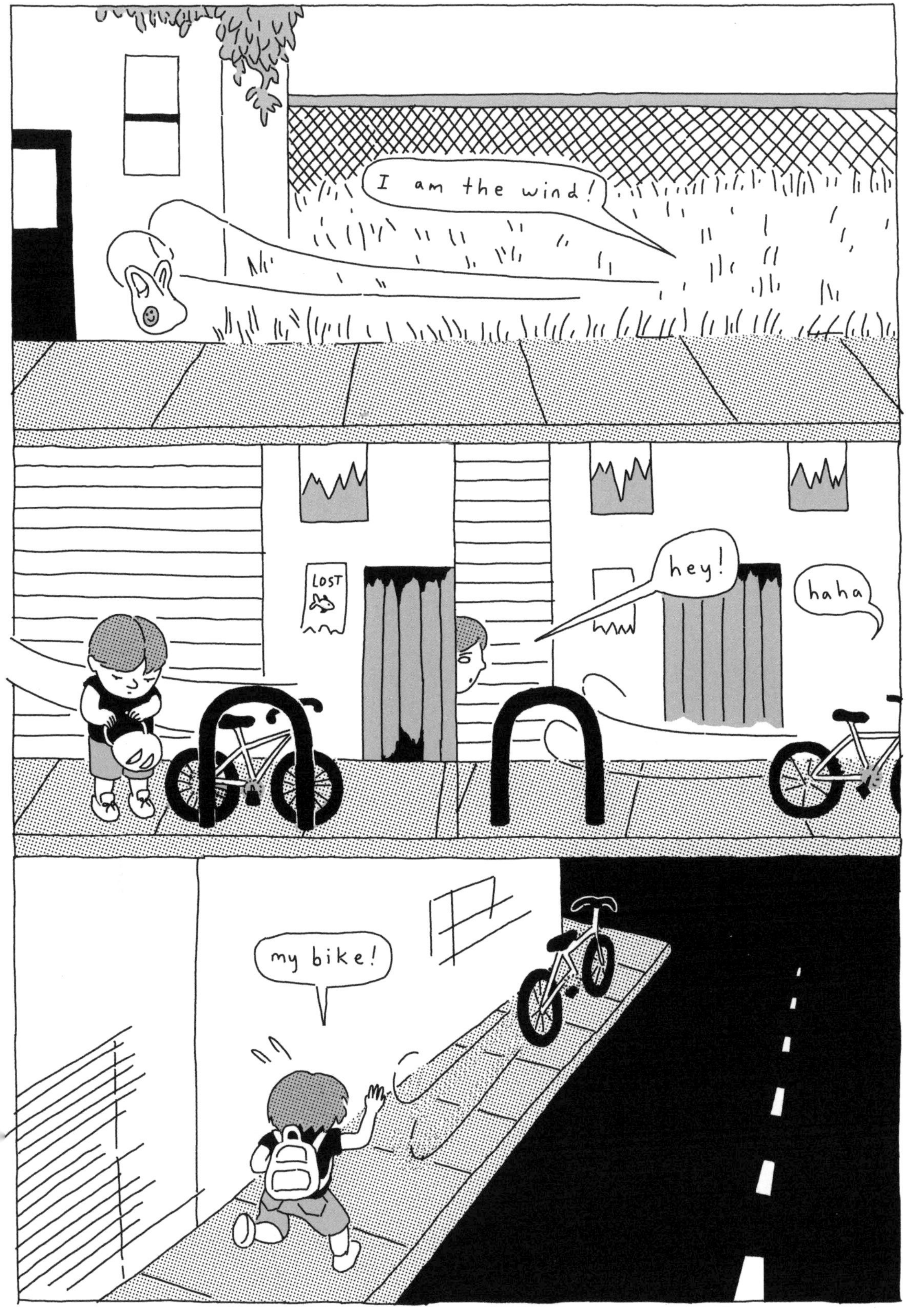
I am the wind!
LOST
hey!
haha
my bike!

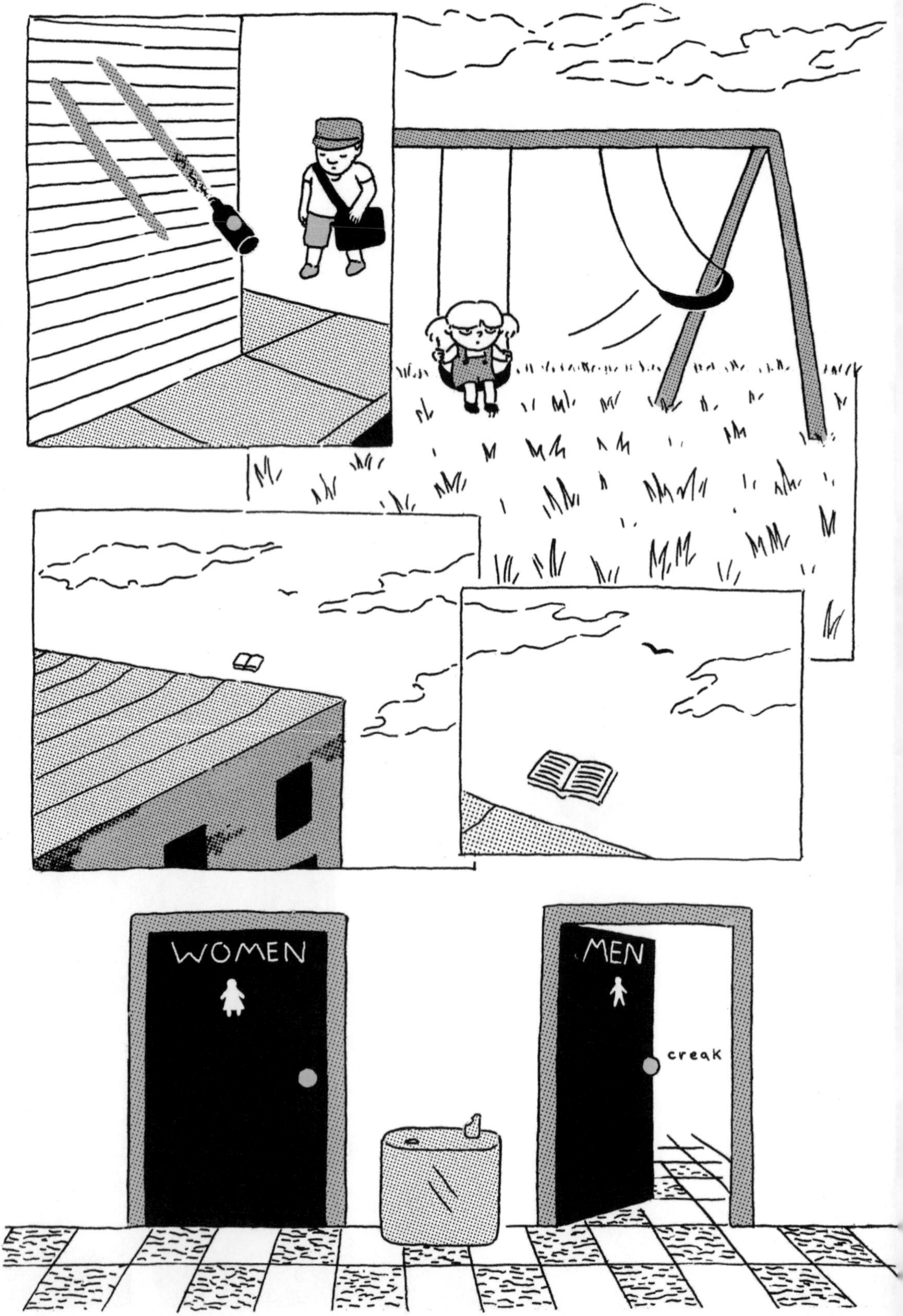
WOMEN
MEN
creak

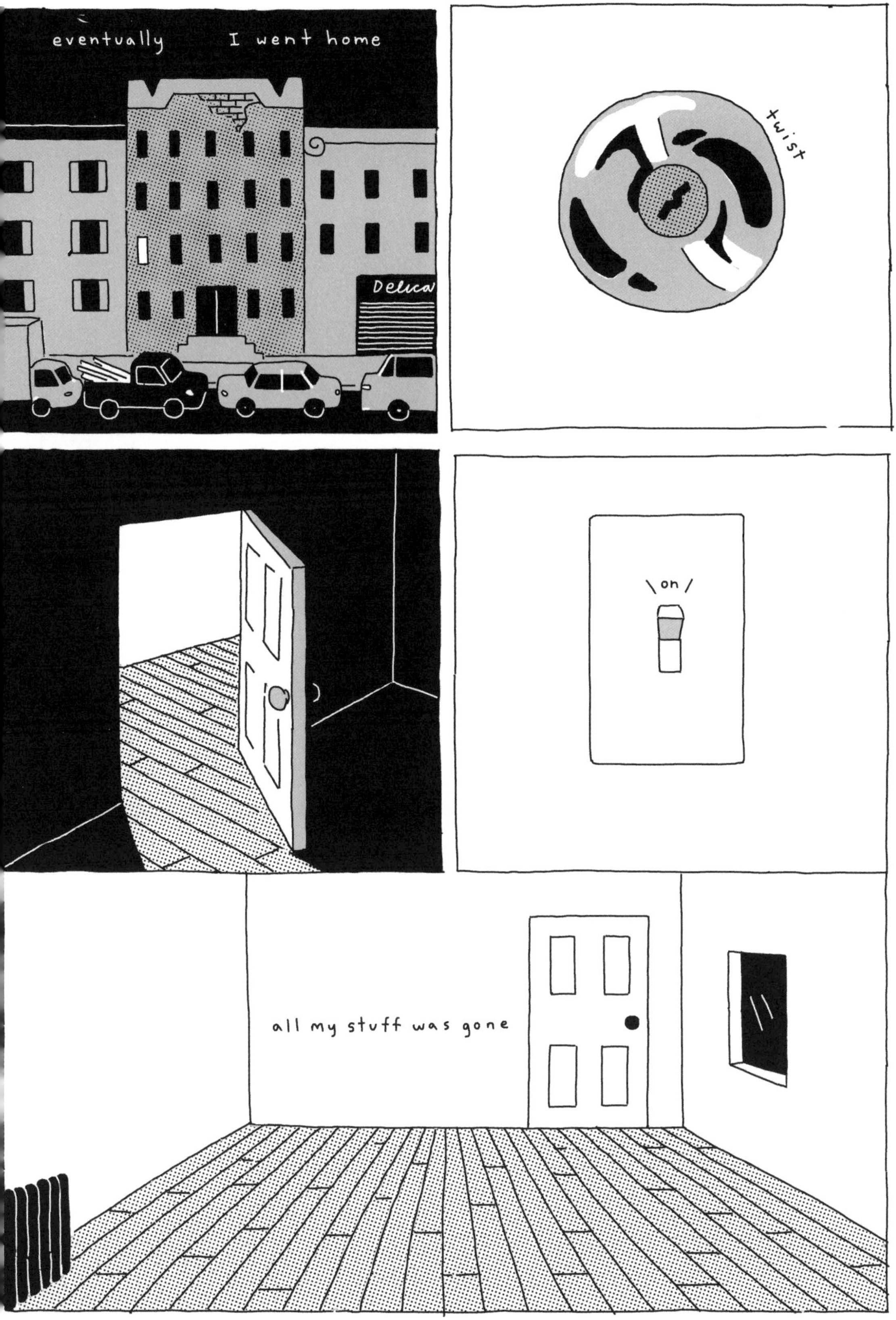
eventually I went home
Delica
twist
on
all my stuff was gone

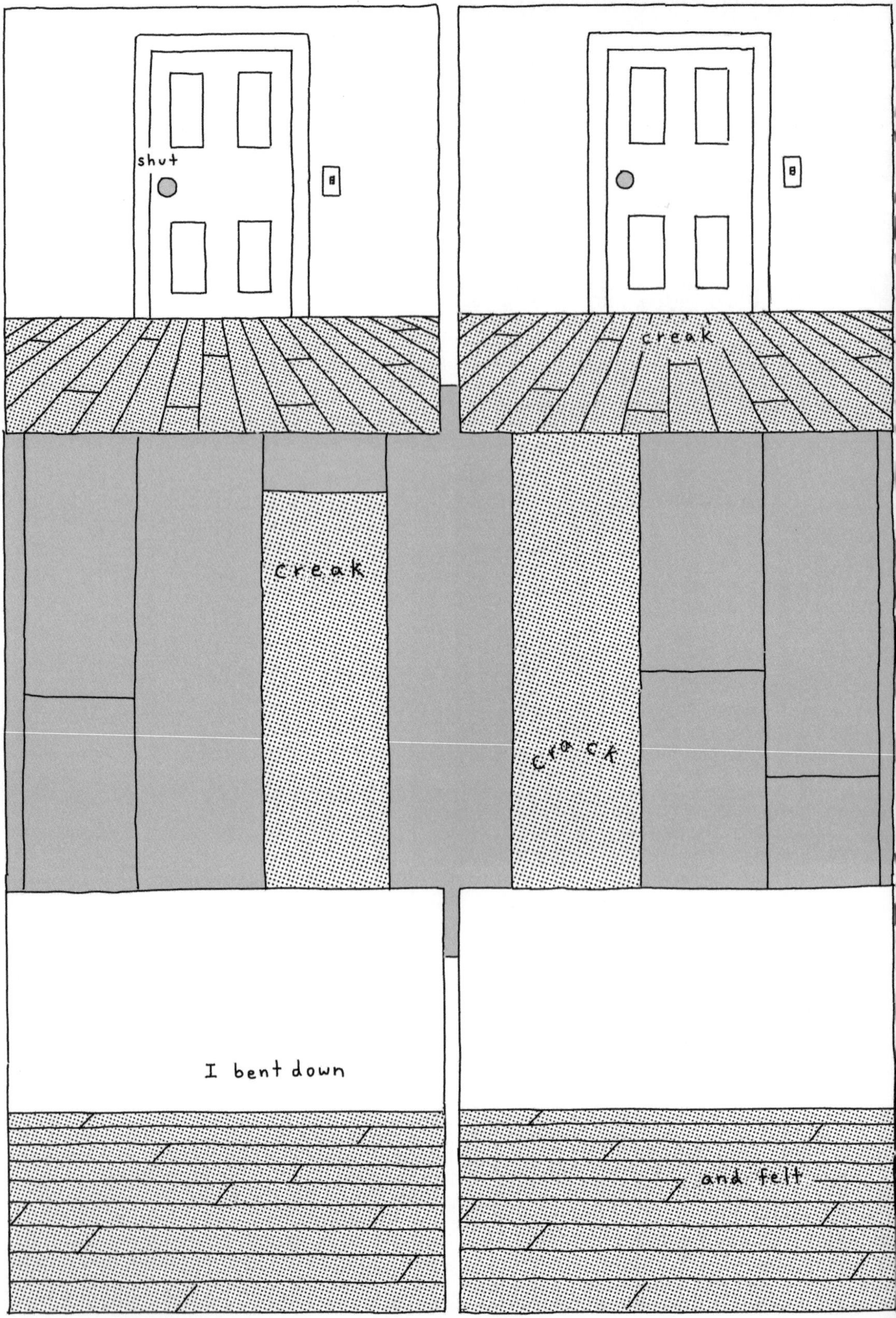
shut
creak
creak
crack
I bent down
and felt

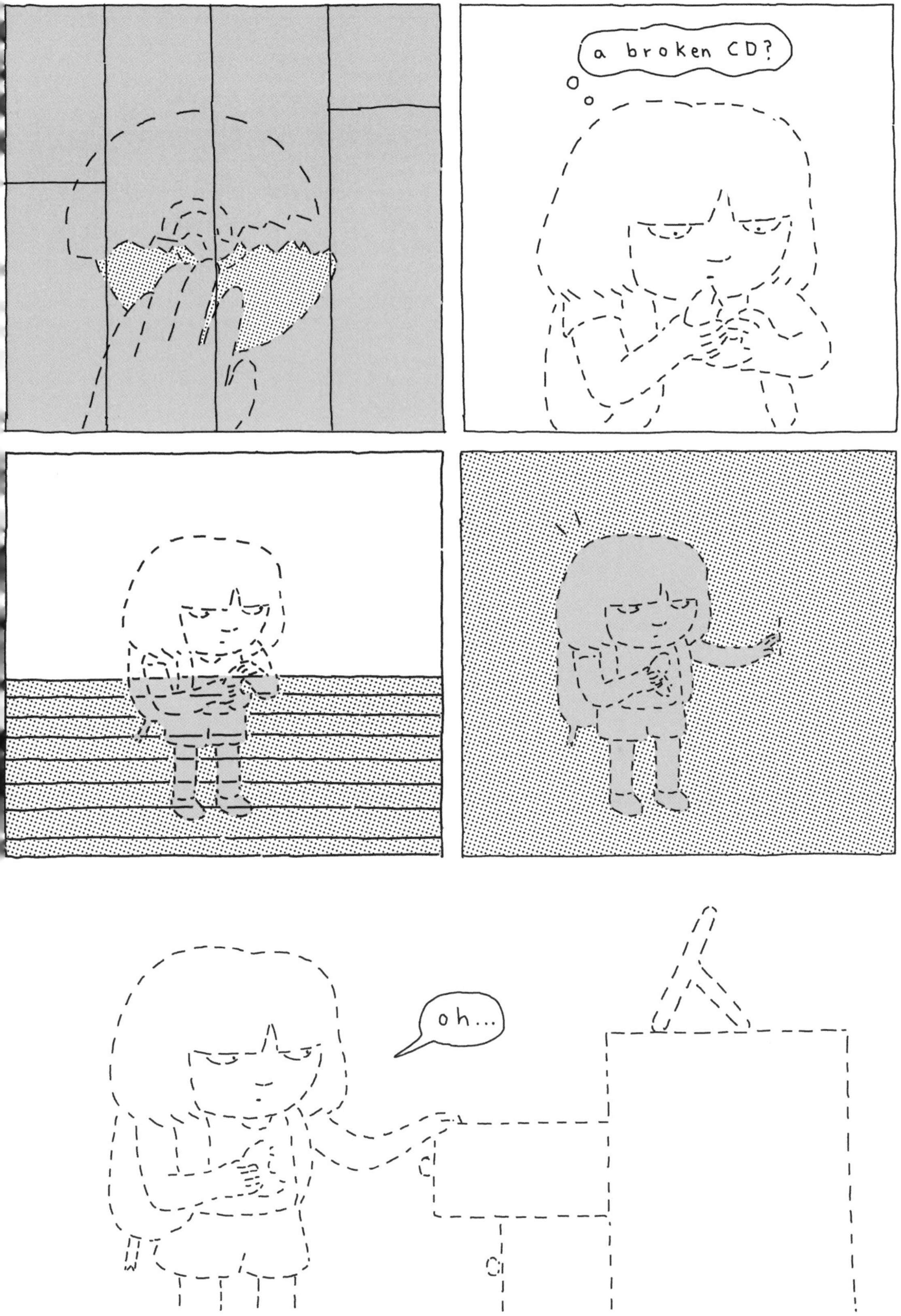
a broken CD?
oh...

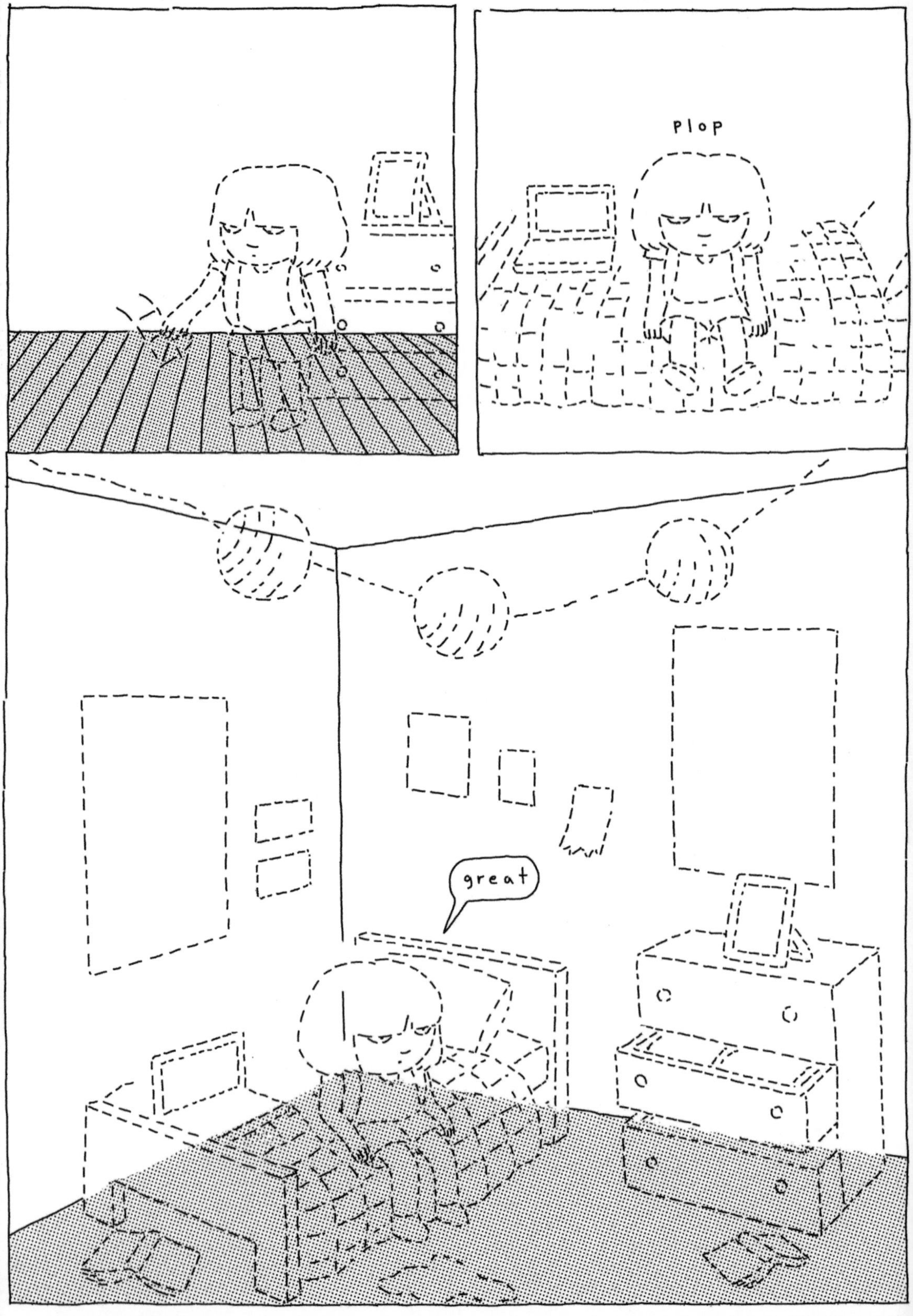
plop
great

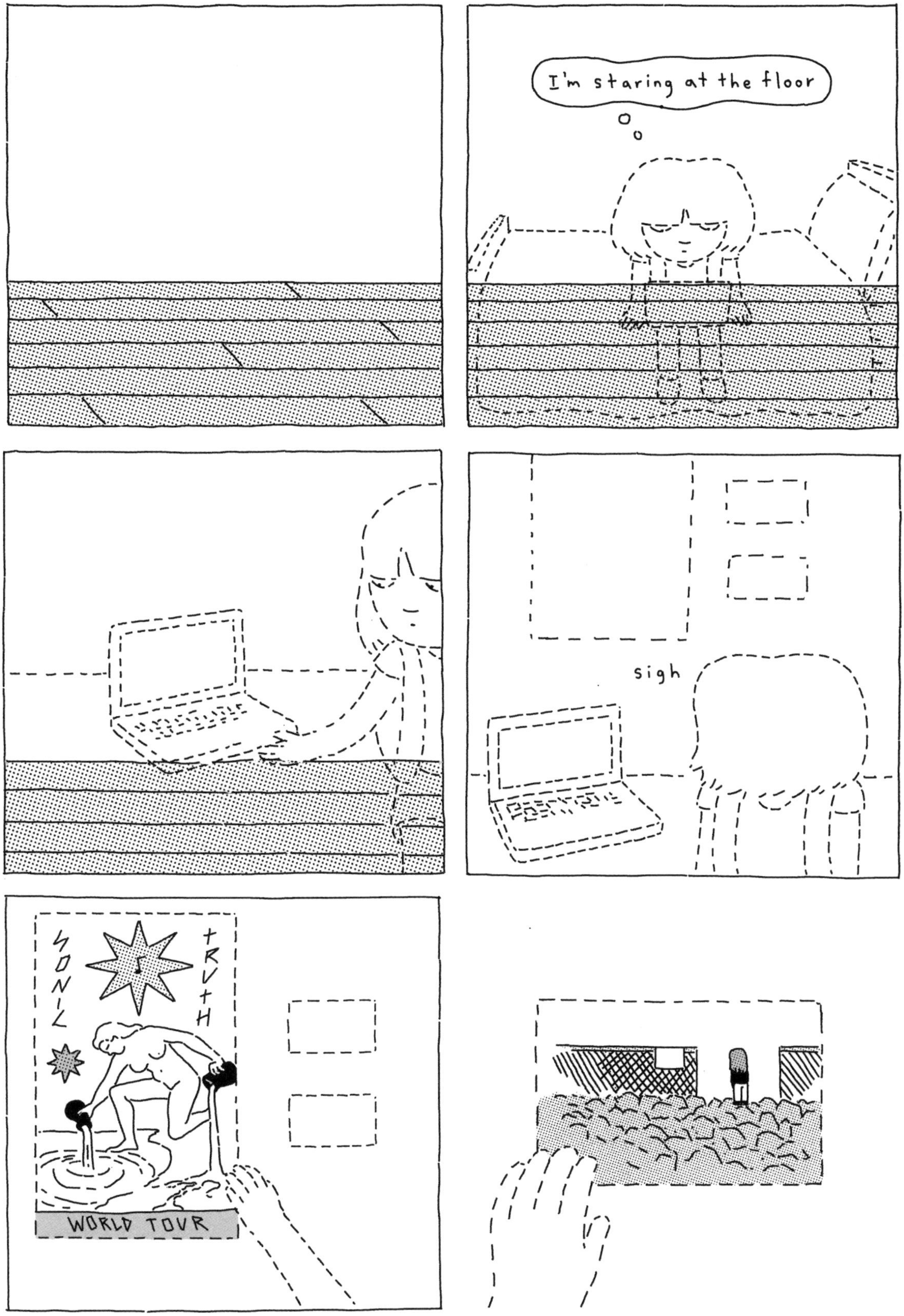
I'm staring at the floor
sigh
SONIC
TRUTH
WORLD TOUR

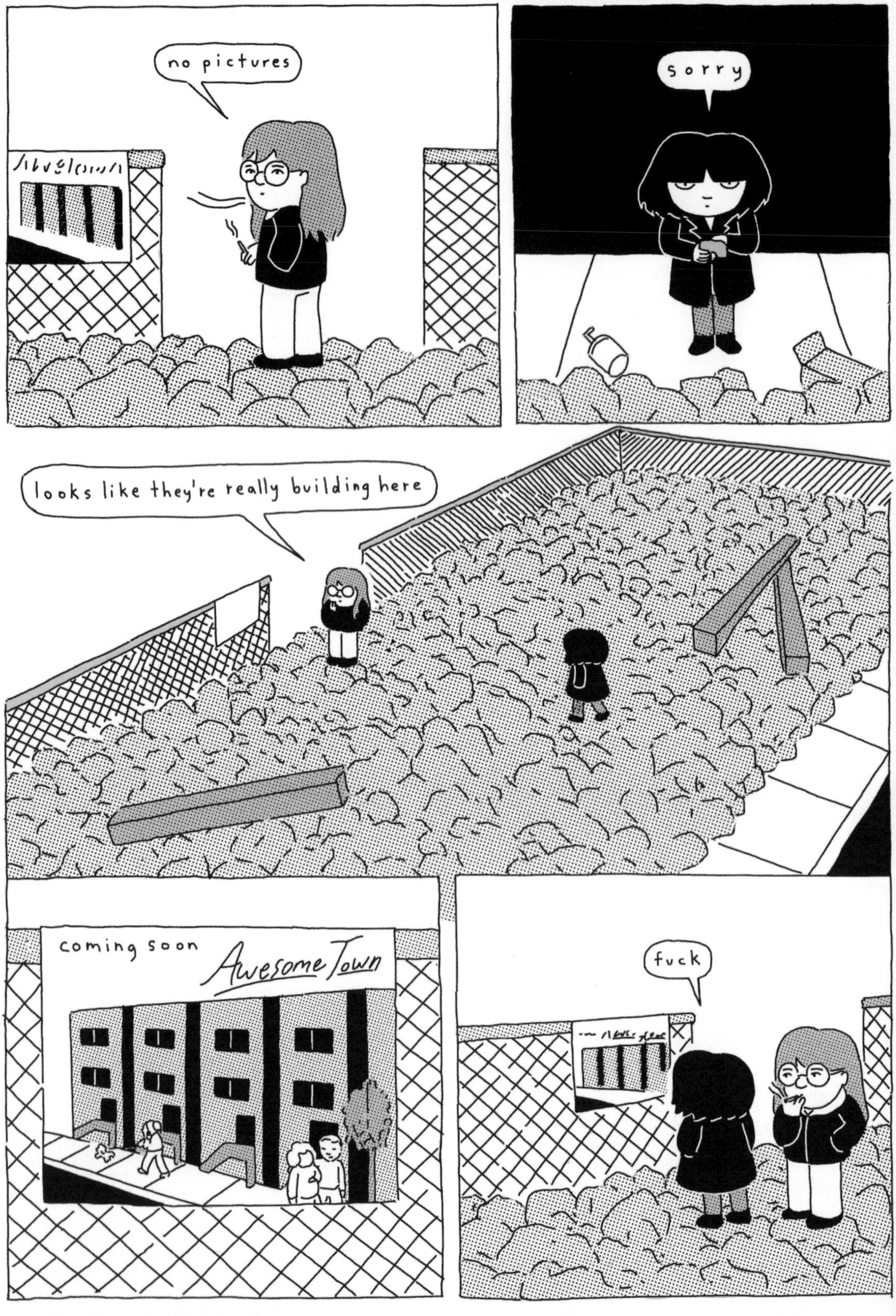
no pictures
sorry
looks like they're really building here
coming soon
Awesome Town
fuck

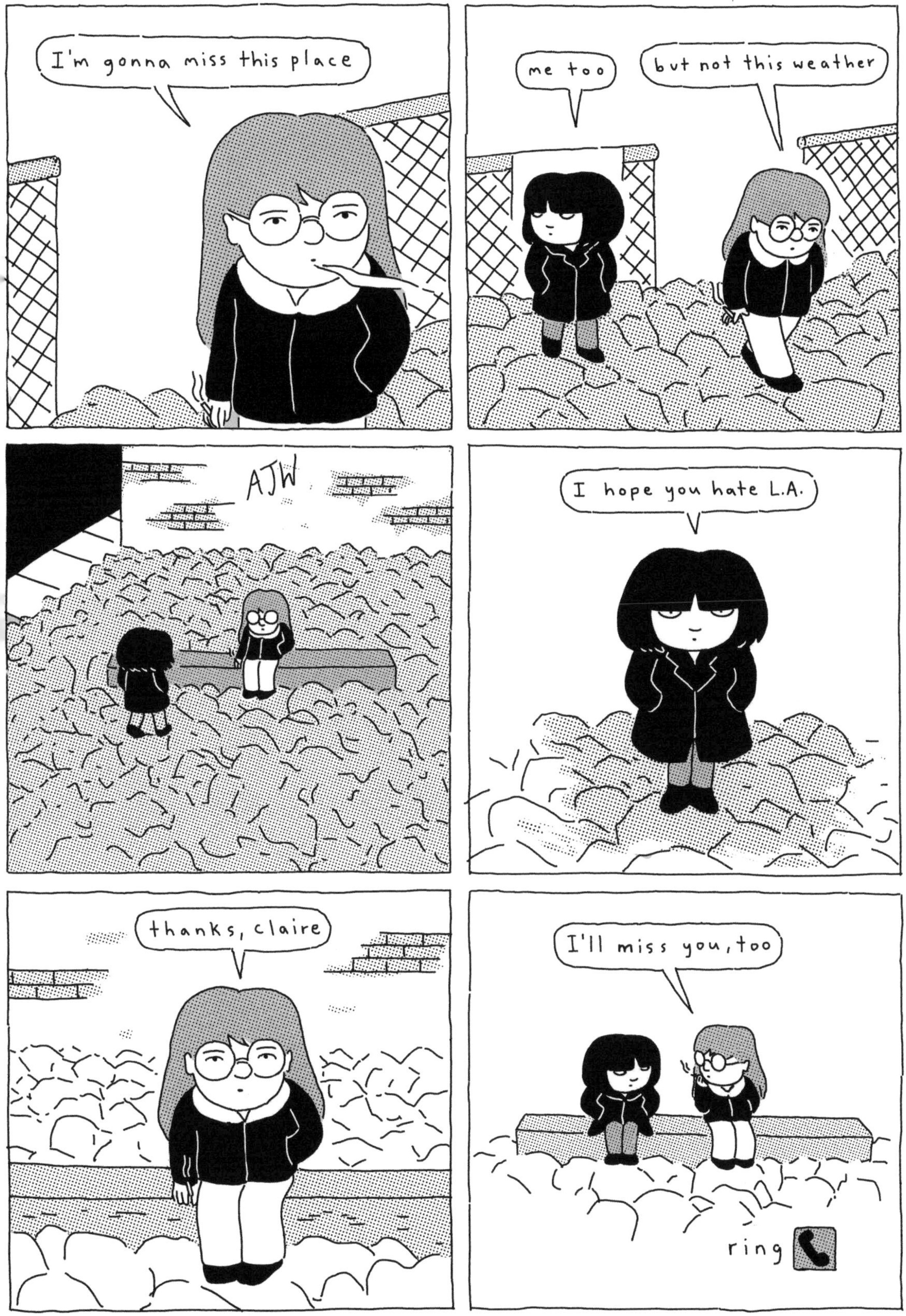
I'm gonna miss this place
me too
but not this weather
AJW
I hope you hate L.A.
thanks, claire
I'll miss you, too
ring

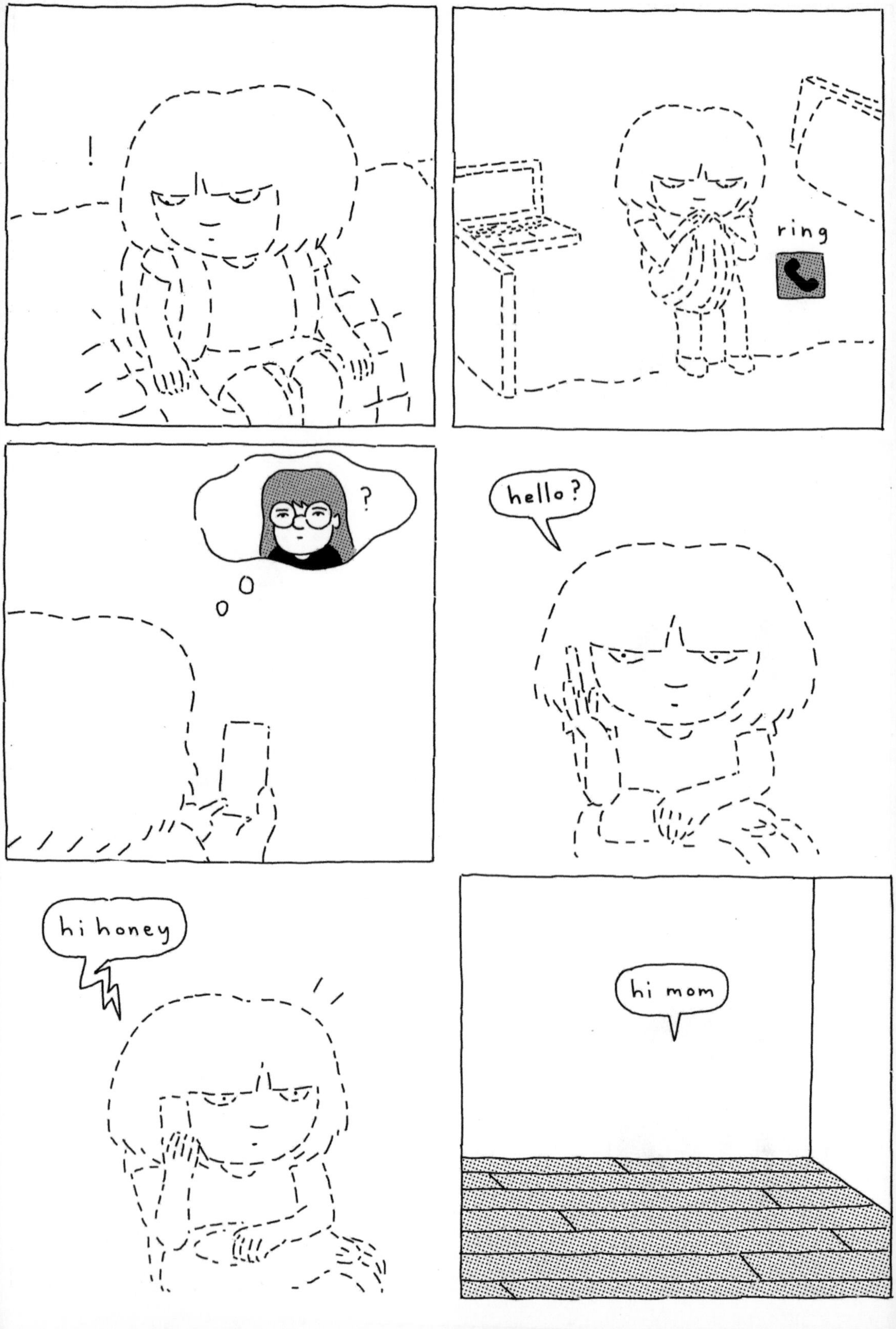
!
ring
?
hello?
hi honey
hi mom

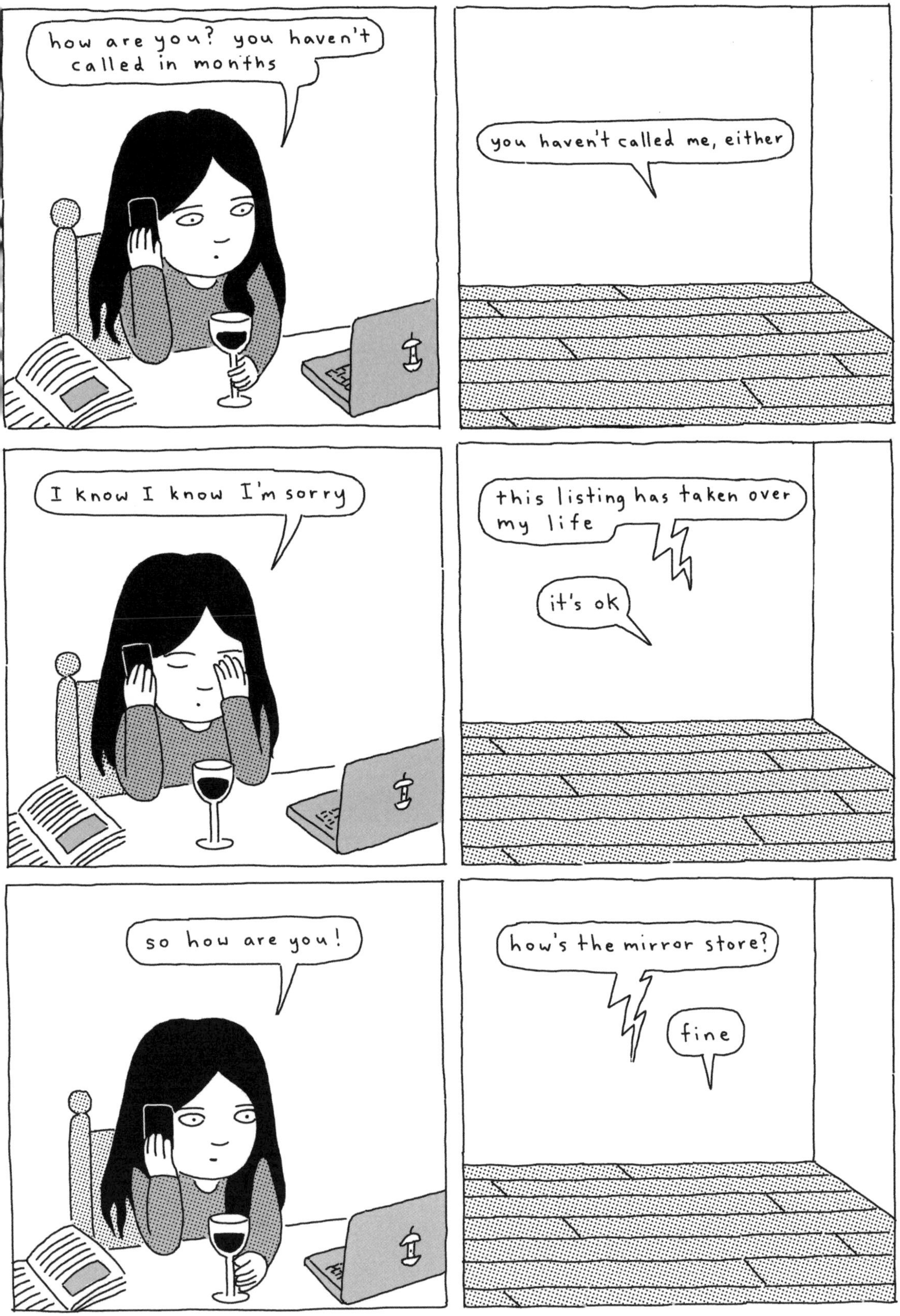
how are you? you haven't called in months
you haven't called me, either
I know I know I'm sorry
this listing has taken over my life
it's ok
so how are you!
how's the mirror store?
fine

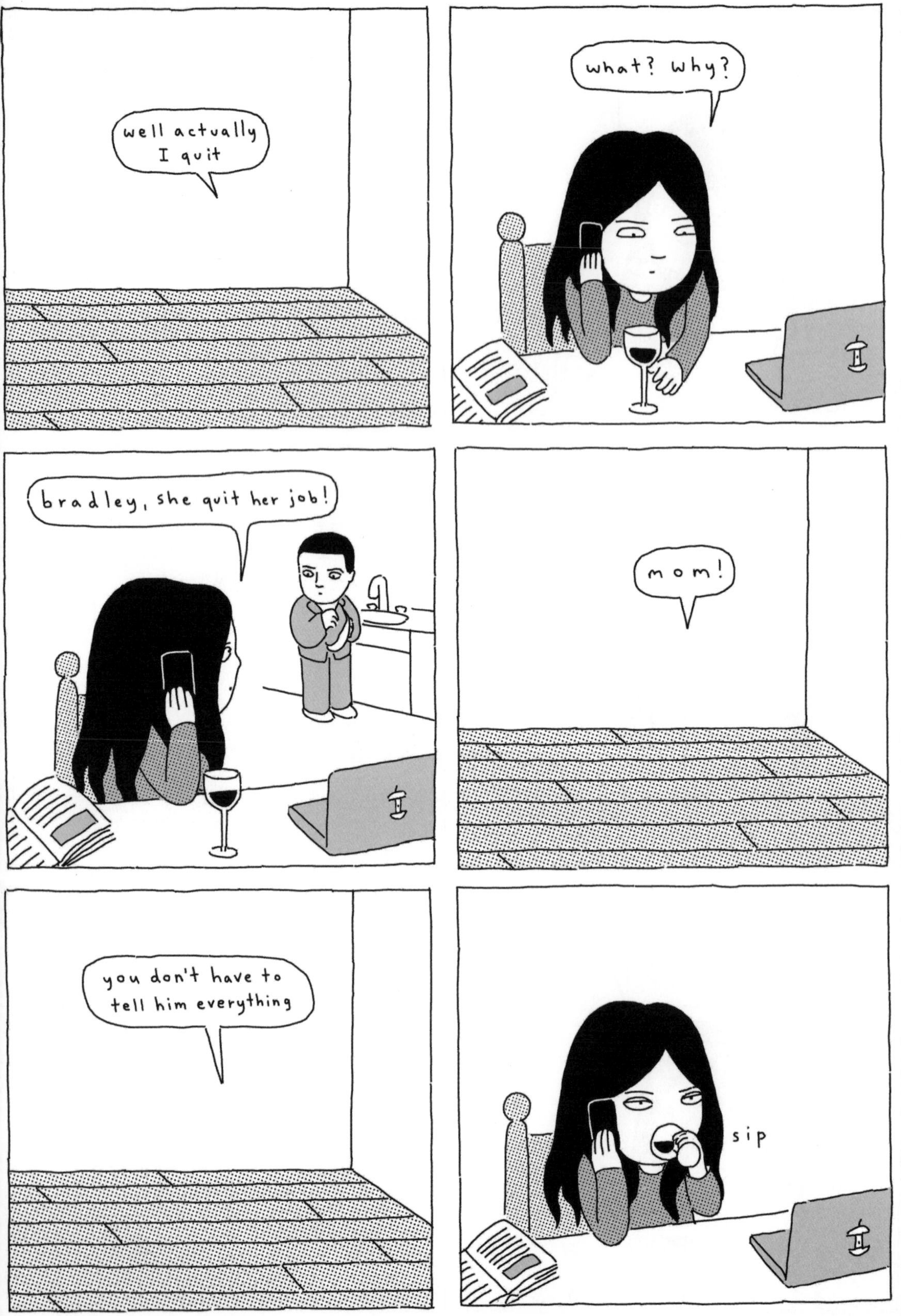
well actually I quit
what? why?
bradley, she quit her job!
mom!
you don't have to tell him everything
sip

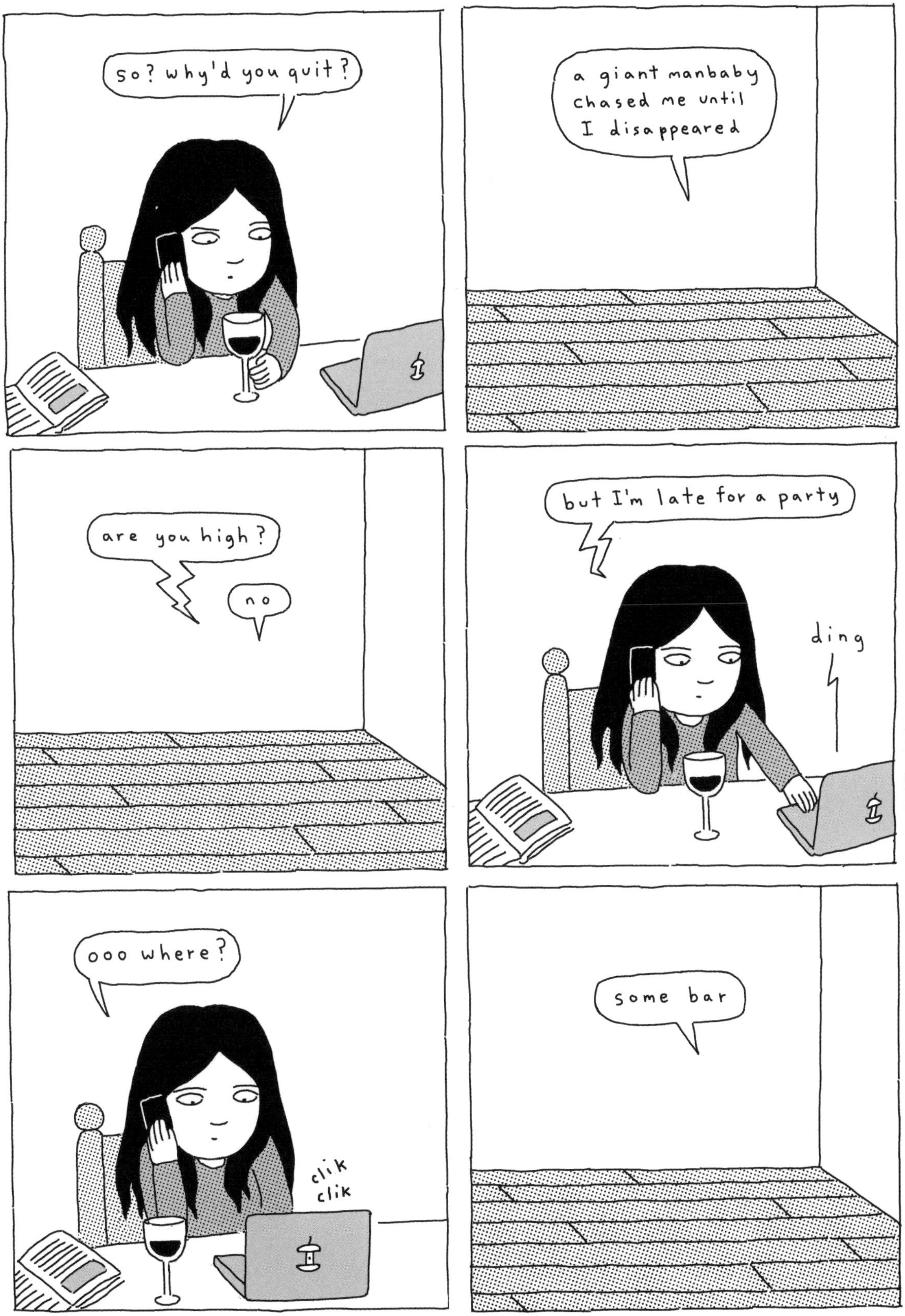
so? why'd you quit?
a giant manbaby chased me until I disappeared
are you high?
no
but I'm late for a party
ding
ooo where?
clik clik
some bar

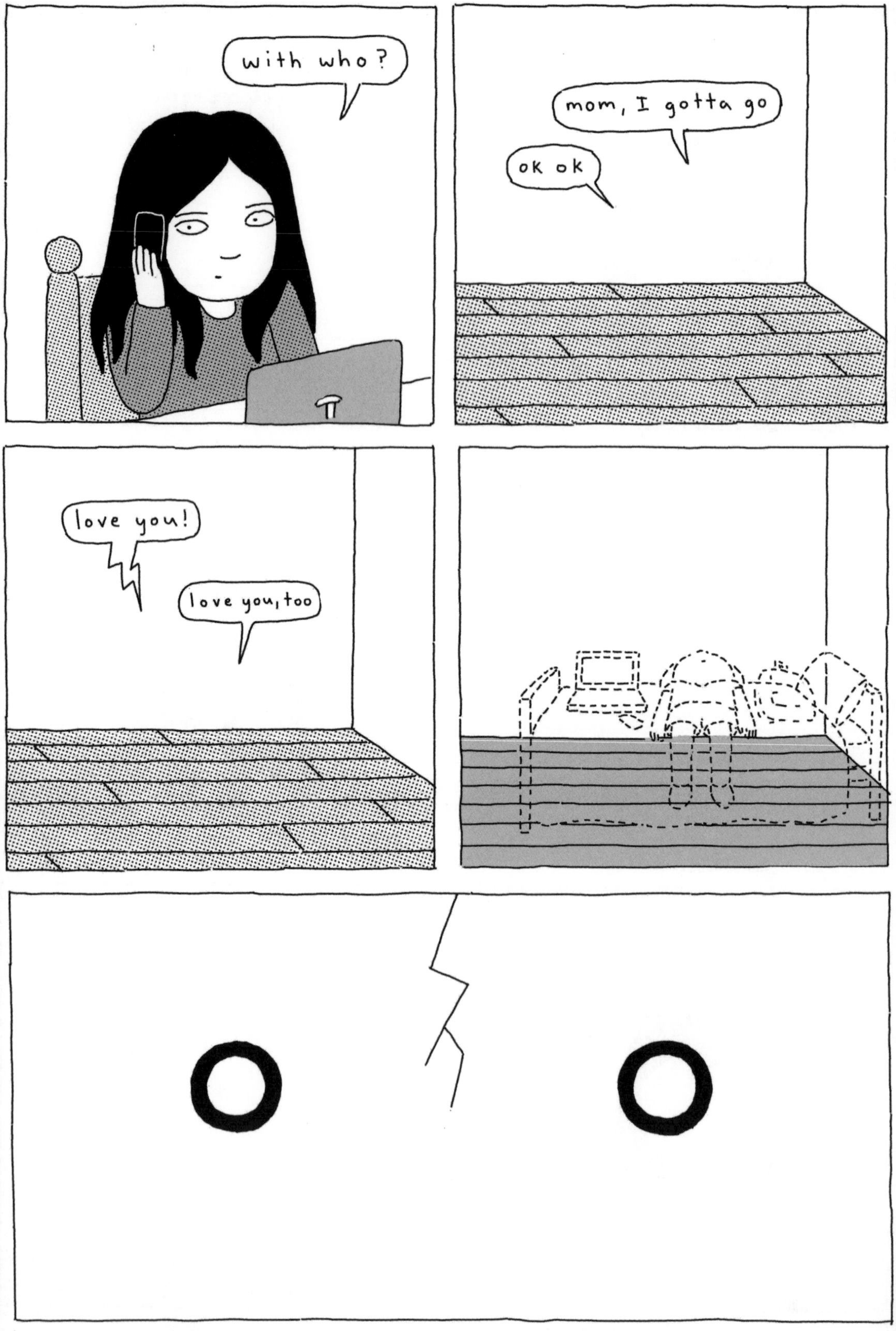
with who?
mom, I gotta go
ok ok
love you!
love you, too

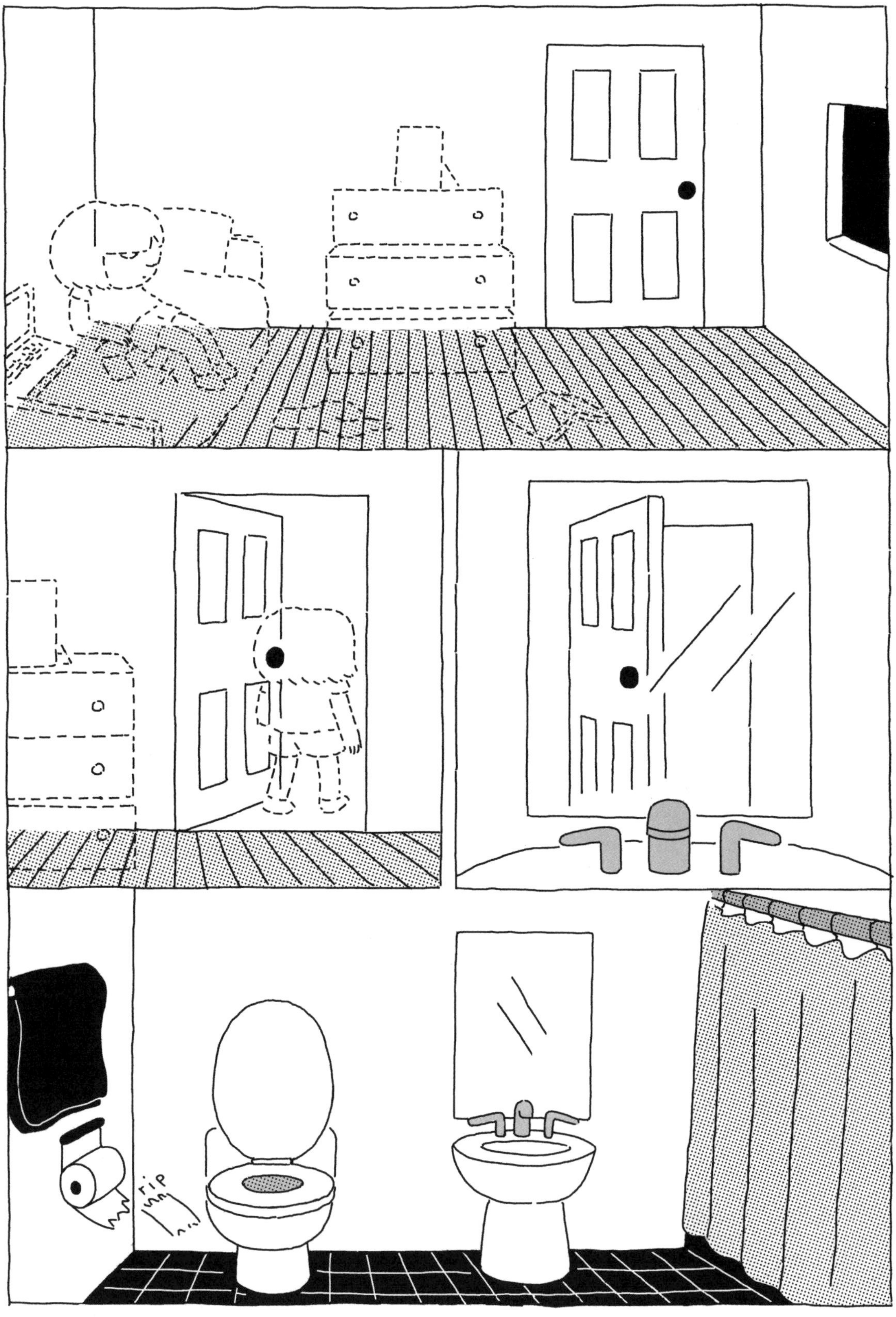
rip

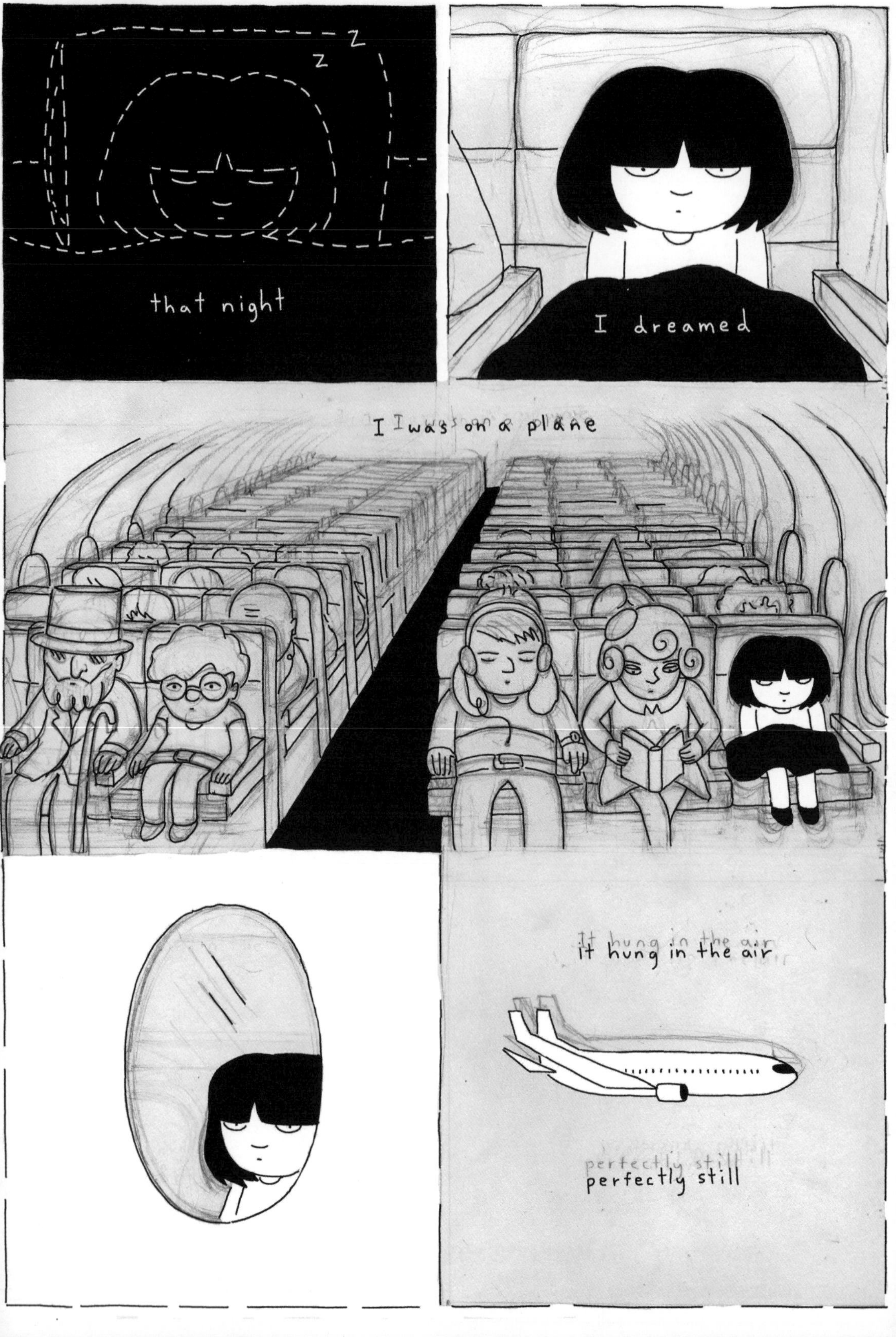
that night
I dreamed
I was on a plane
it hung in the air
perfectly still

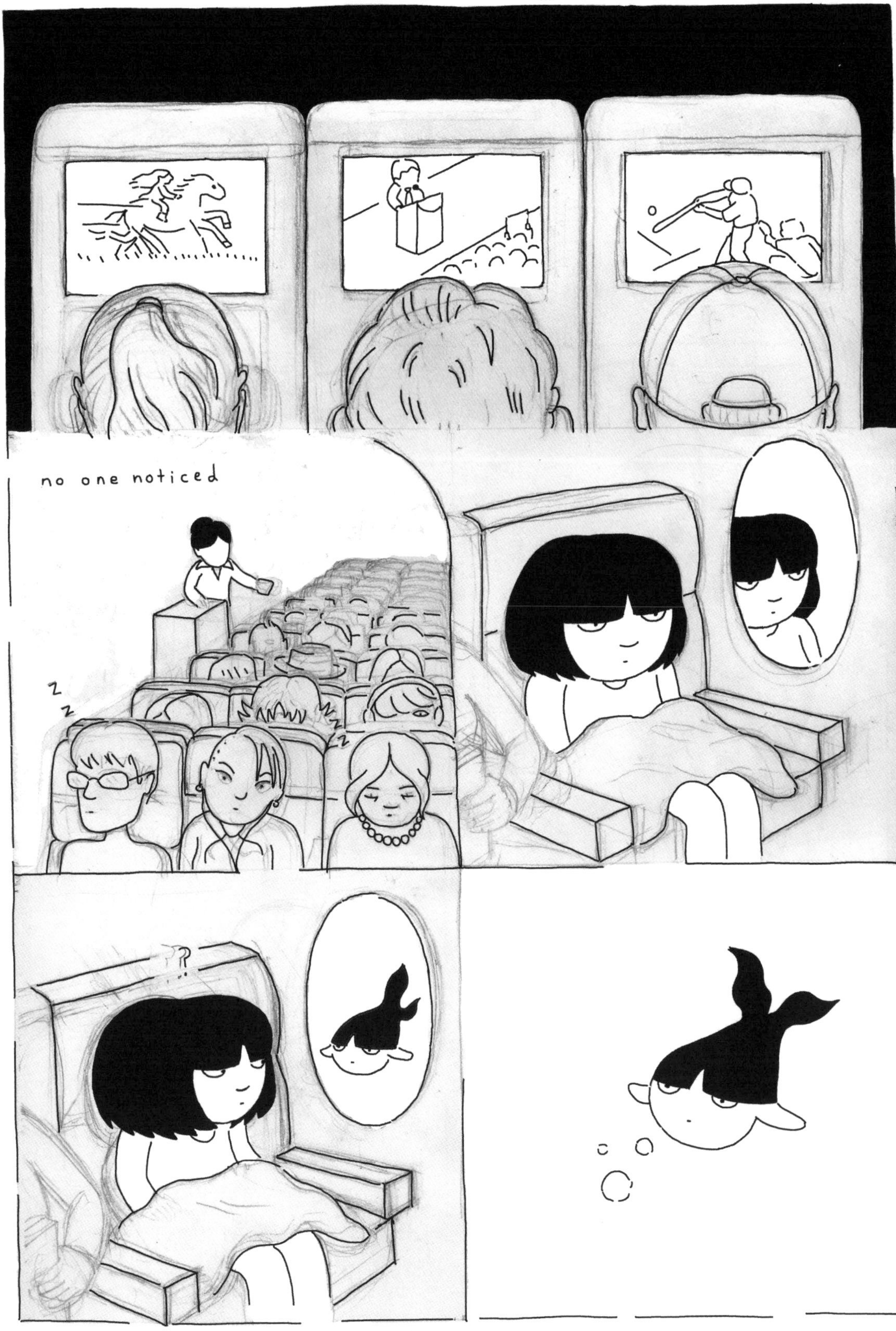
no one noticed

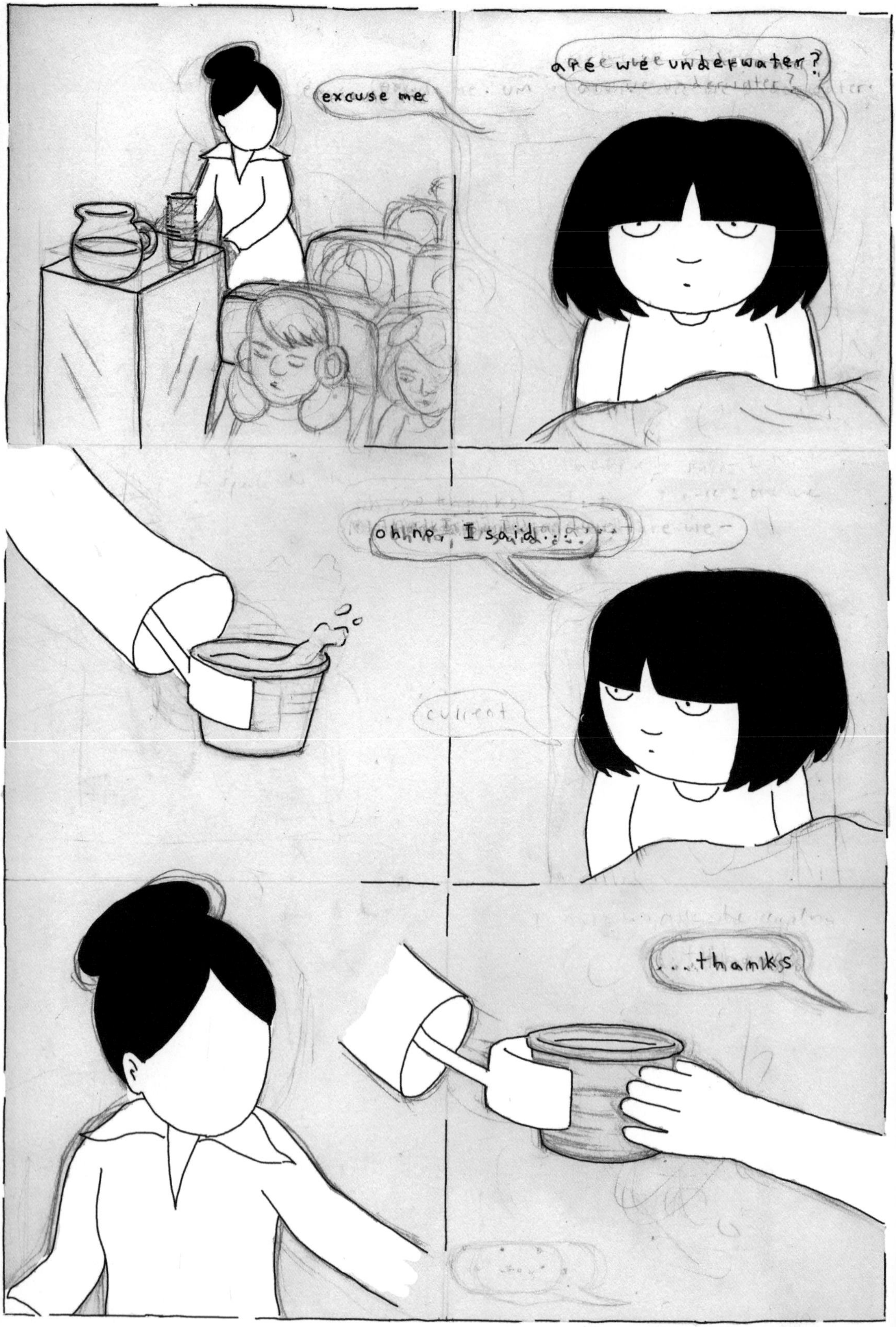
excuse me
are we underwater?
oh no, I said...
...thanks

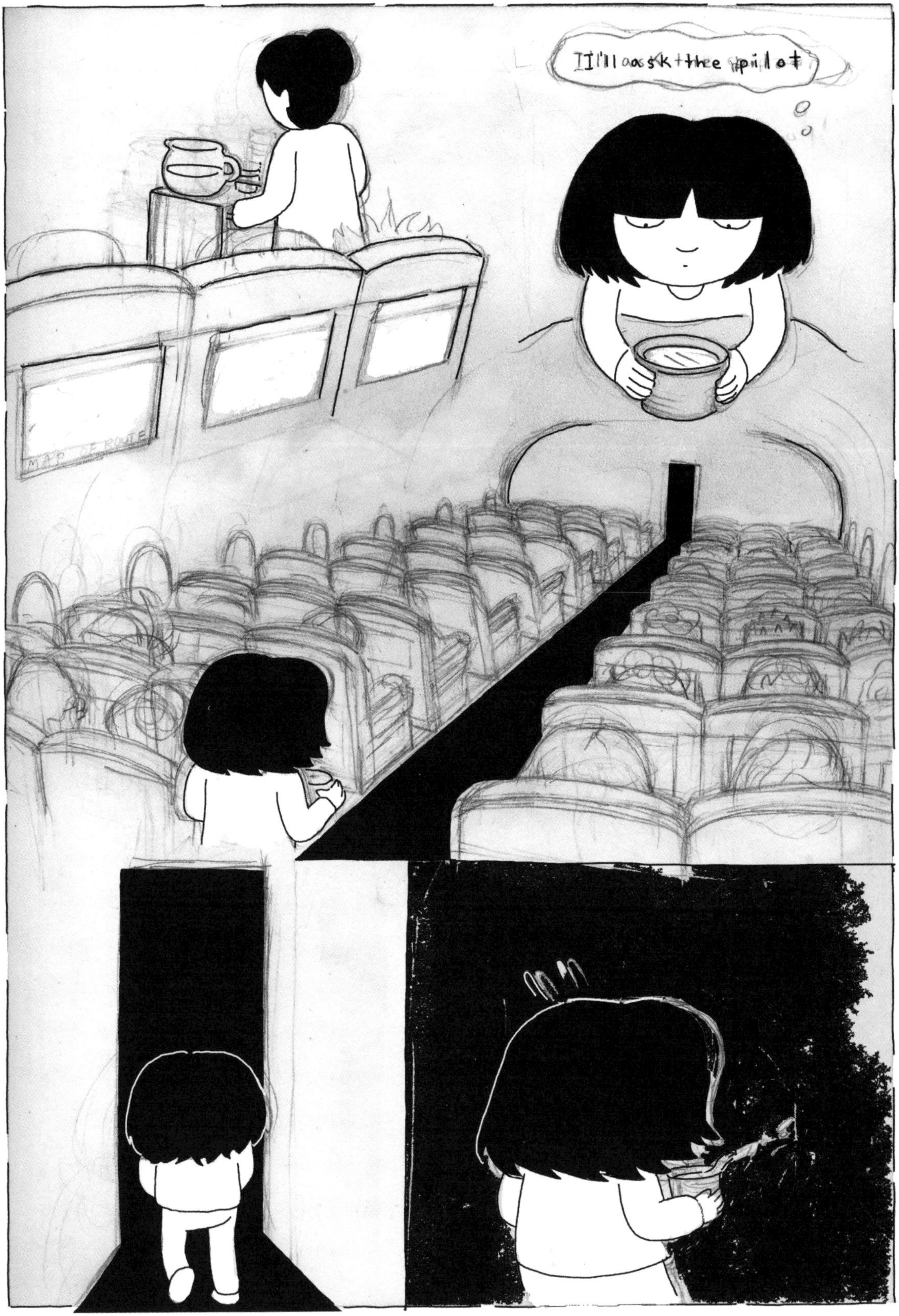
I'll ask the pilot
MAP OF ROUTE

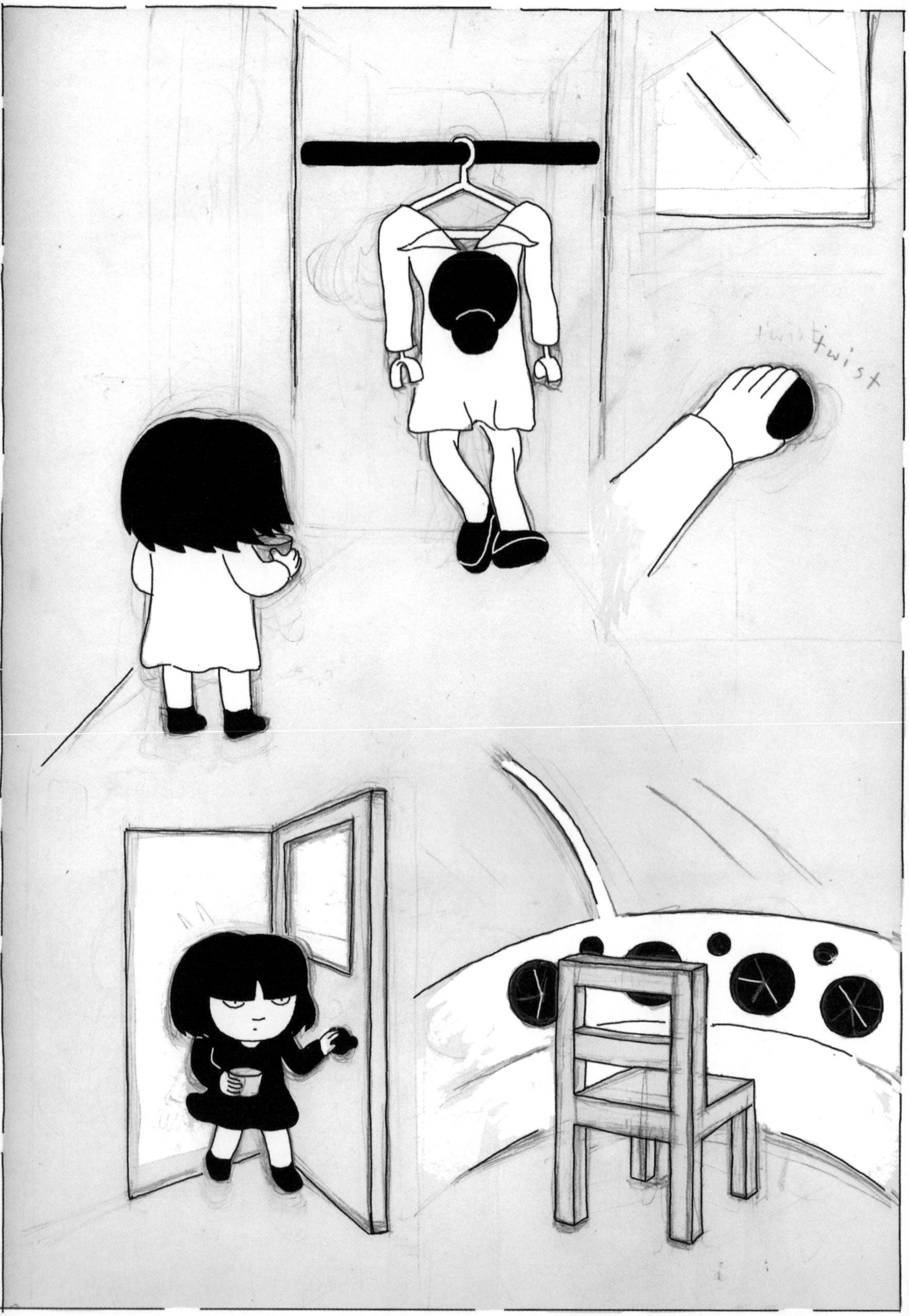
twist twist

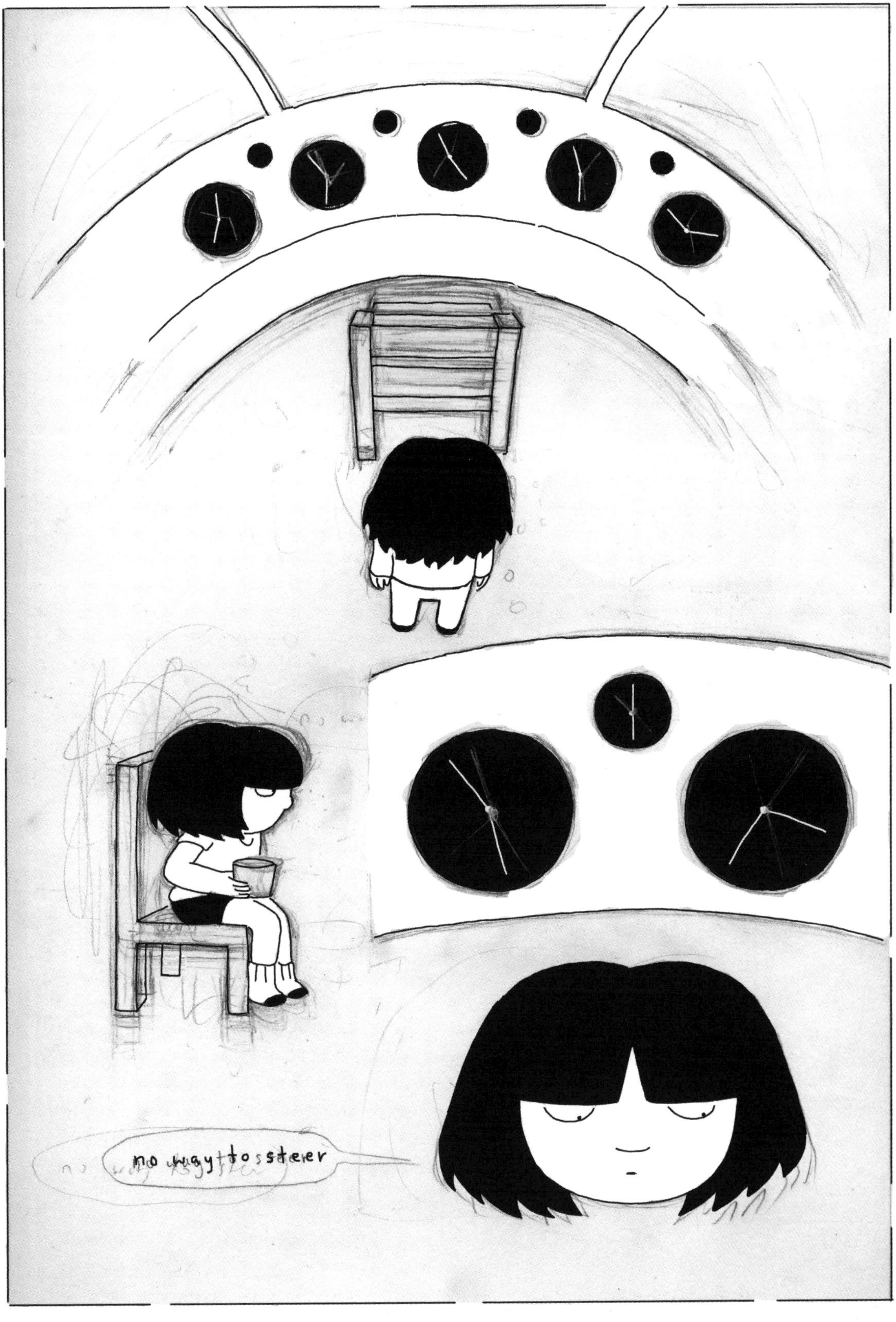

no way to steer

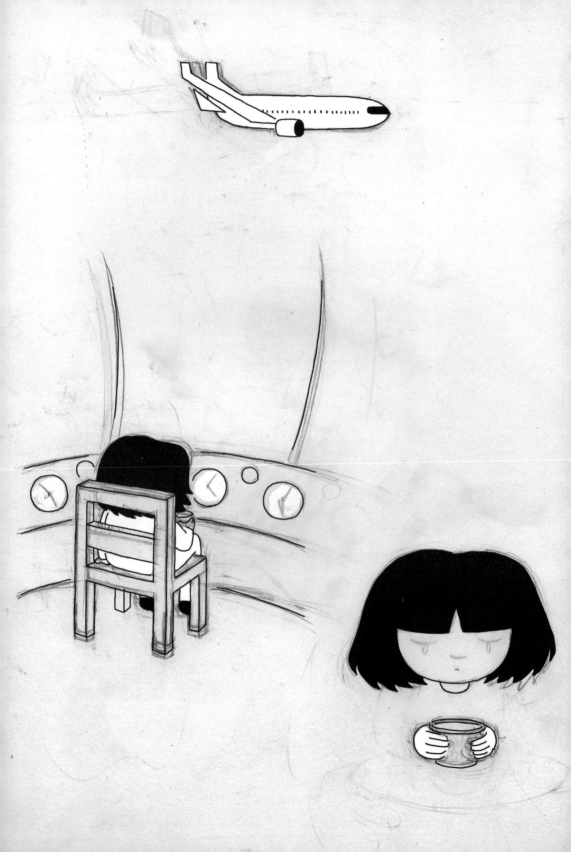

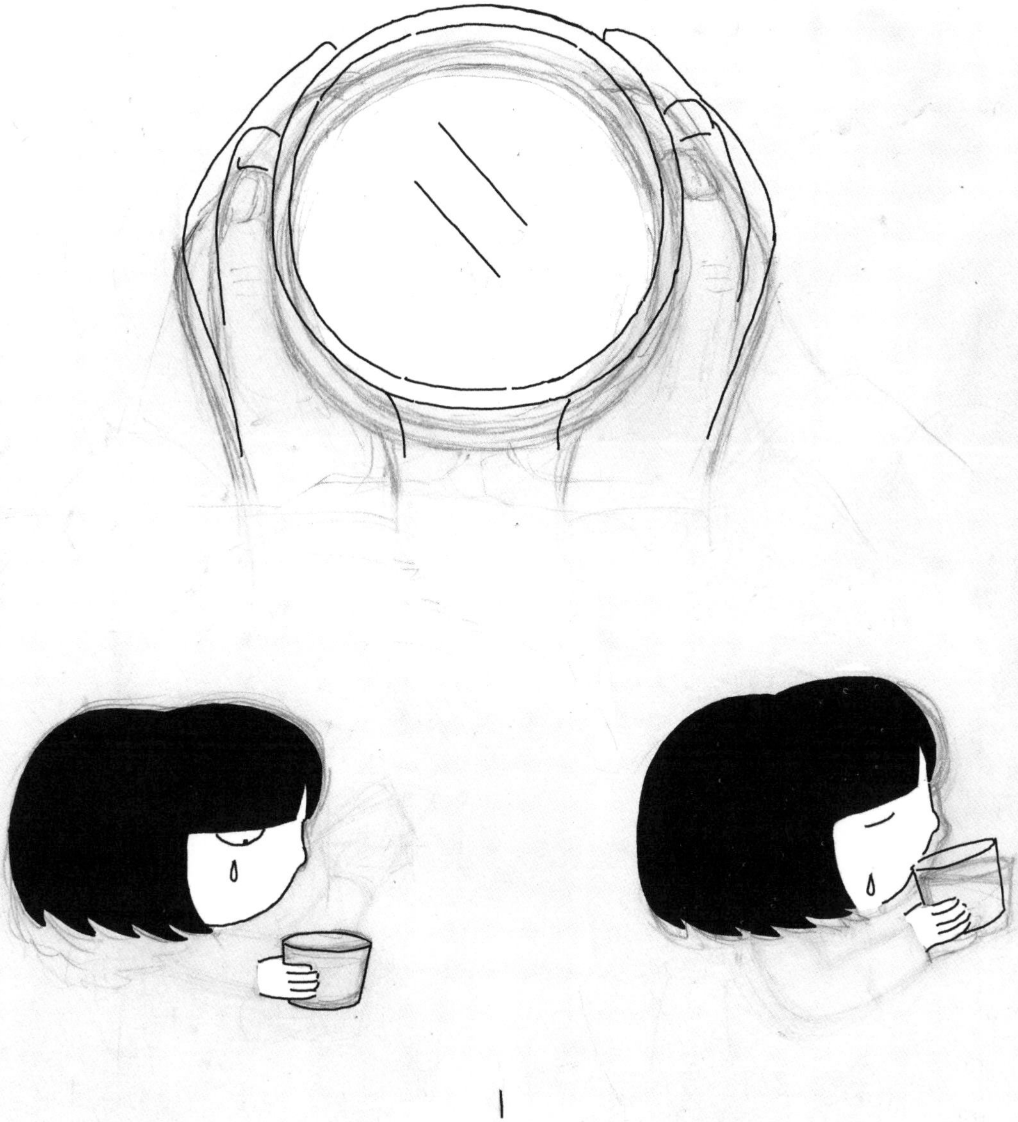
!

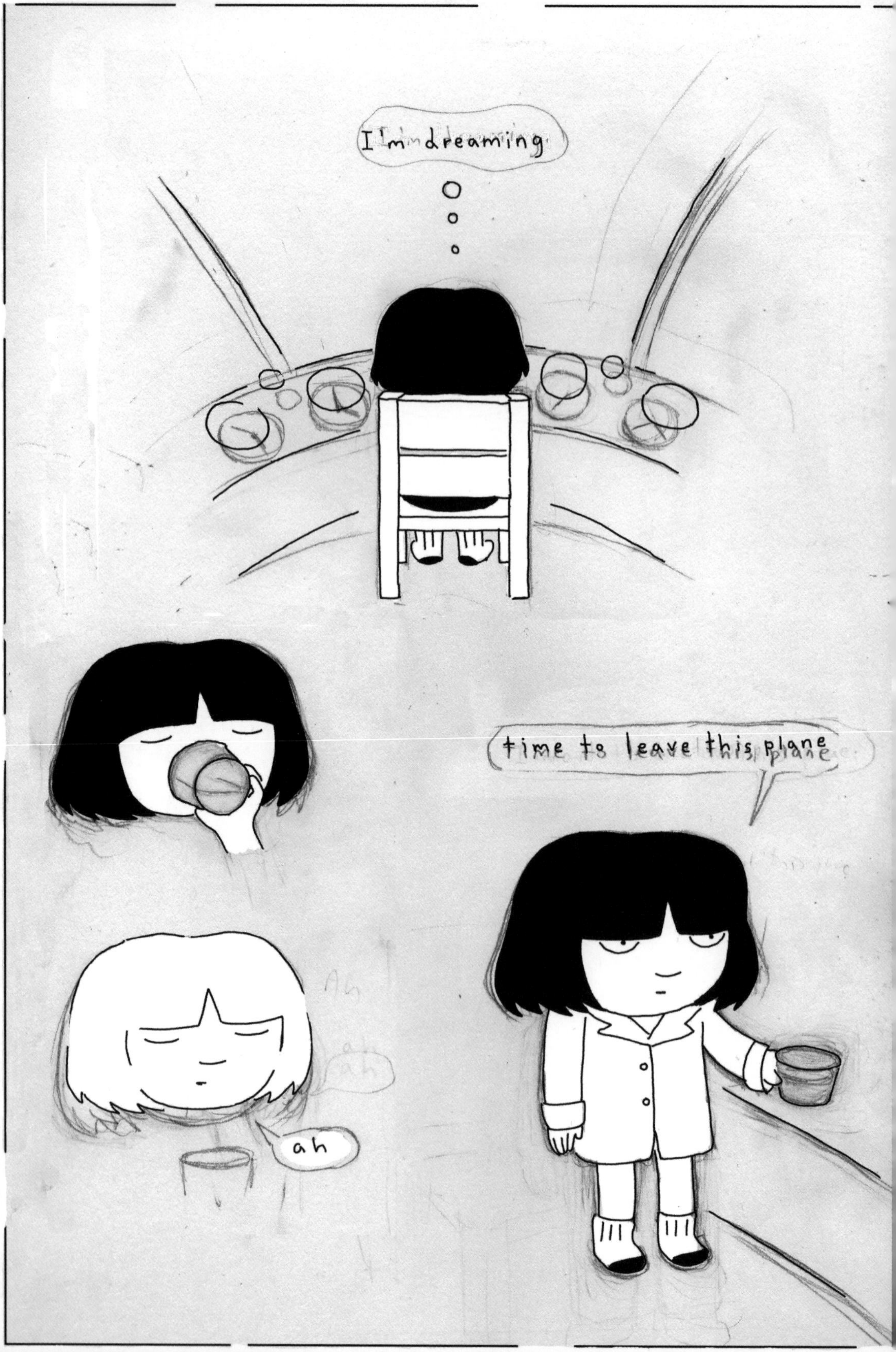
I'm dreaming
time to leave this plane
ah

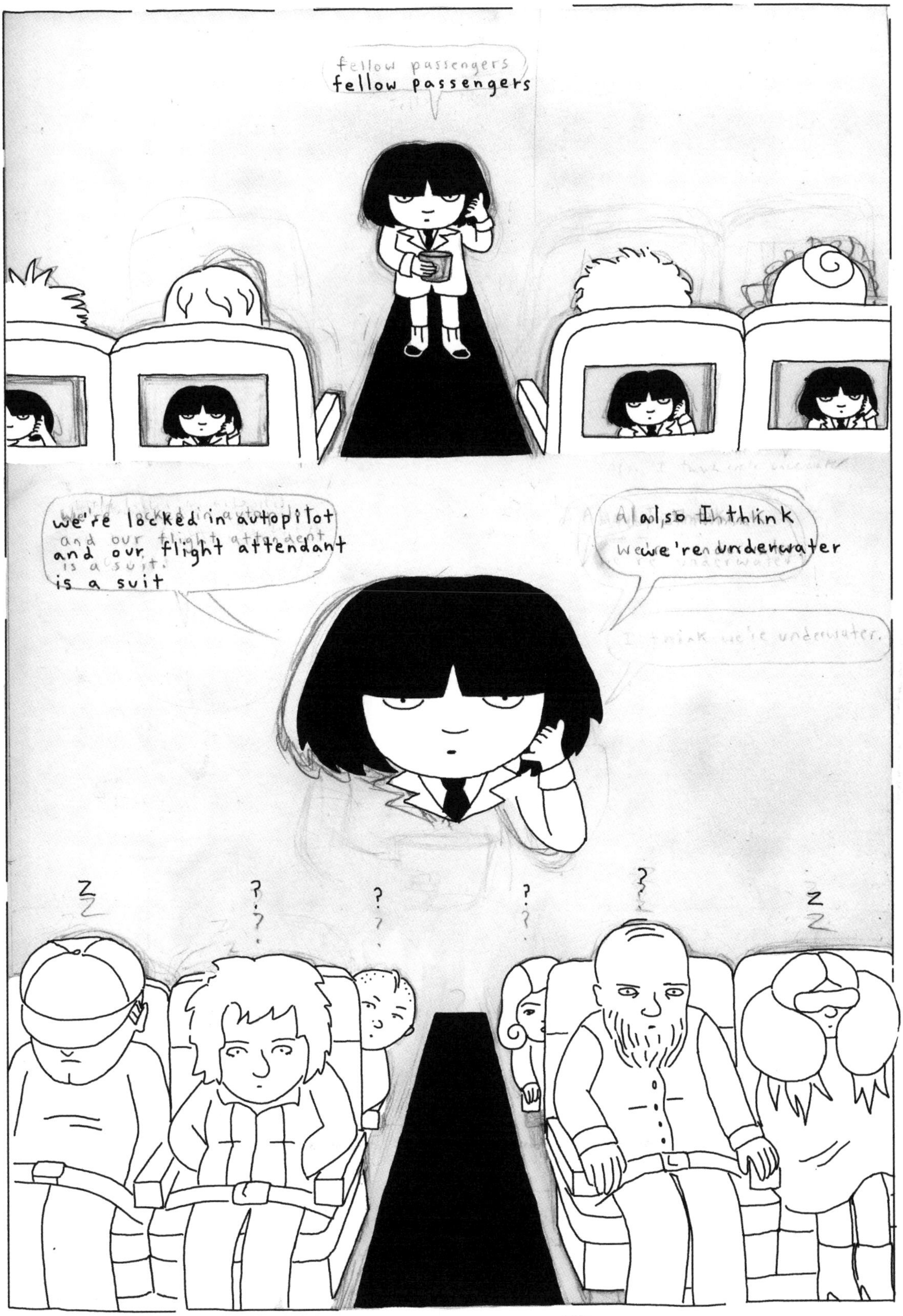
fellow passengers
fellow passengers
we're locked in autopilot and our flight attendant is a suit
also I think we're underwater
Z Z
? ? ?
? ? ?
? ?
?
Z Z

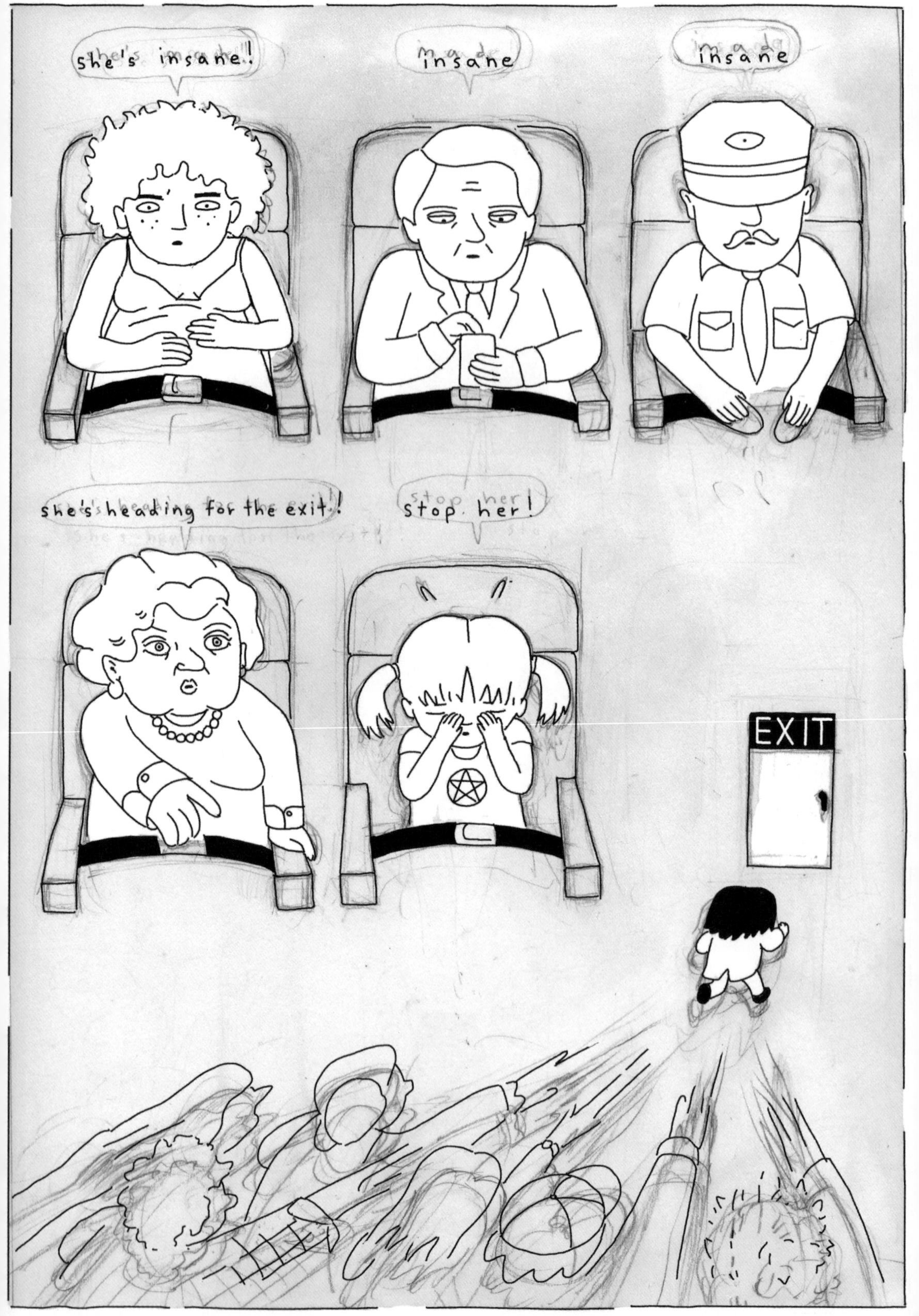
she's insane!
insane
insane
she's heading for the exit!
stop her!
EXIT

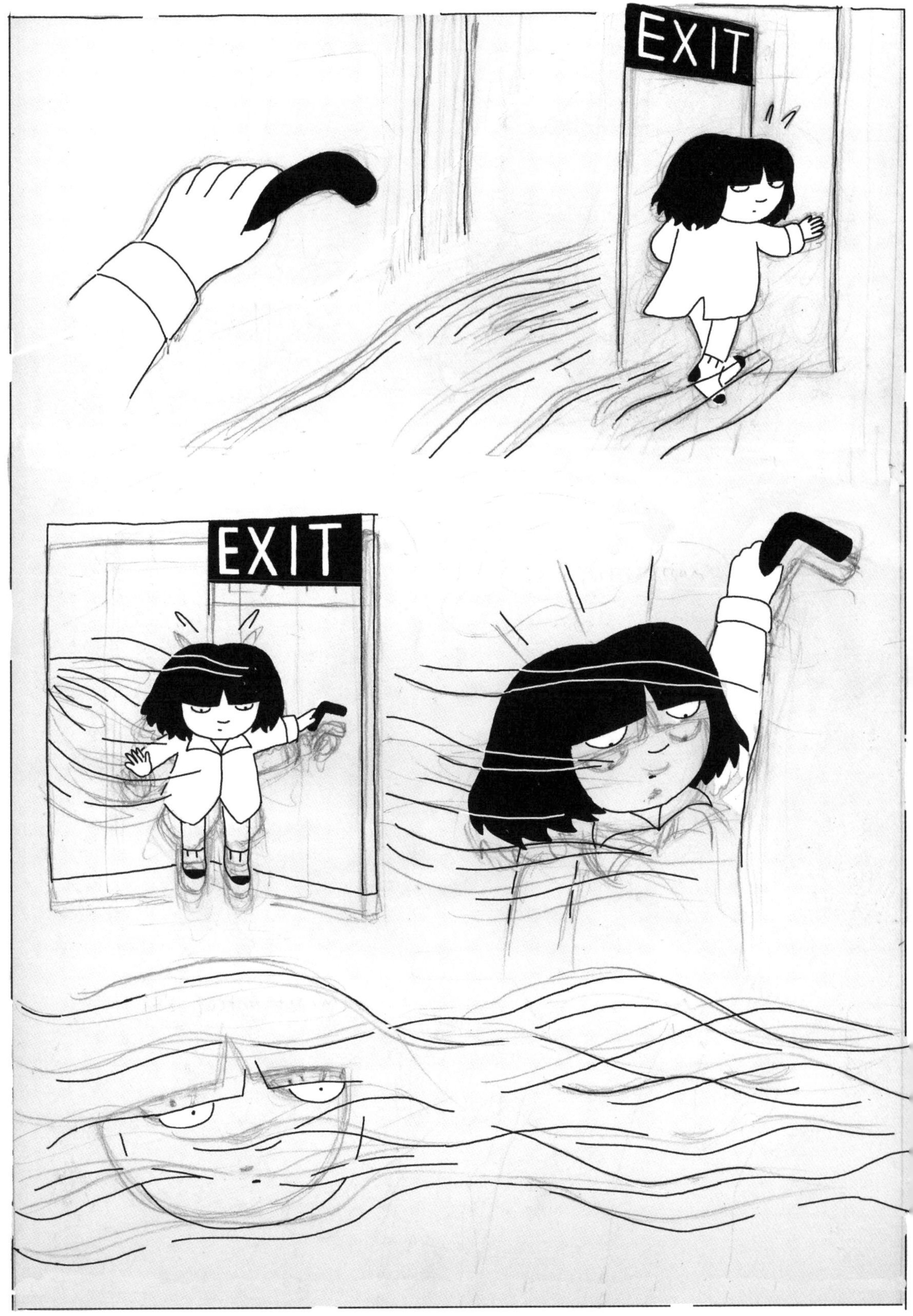
EXIT
EXIT

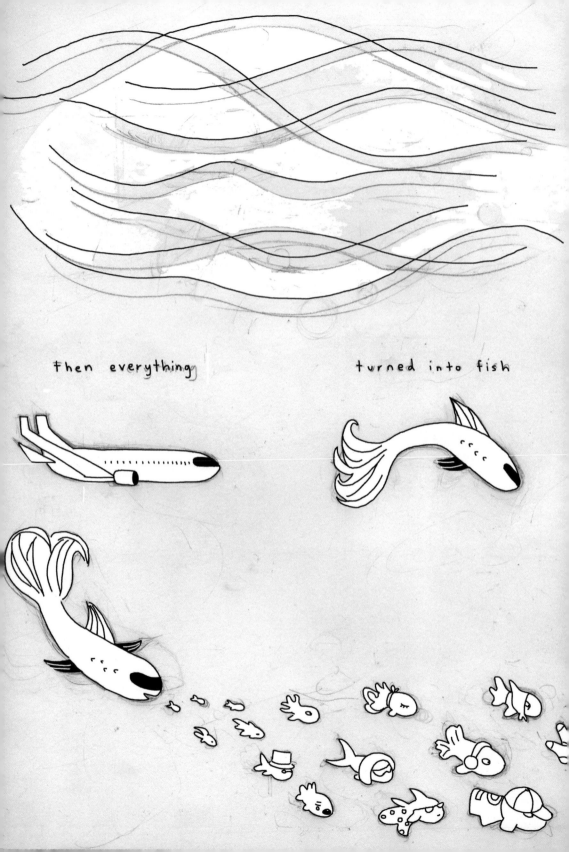

then everything   turned into fish

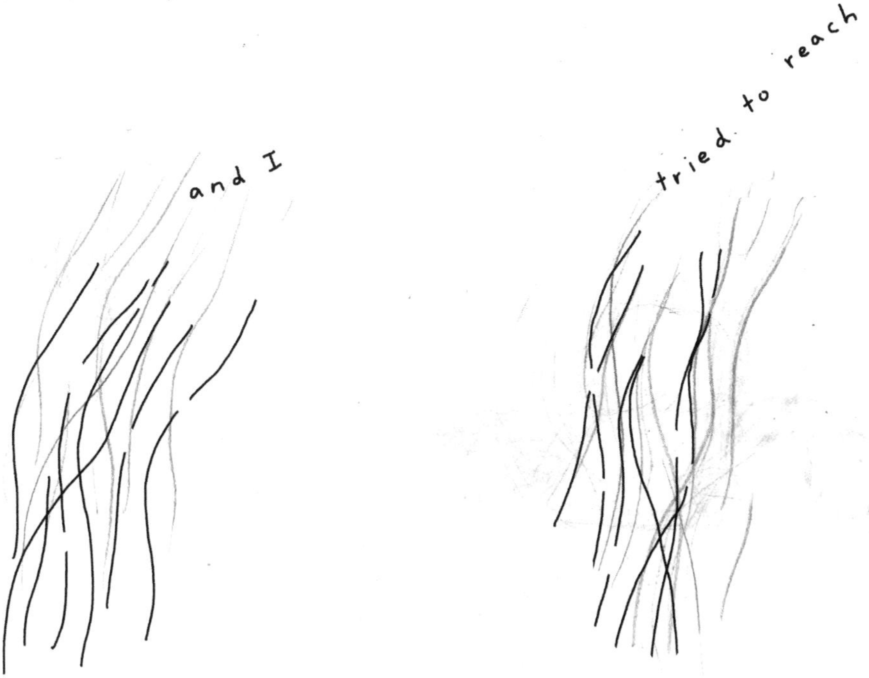
and I
tried to reach

the surface

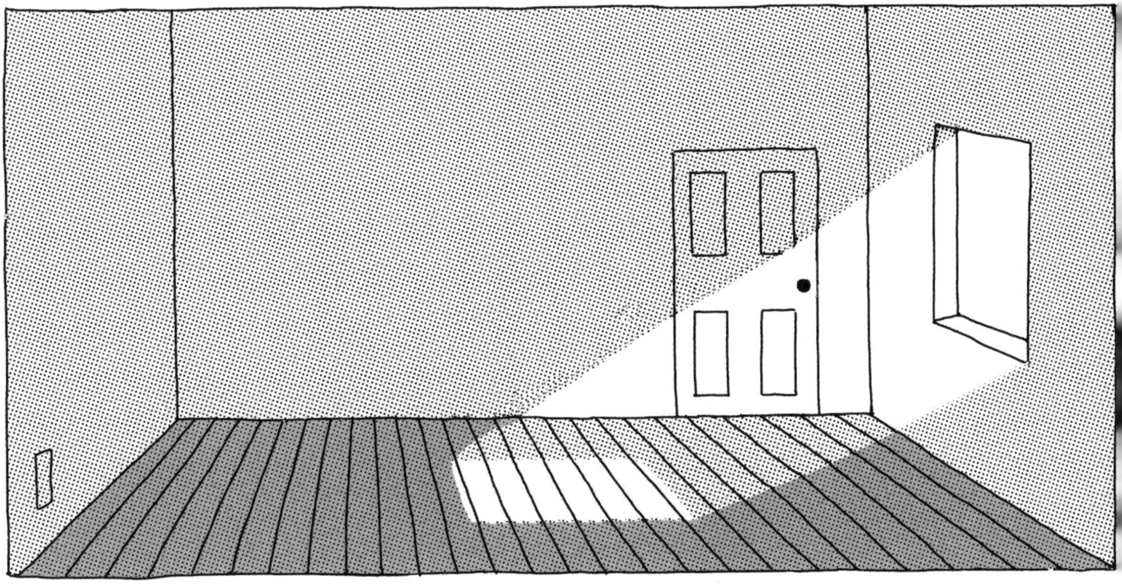

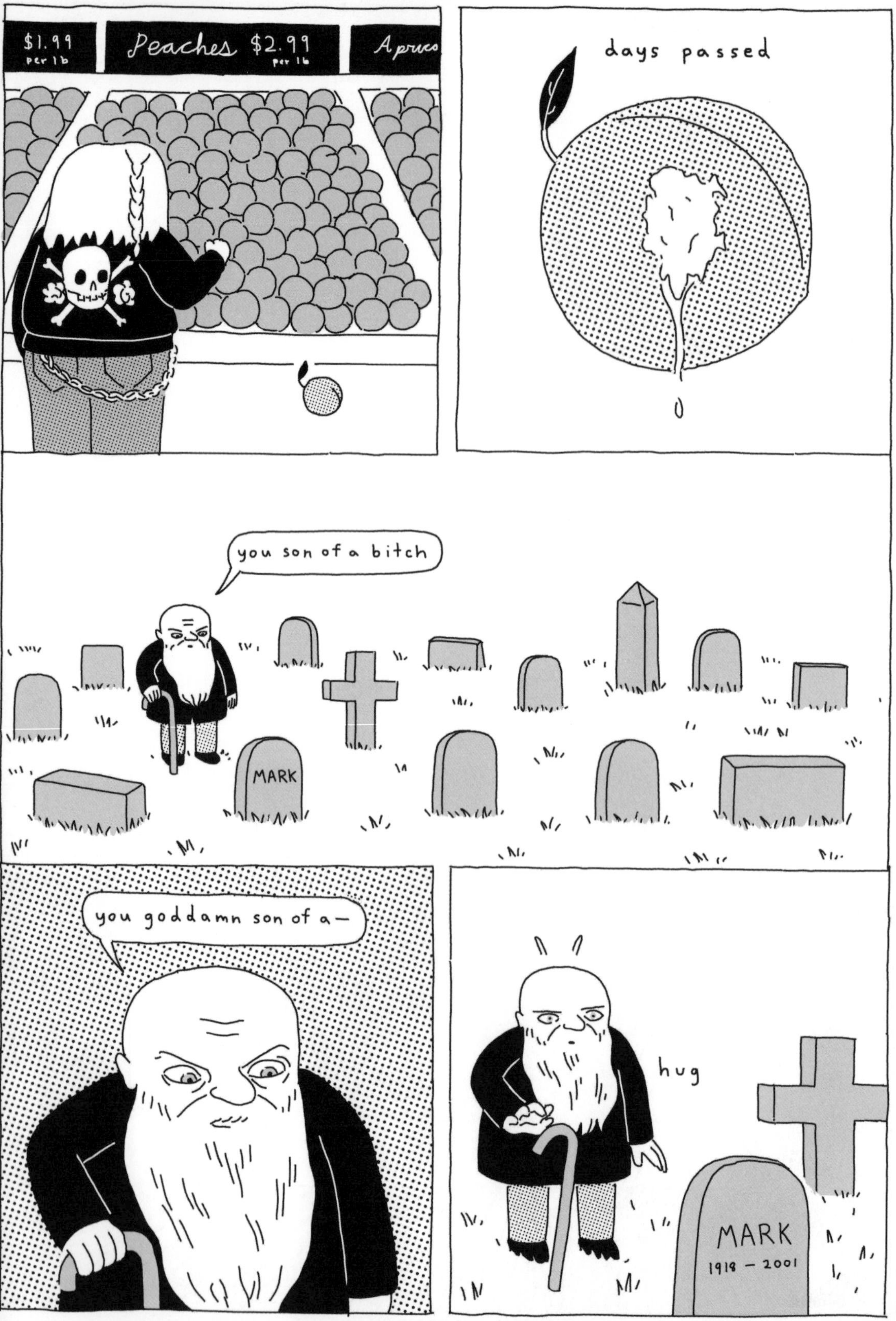
$1.99 per lb
Peaches $2.99 per lb
Aprico
days passed
you son of a bitch
MARK
you goddamn son of a—
hug
MARK
1918 — 2001

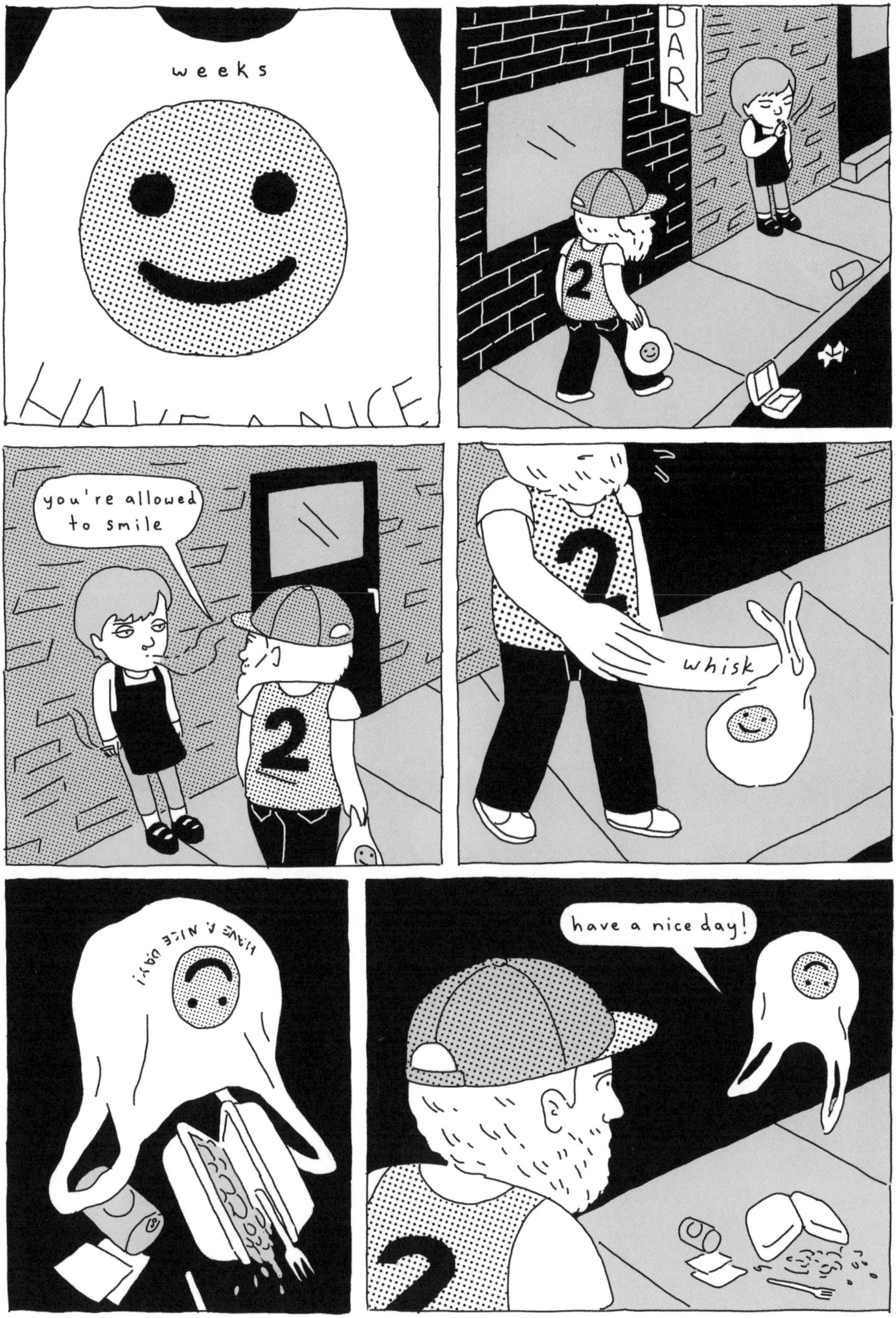
weeks
BAR
you're allowed to smile
whisk
HAVE A NICE DAY!
have a nice day!

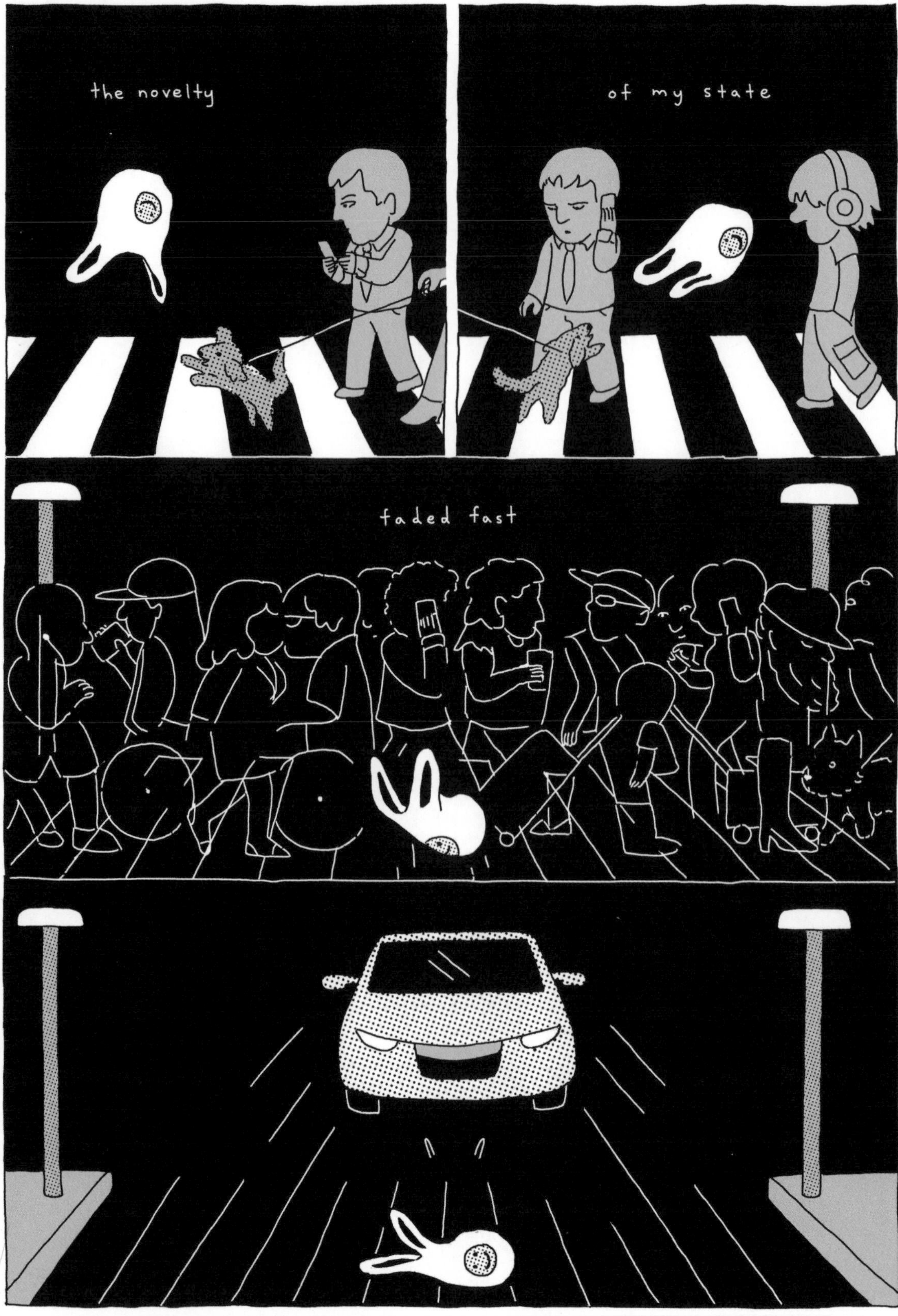
the novelty
of my state
faded fast

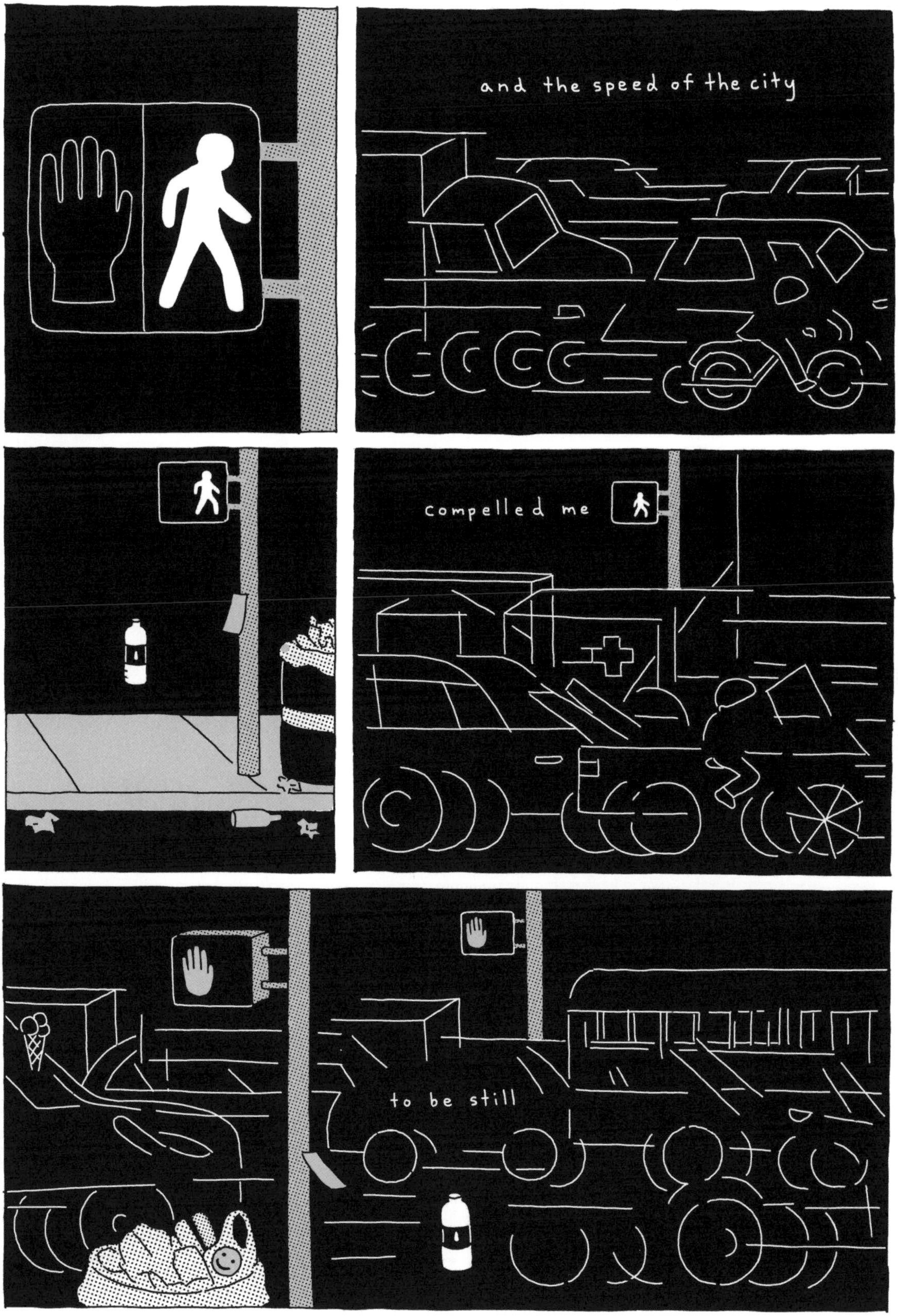
and the speed of the city
compelled me
to be still

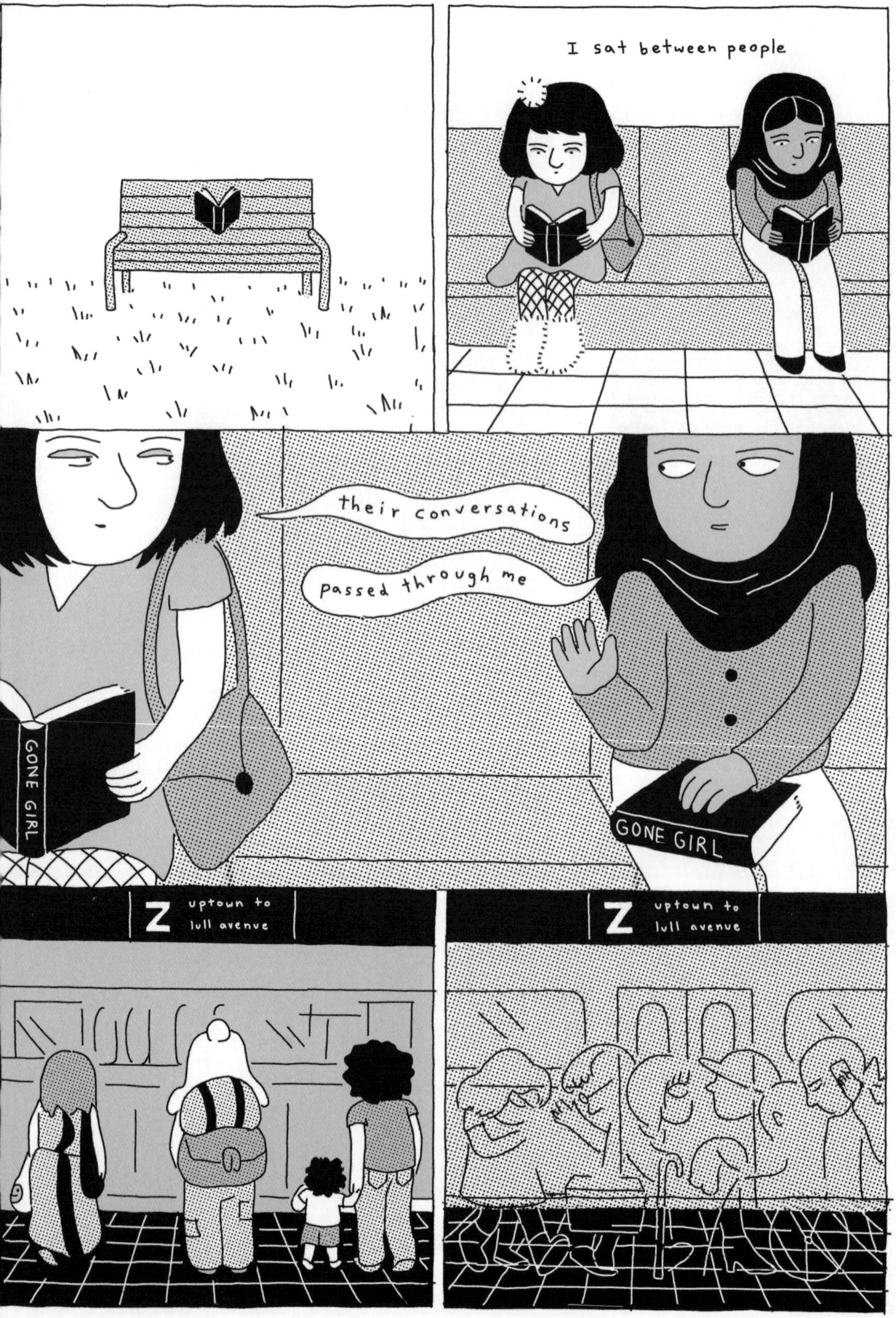

I sat between people
their conversations
passed through me
GONE GIRL
GONE GIRL
Z uptown to lull avenue
Z uptown to lull avenue

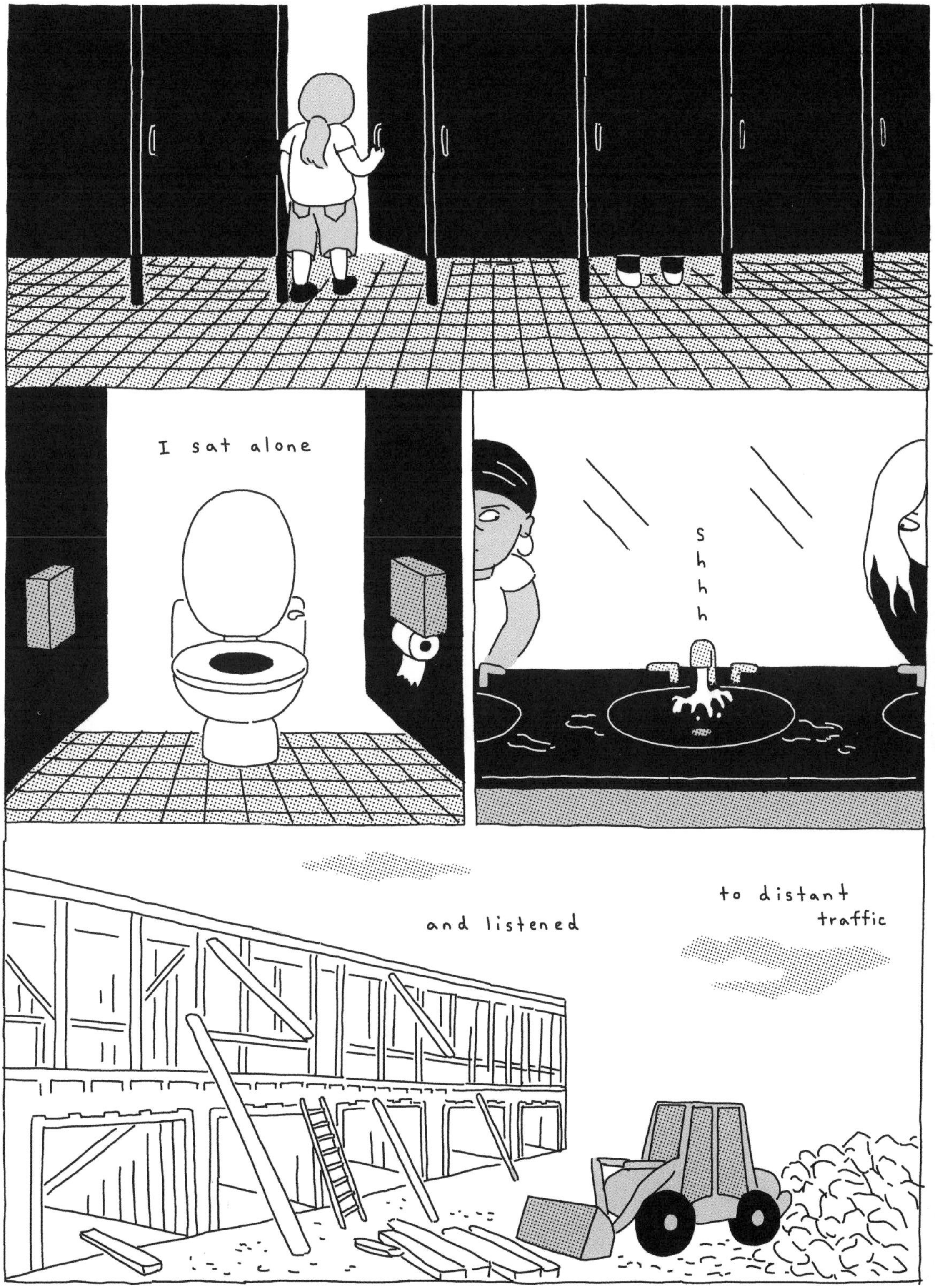
I sat alone
S h h h
and listened
to distant traffic

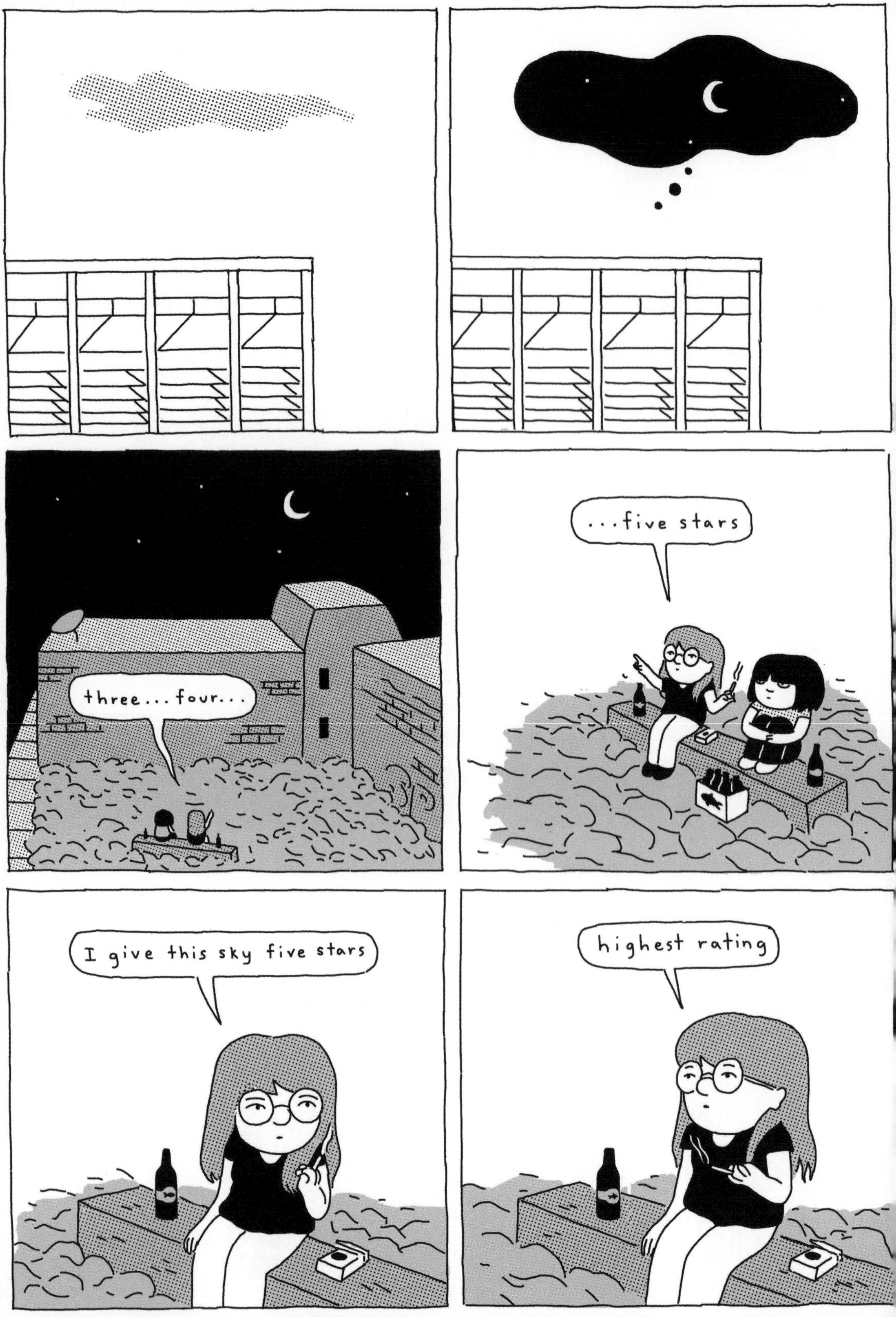
three... four...
...five stars
I give this sky five stars
highest rating

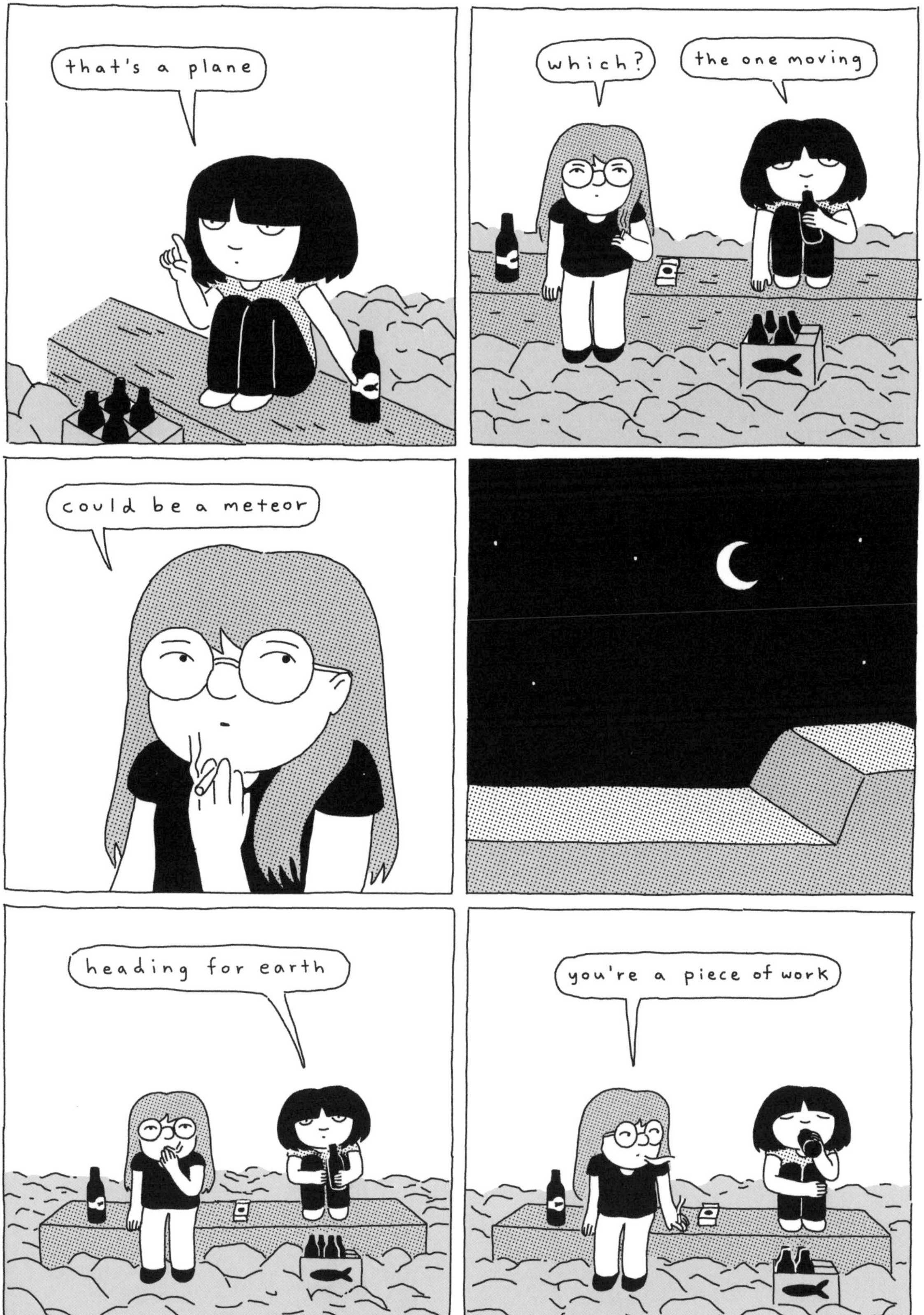
that's a plane
which?
the one moving
could be a meteor
heading for earth
you're a piece of work

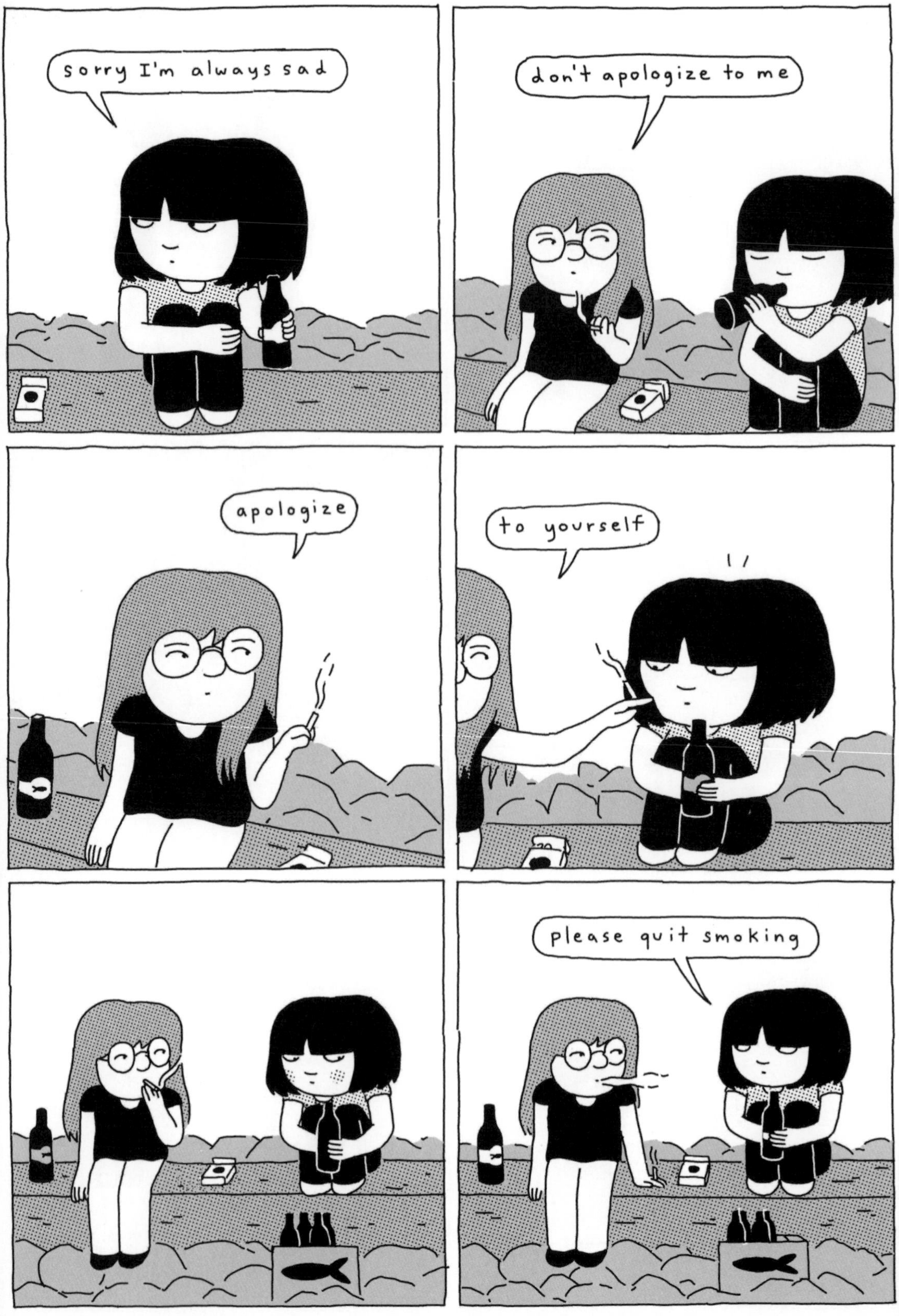
sorry I'm always sad
don't apologize to me
apologize
to yourself
please quit smoking

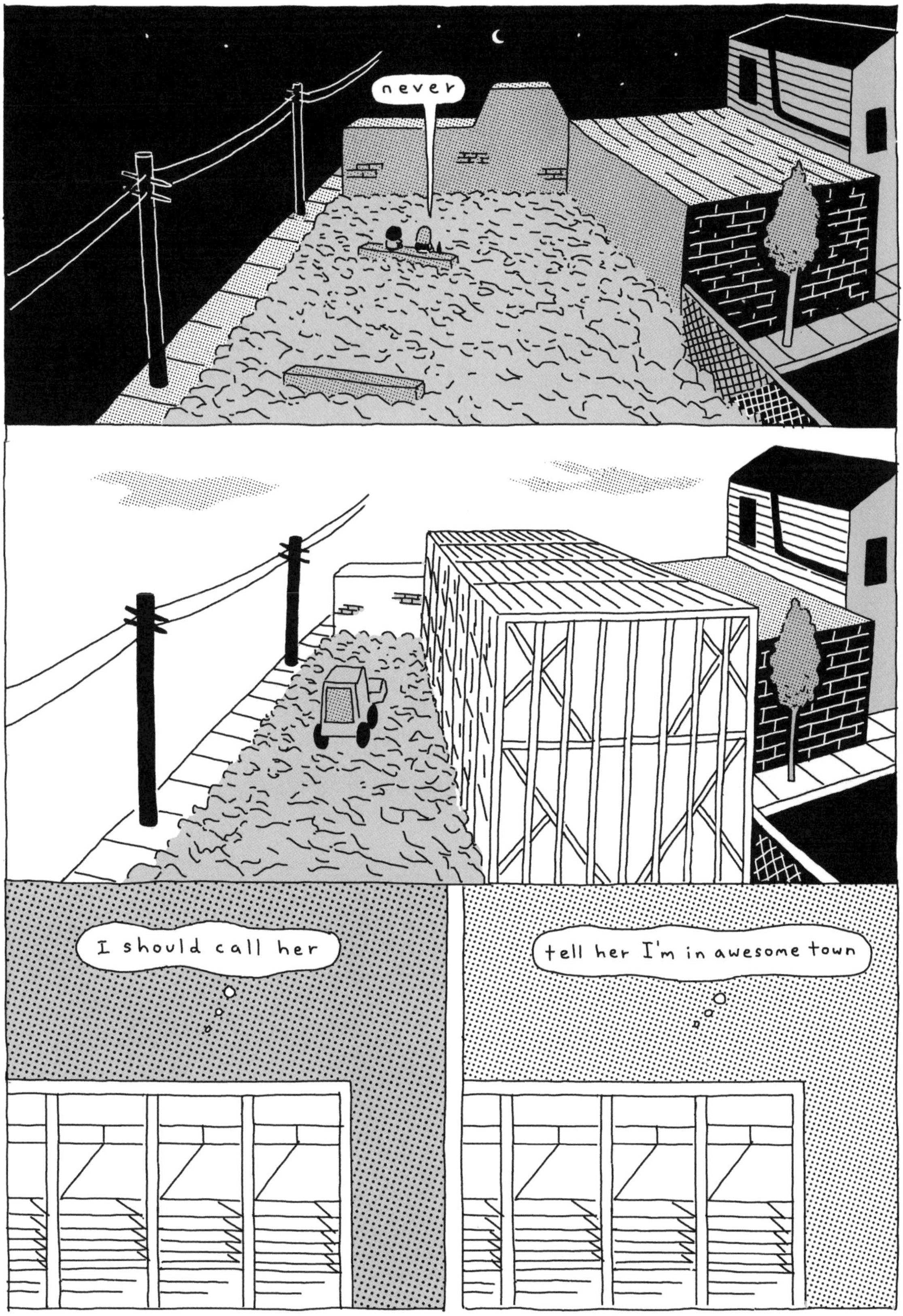
never
I should call her
tell her I'm in awesome town

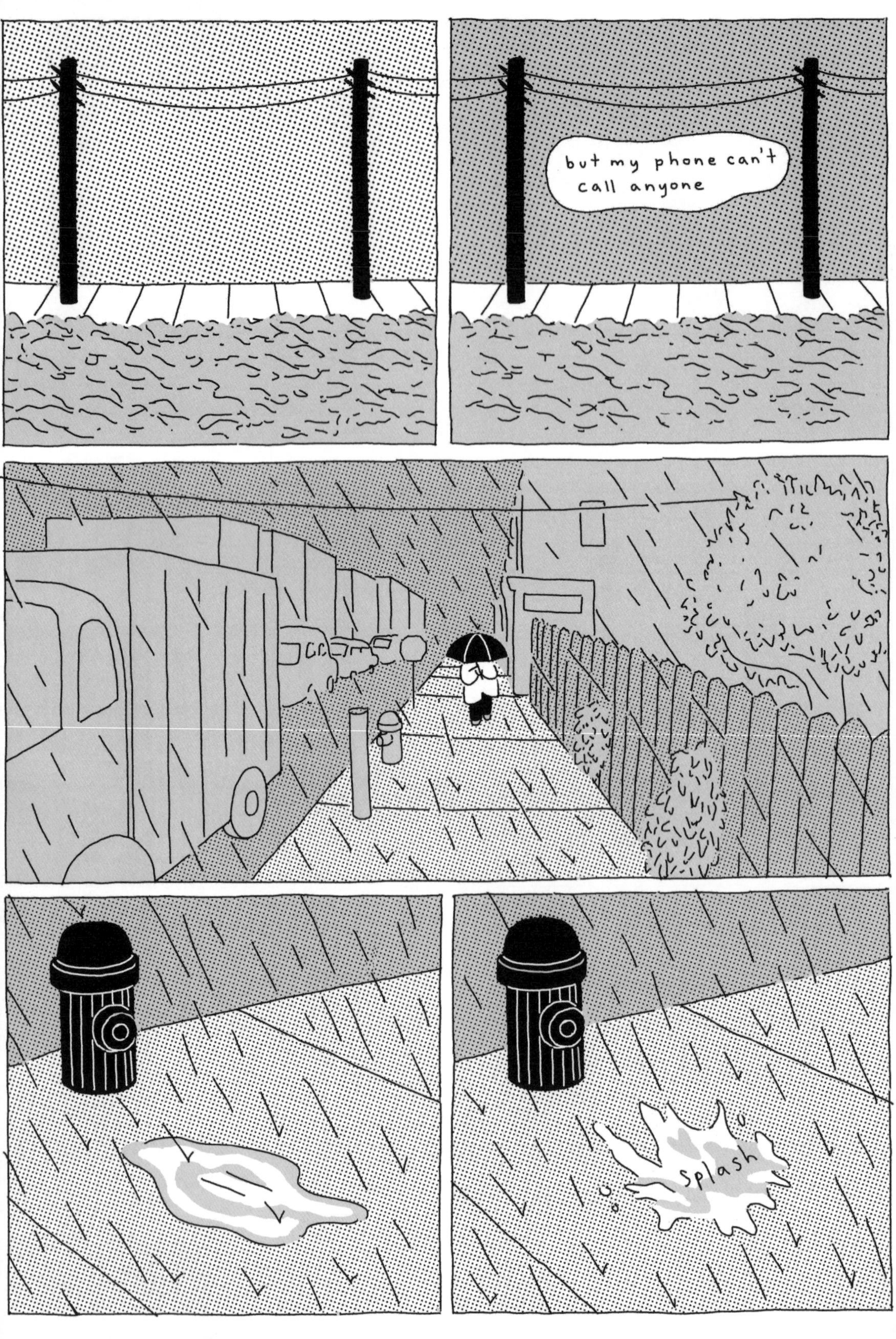
but my phone can't call anyone
splash

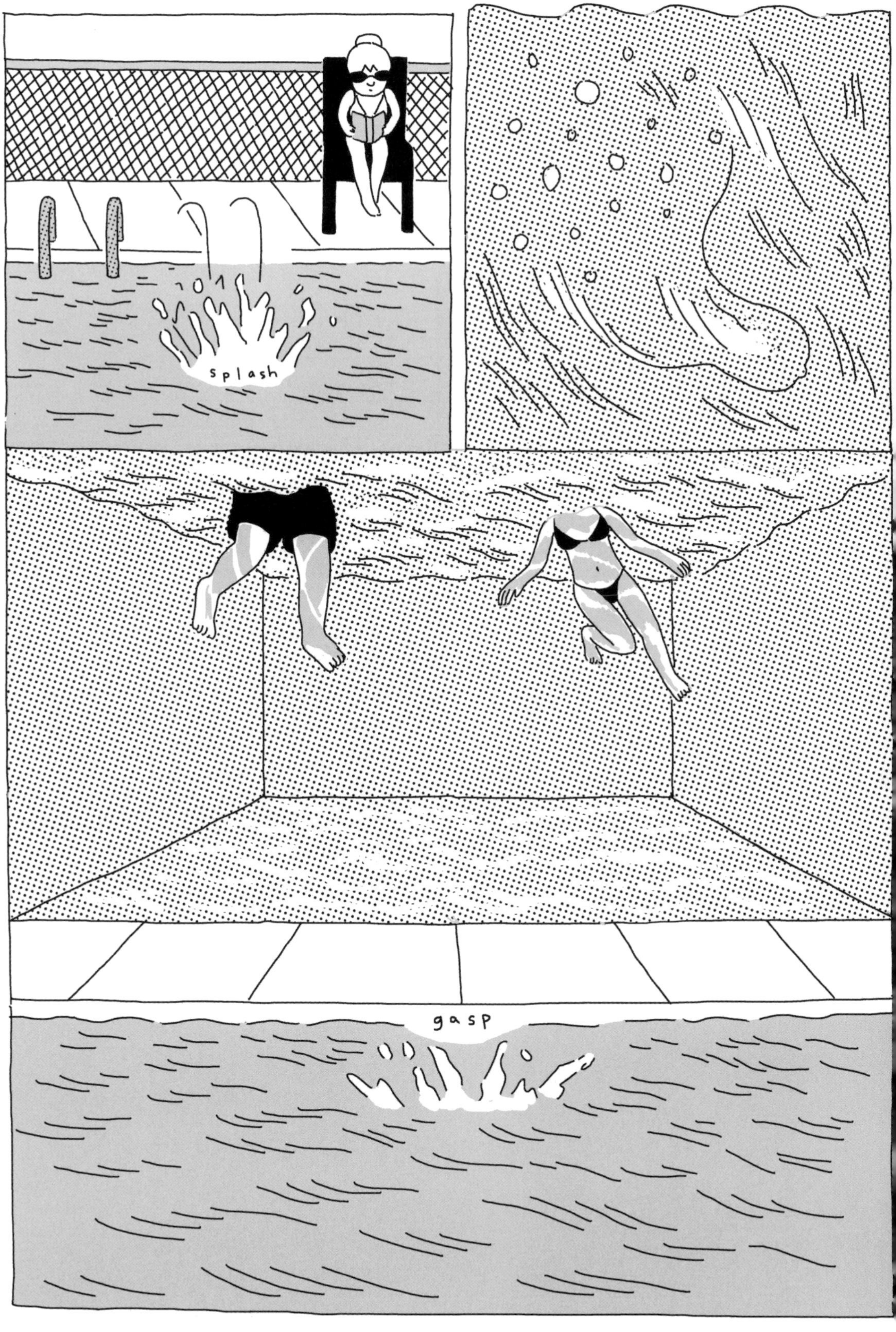
splash
gasp

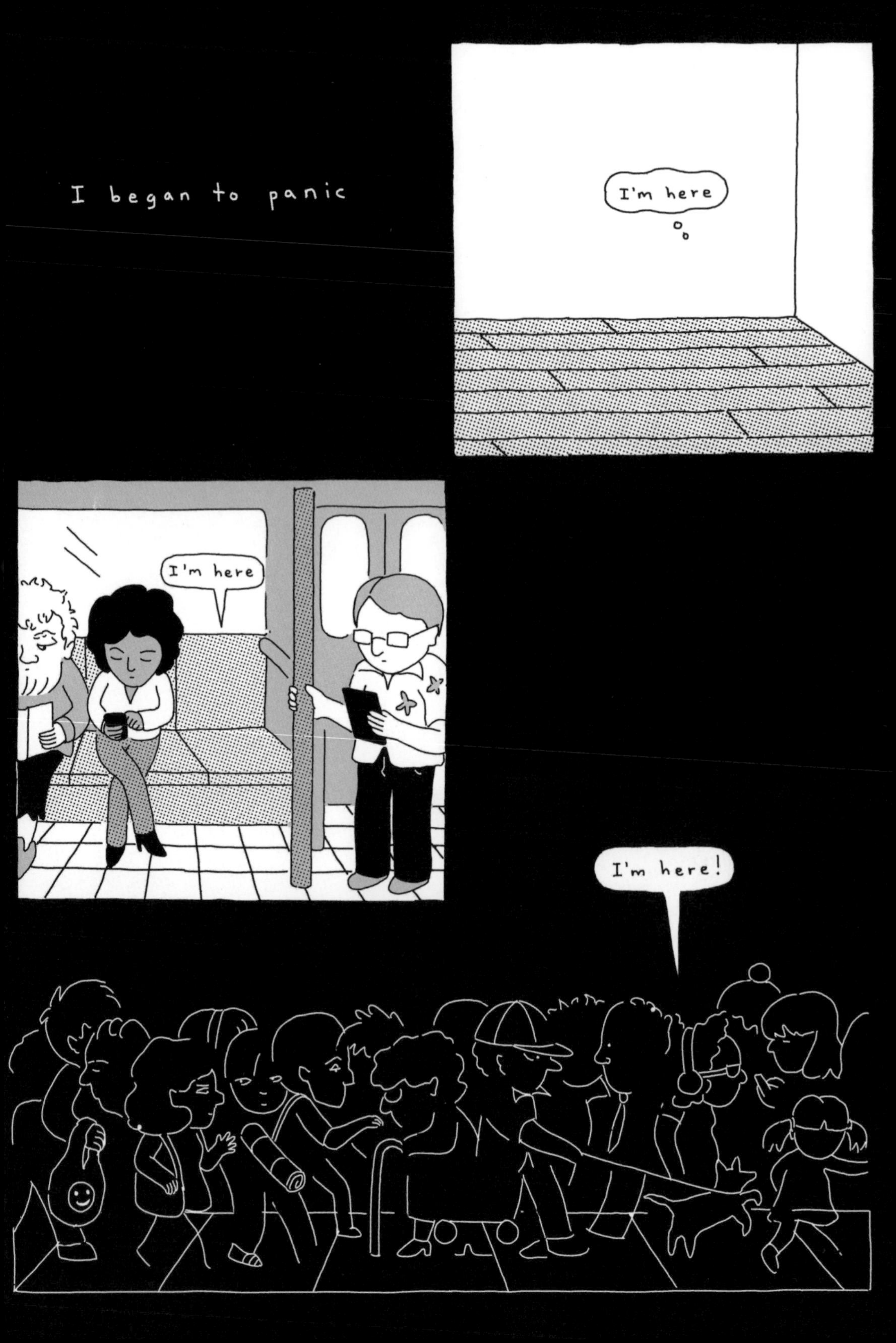
I began to panic
I'm here
I'm here
I'm here!

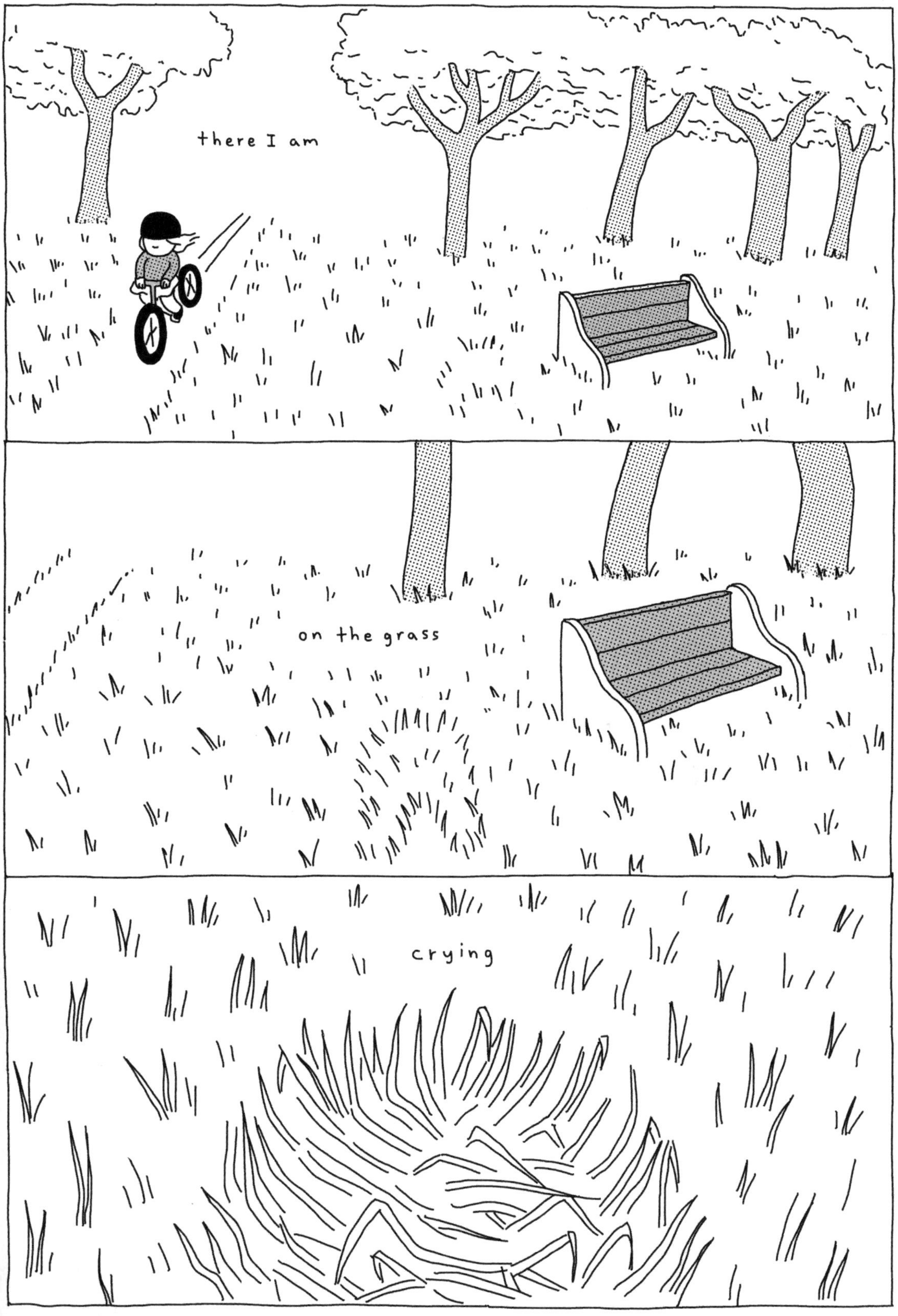
there I am
on the grass
crying

snff

I'm not dead

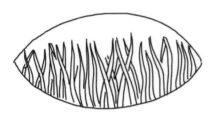

but I might as well be

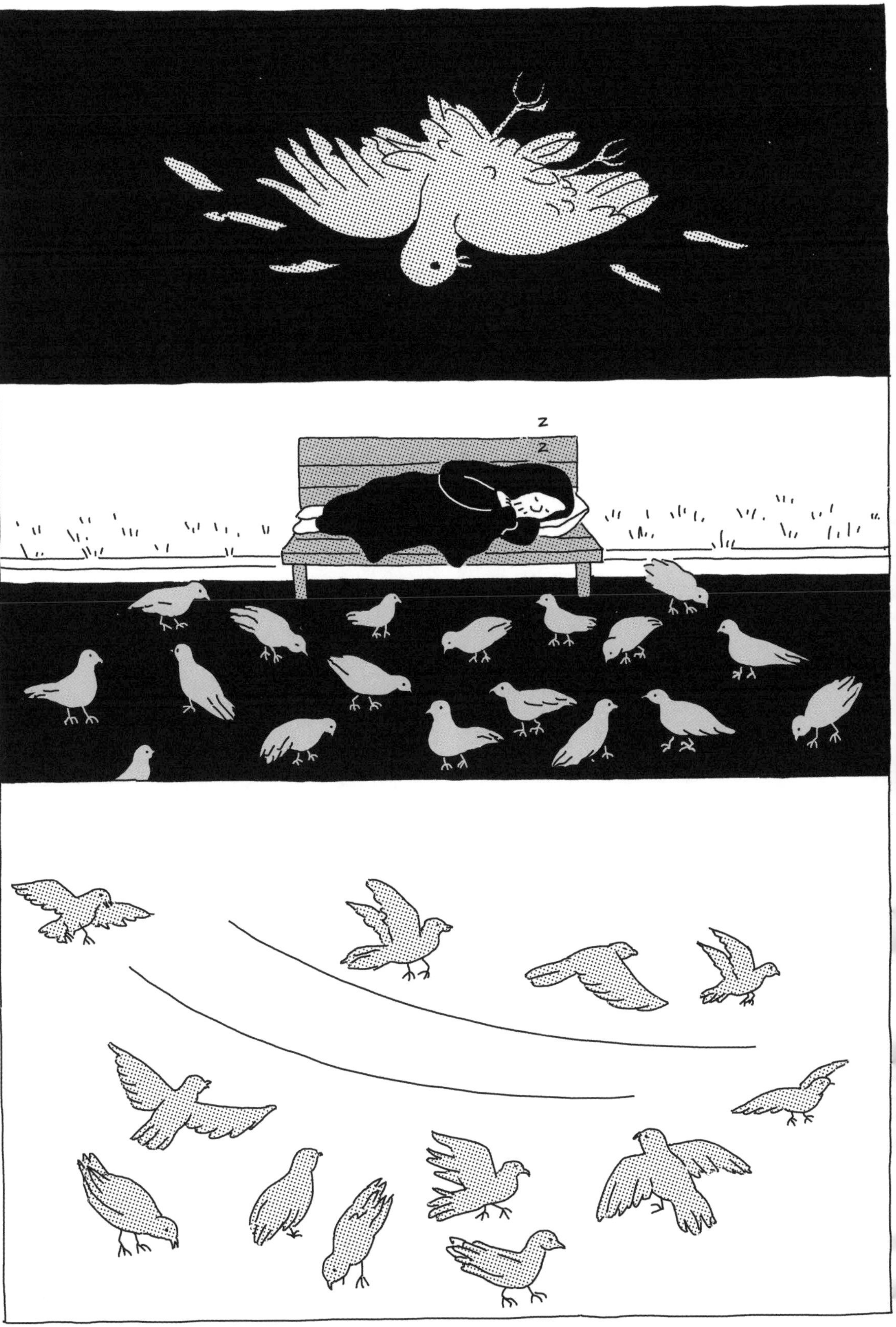
z
z

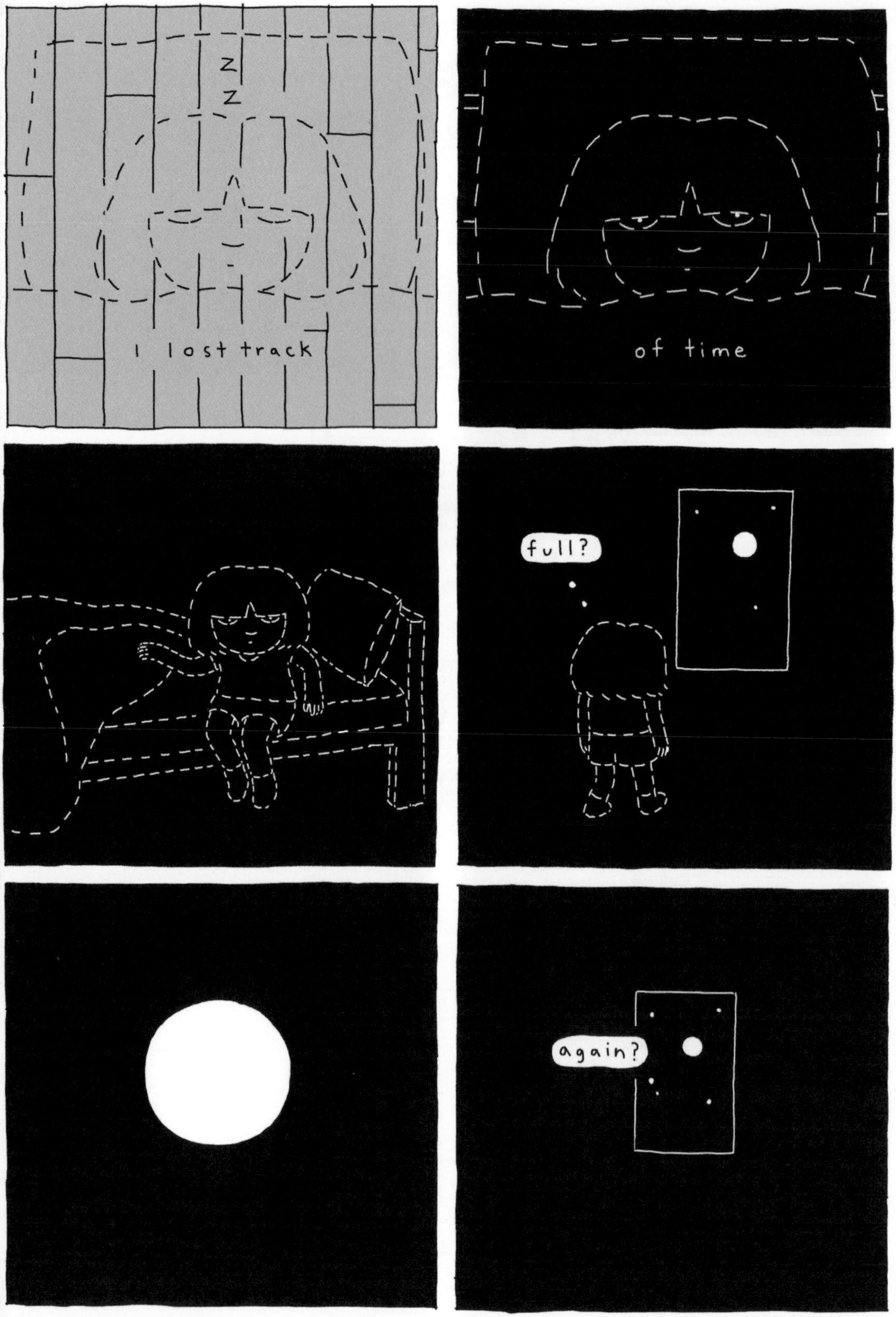
Z
Z
I lost track
of time
full?
again?

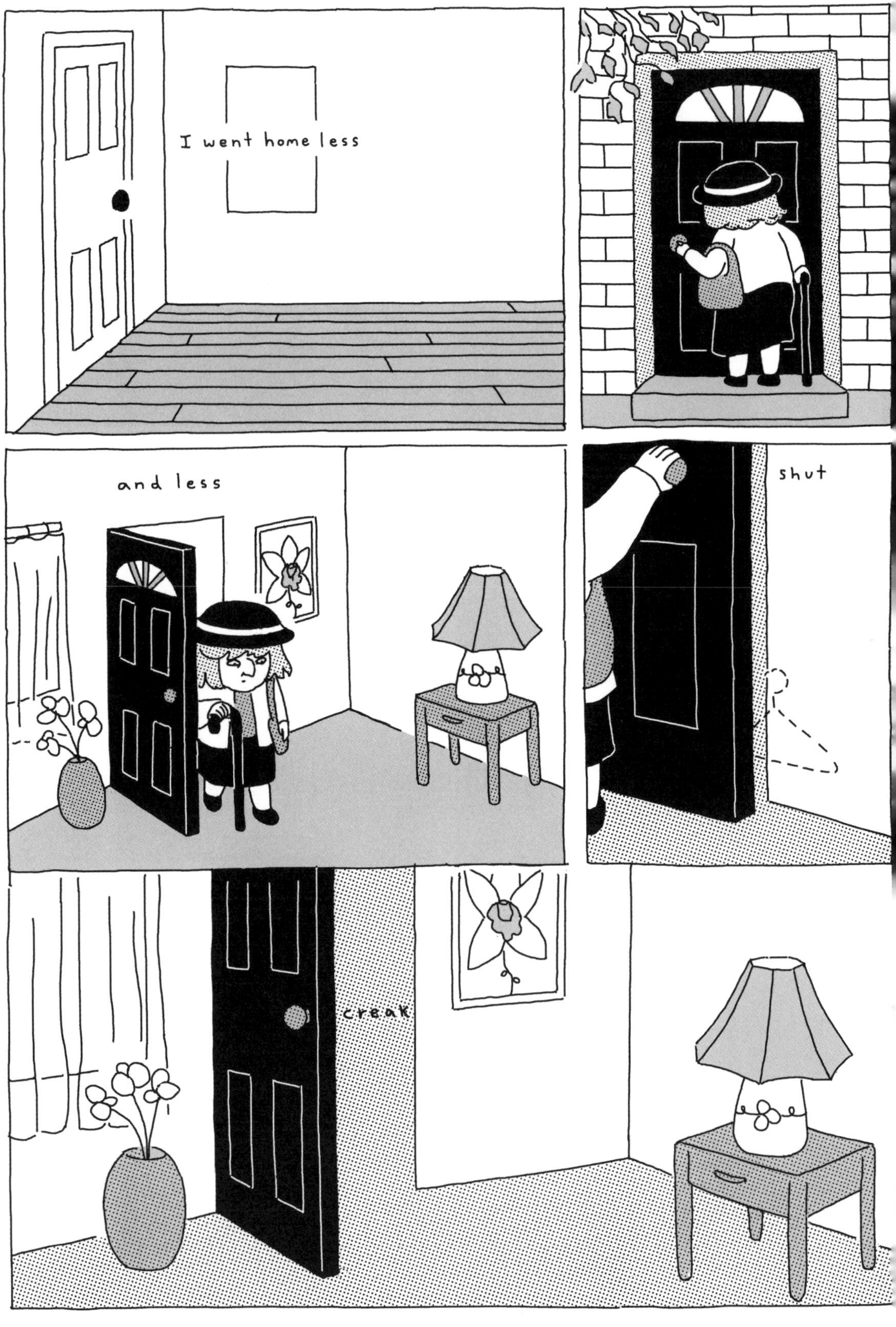
I went home less
and less
shut
creak

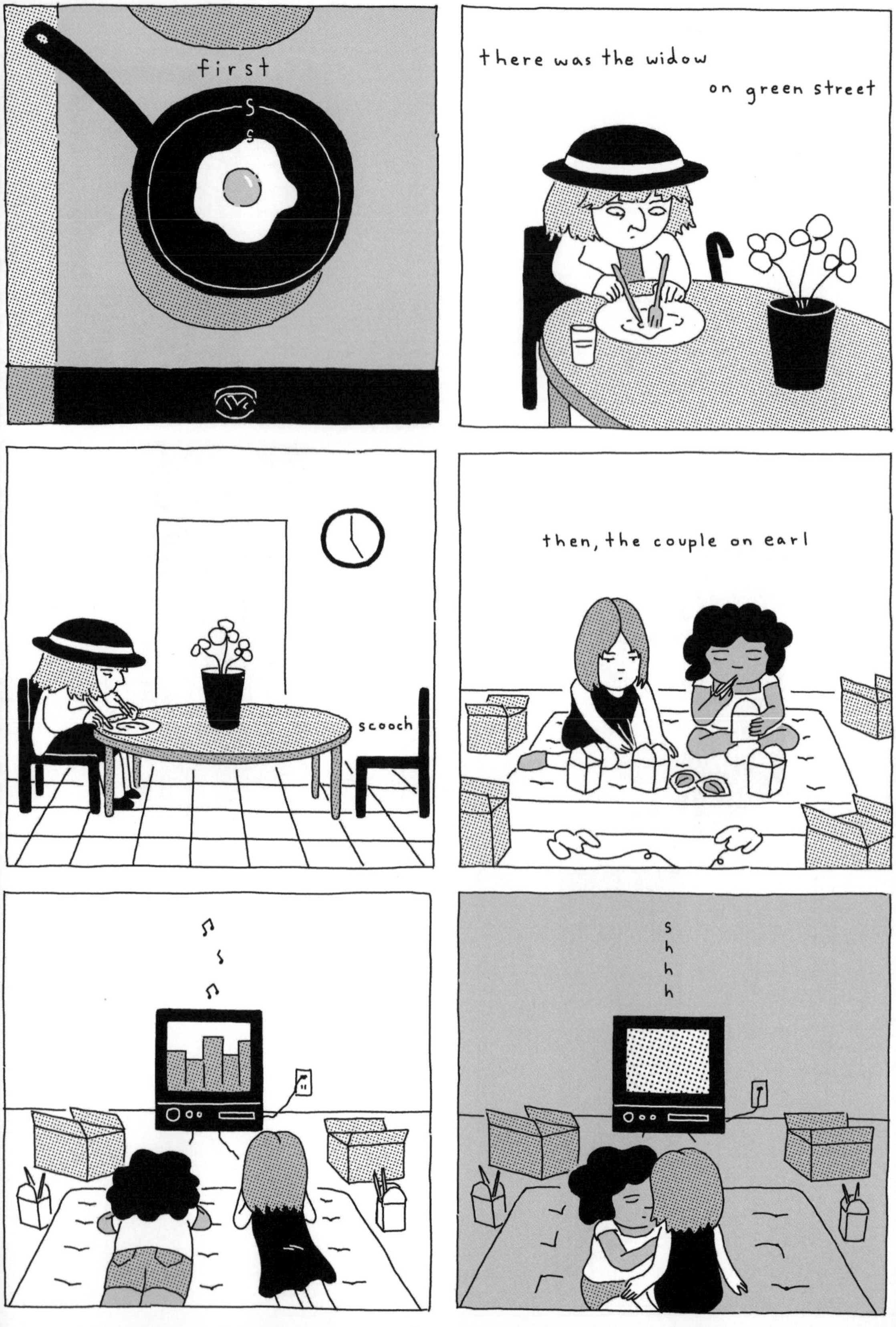
first
s
s
there was the widow
on green street
scooch
then, the couple on earl
s
h
h
h

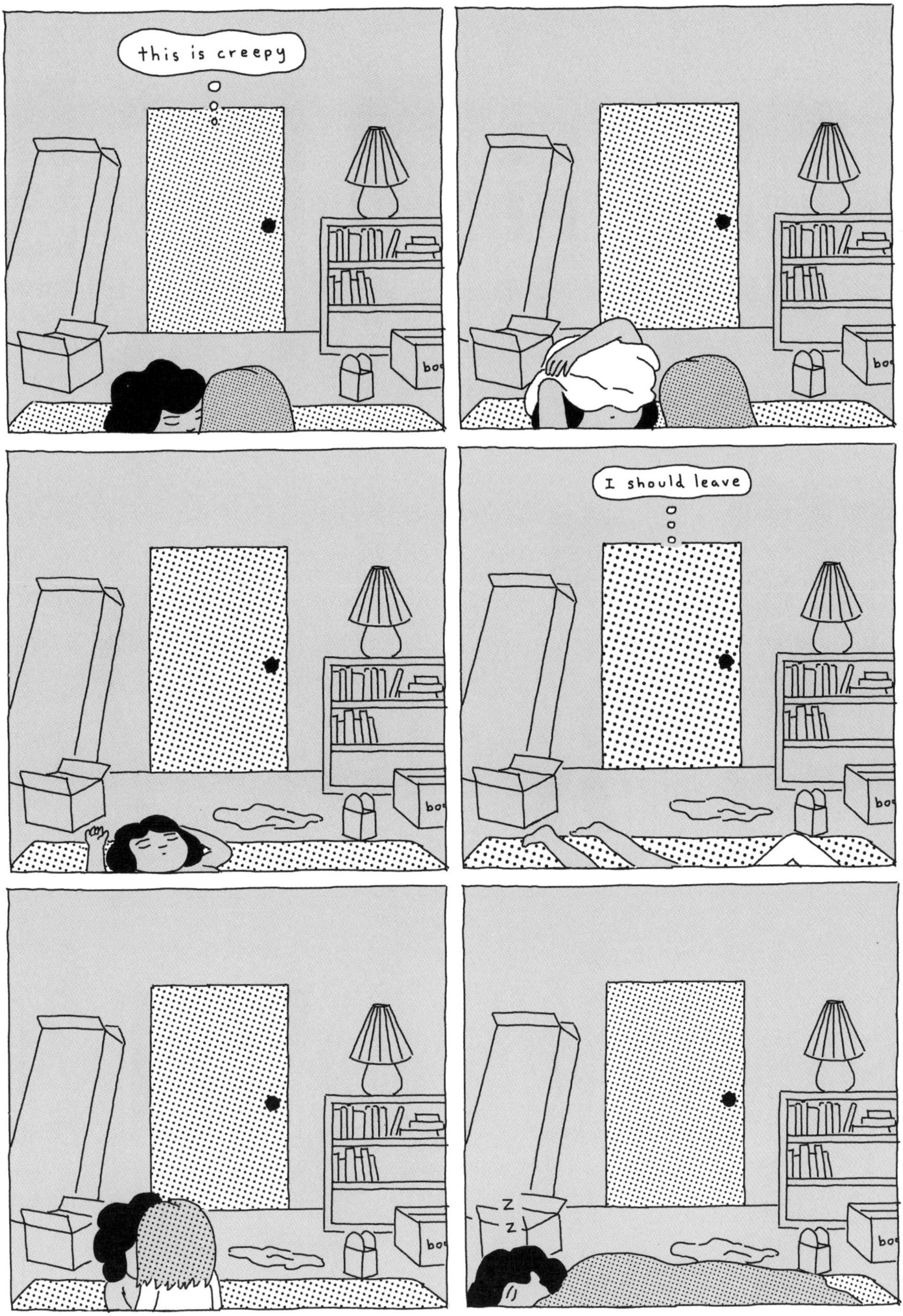
this is creepy
I should leave
Z
Z

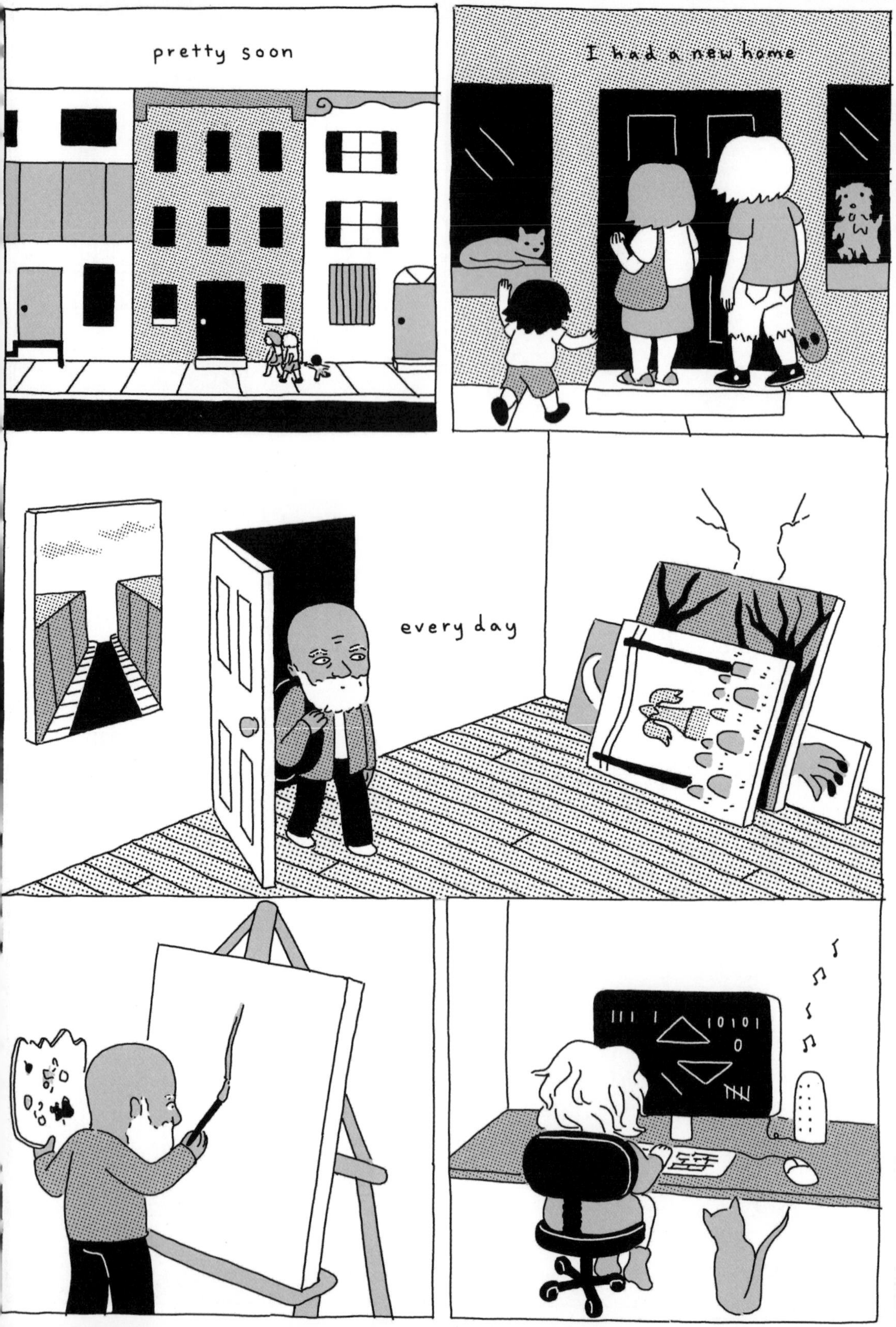
pretty soon
I had a new home
every day

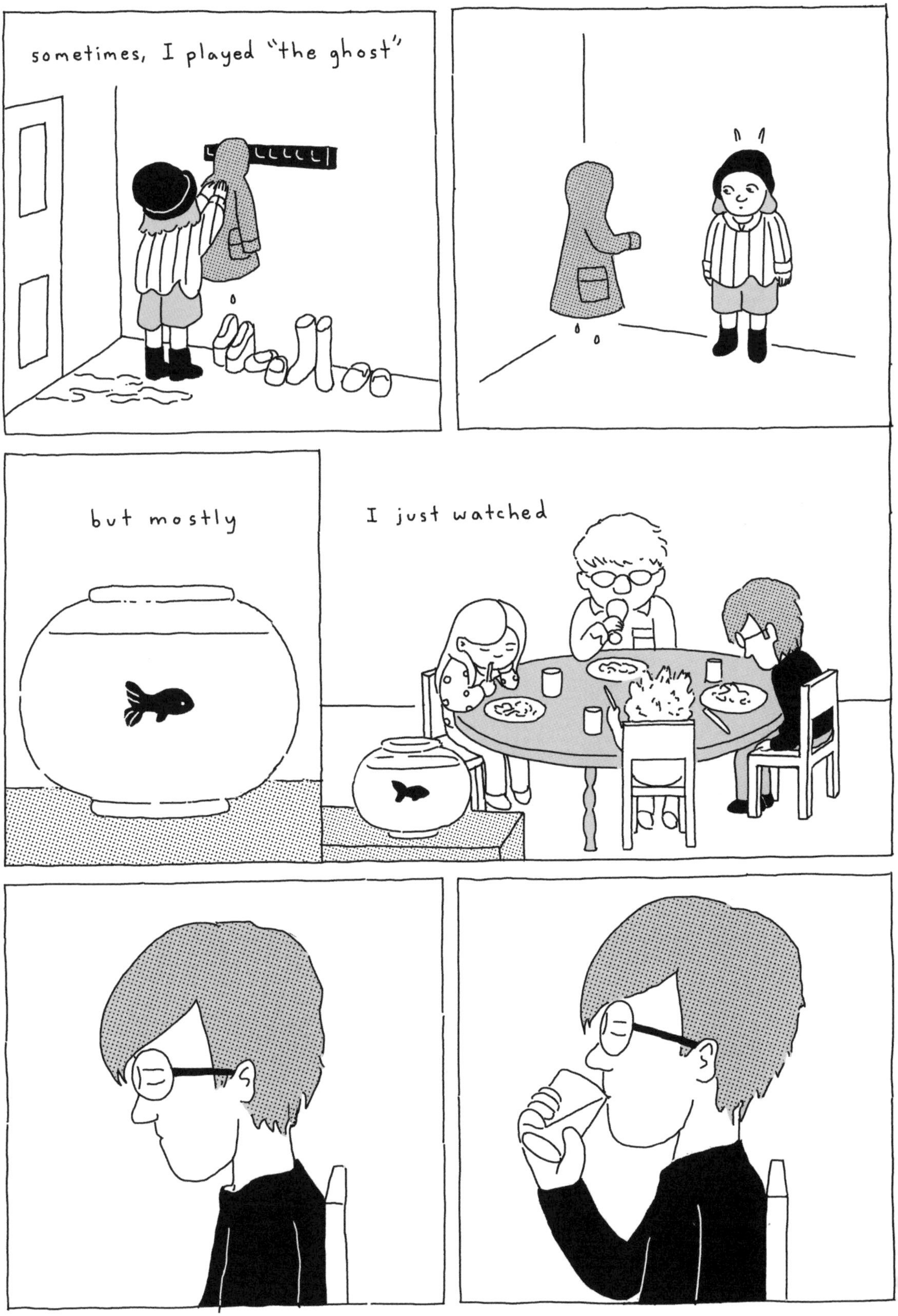
sometimes, I played "the ghost"
but mostly
I just watched

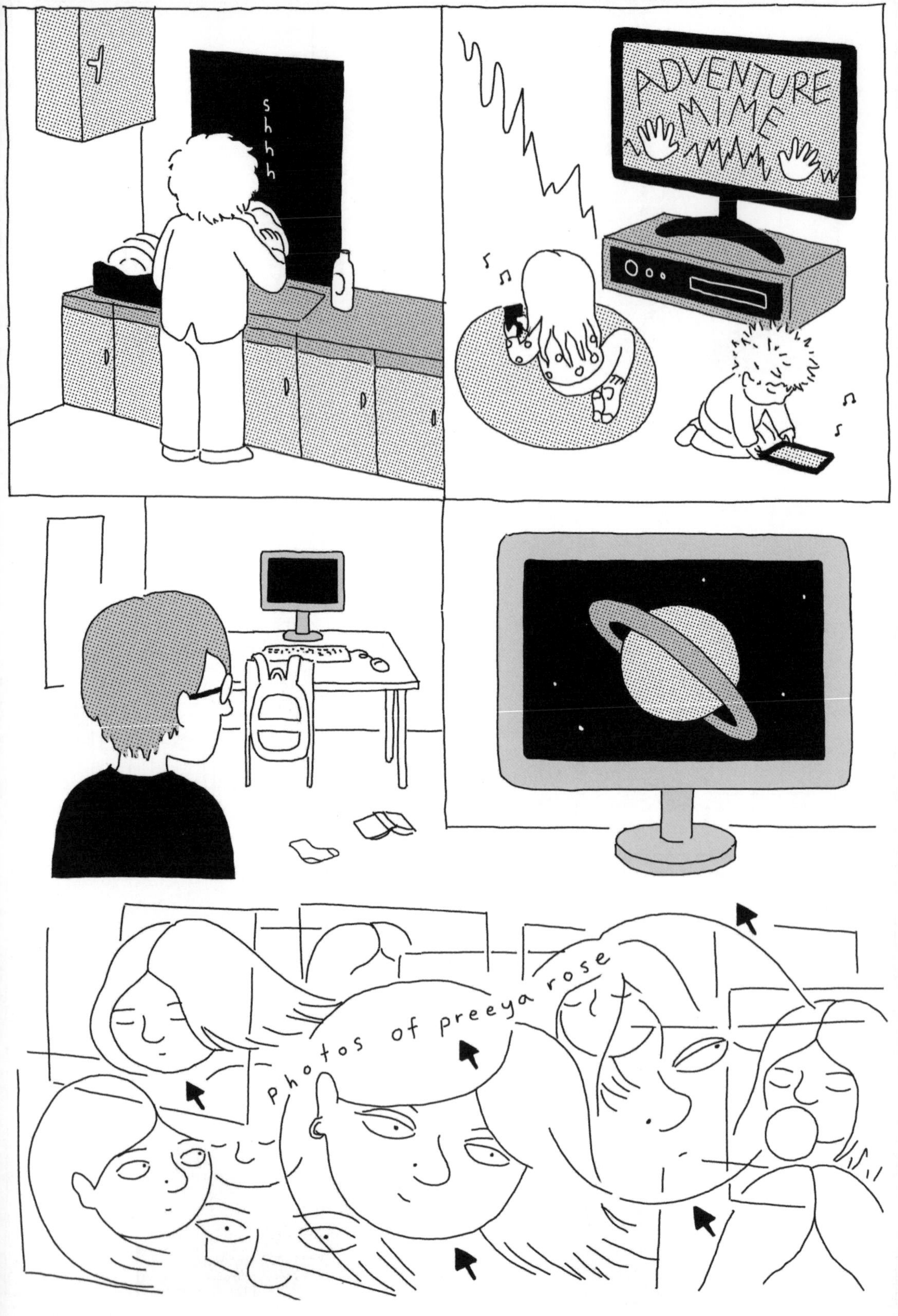
shhh
ADVENTURE MIME
photos of preeya rose

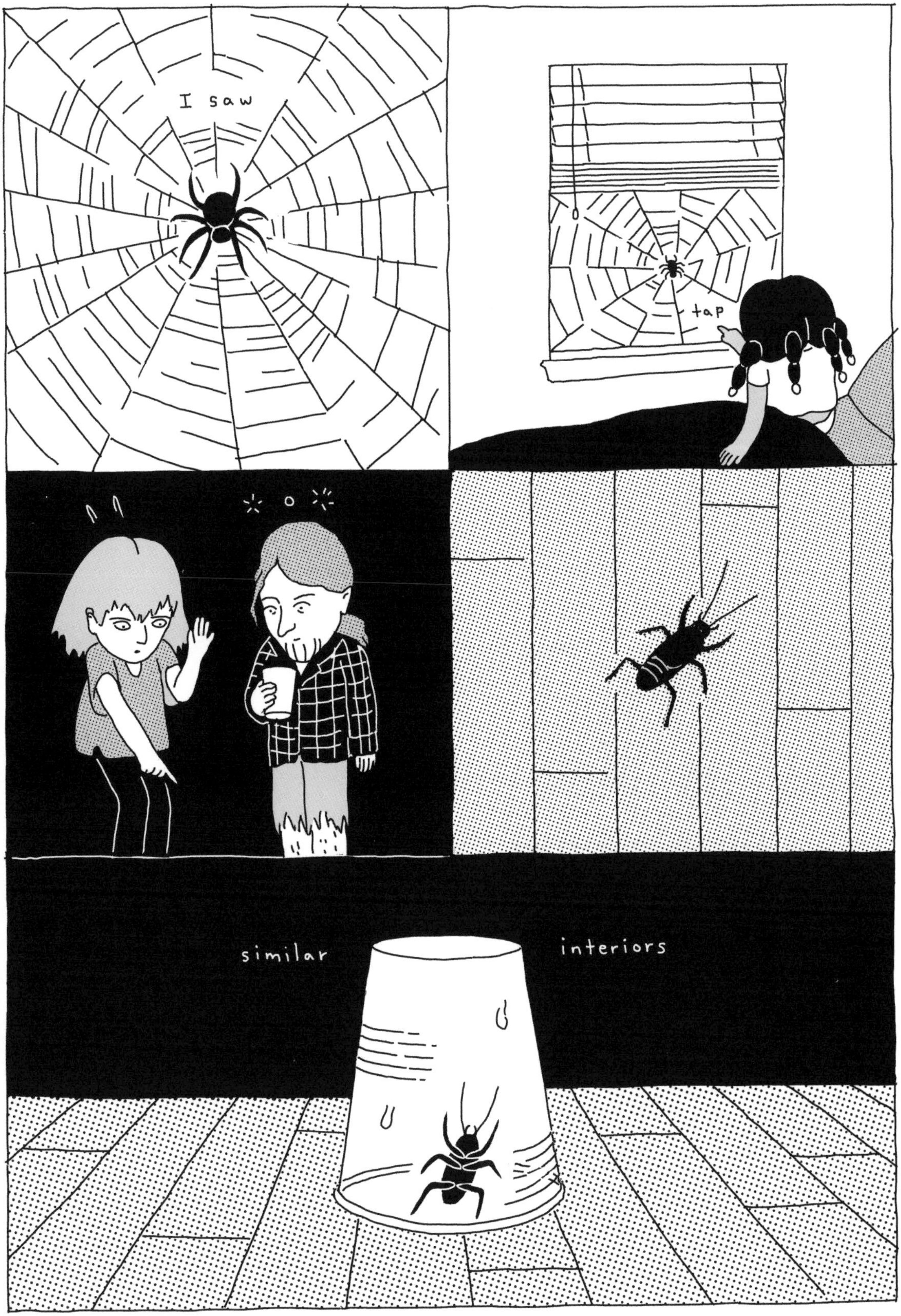
I saw
tap
similar
interiors

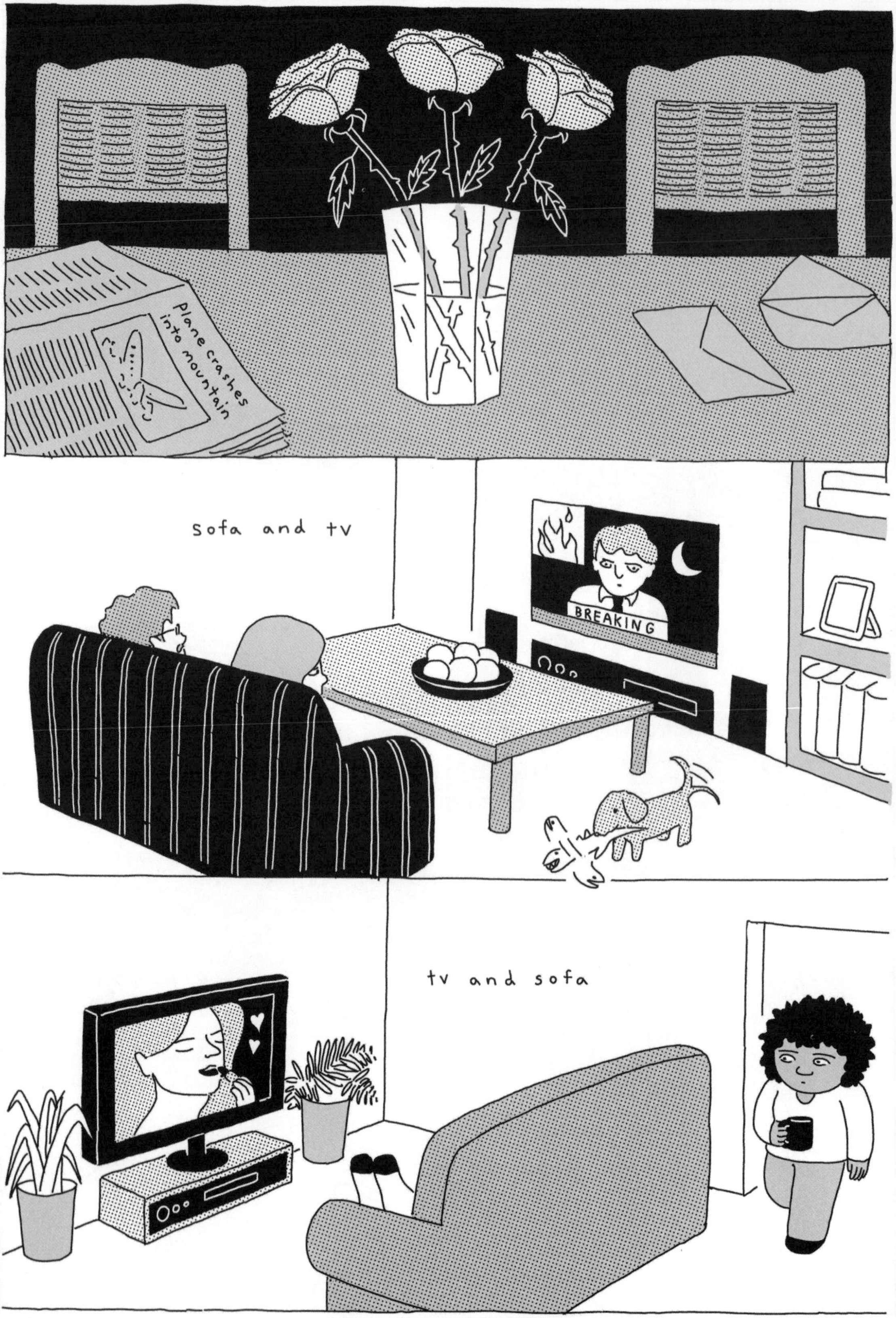
Plane crashes into mountain
sofa and tv
BREAKING
tv and sofa

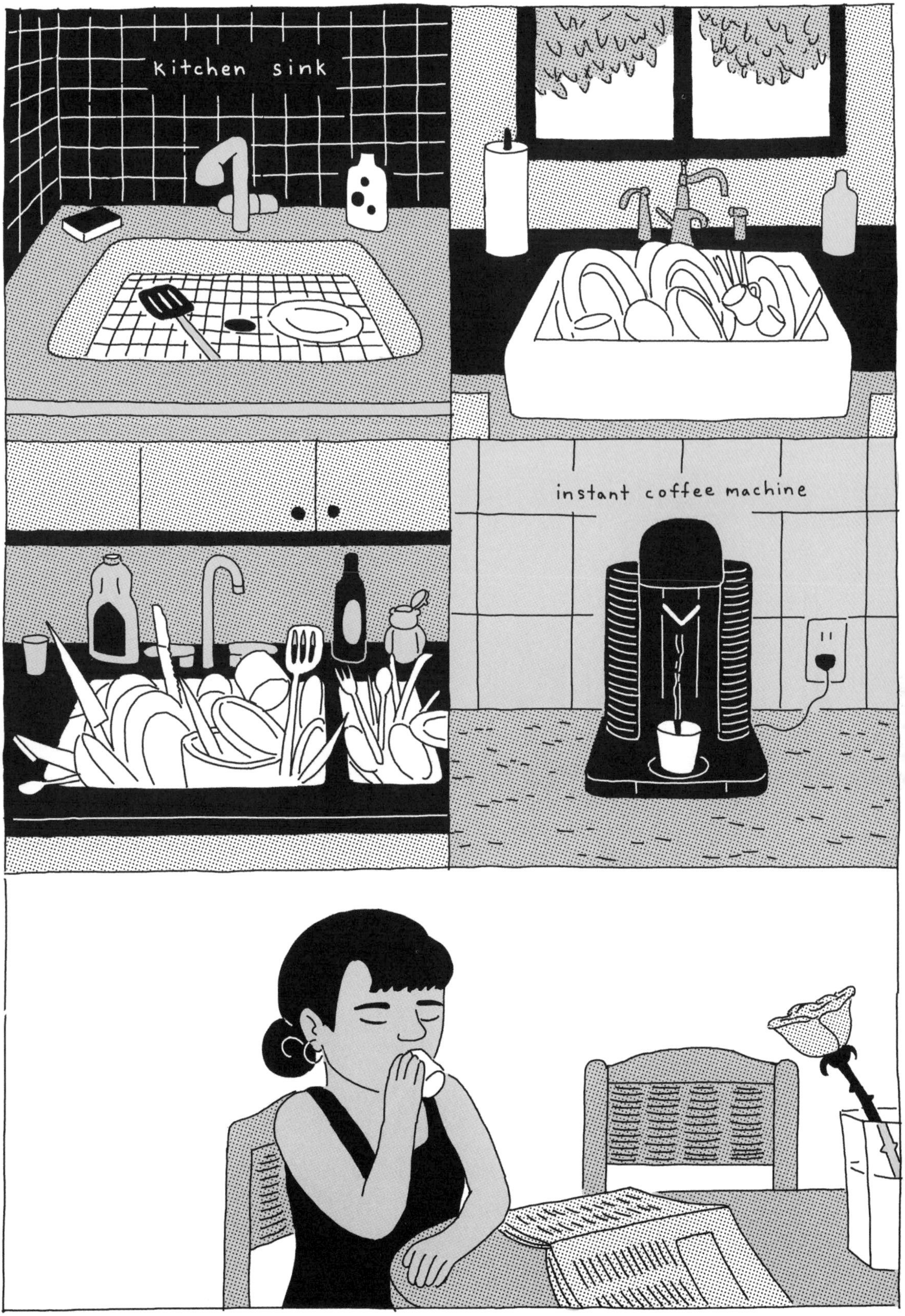
kitchen sink
instant coffee machine

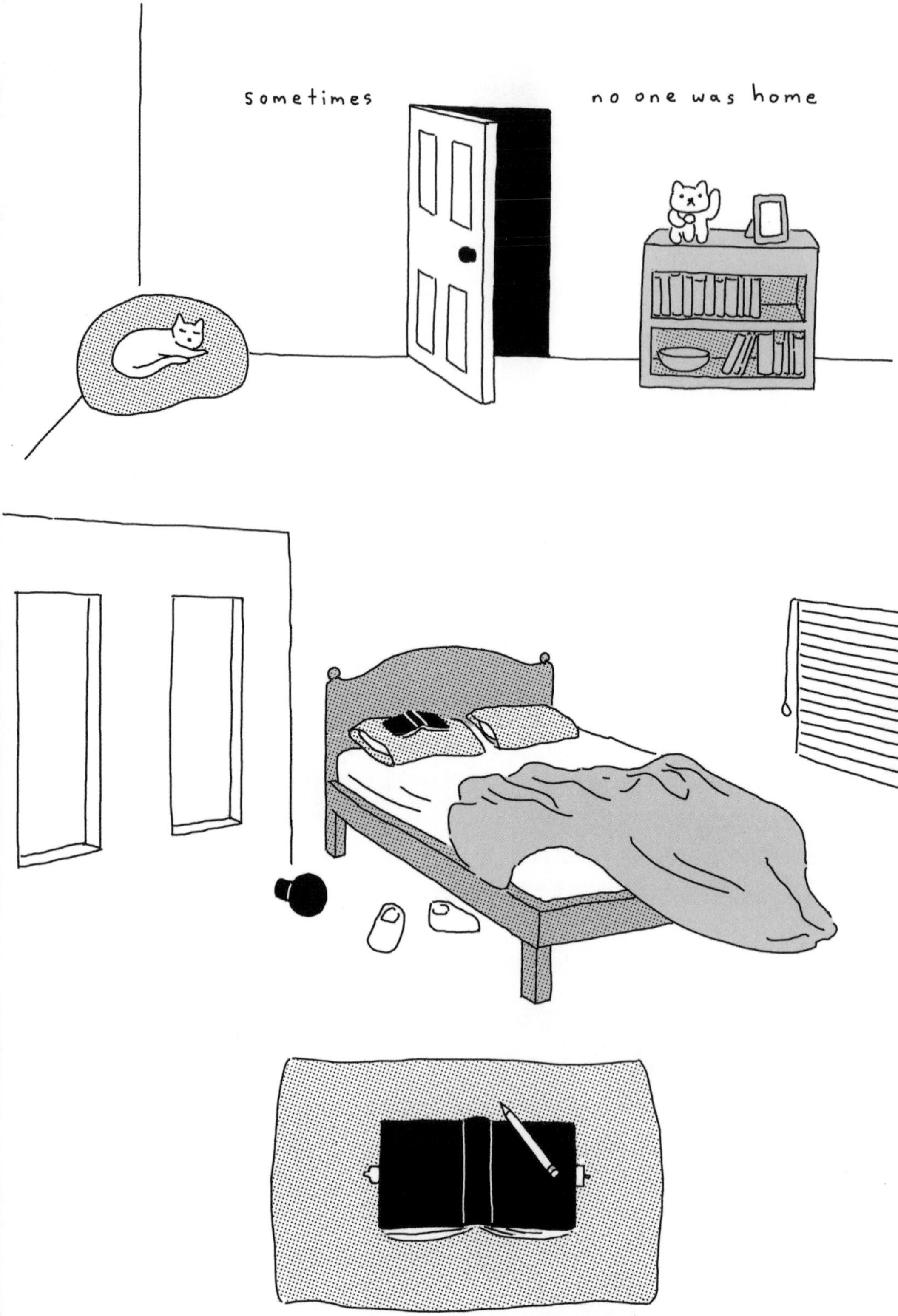
sometimes
no one was home

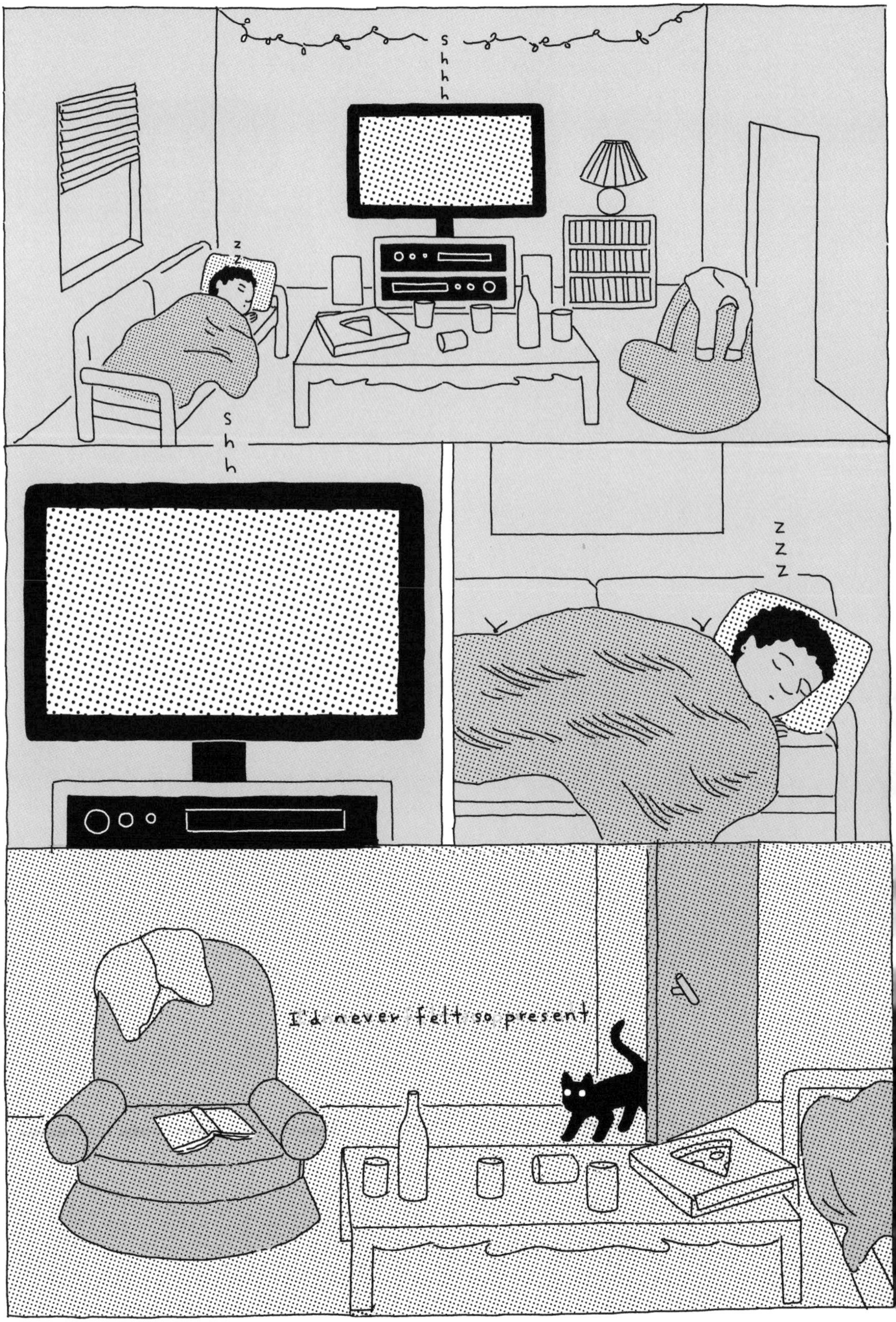
s
h
h
h
z
z
s
h
h
z
z
z
I'd never felt so present.

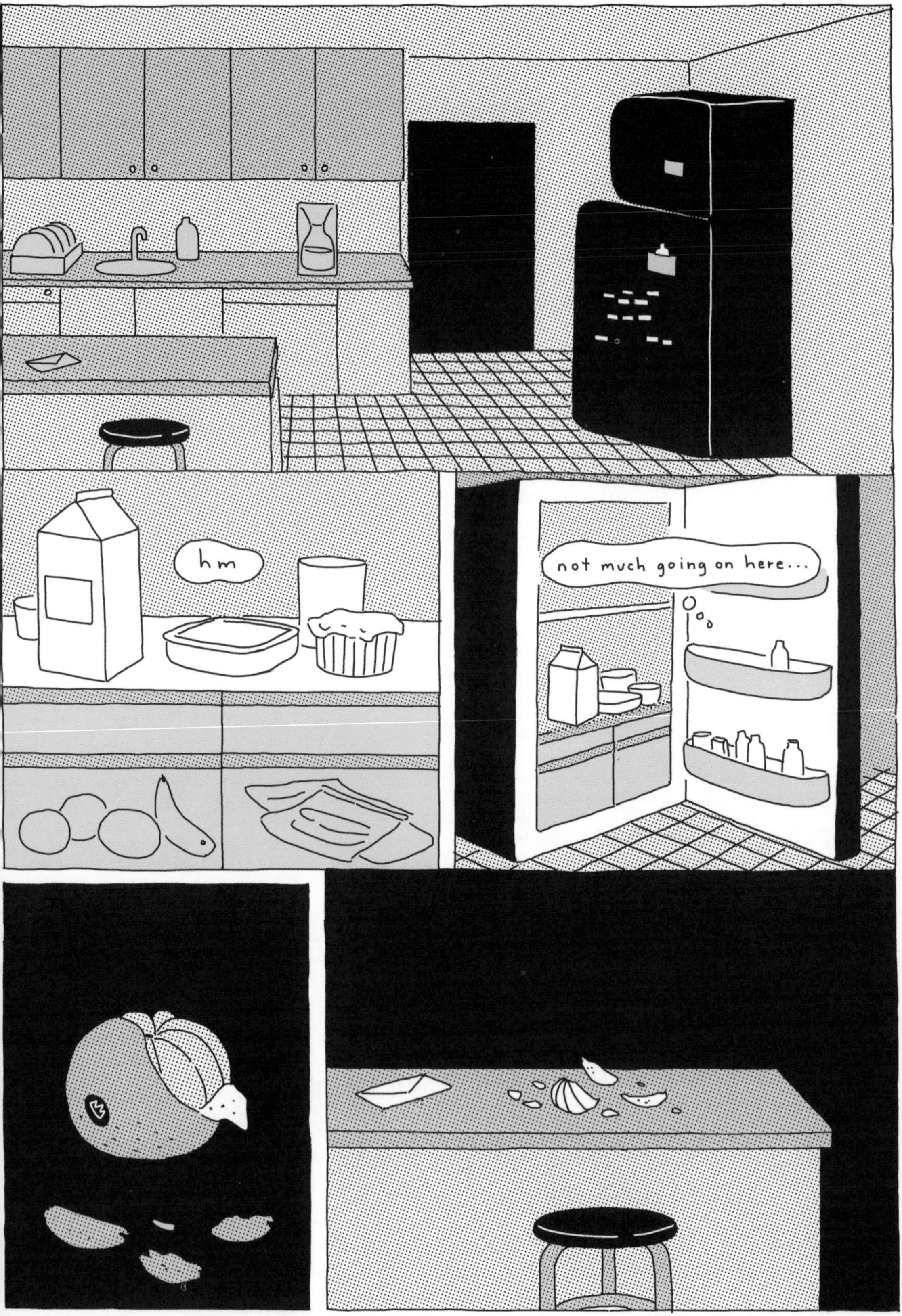
hm
not much going on here...

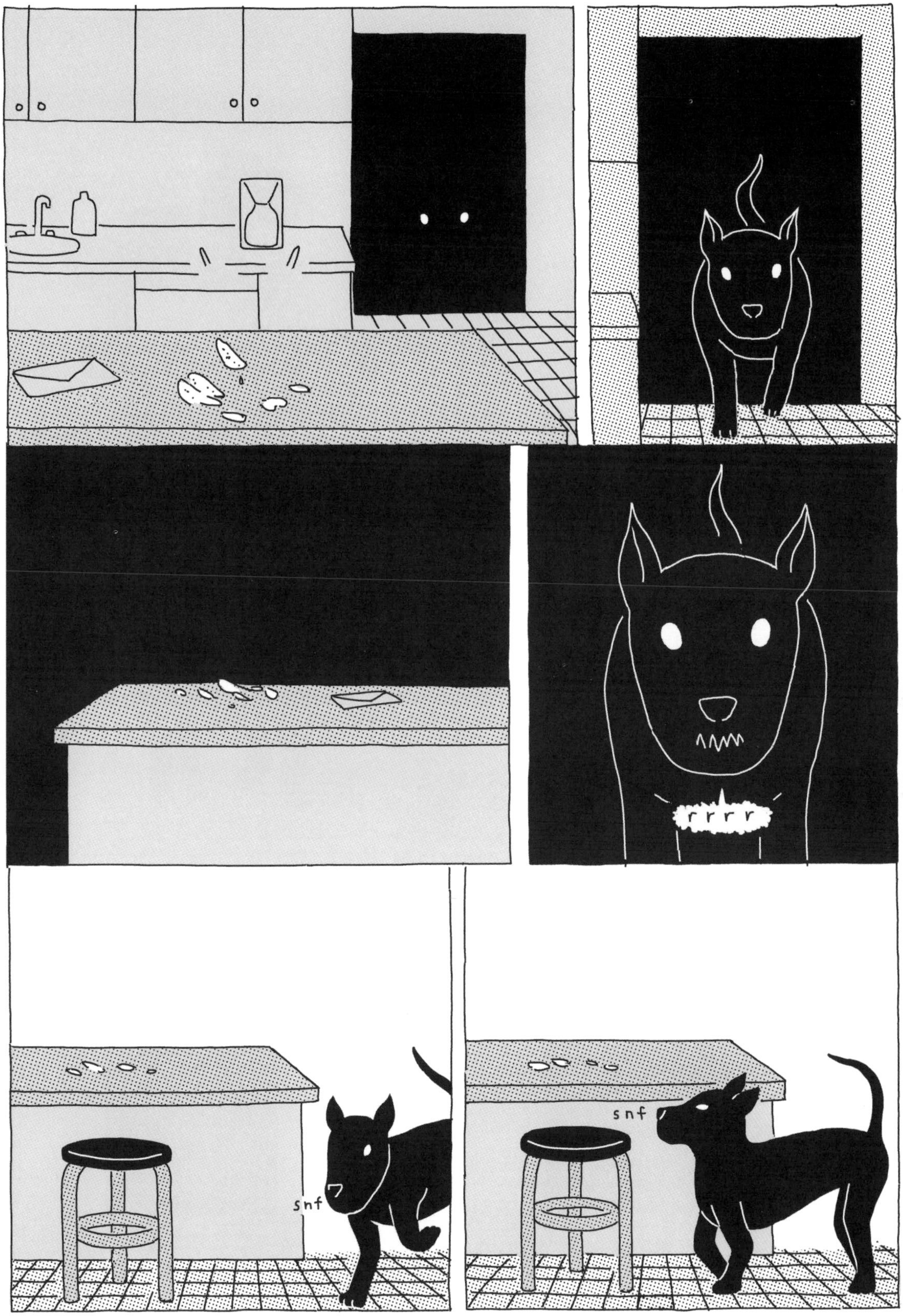
rrrr
snf
snf

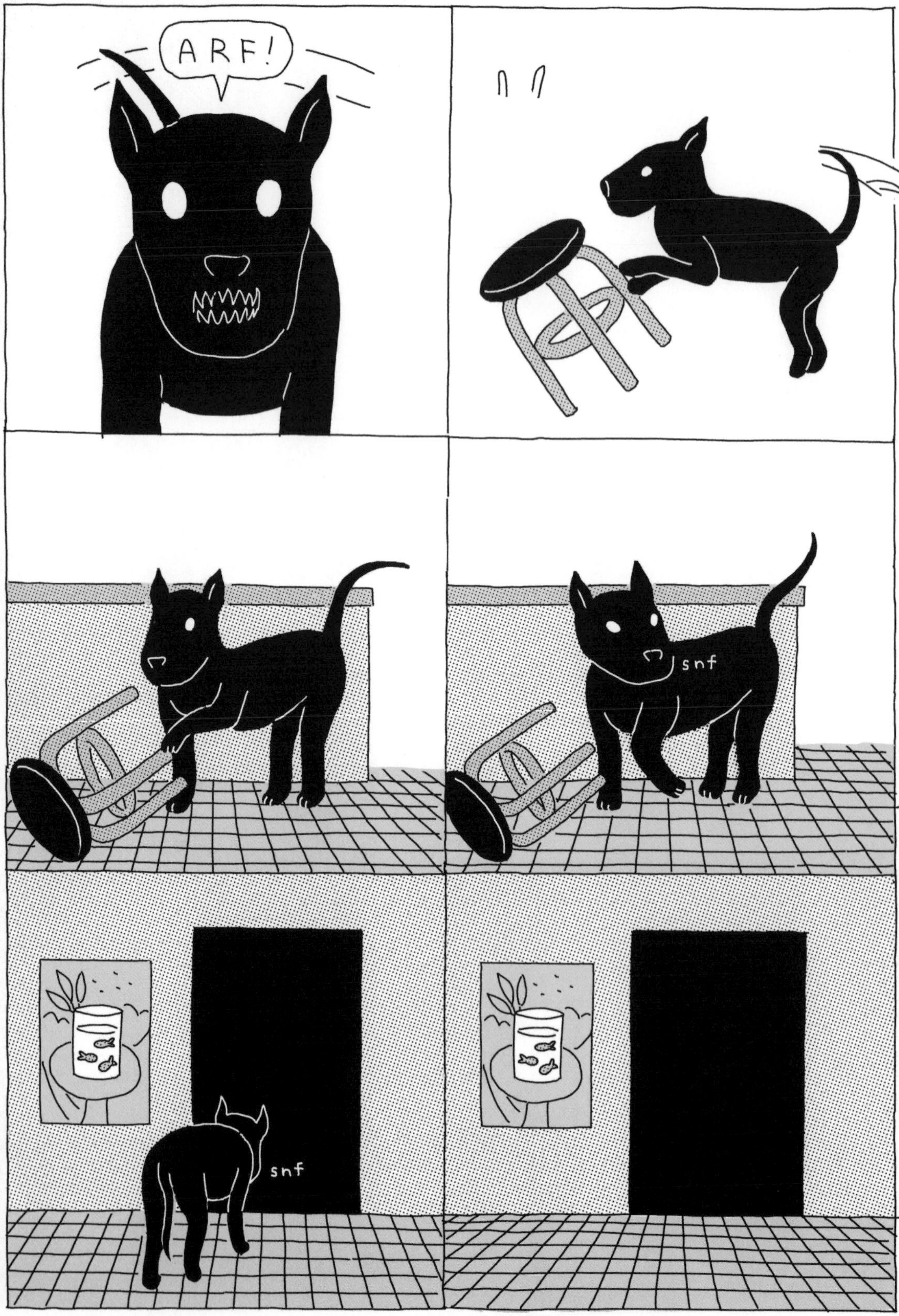
ARF!
snf
snf

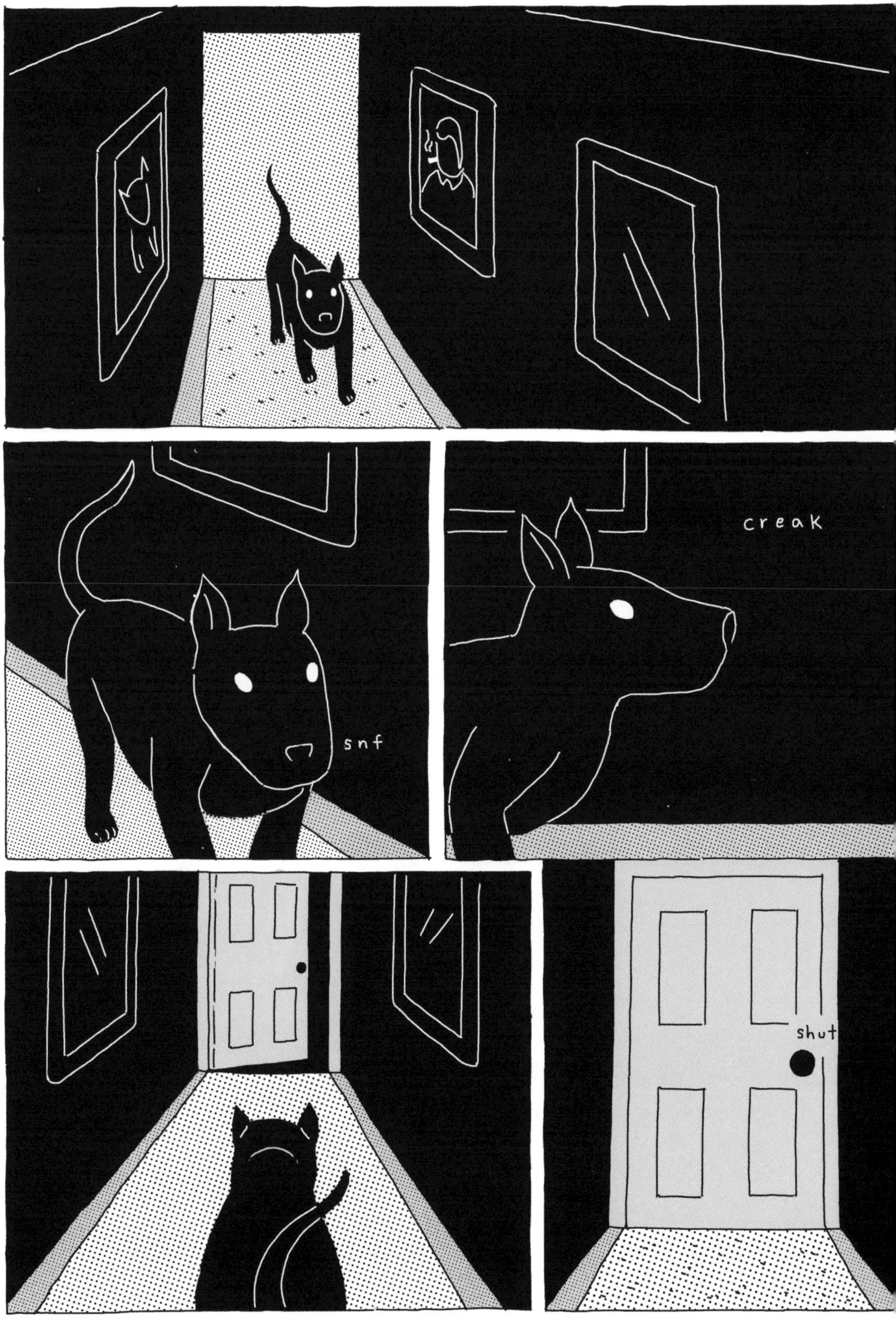
snf
creak
shut

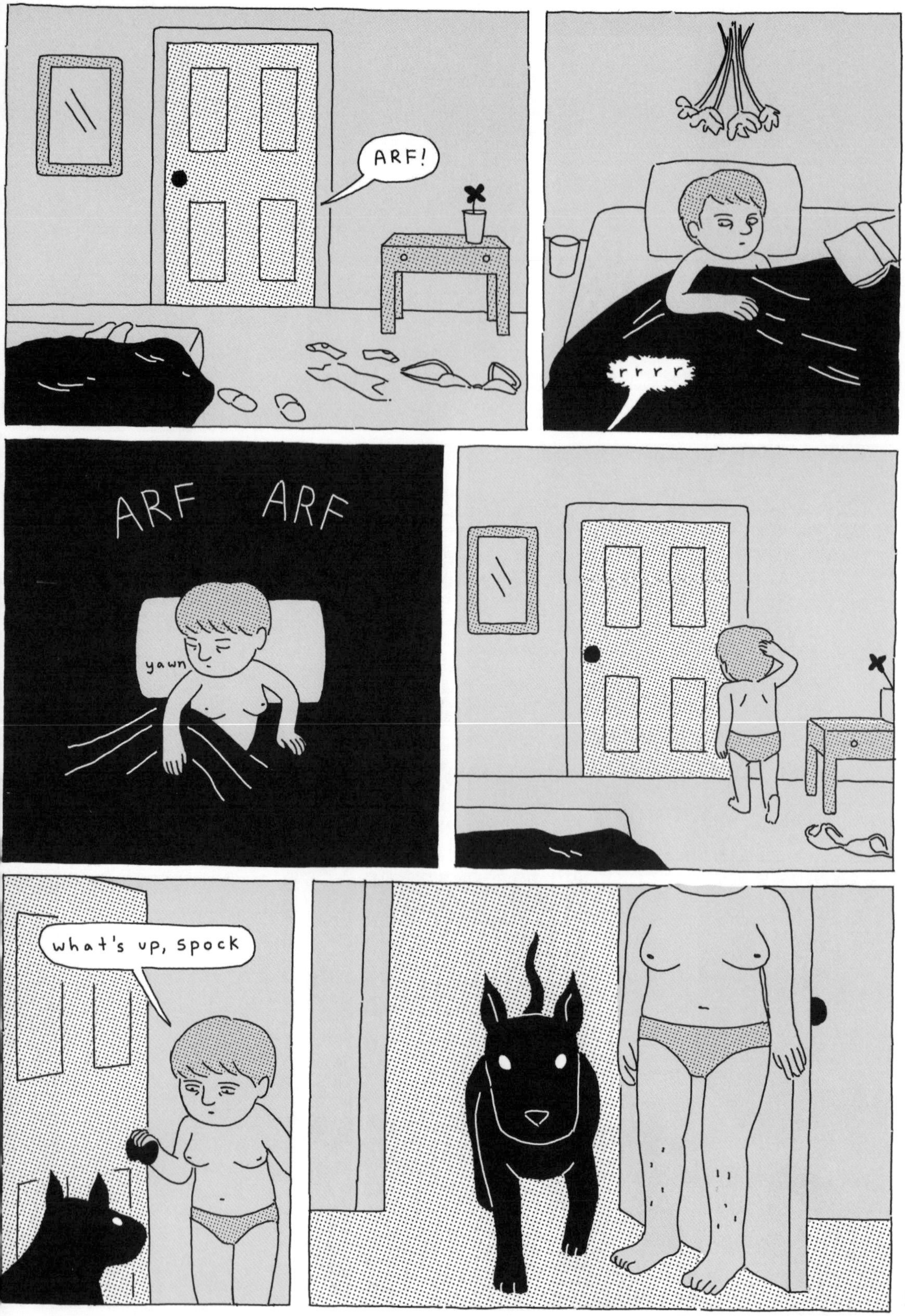
ARF!
rrrr
ARF ARF
yawn
what's up, spock

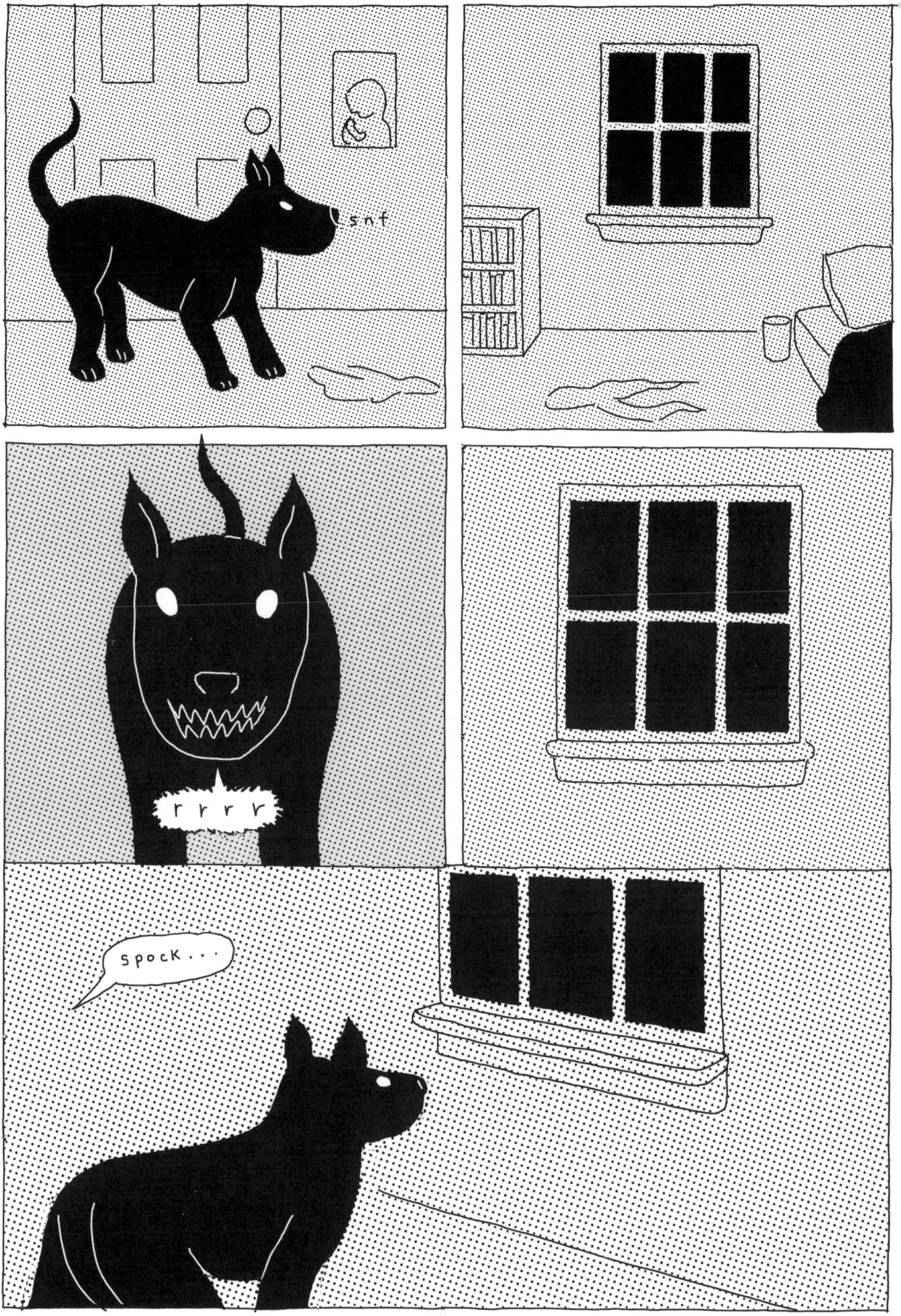
snf
rrrr
spock...

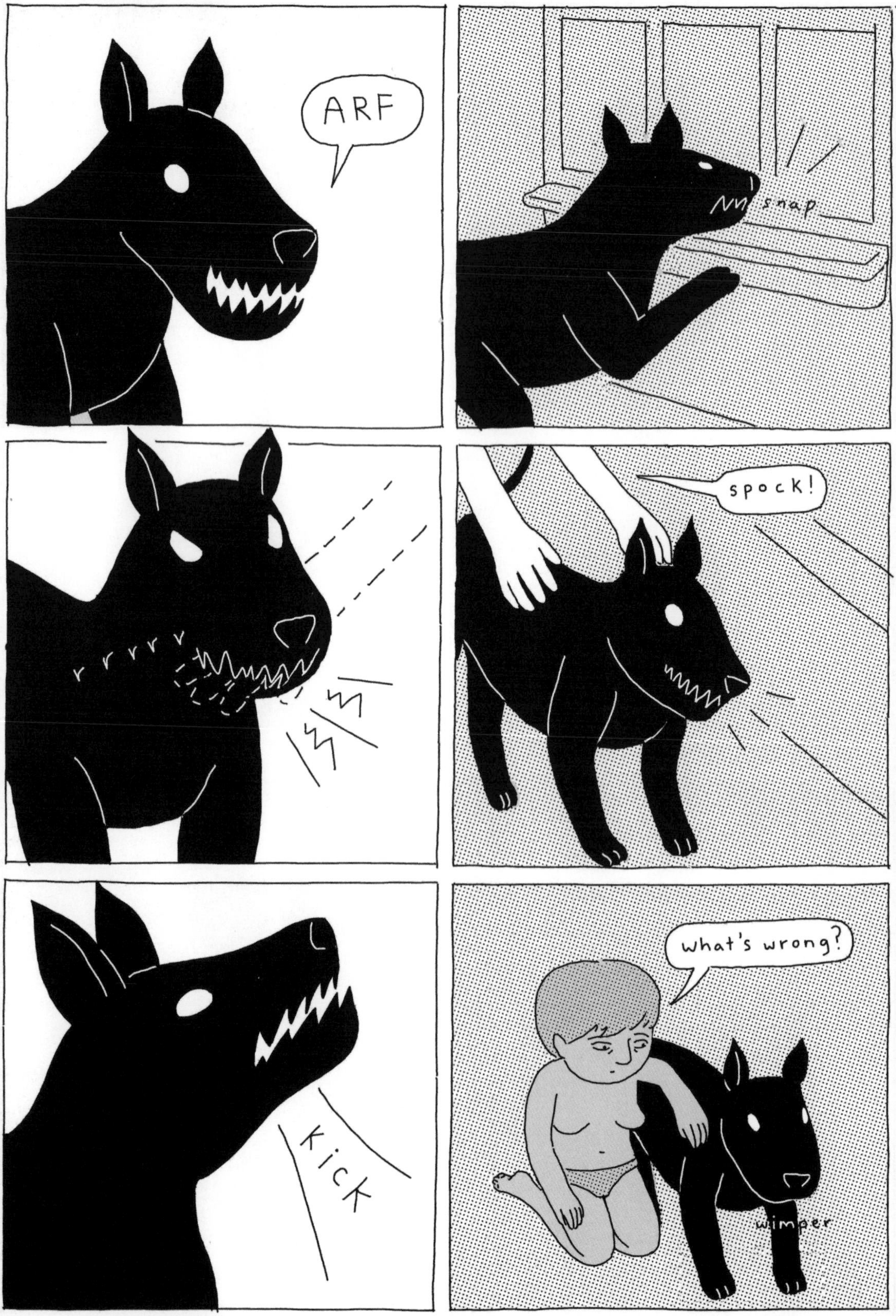
ARF
snap
r r r r r
spock!
KICK
what's wrong?
wimper

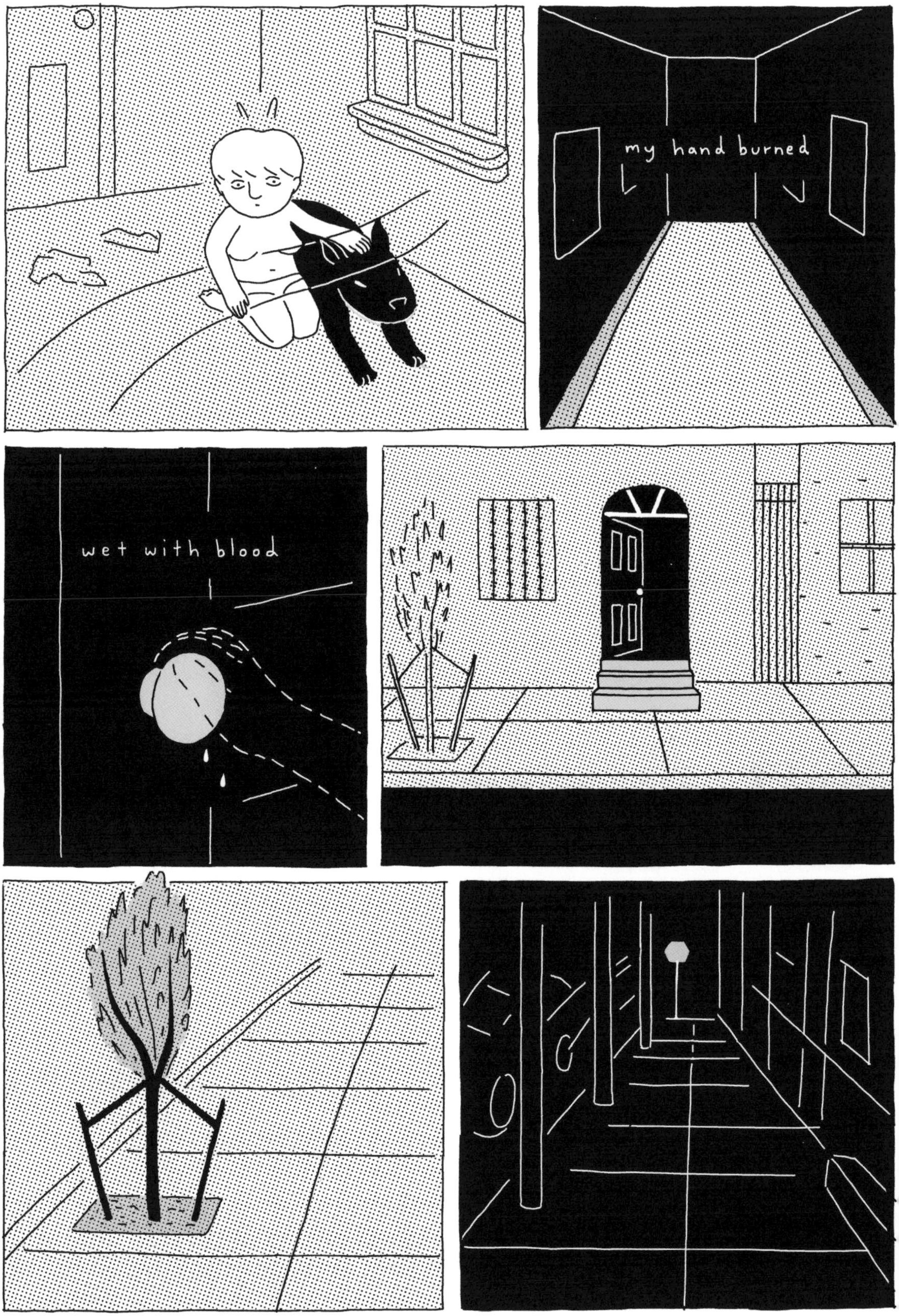
my hand burned
wet with blood

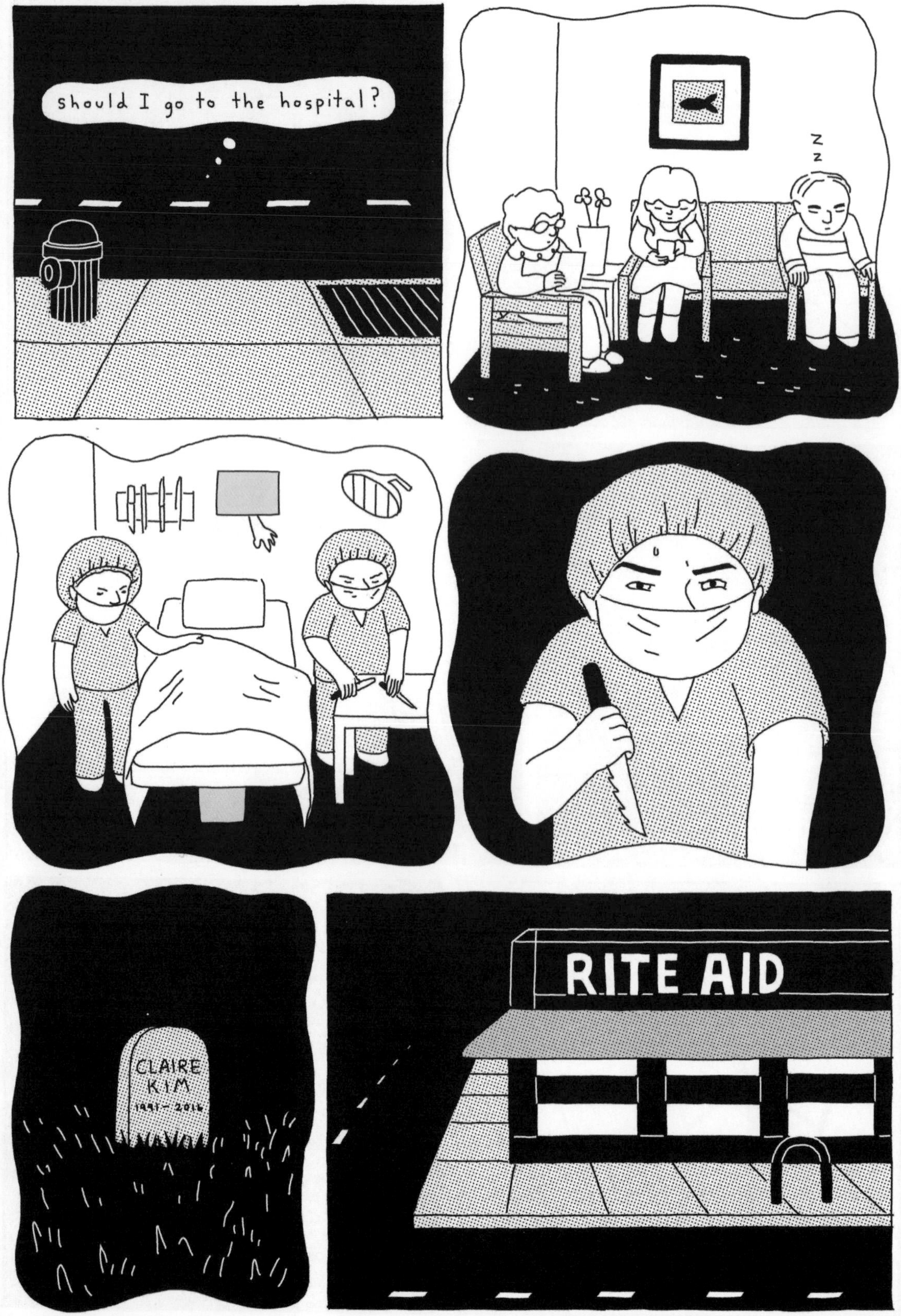
should I go to the hospital?
Z
Z
CLAIRE
KIM
1991 – 2016
RITE AID

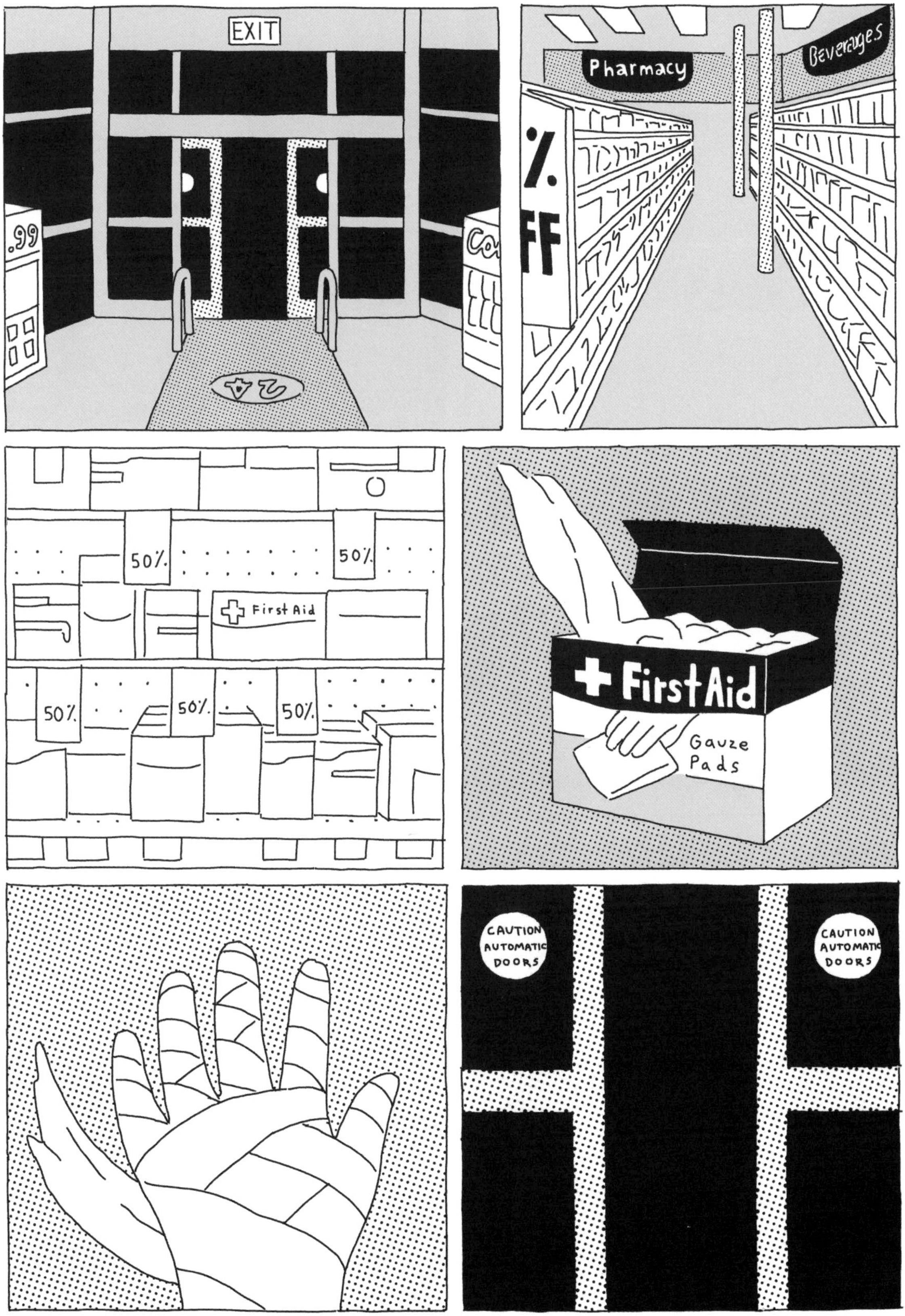
EXIT
.99
Pharmacy
Beverages
50%
50%
First Aid
50%
50%
50%
First Aid
Gauze Pads
CAUTION AUTOMATIC DOORS
CAUTION AUTOMATIC DOORS

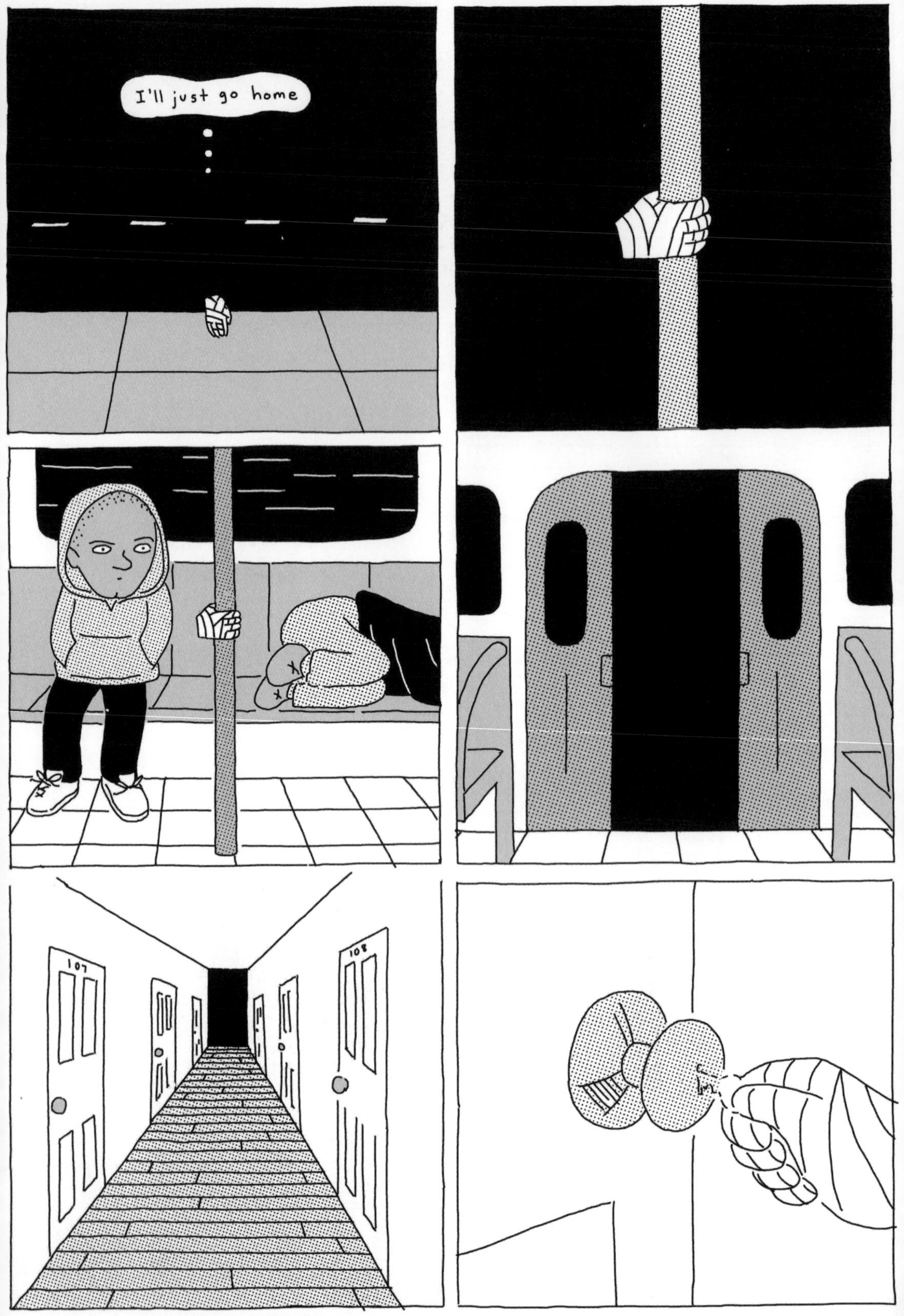
I'll just go home
107
108

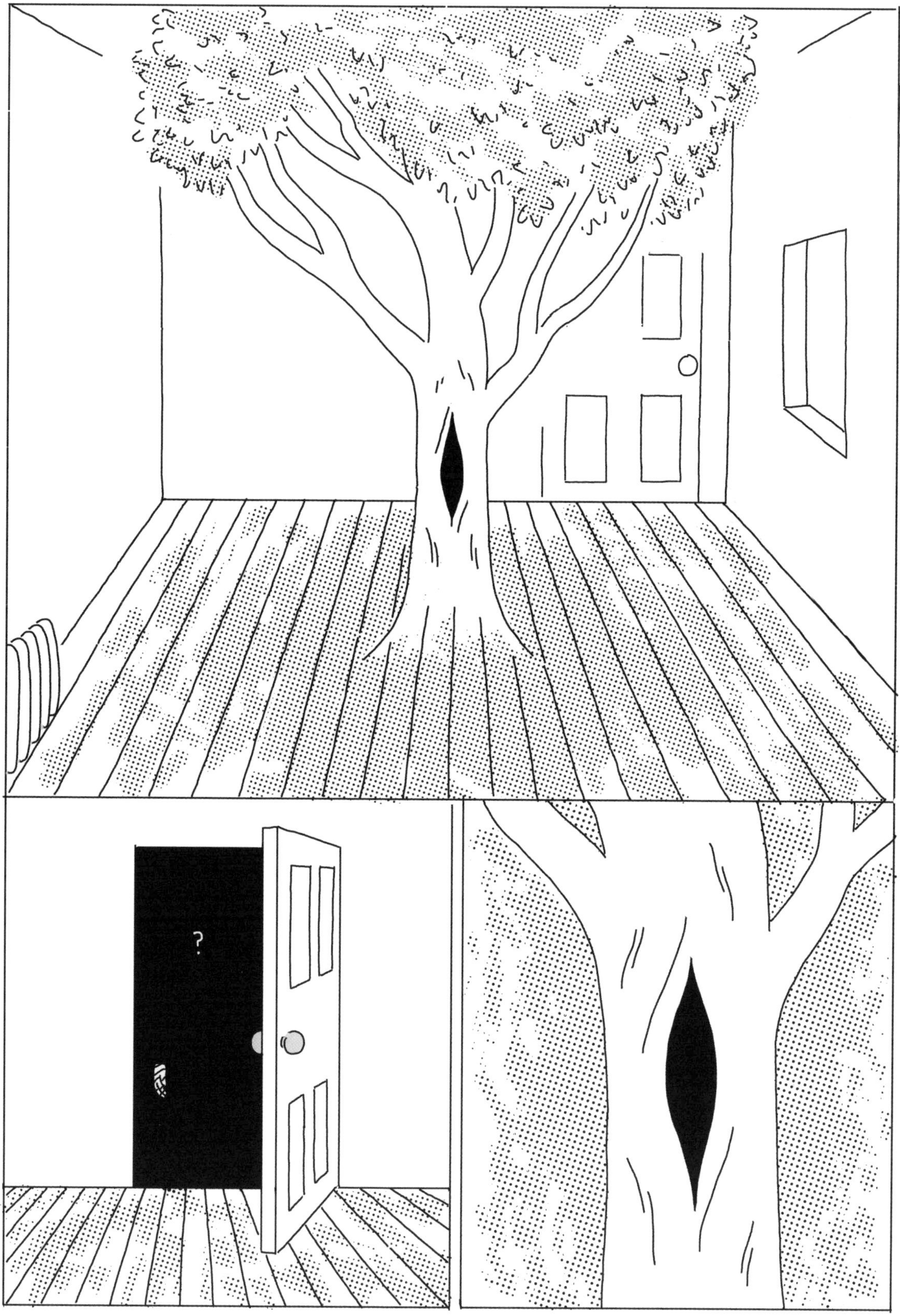
?

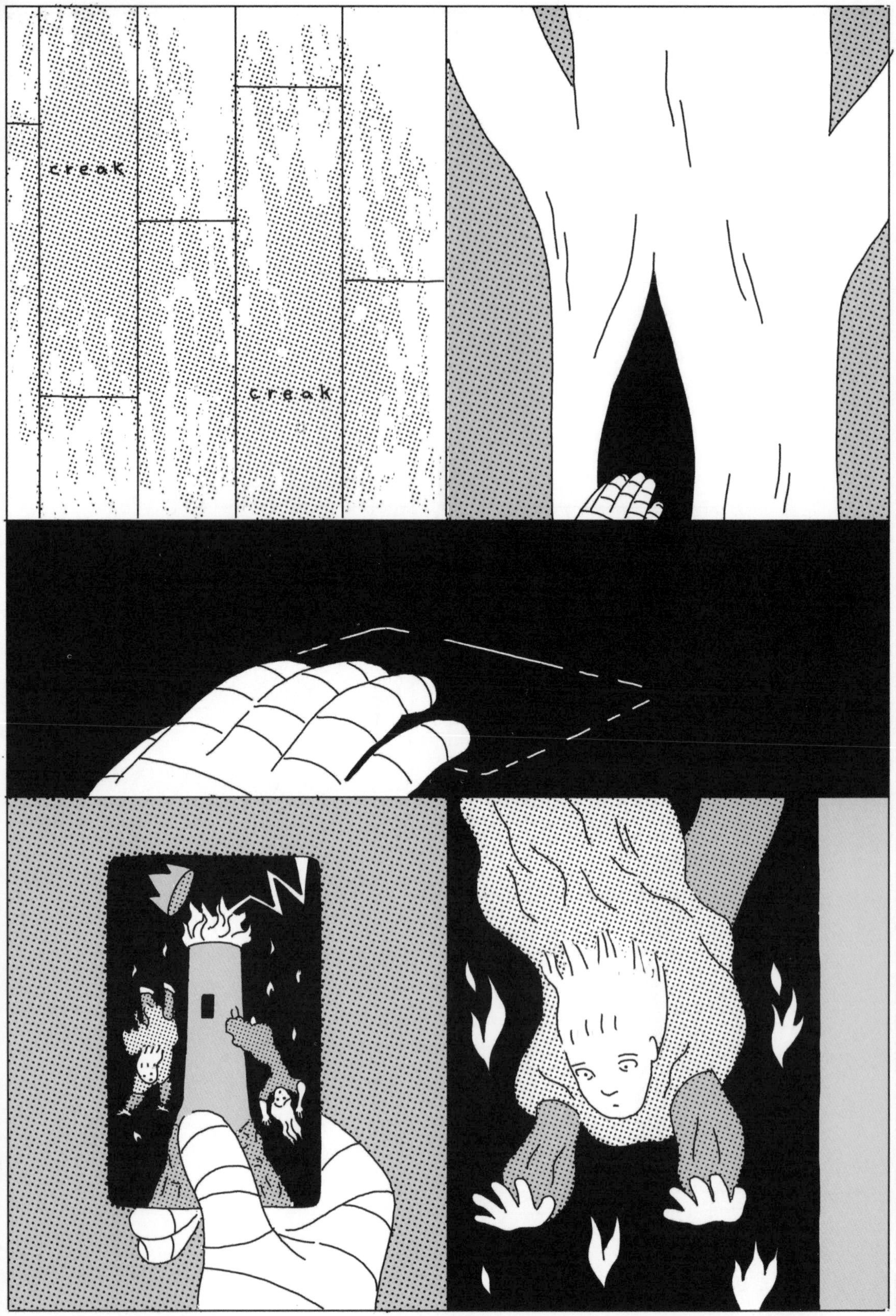
creak
creak

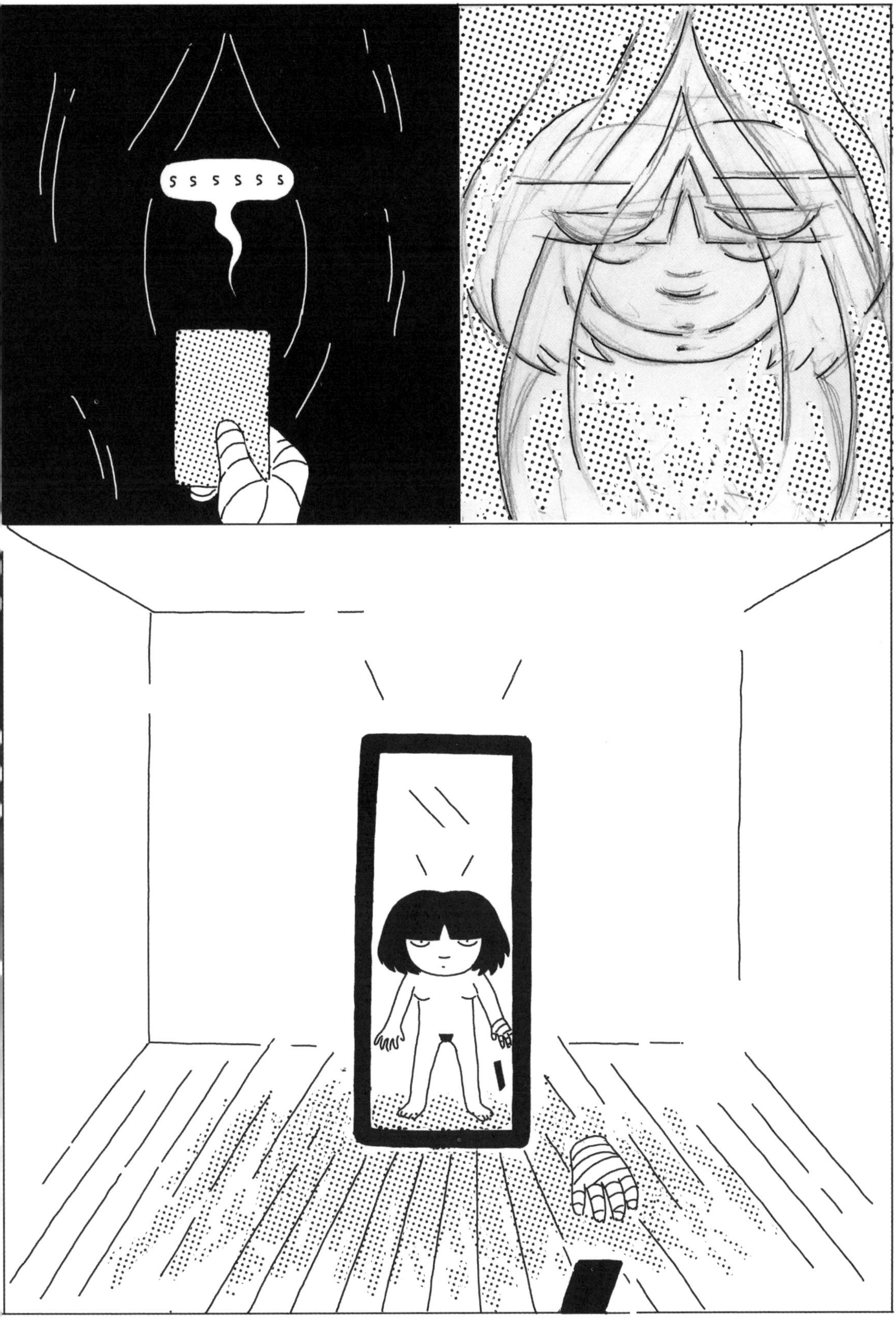
s s s s s s

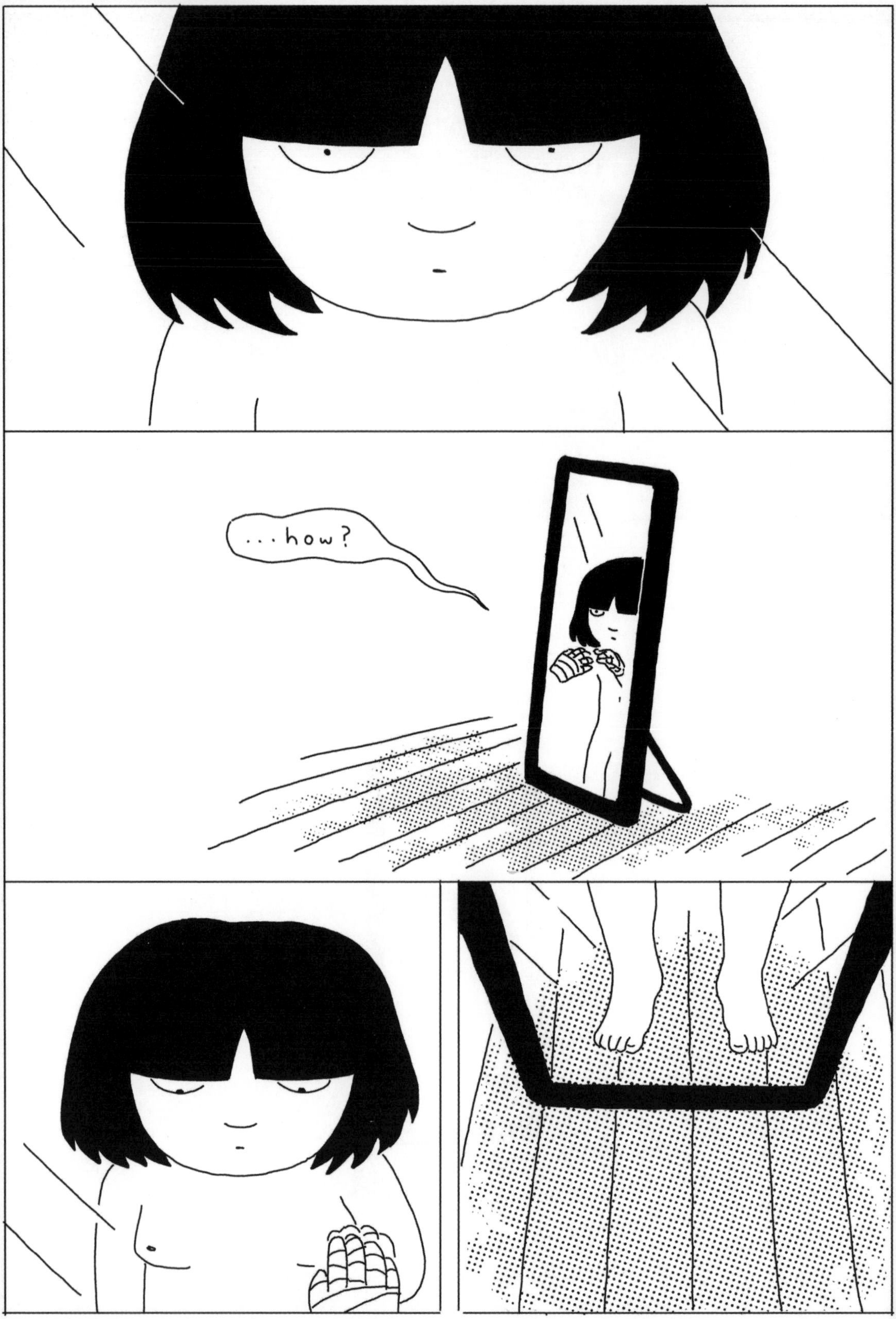
...how?

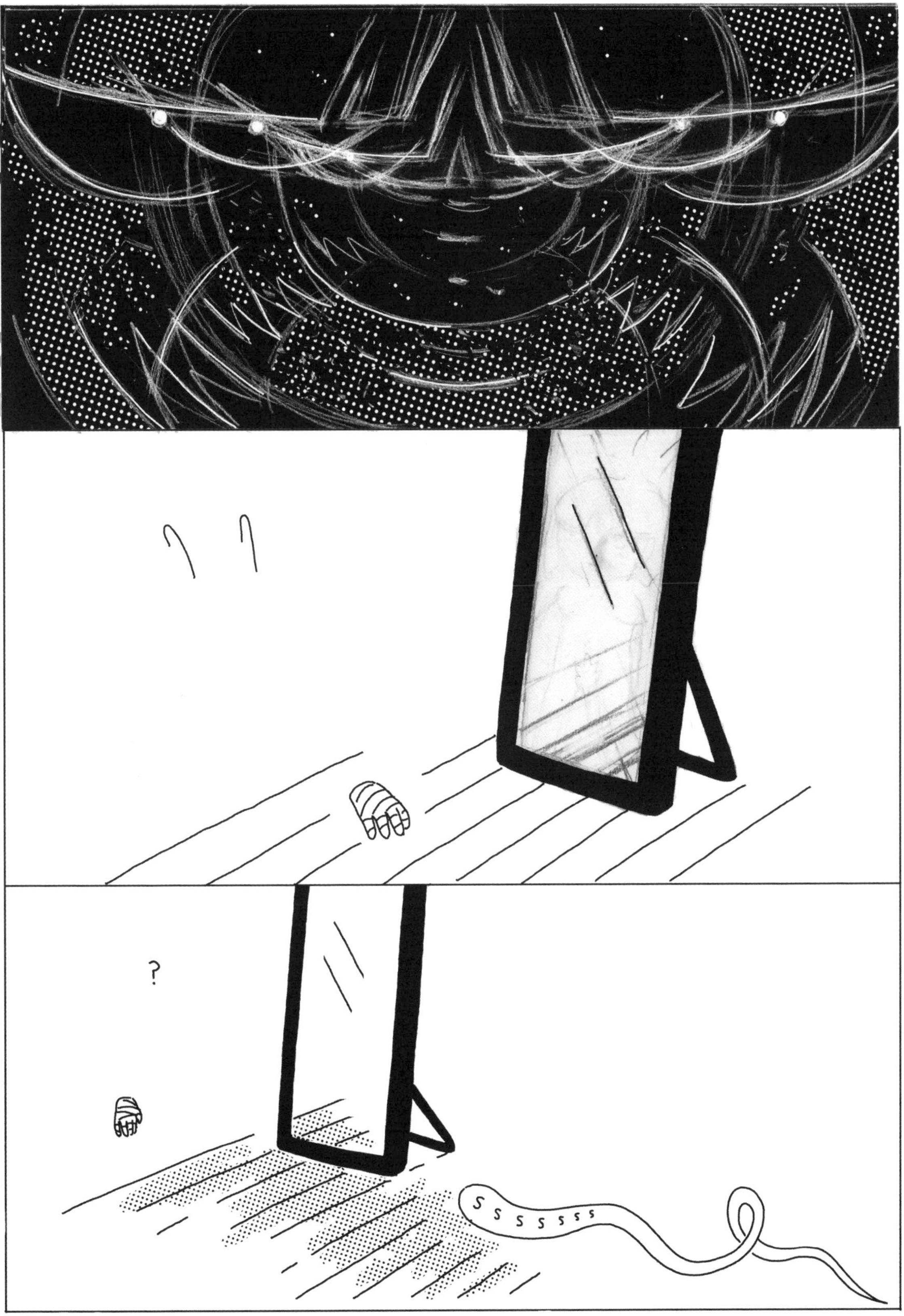
?
Sssssss

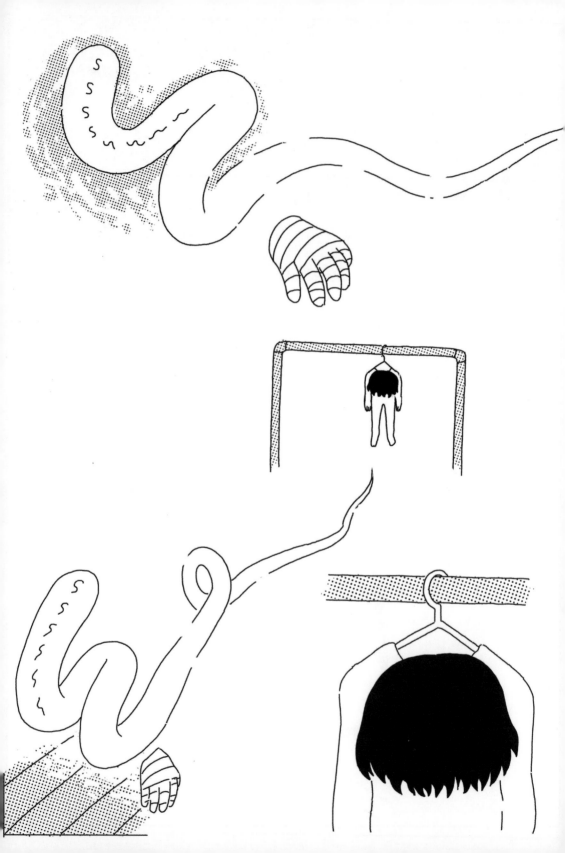

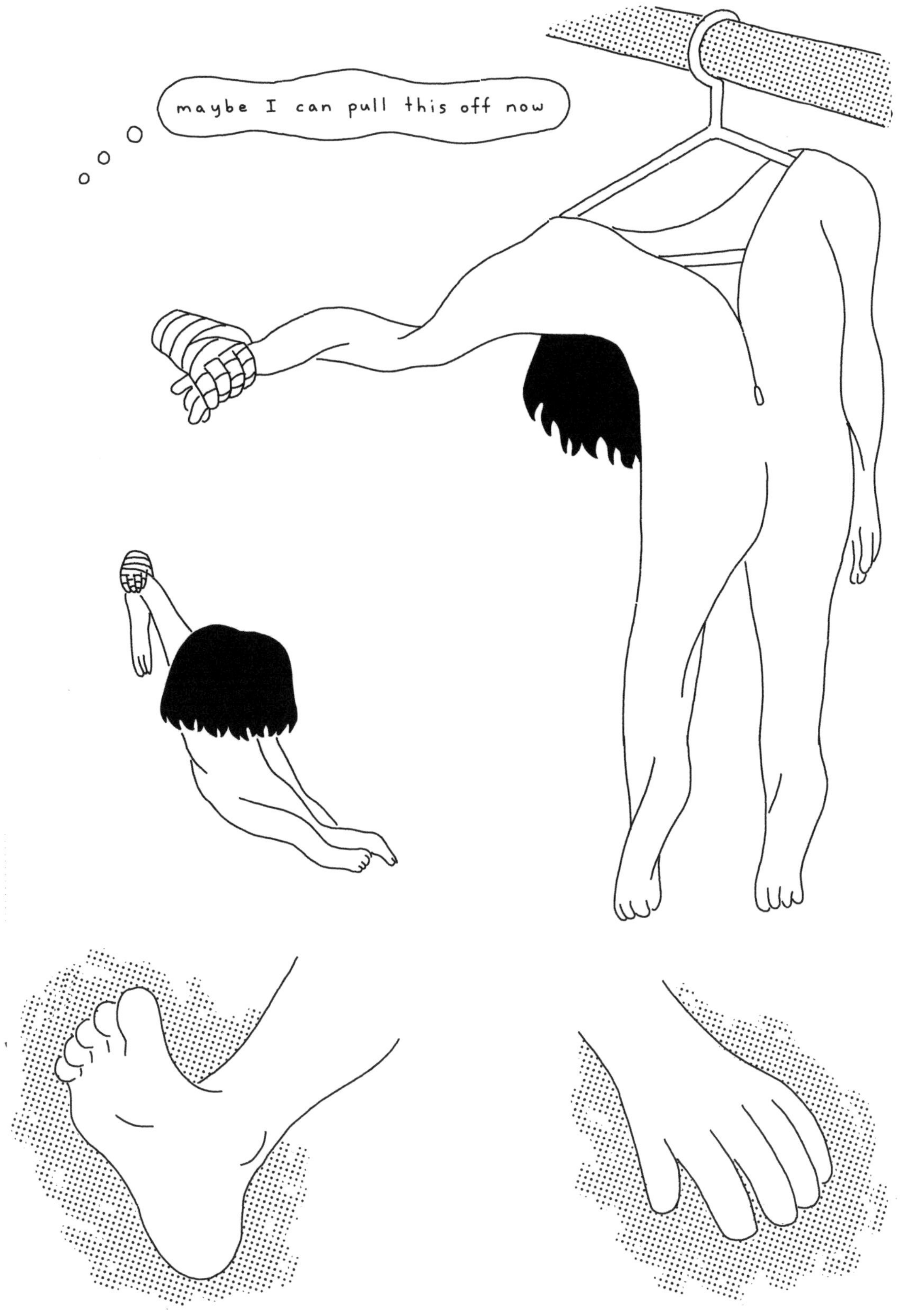
maybe I can pull this off now

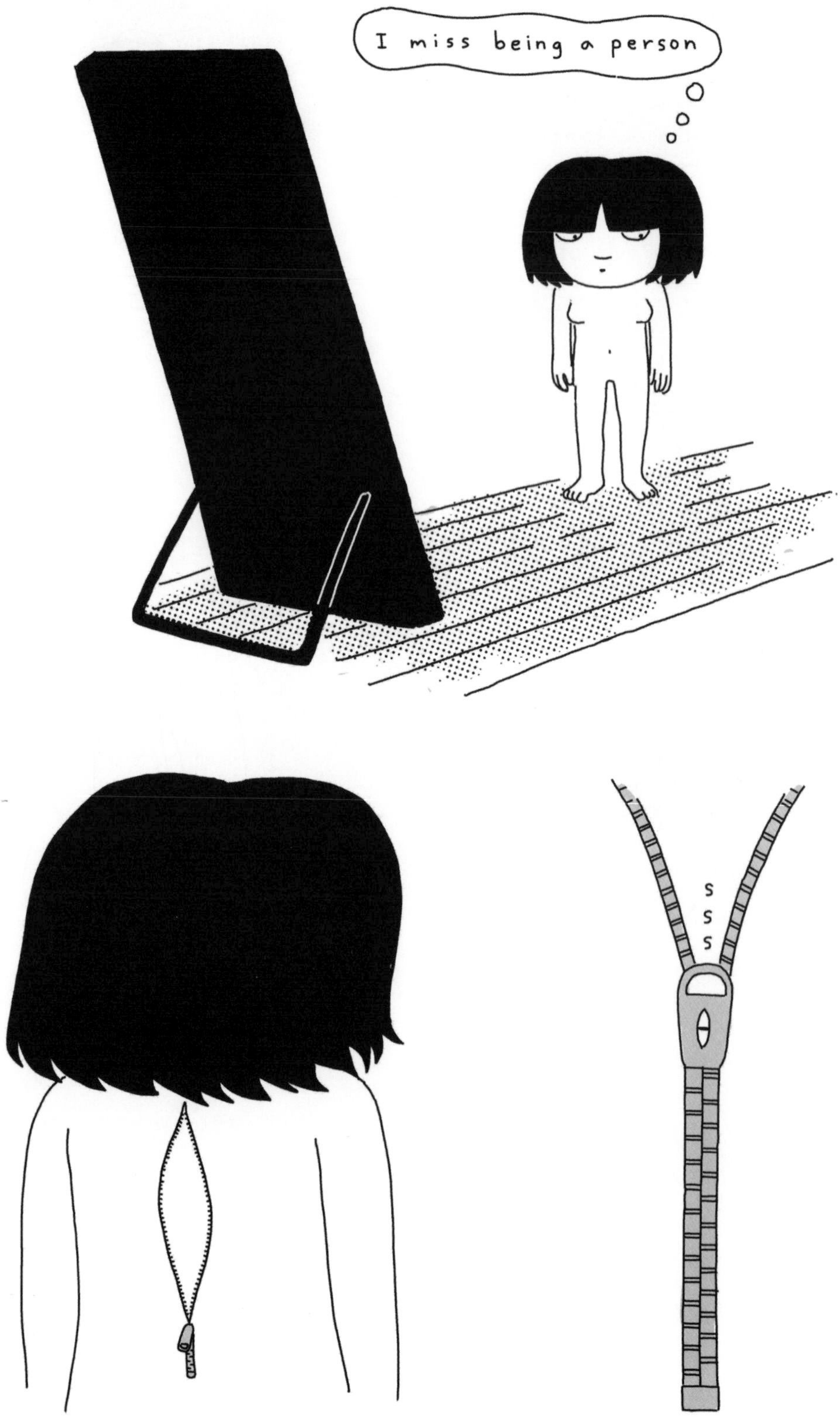
I miss being a person
s
s
s

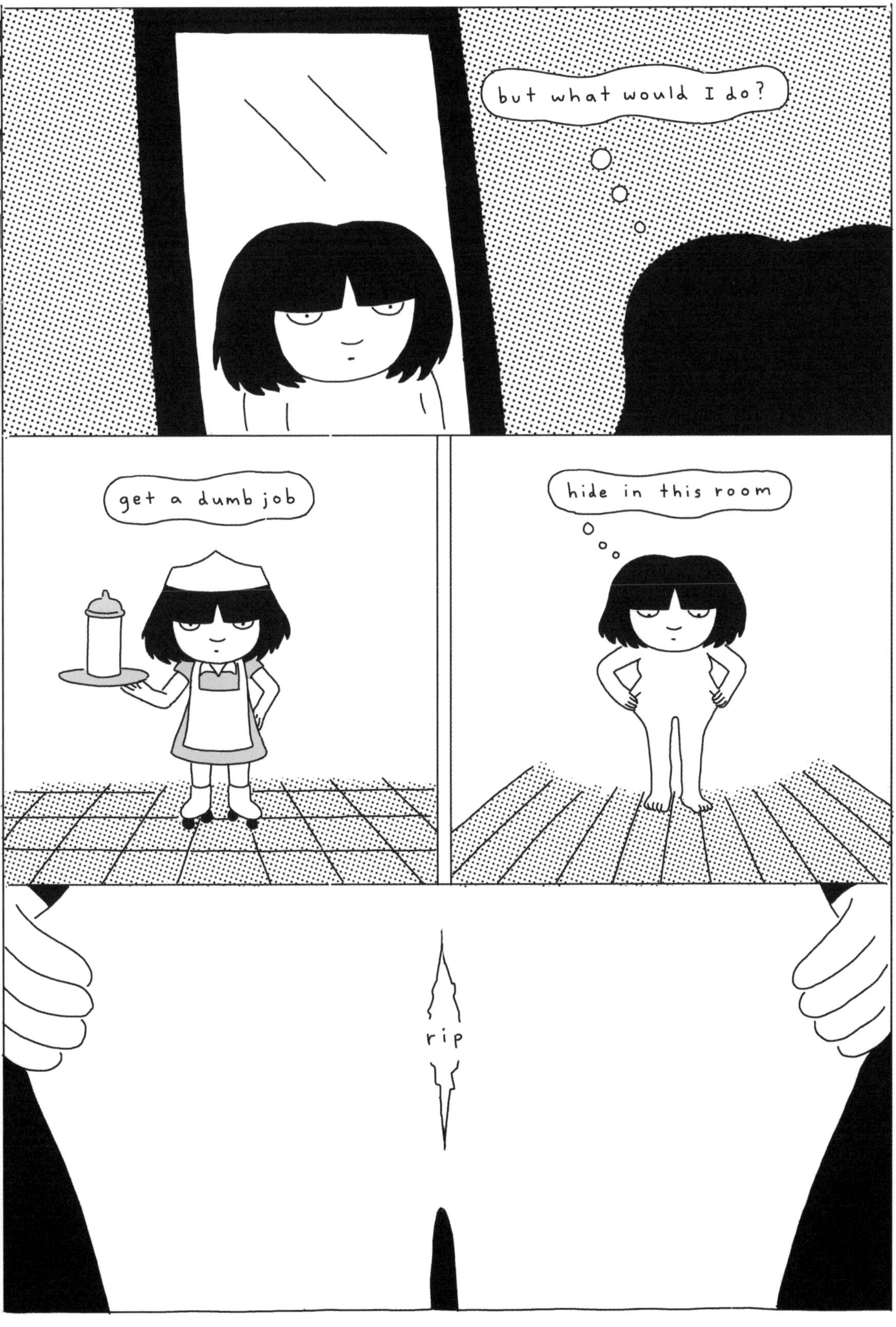
but what would I do?
get a dumb job
hide in this room
rip

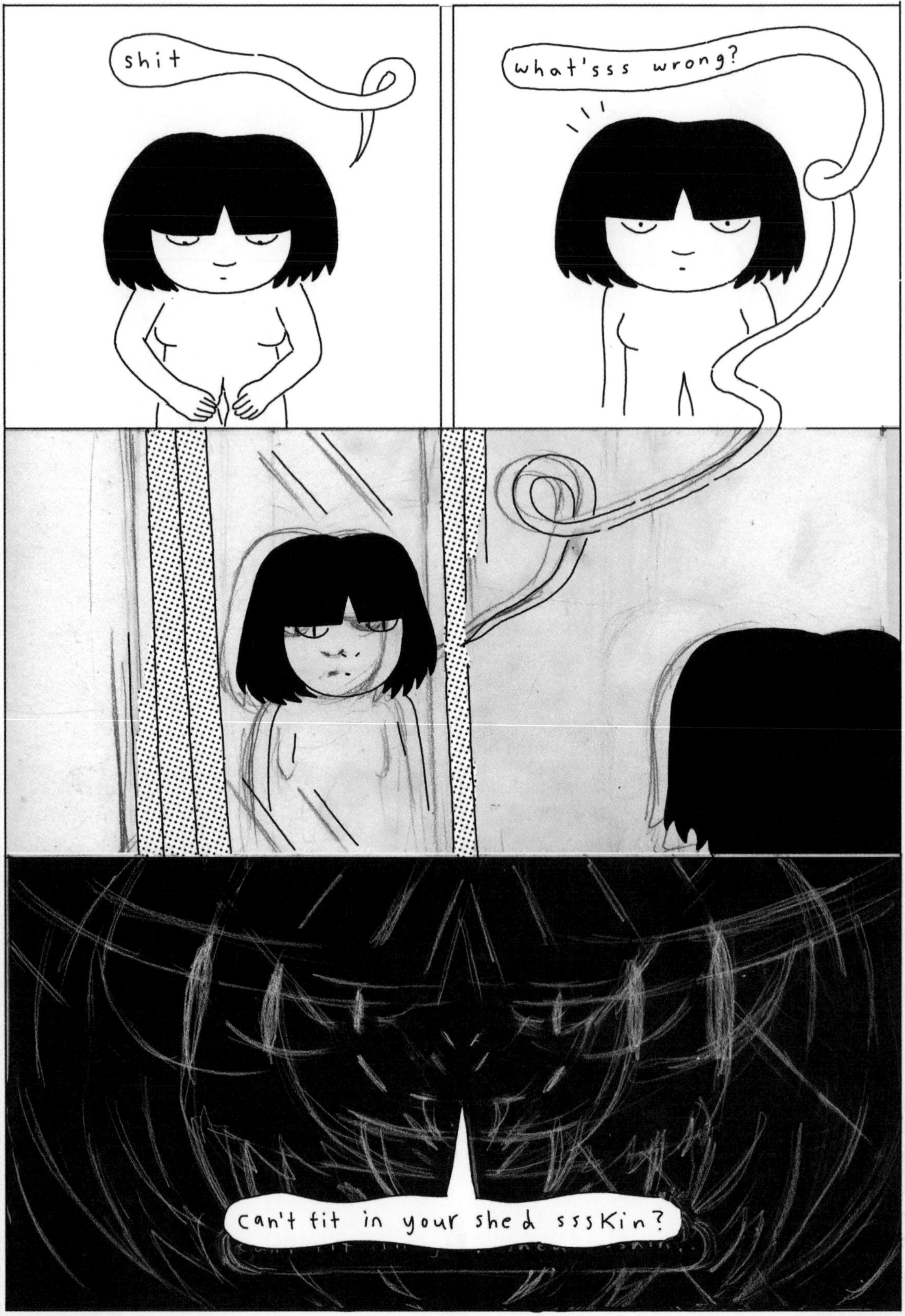
shit
what'sss wrong?
can't fit in your shed sssKin?

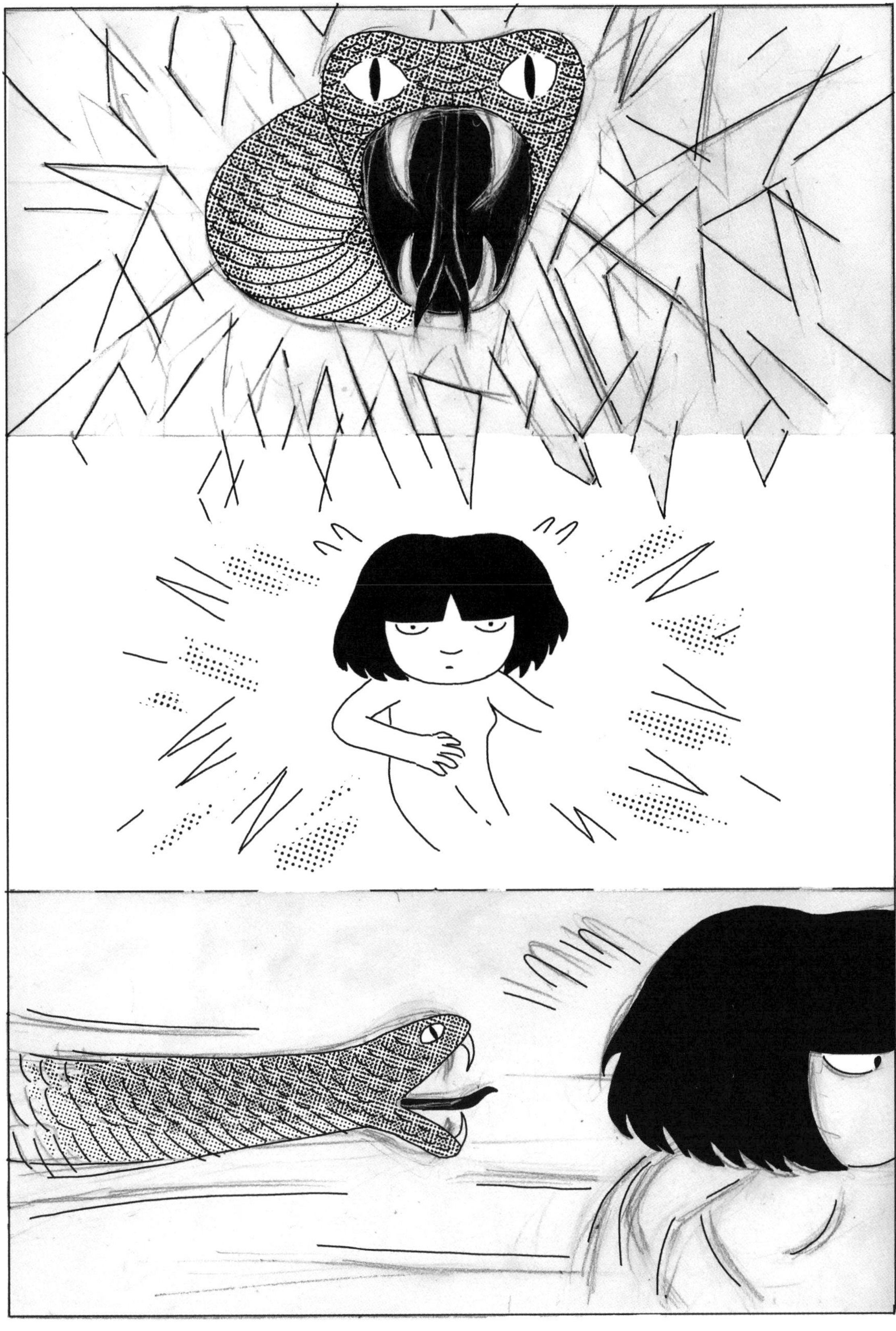

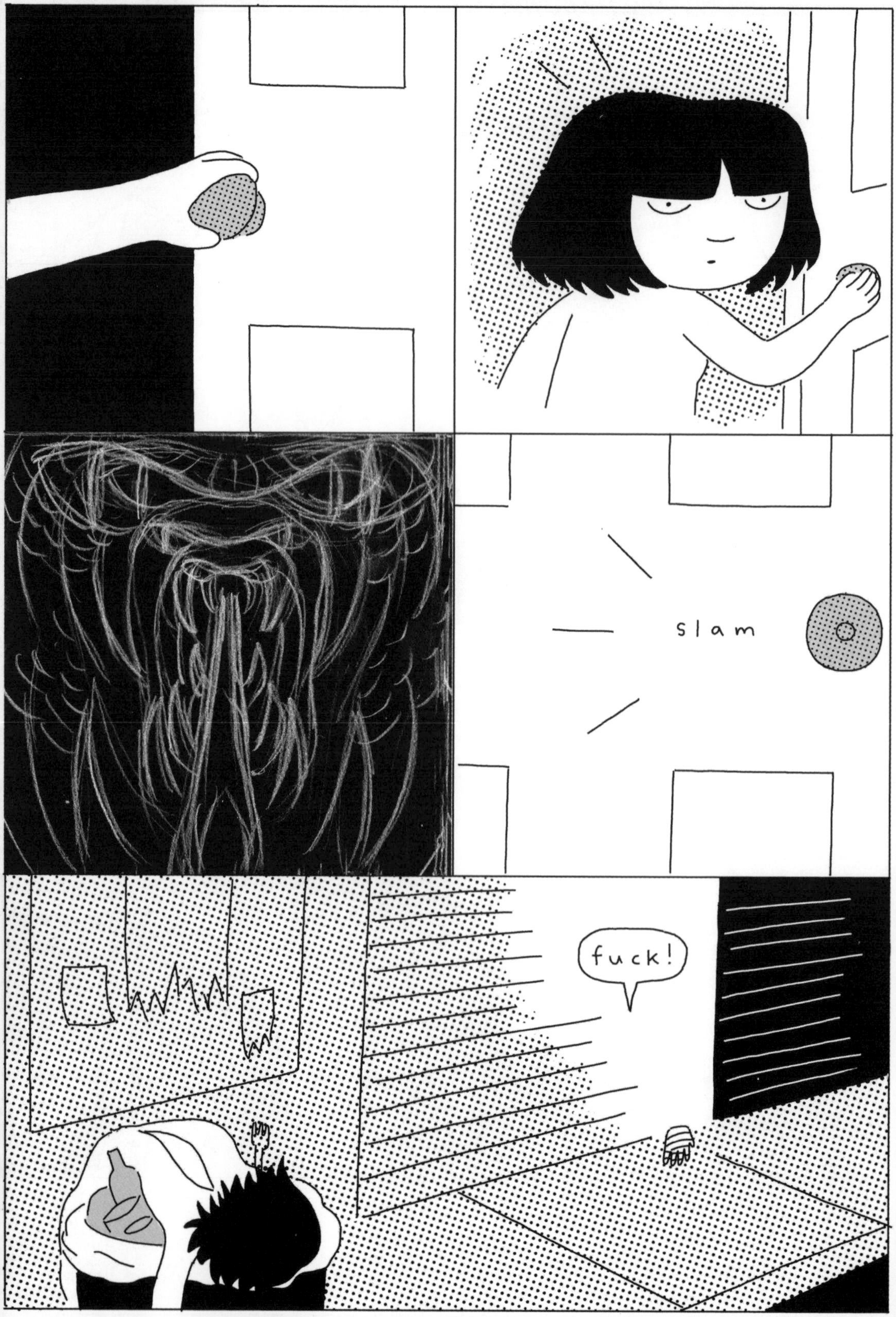
slam
fuck!

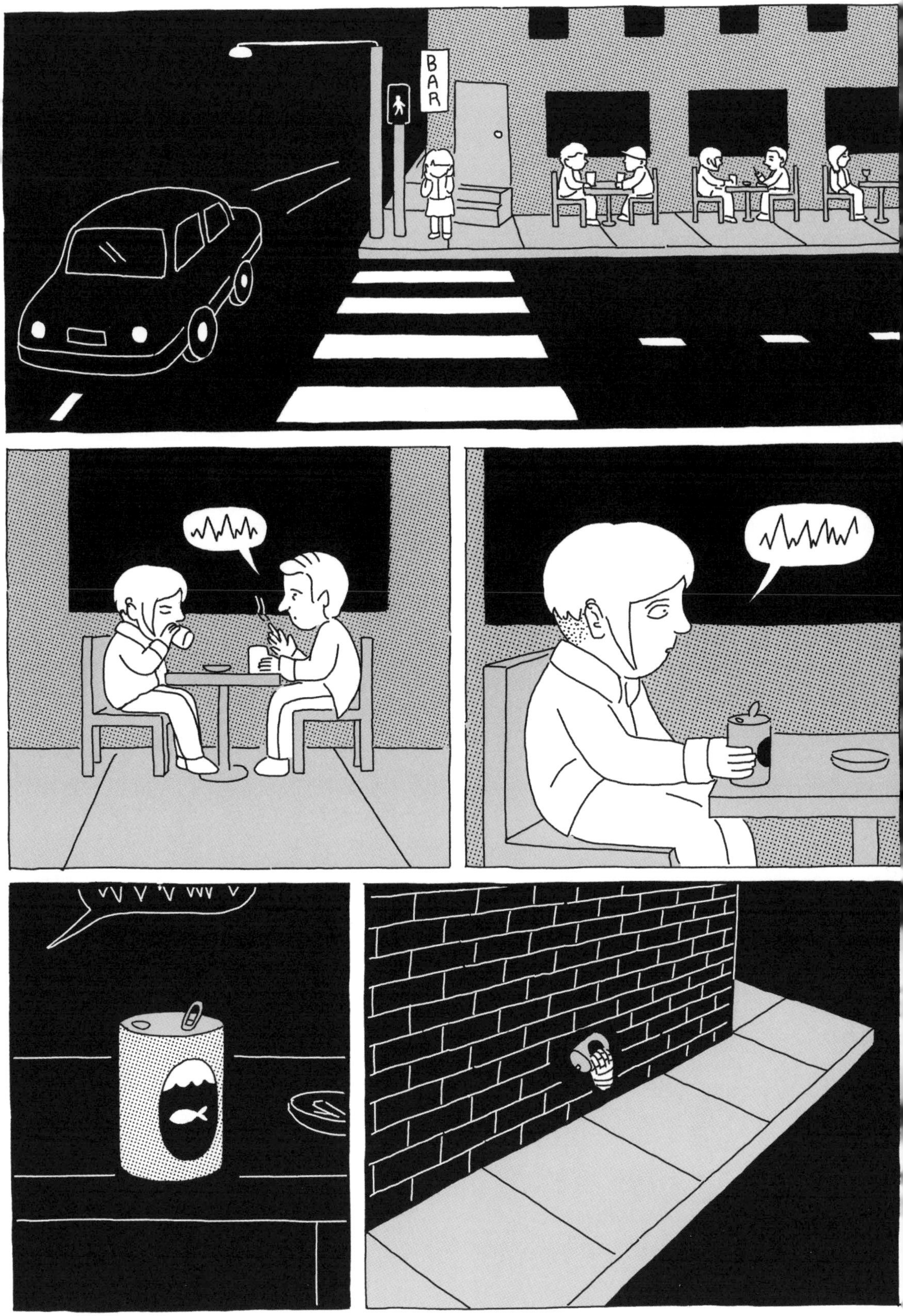
BAR

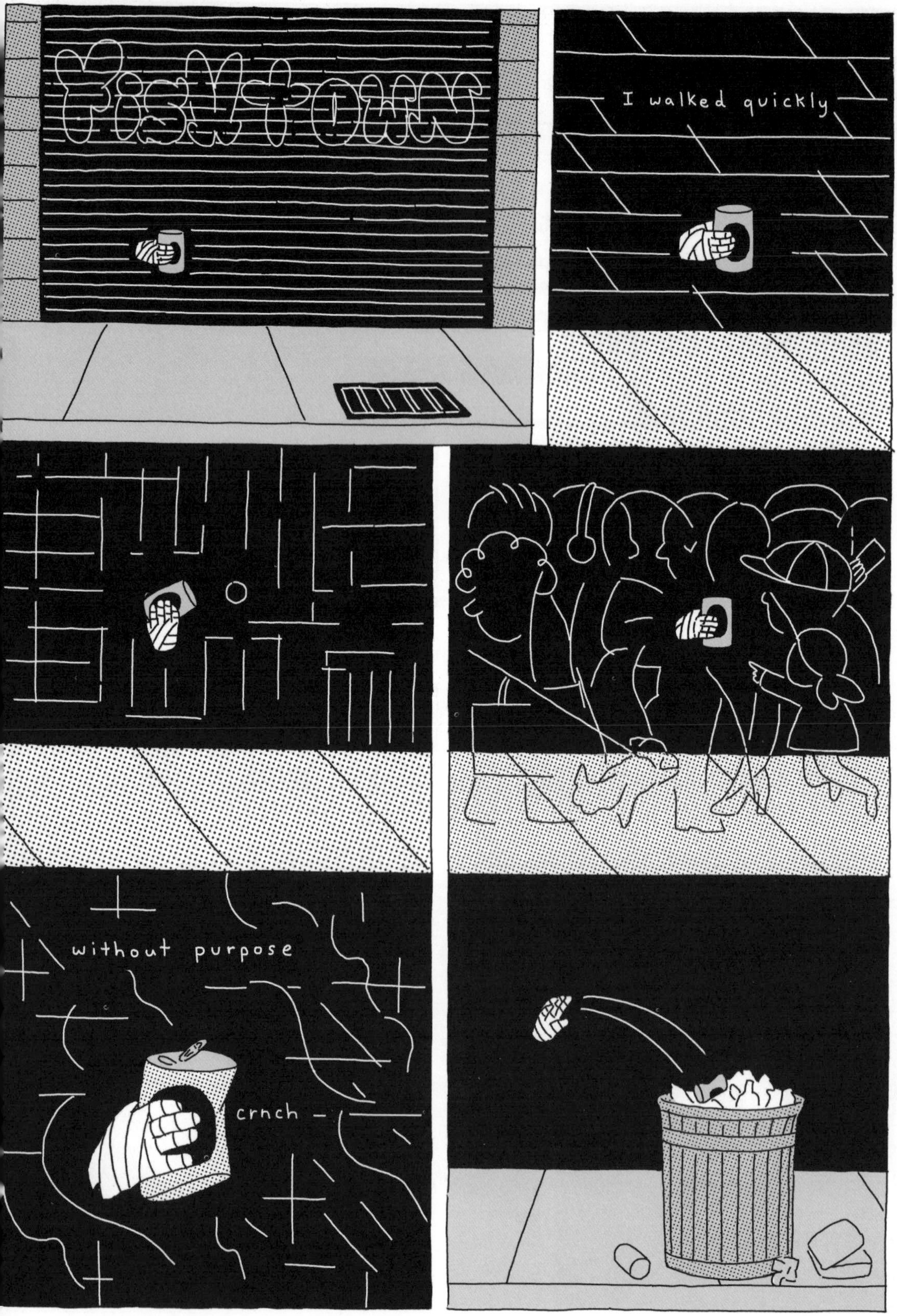
I walked quickly
without purpose
crnch

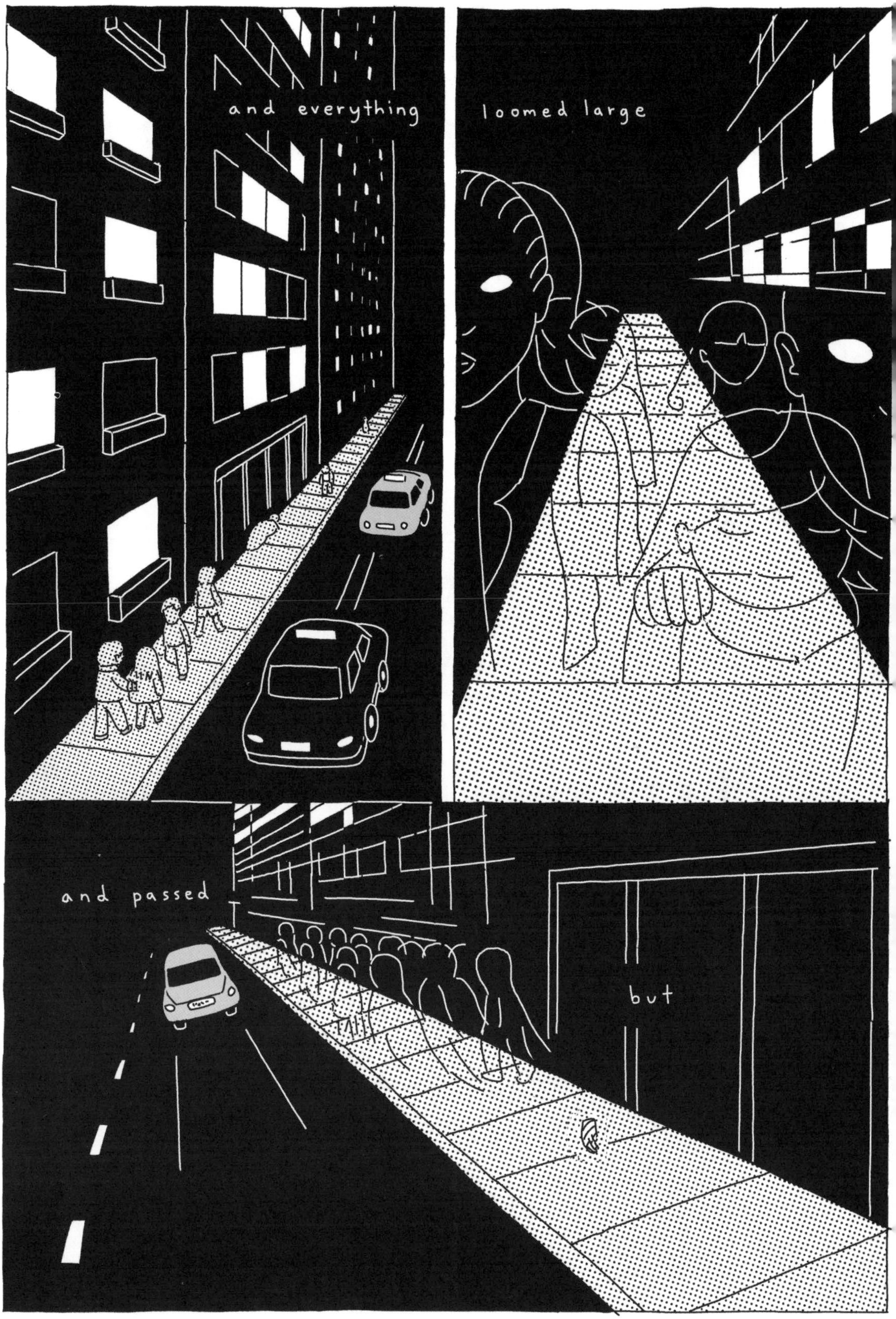
and everything
loomed large
and passed
but

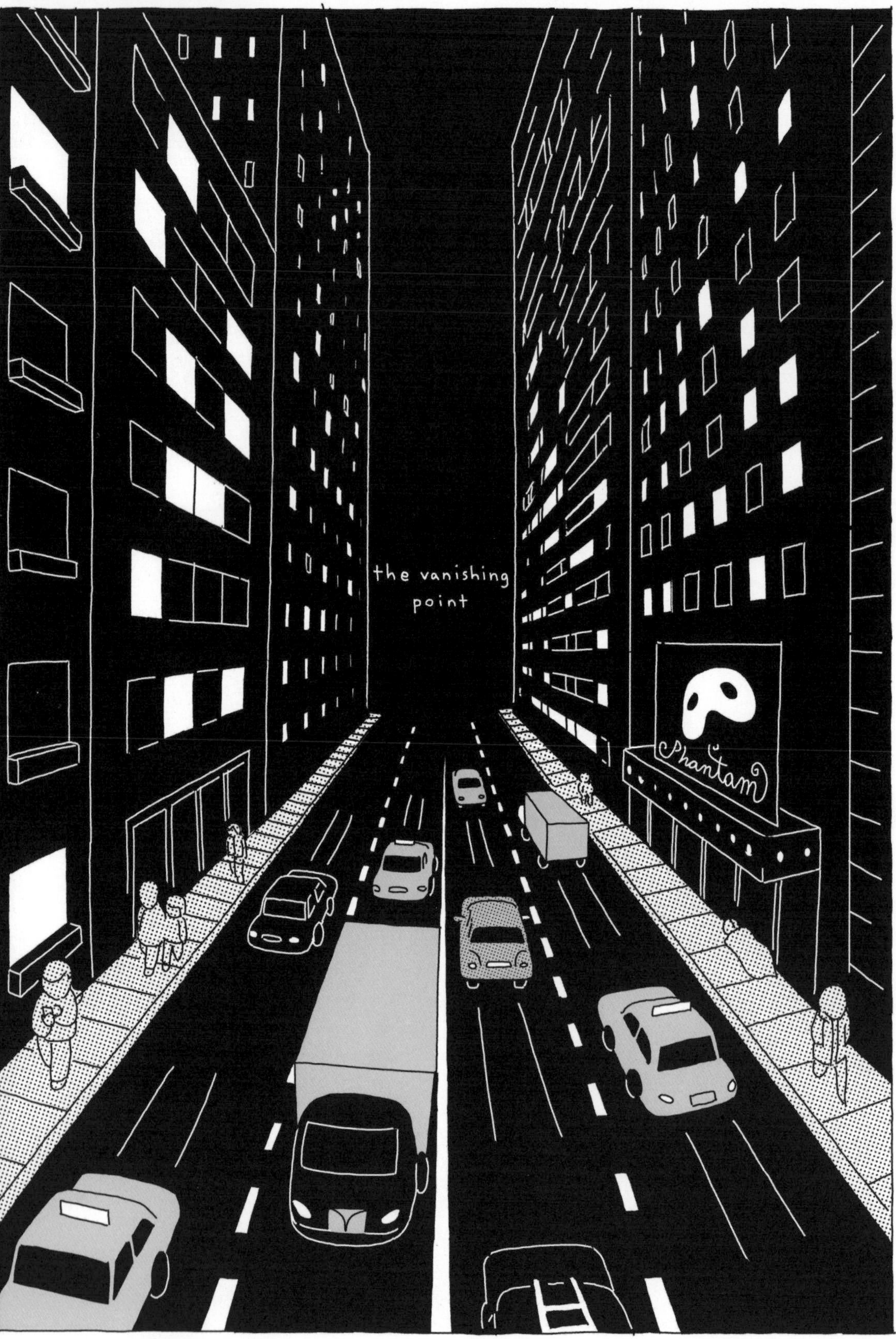
the vanishing point
Phantom

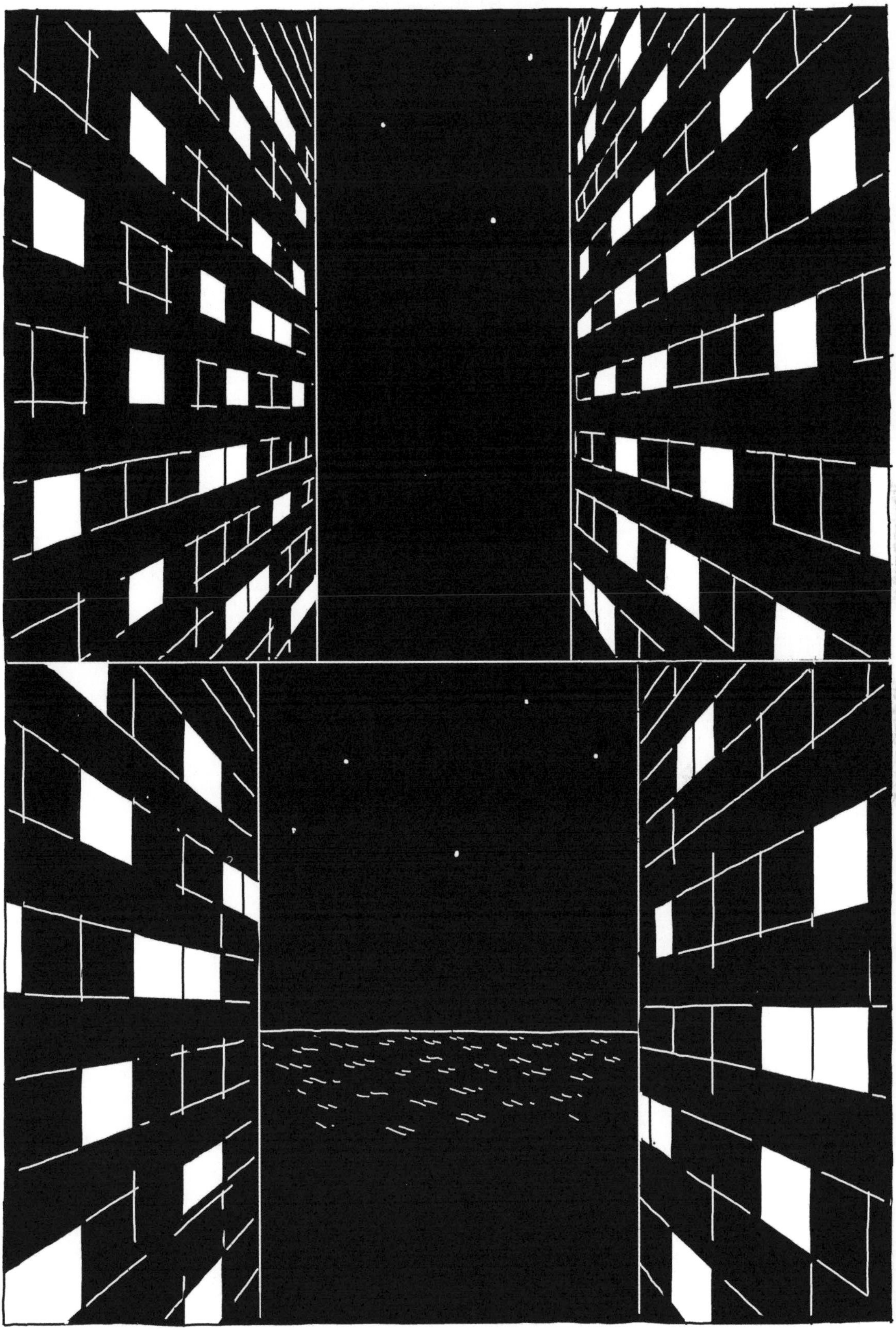

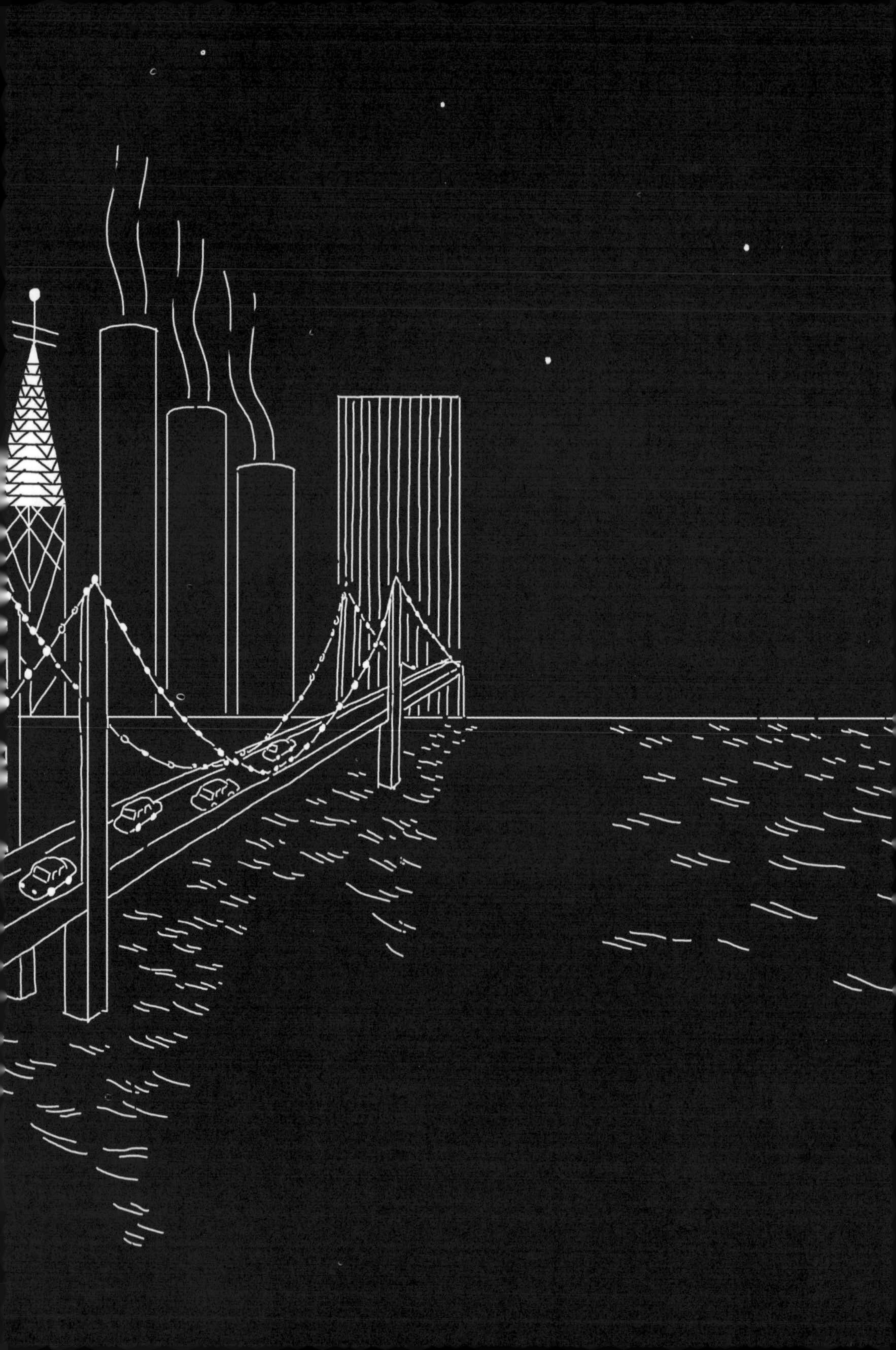

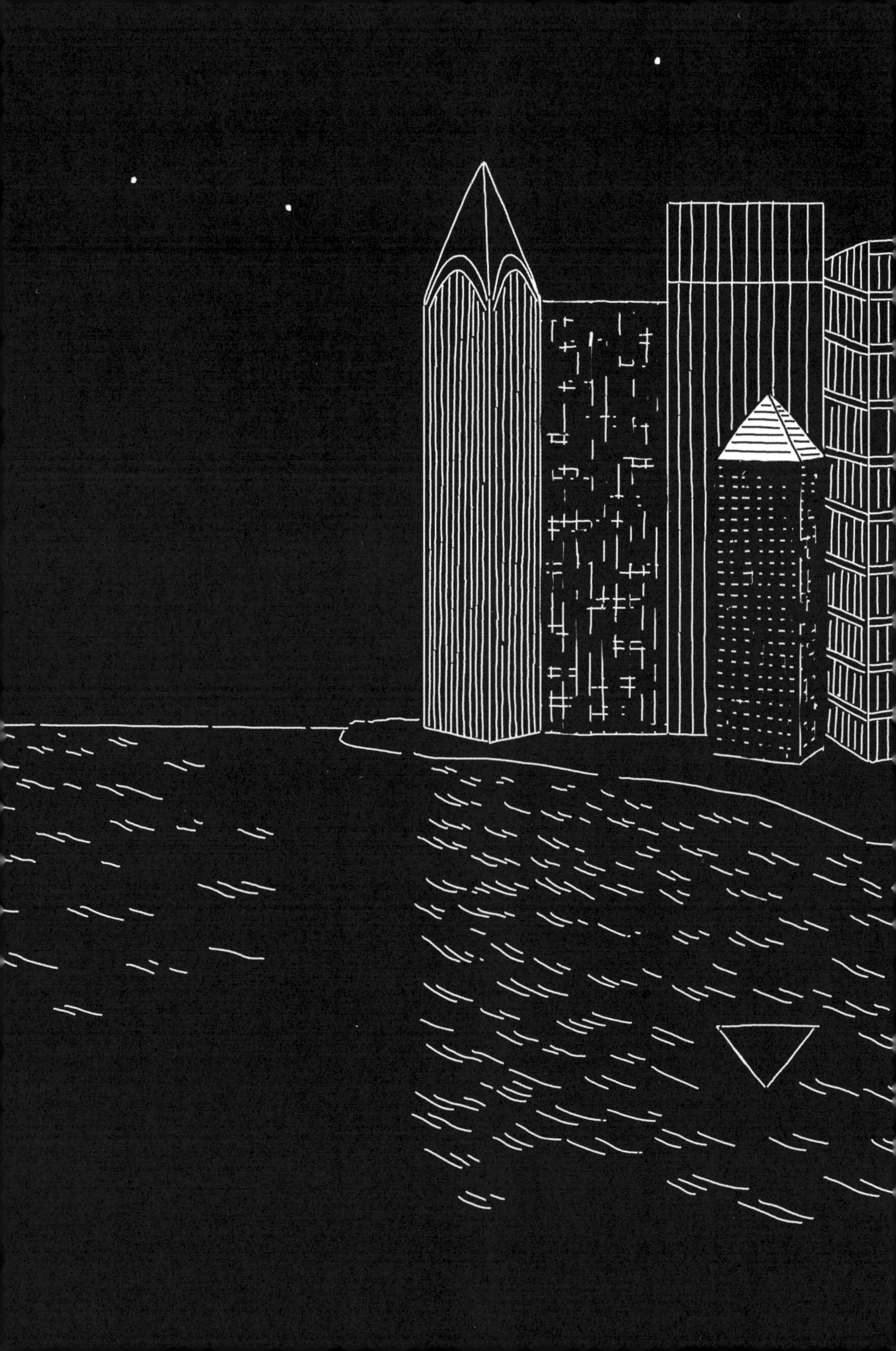

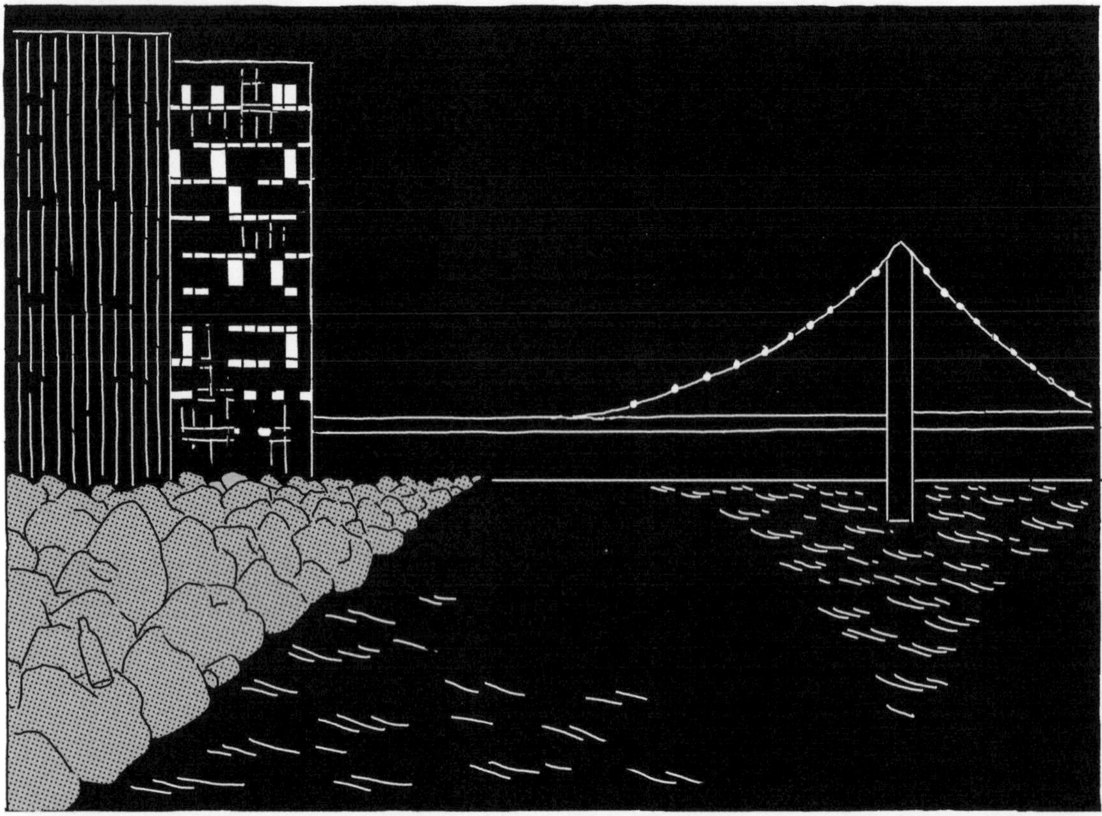
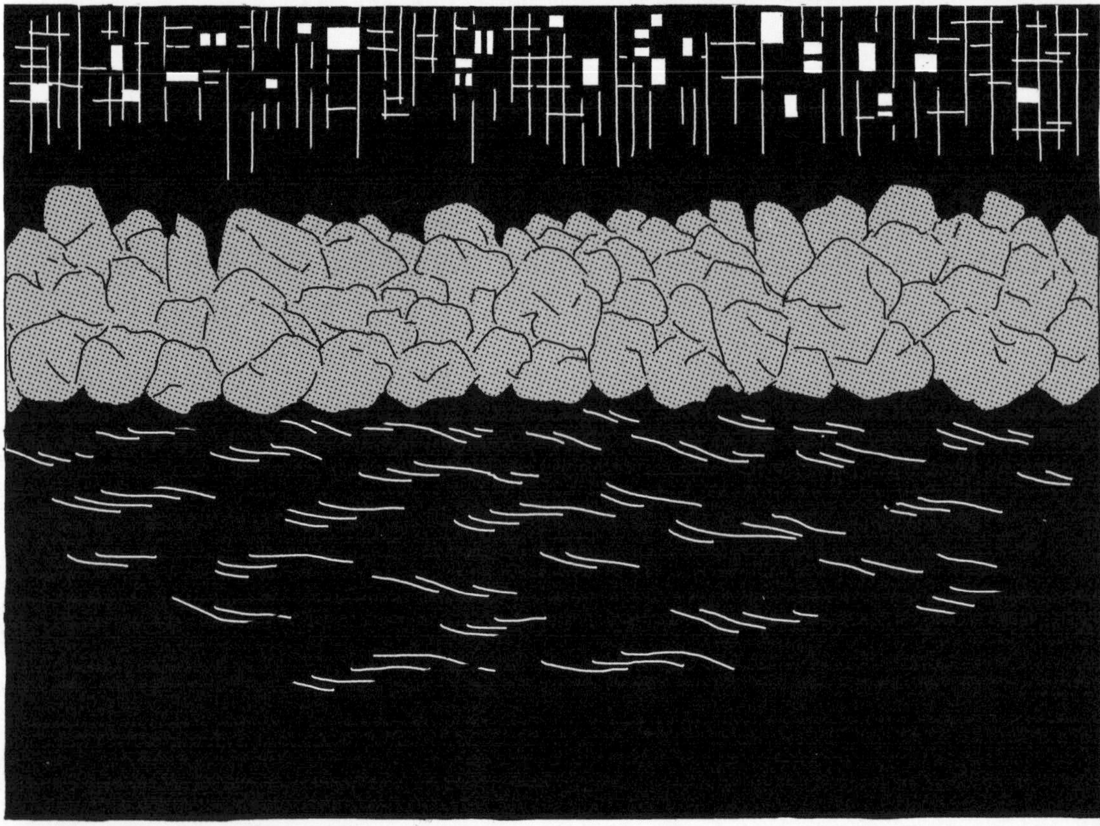

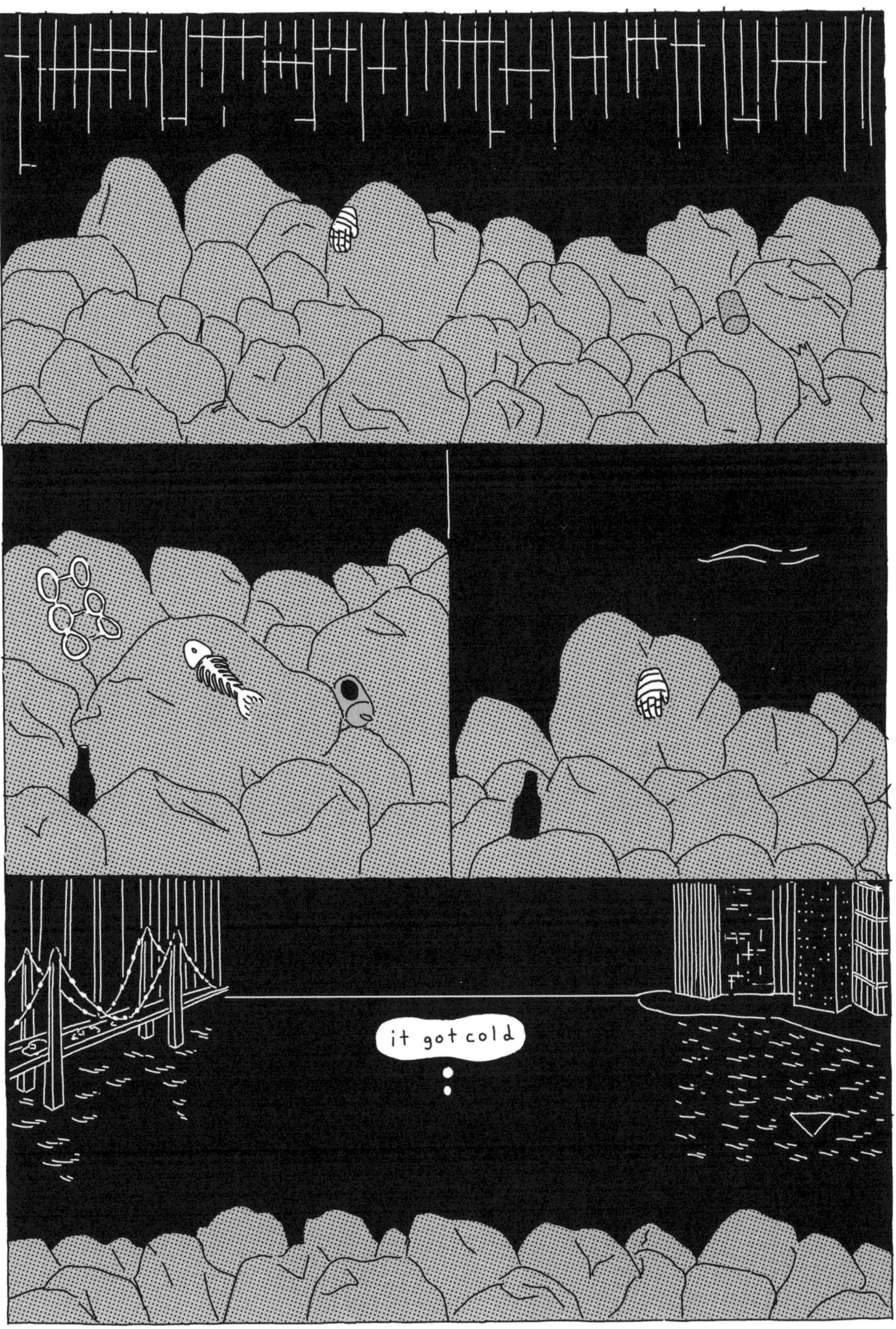
it got cold

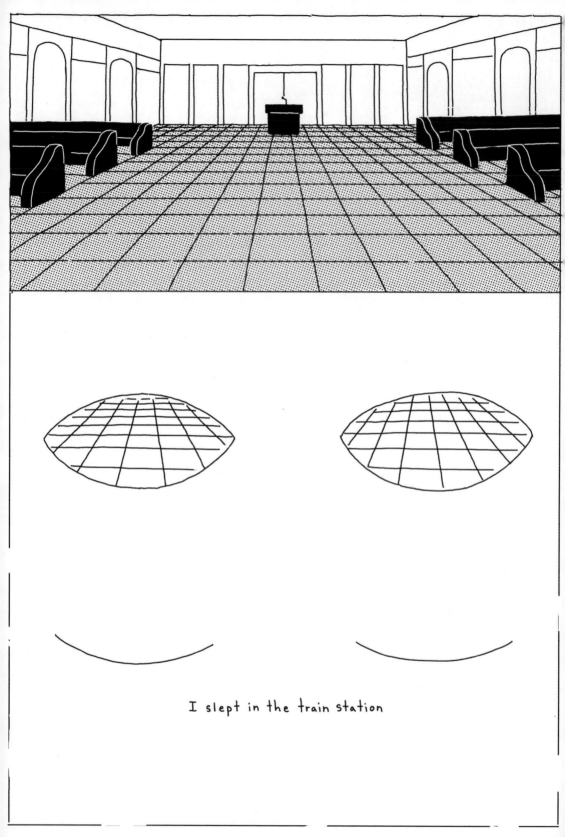

I slept in the train station

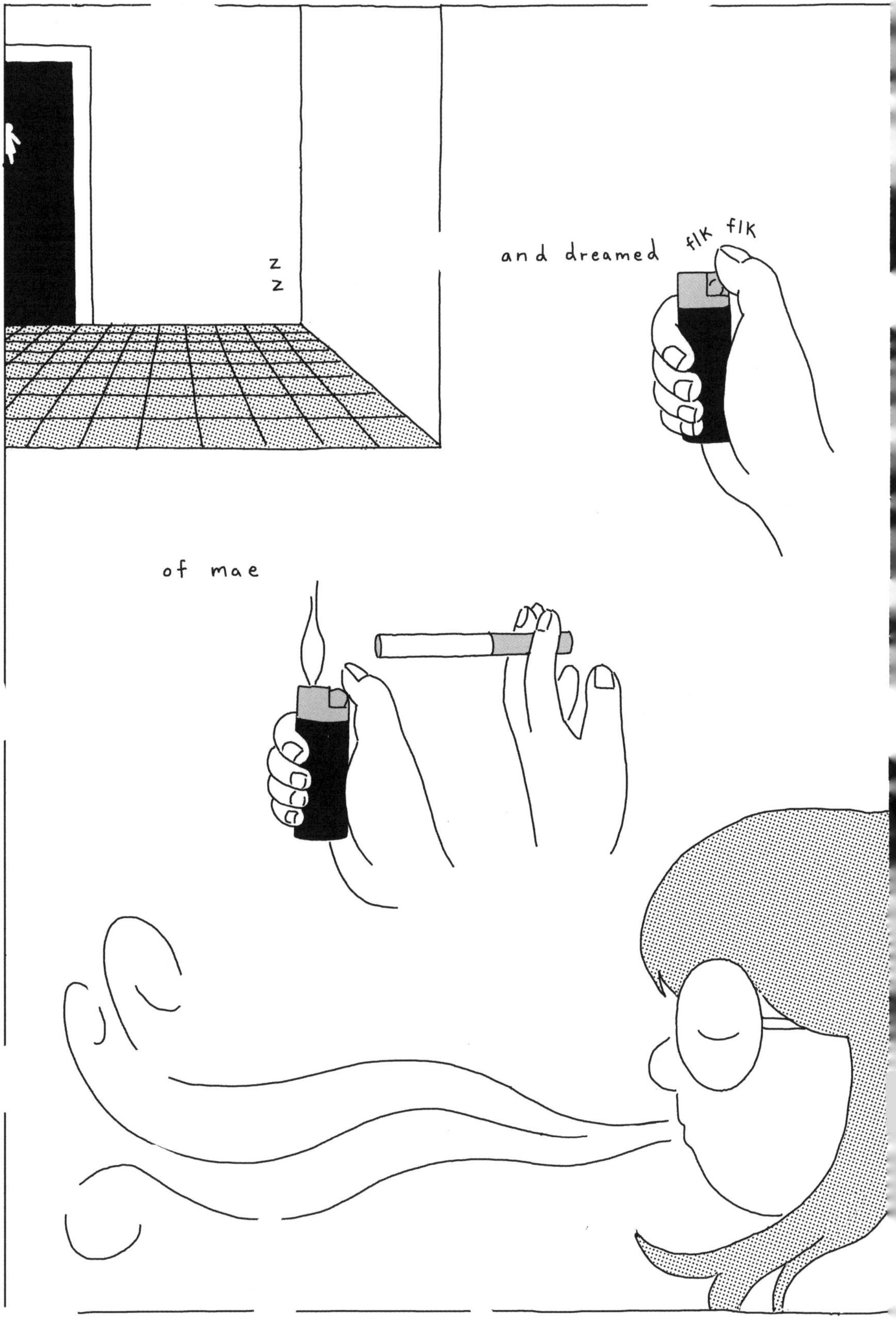

z
z
and dreamed
flk flk
of mae

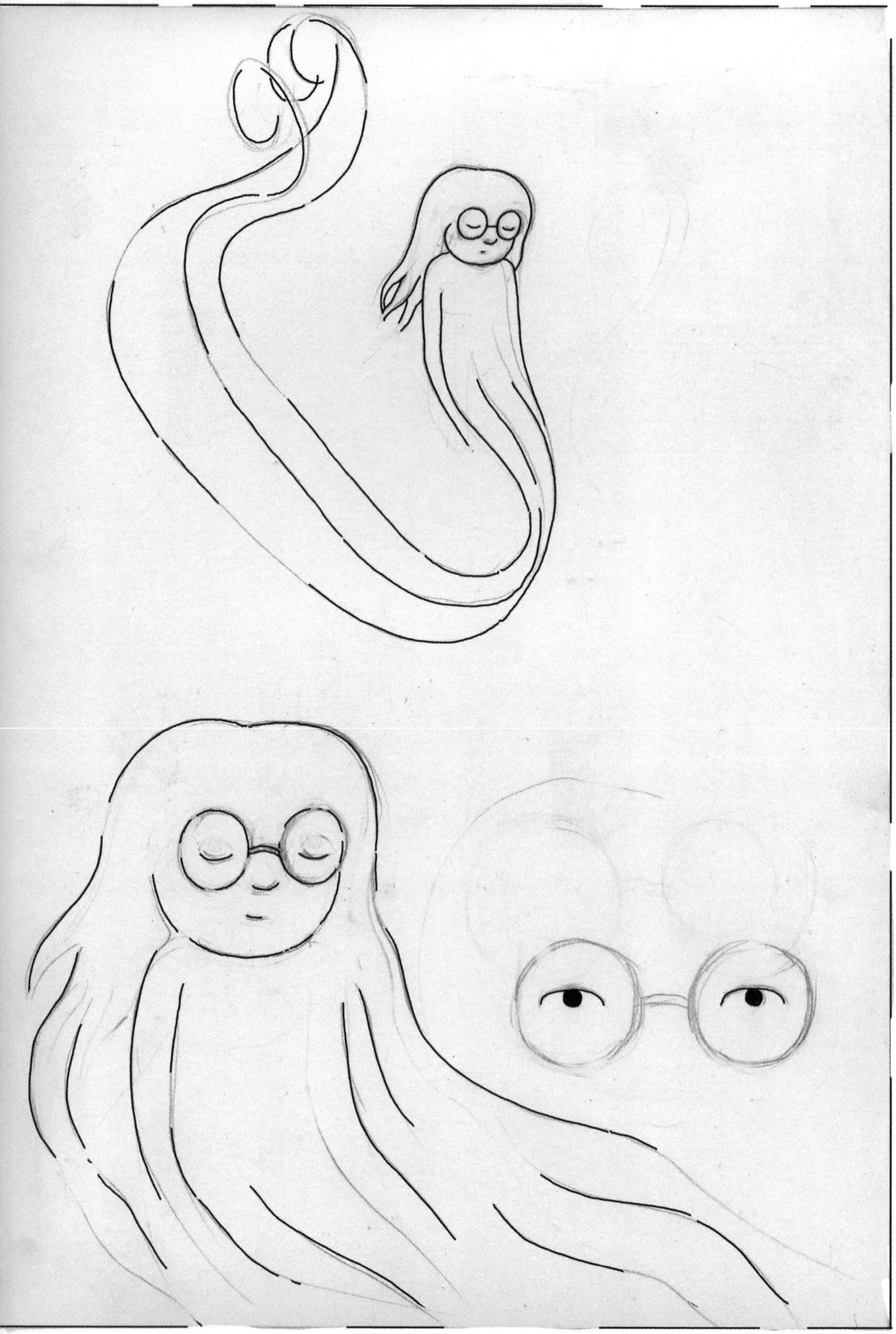

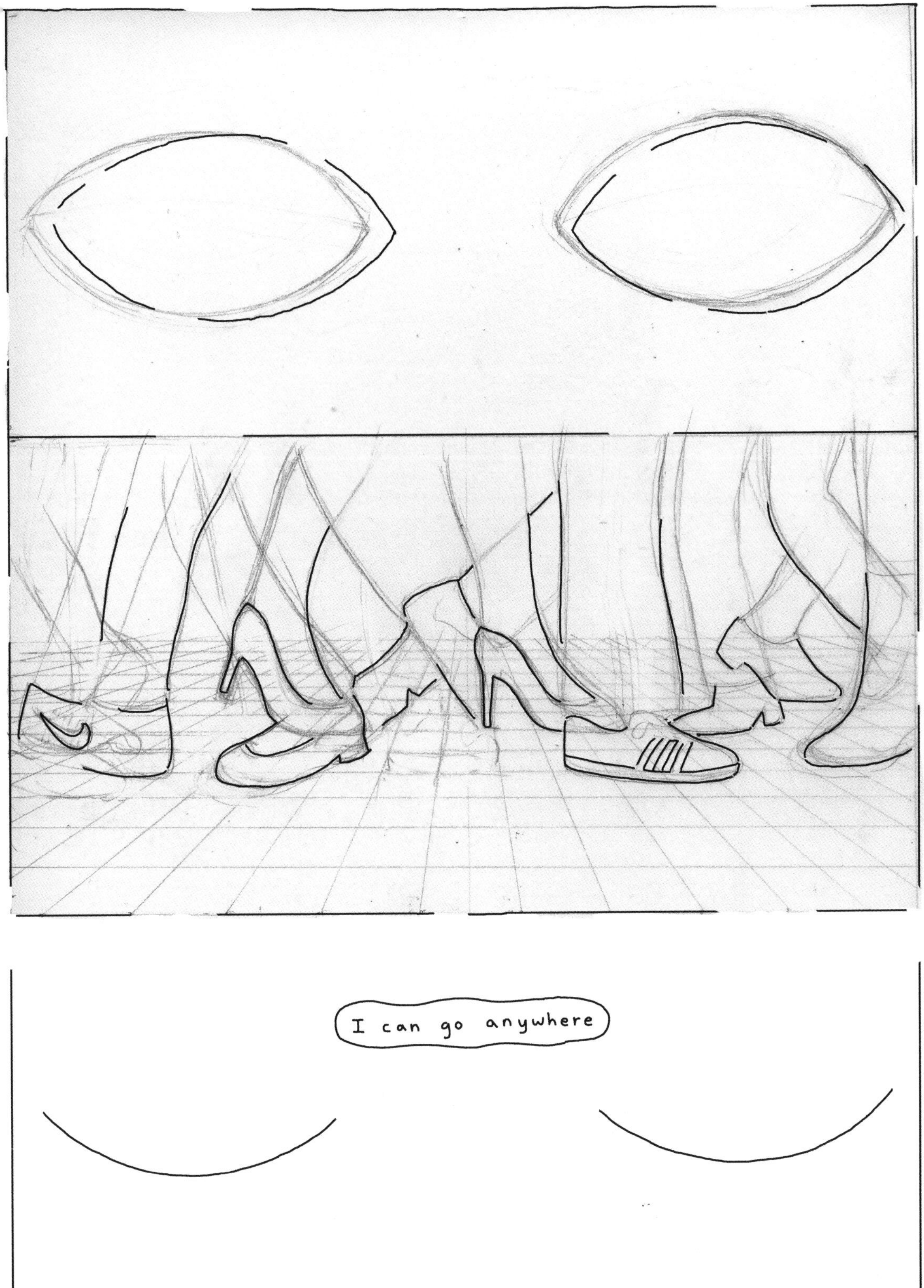
I can go anywhere

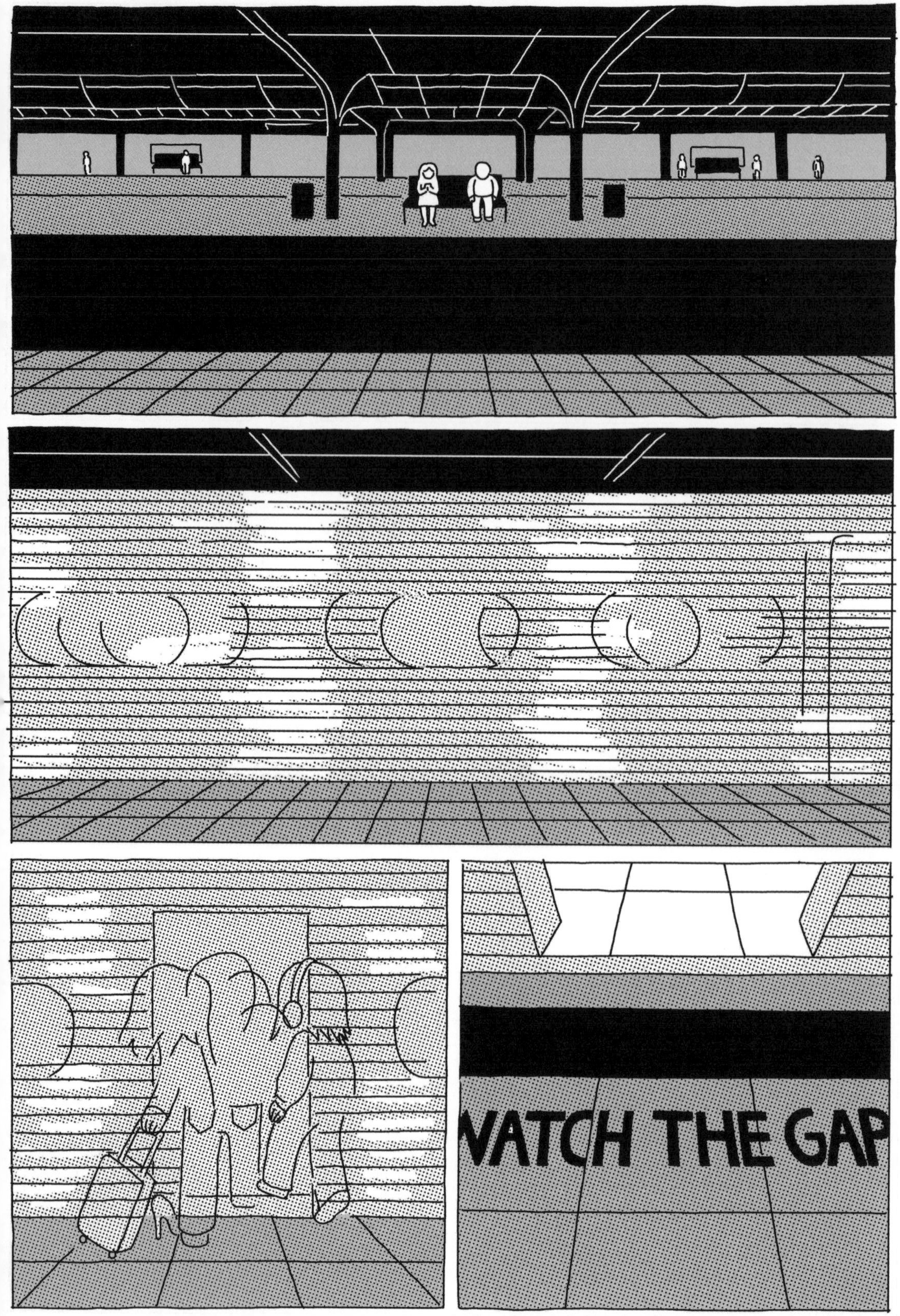
WATCH THE GAP

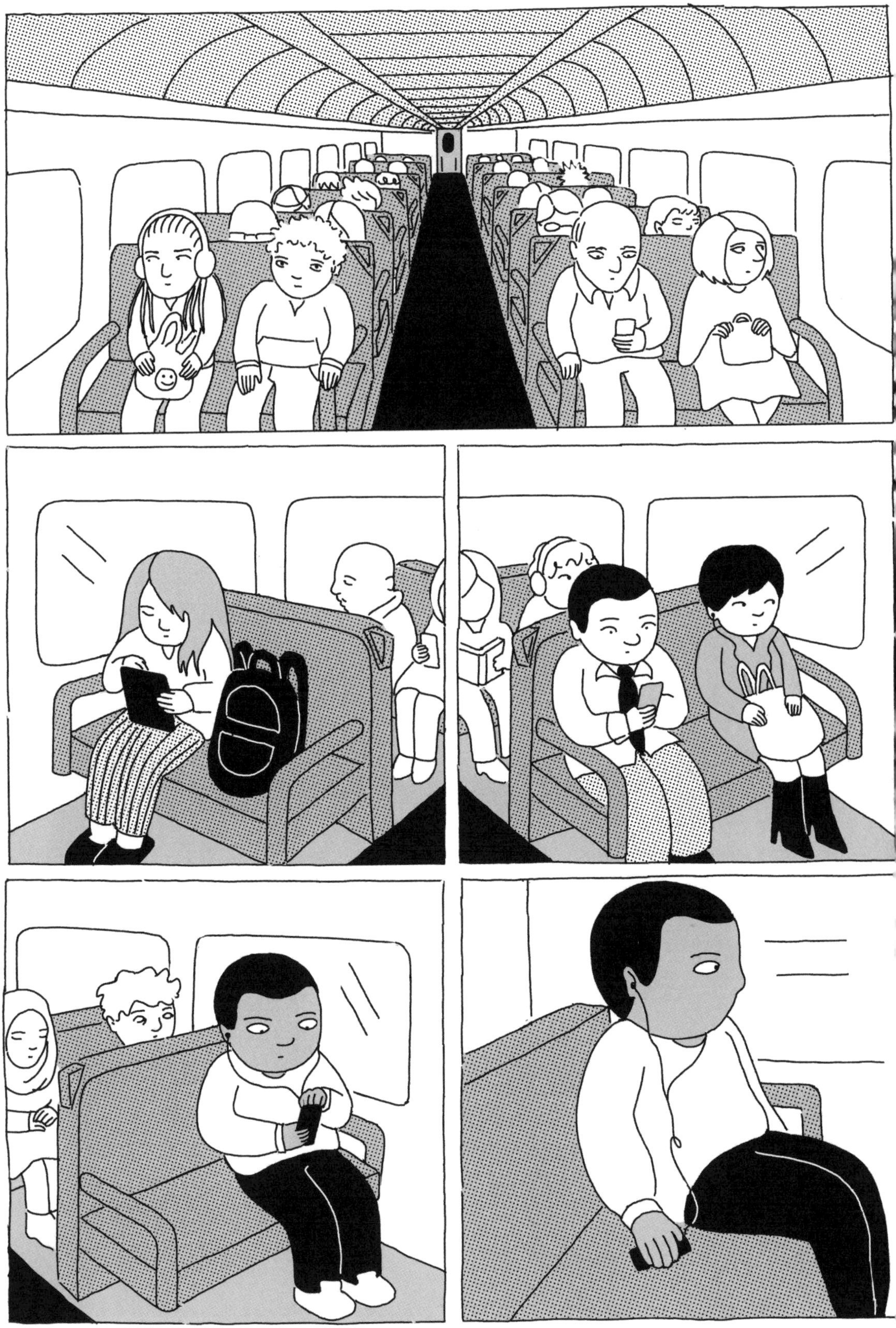

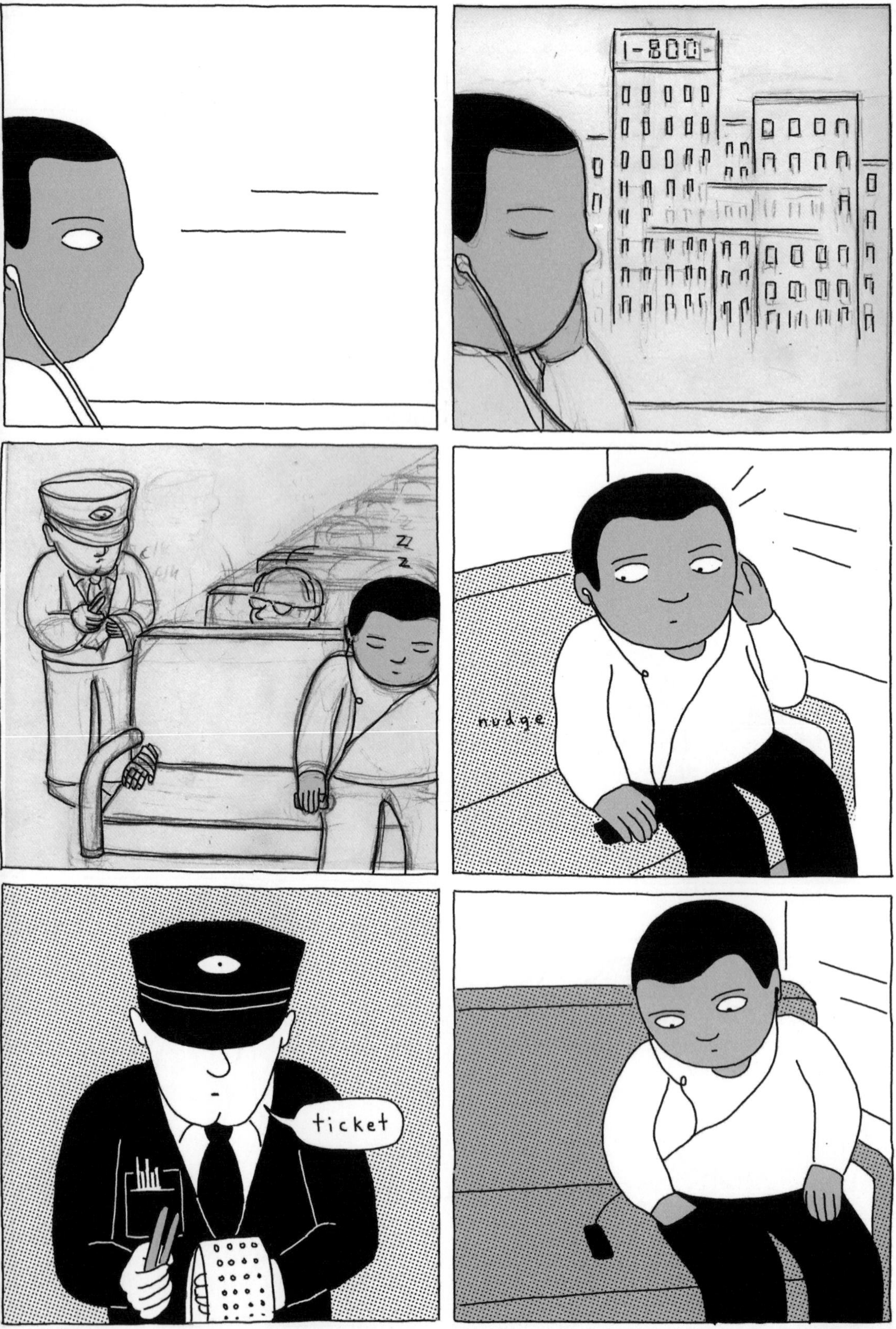
1-800
nudge
ticket

where you headed?
bristol
you're short two fifty

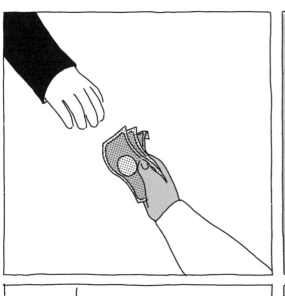

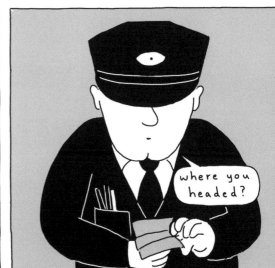

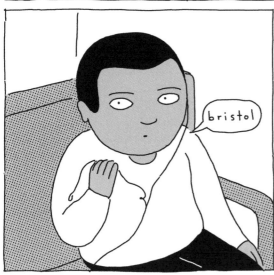

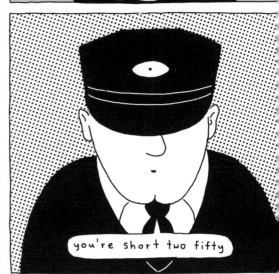

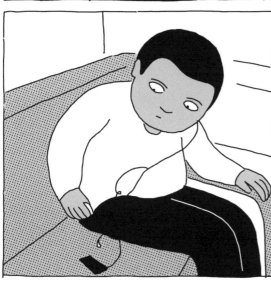

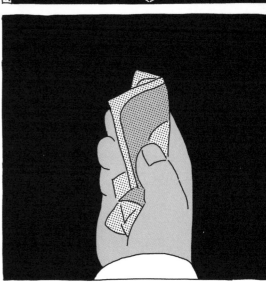

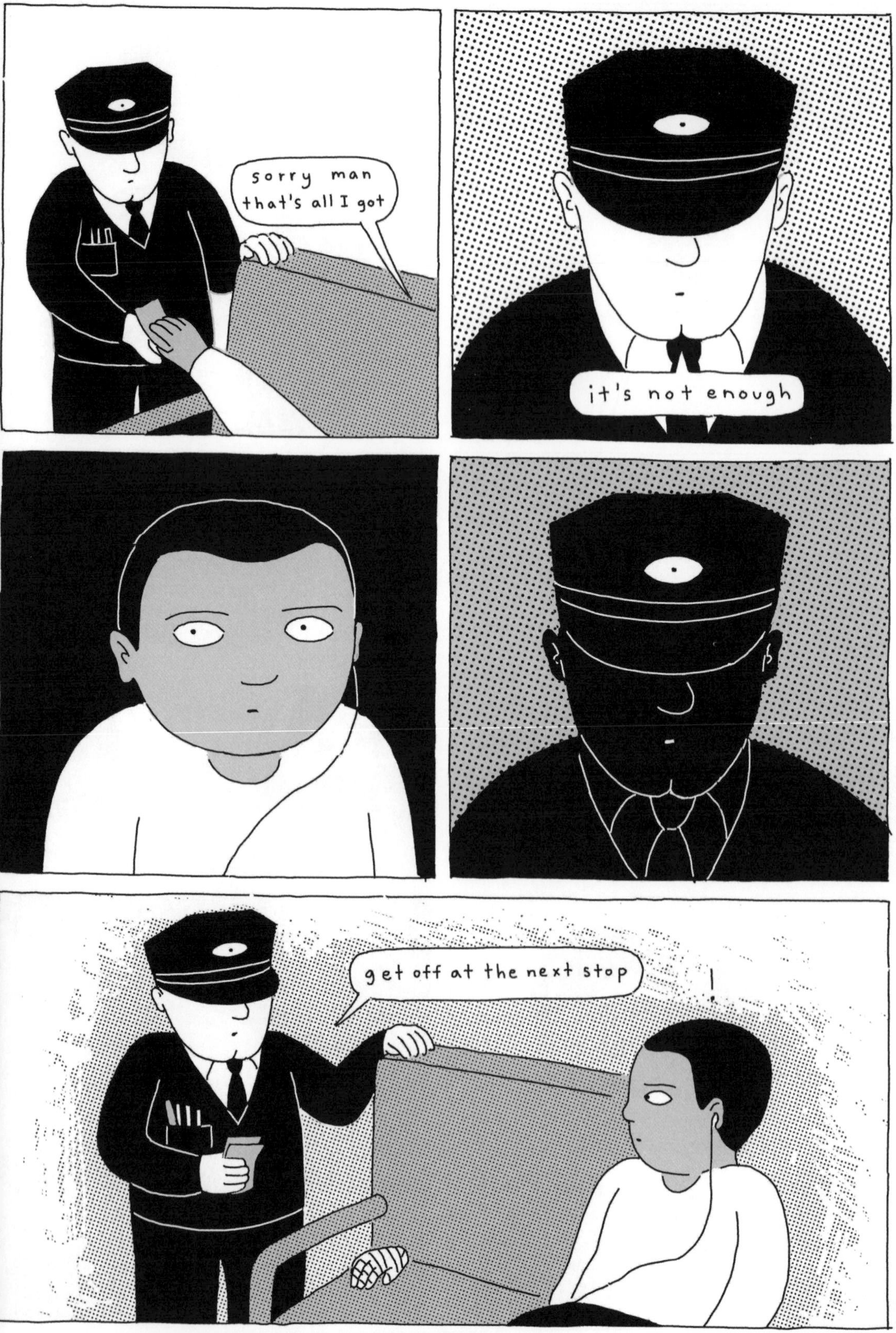

sorry man
that's all I got
it's not enough
get off at the next stop

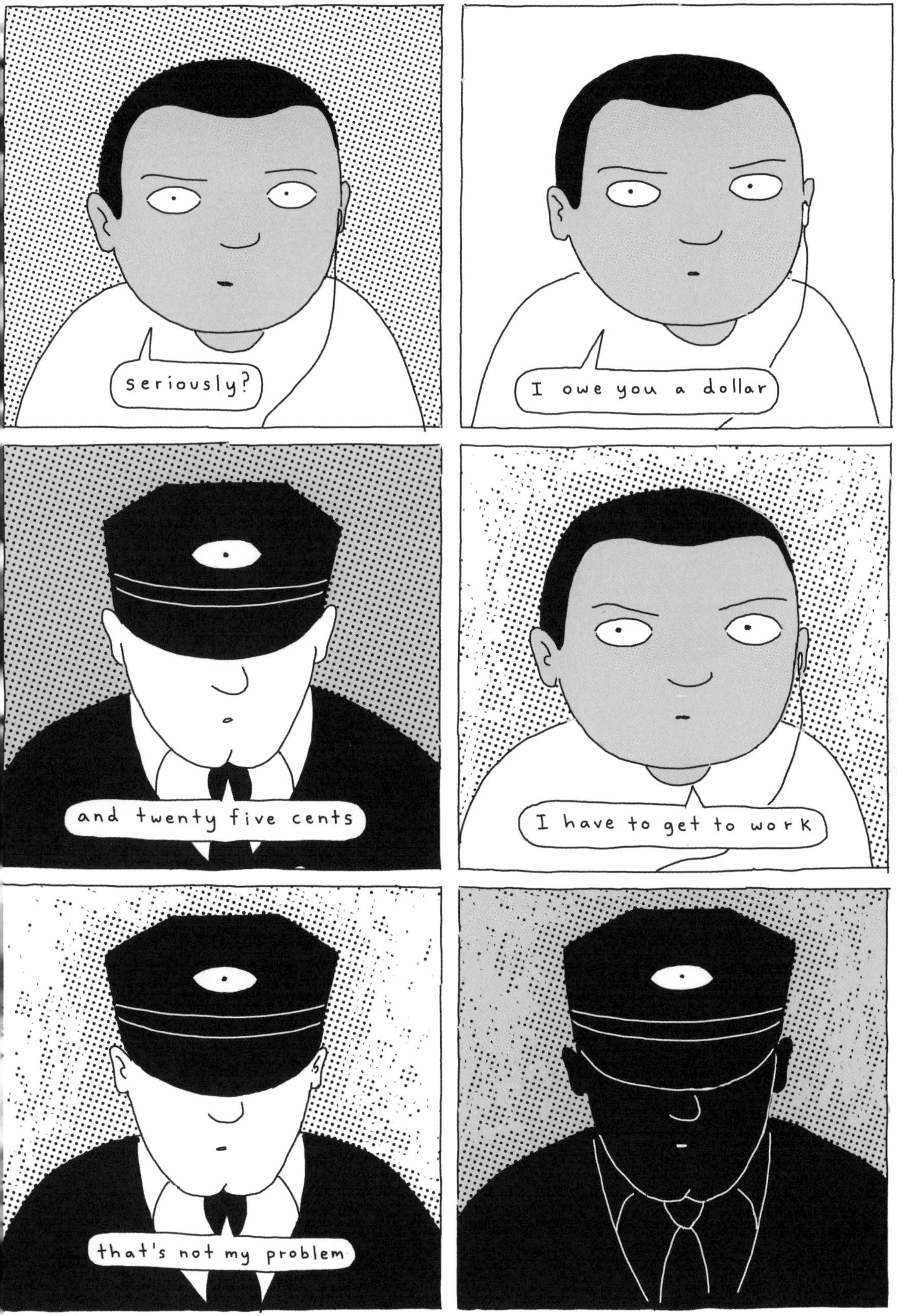
seriously?
I owe you a dollar
and twenty five cents
I have to get to work
that's not my problem

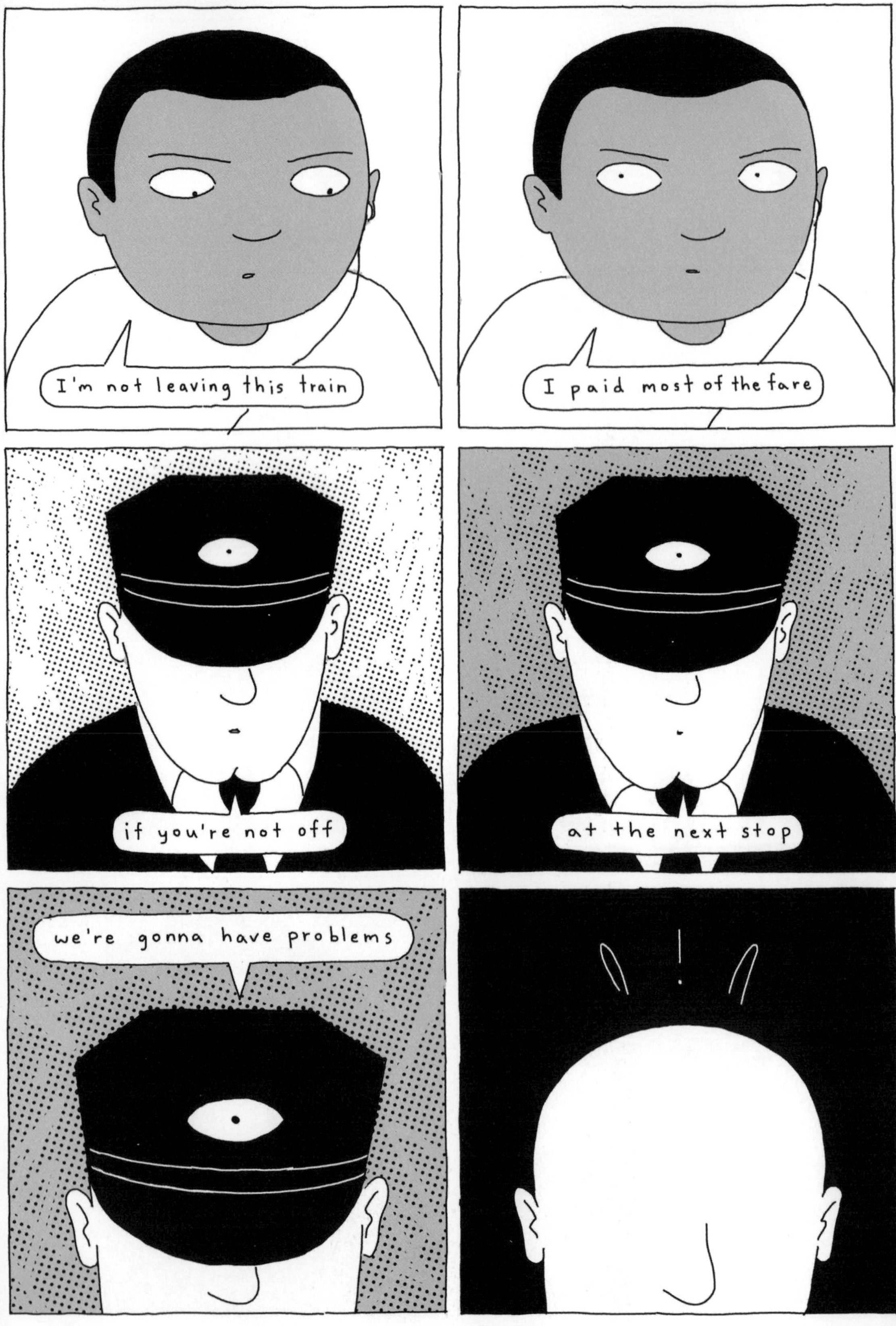
I'm not leaving this train
I paid most of the fare
if you're not off
at the next stop
we're gonna have problems
!

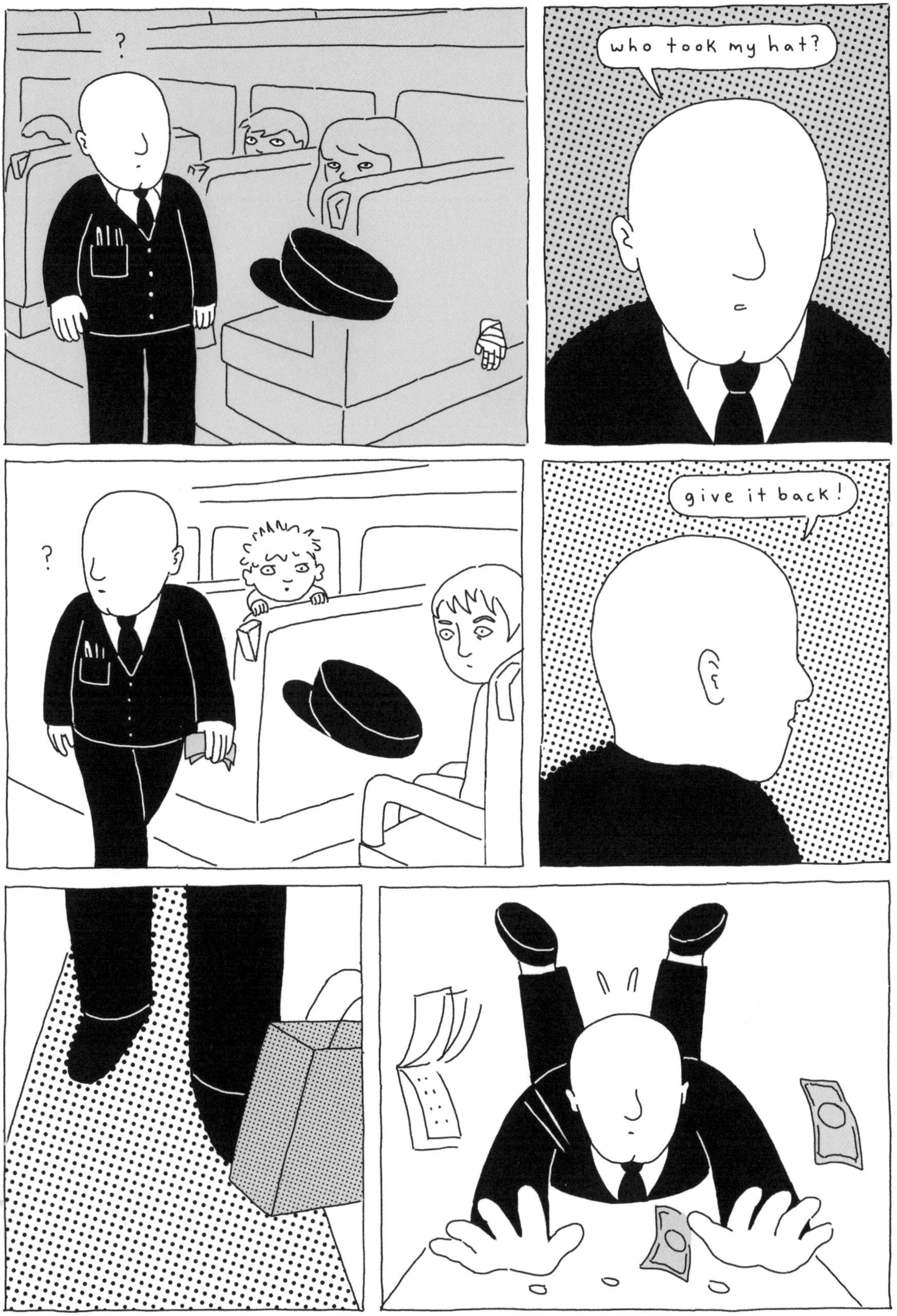
?
who took my hat?
?
give it back!

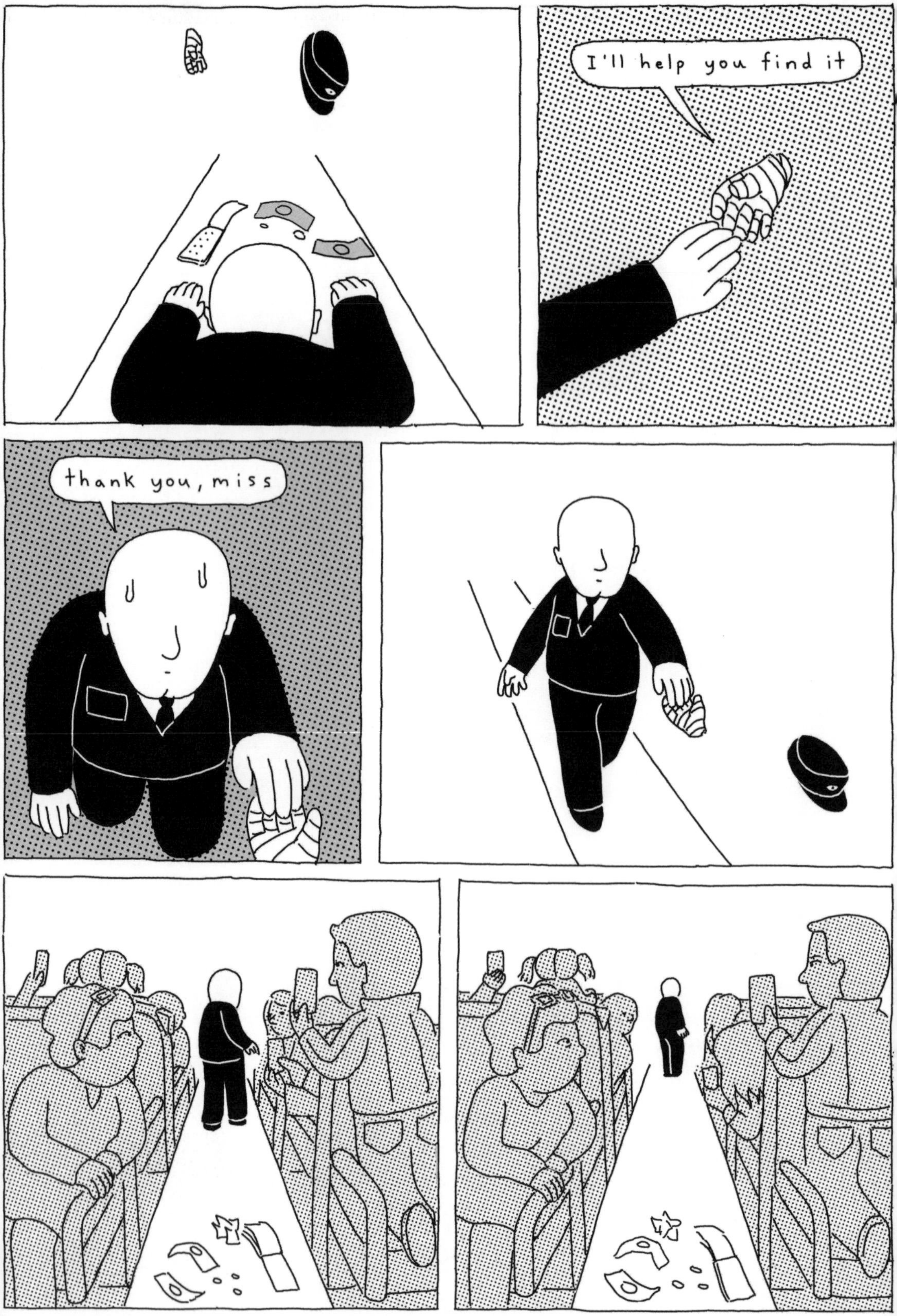

I'll help you find it
thank you, miss

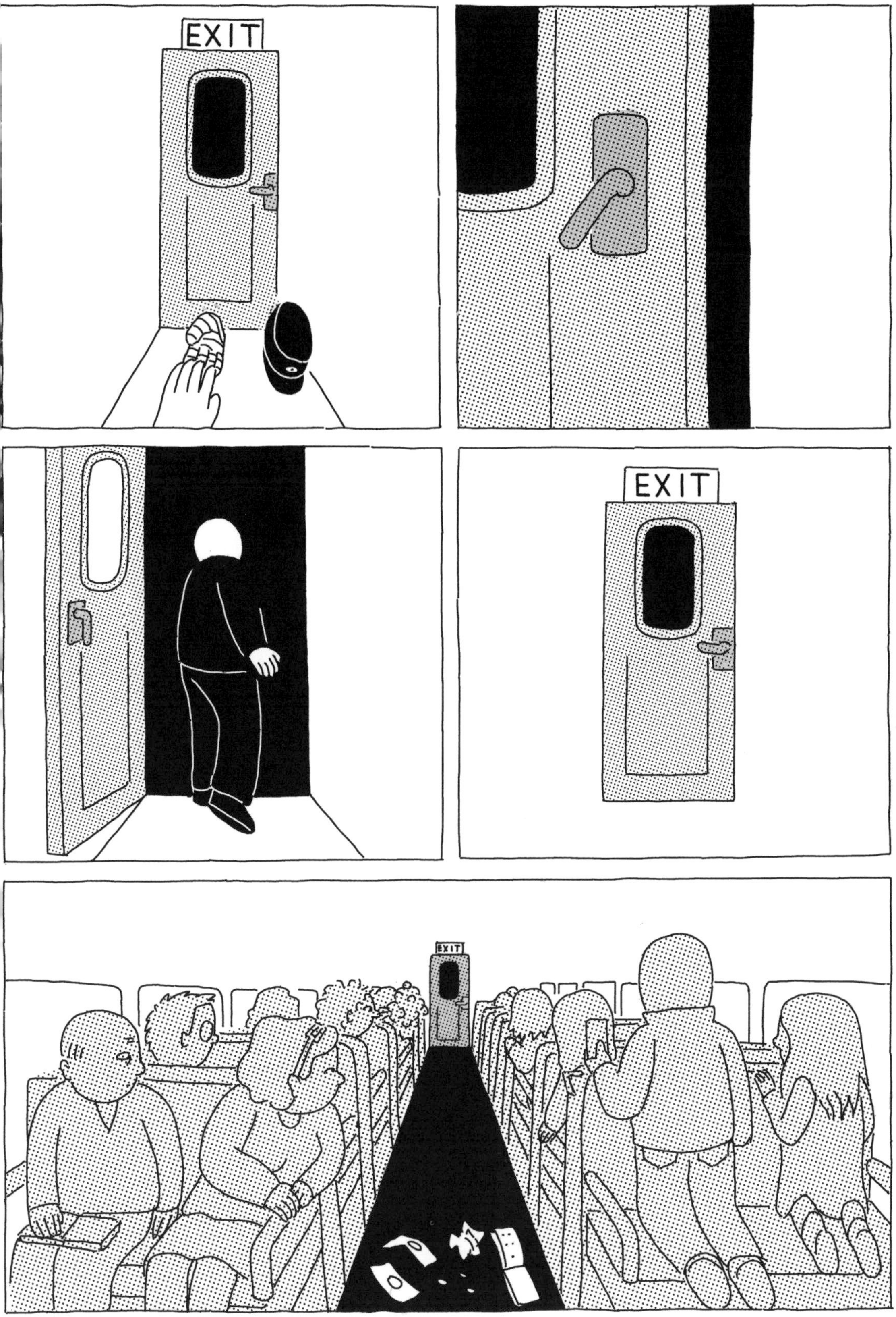
EXIT
EXIT
EXIT

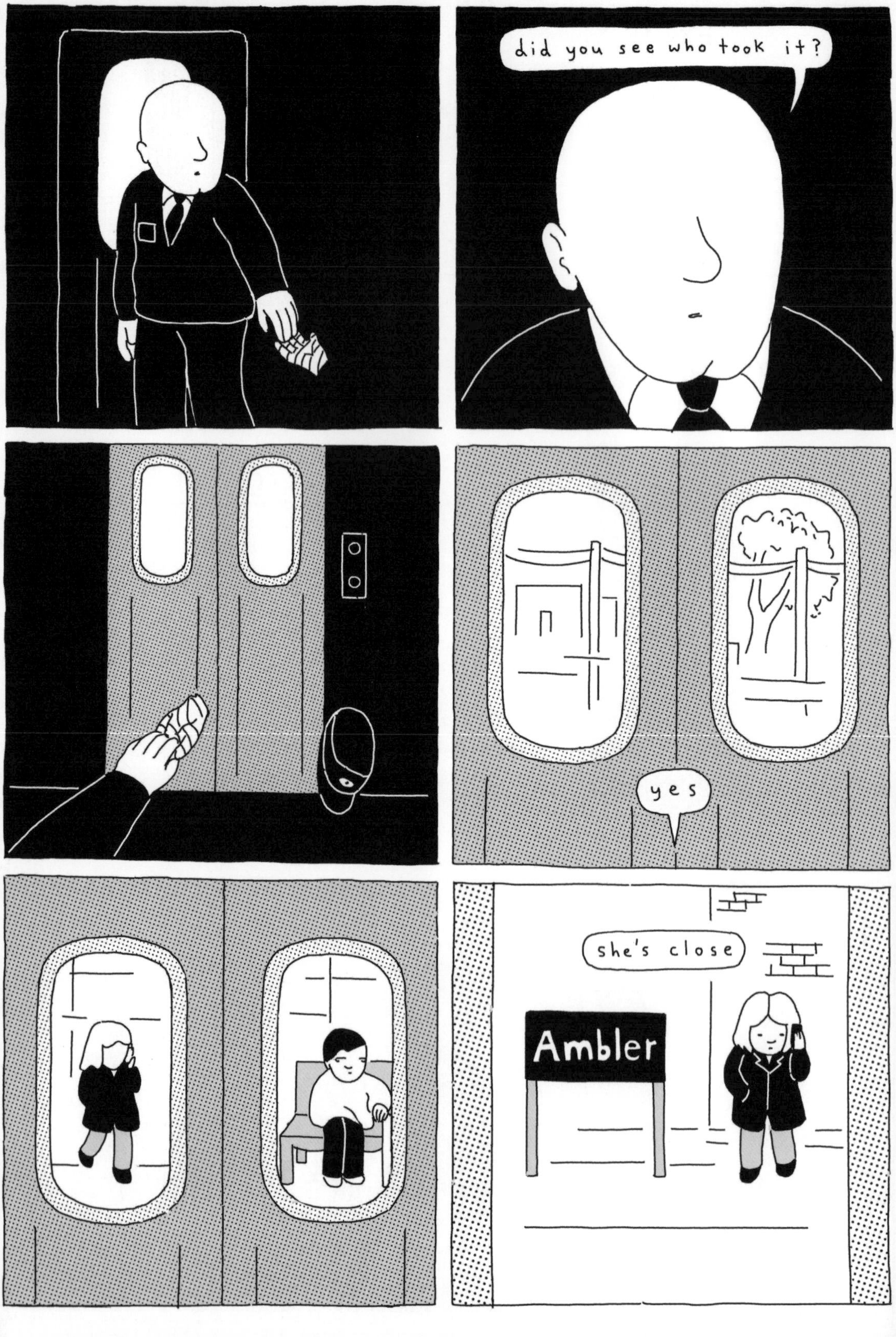
did you see who took it?
yes
she's close
Ambler

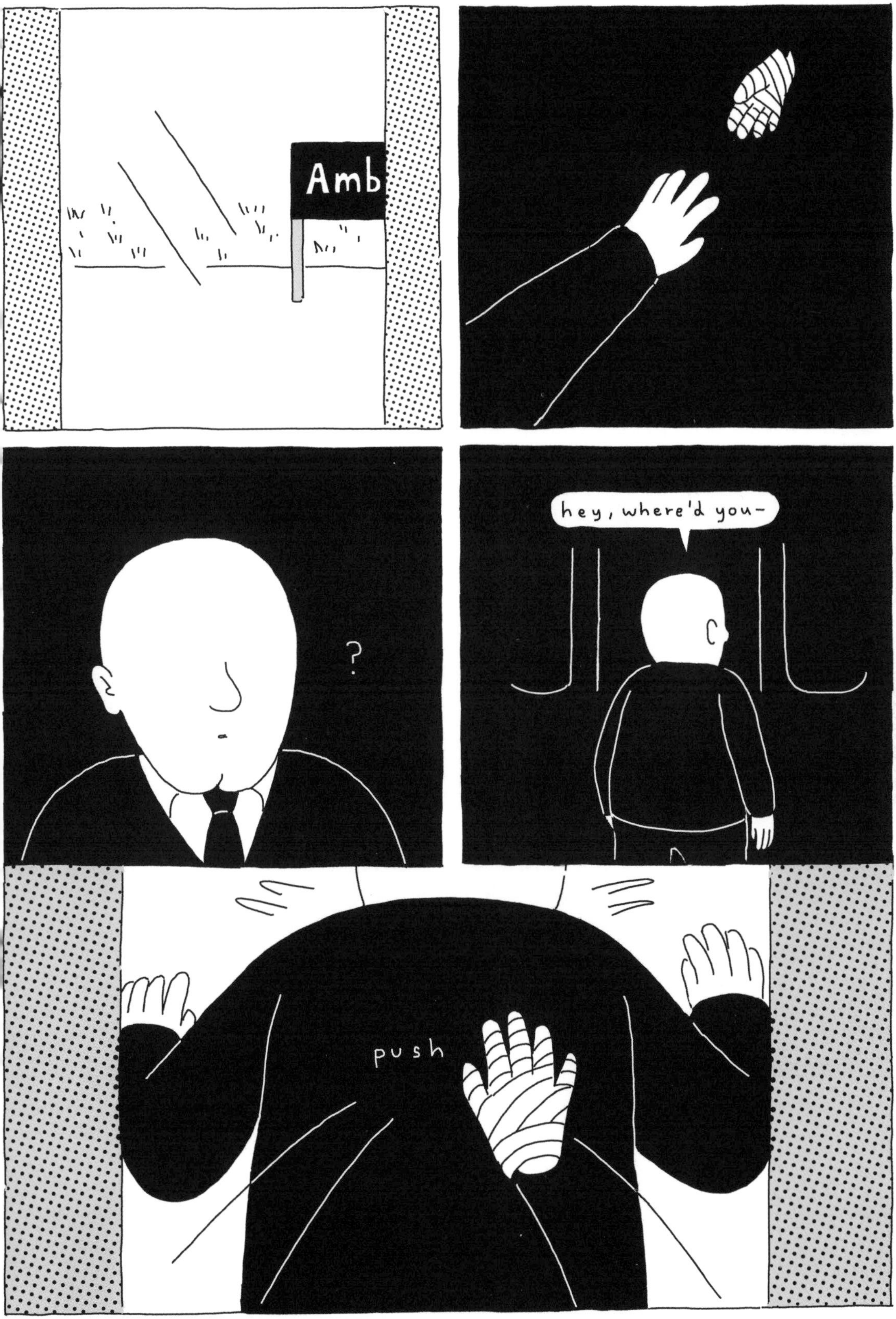
Amb
?
hey, where'd you-
push

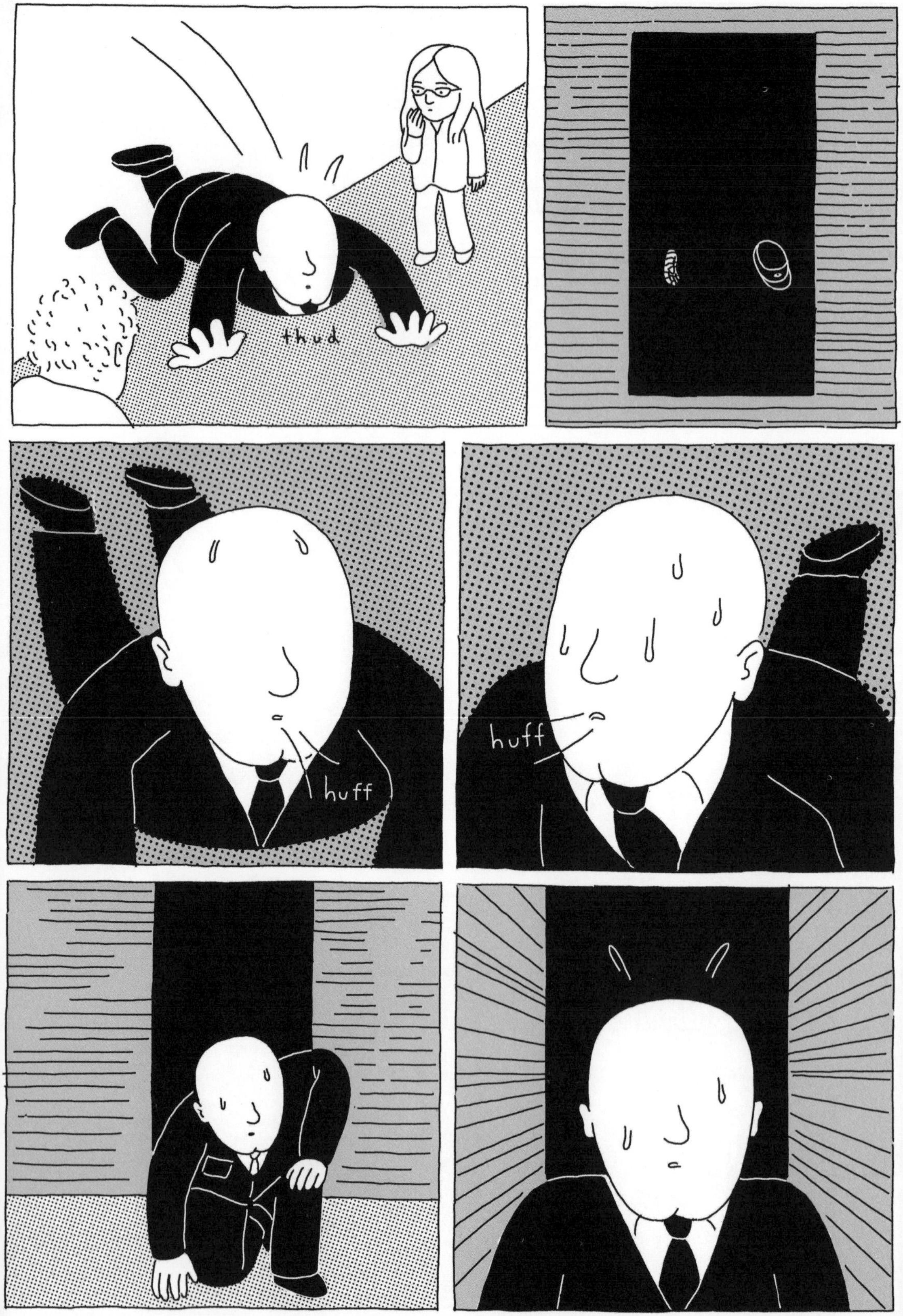
thud
huff
huff

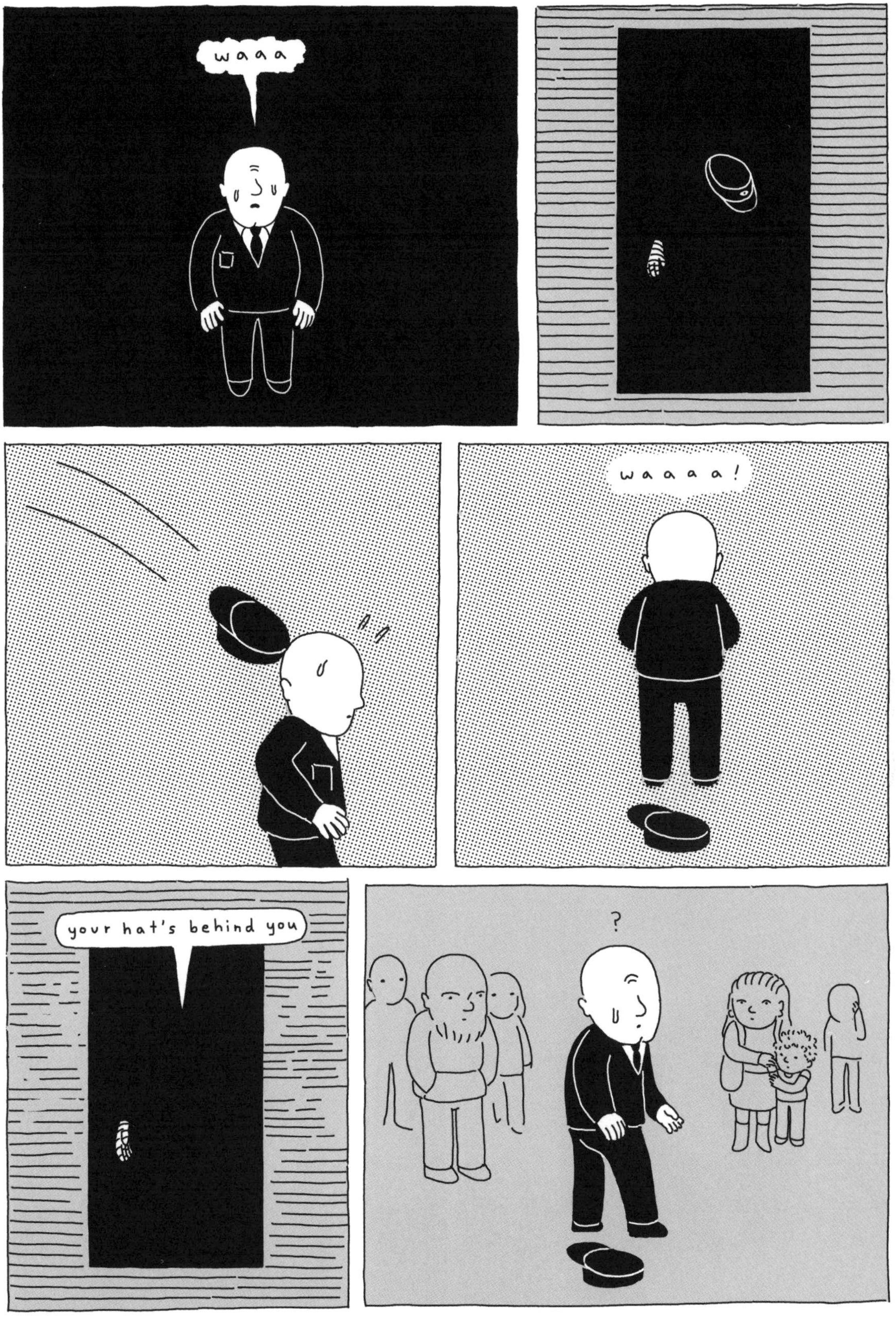
waaa
waaaa!
your hat's behind you
?

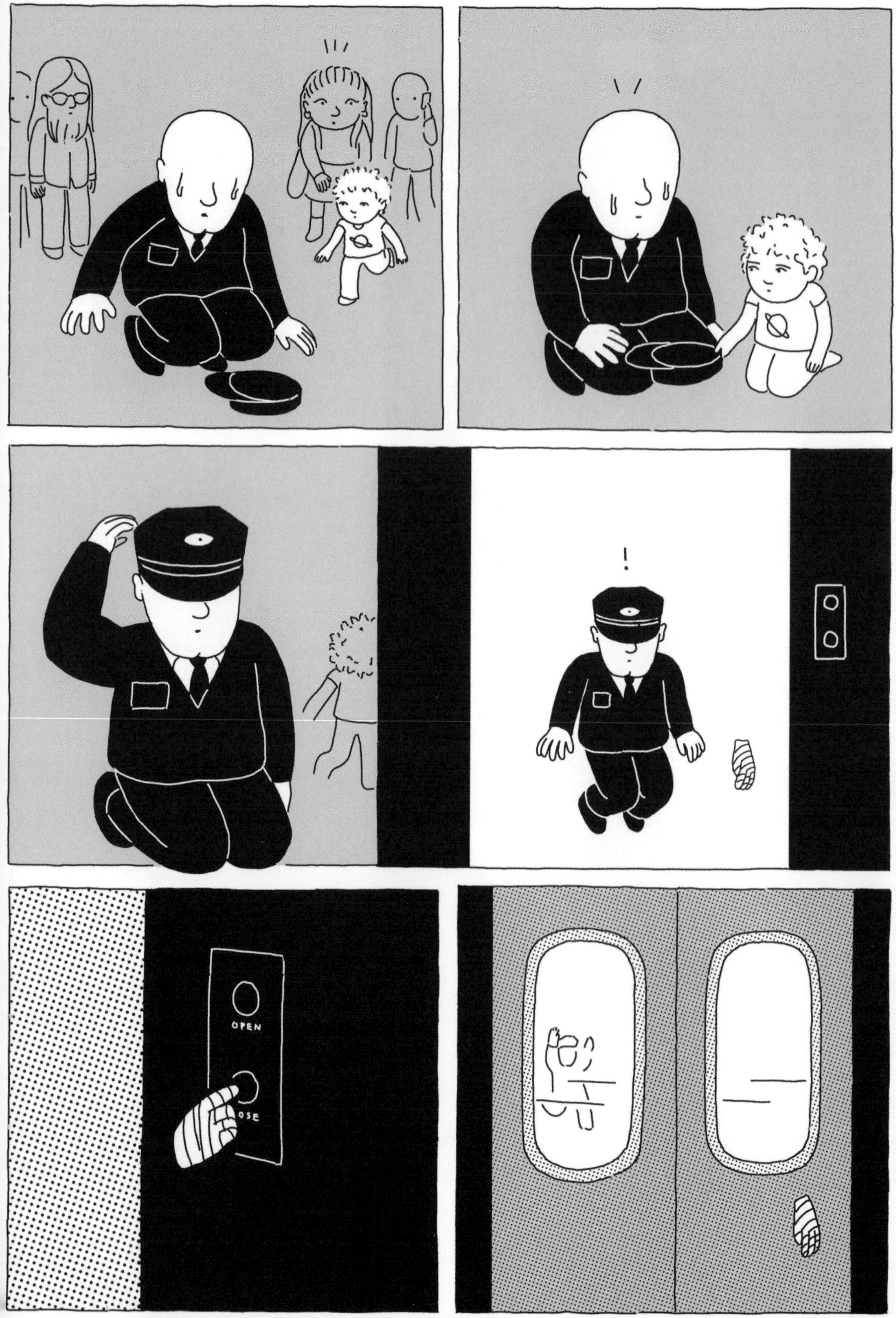
!
OPEN
OSE

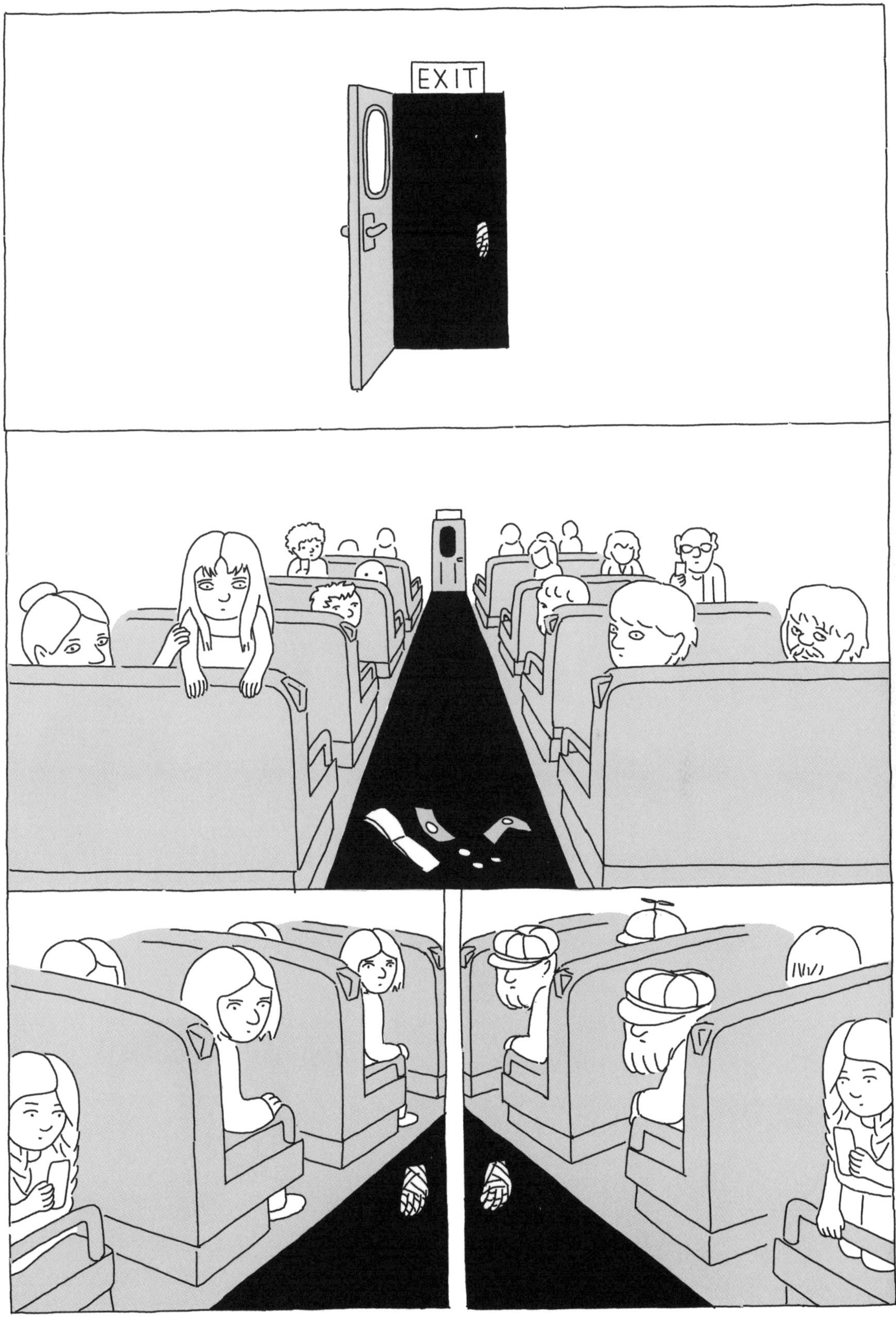
EXIT

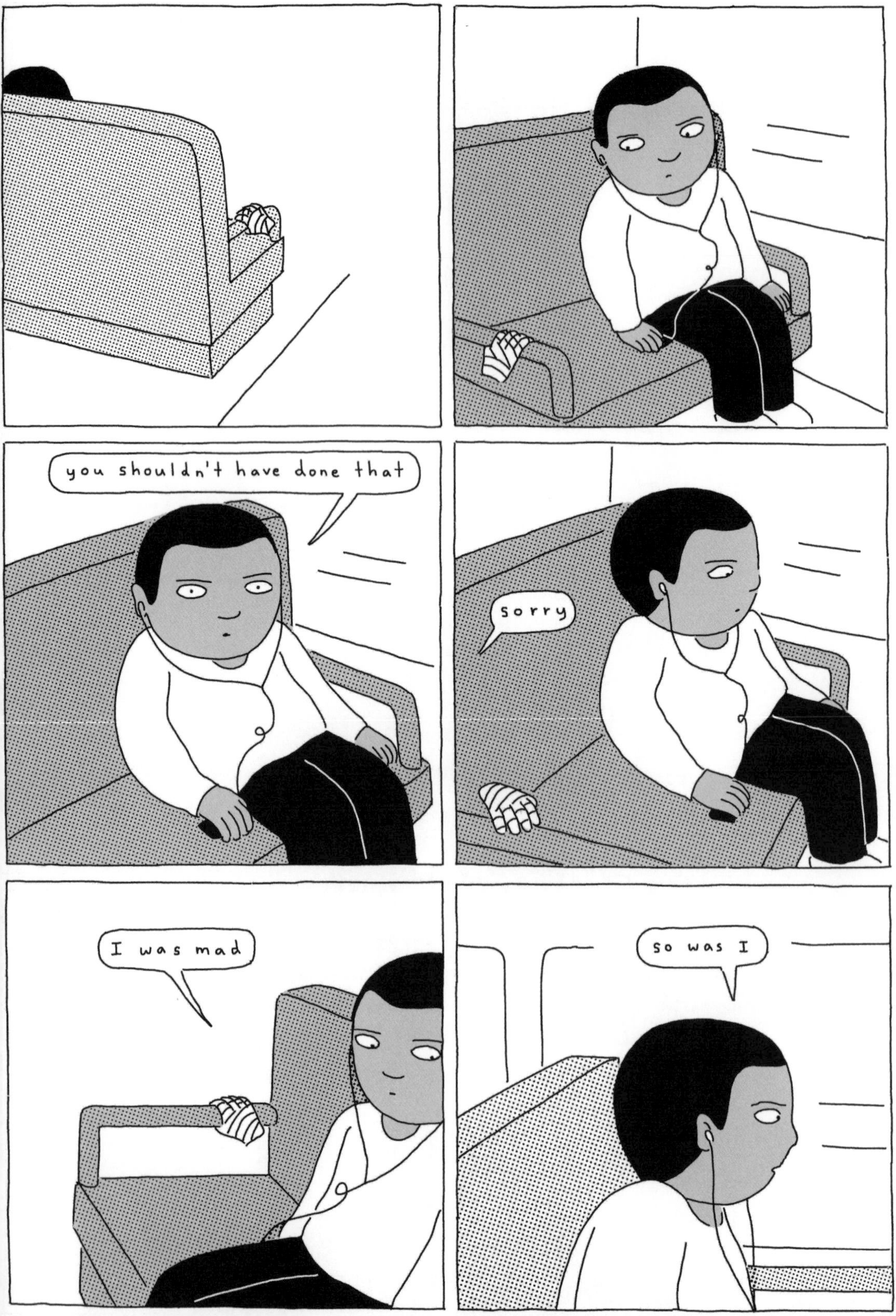
you shouldn't have done that
sorry
I was mad
so was I

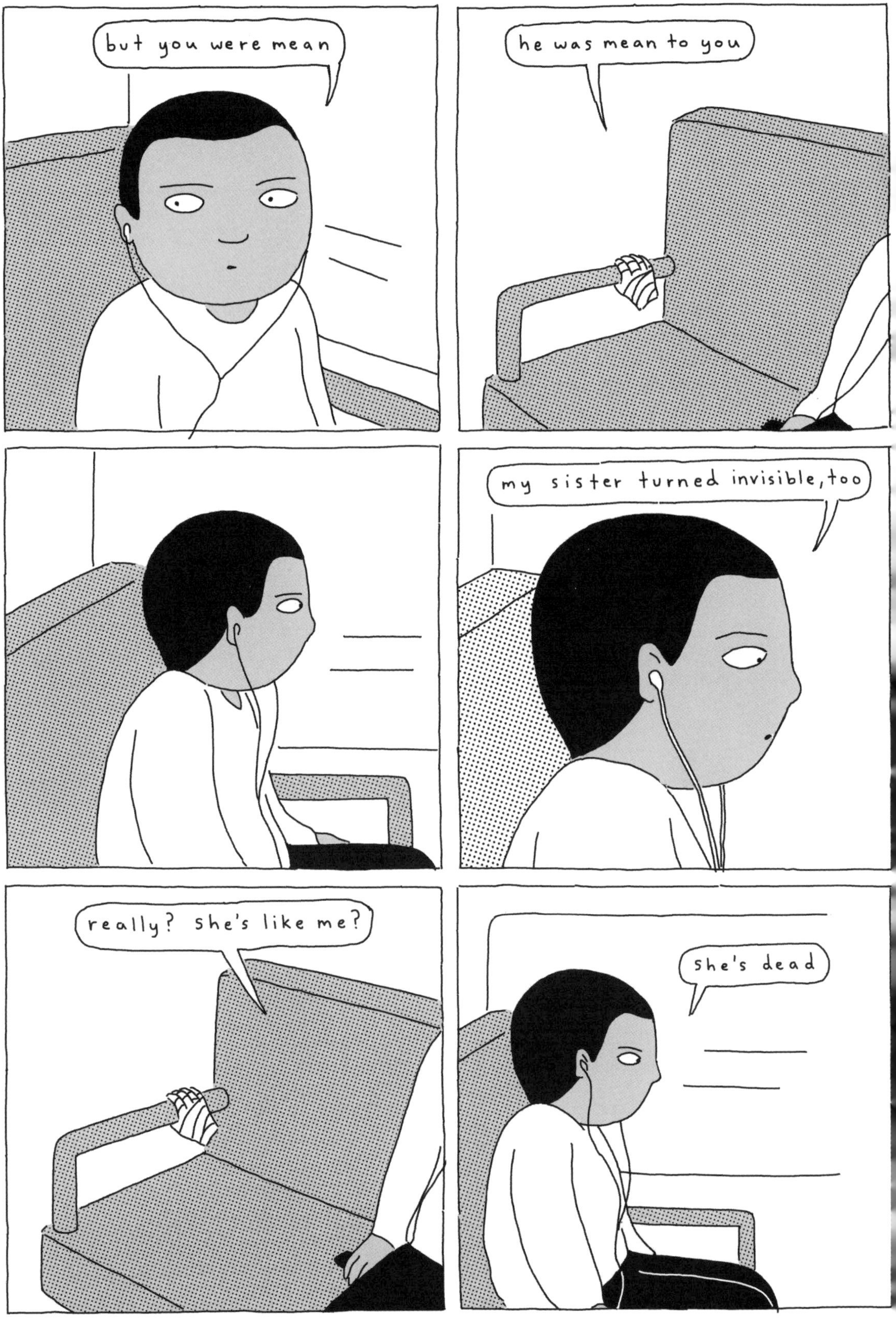
but you were mean
he was mean to you
my sister turned invisible, too
really? she's like me?
she's dead

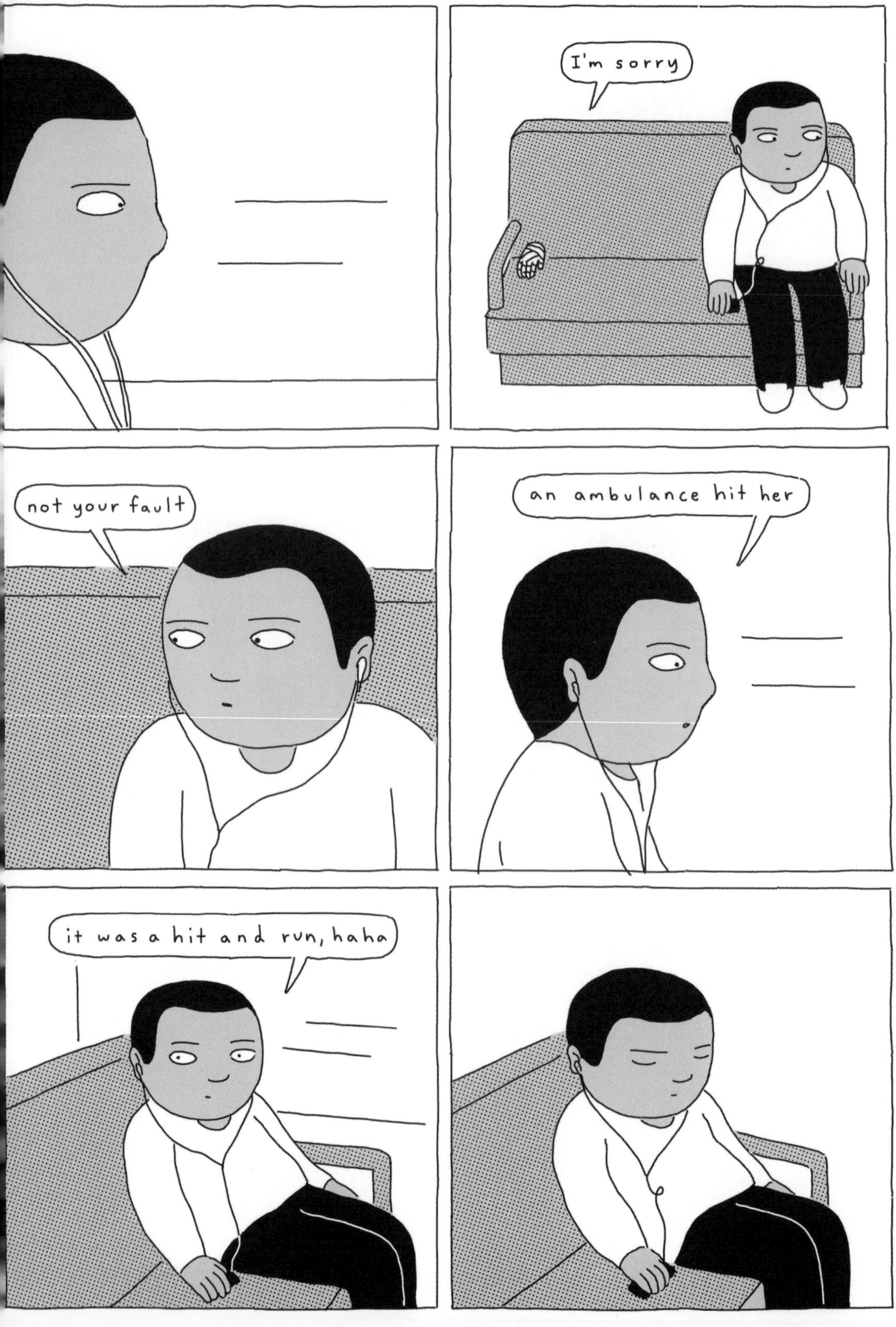
I'm sorry
not your fault
an ambulance hit her
it was a hit and run, haha

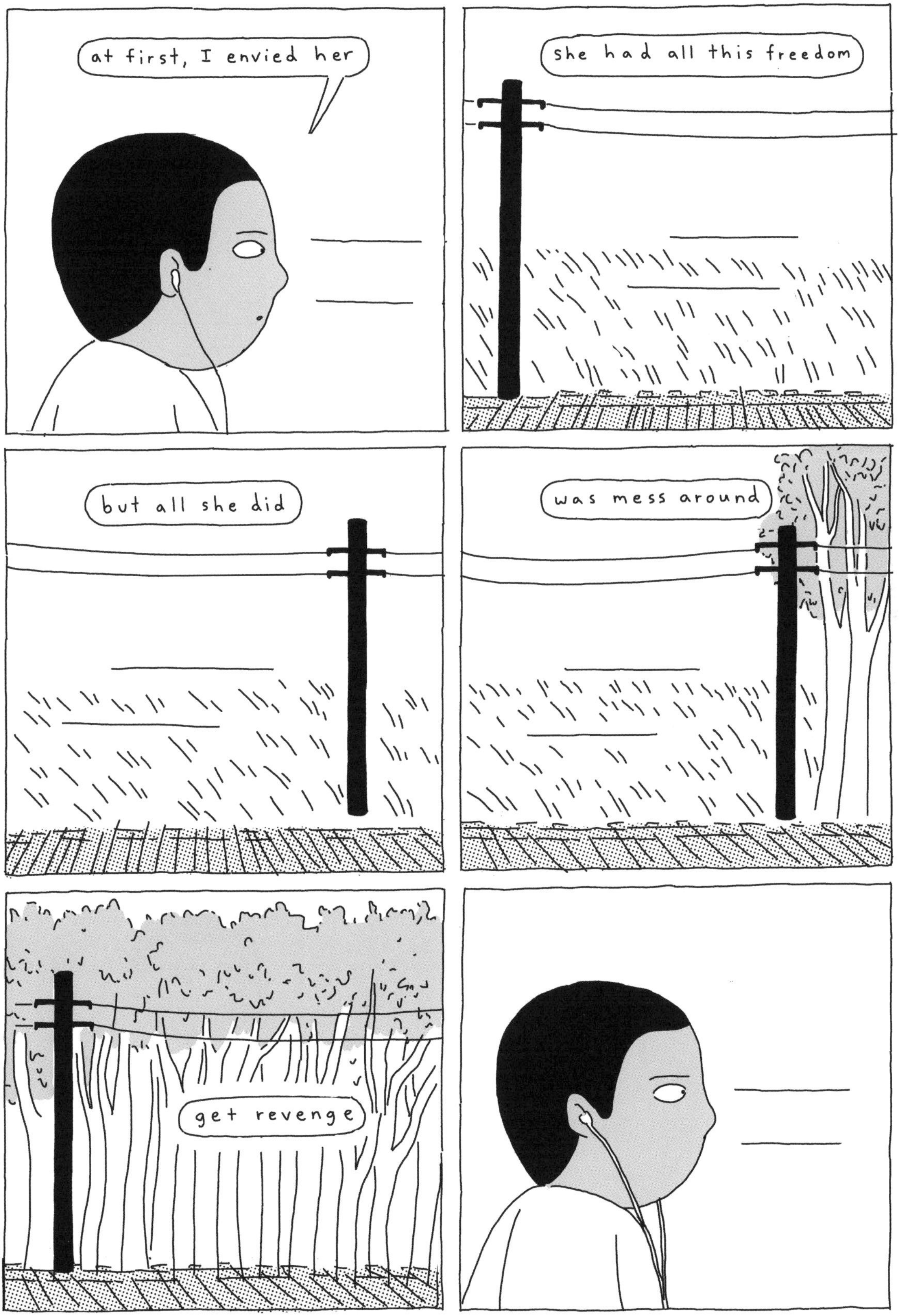
at first, I envied her
she had all this freedom
but all she did
was mess around
get revenge

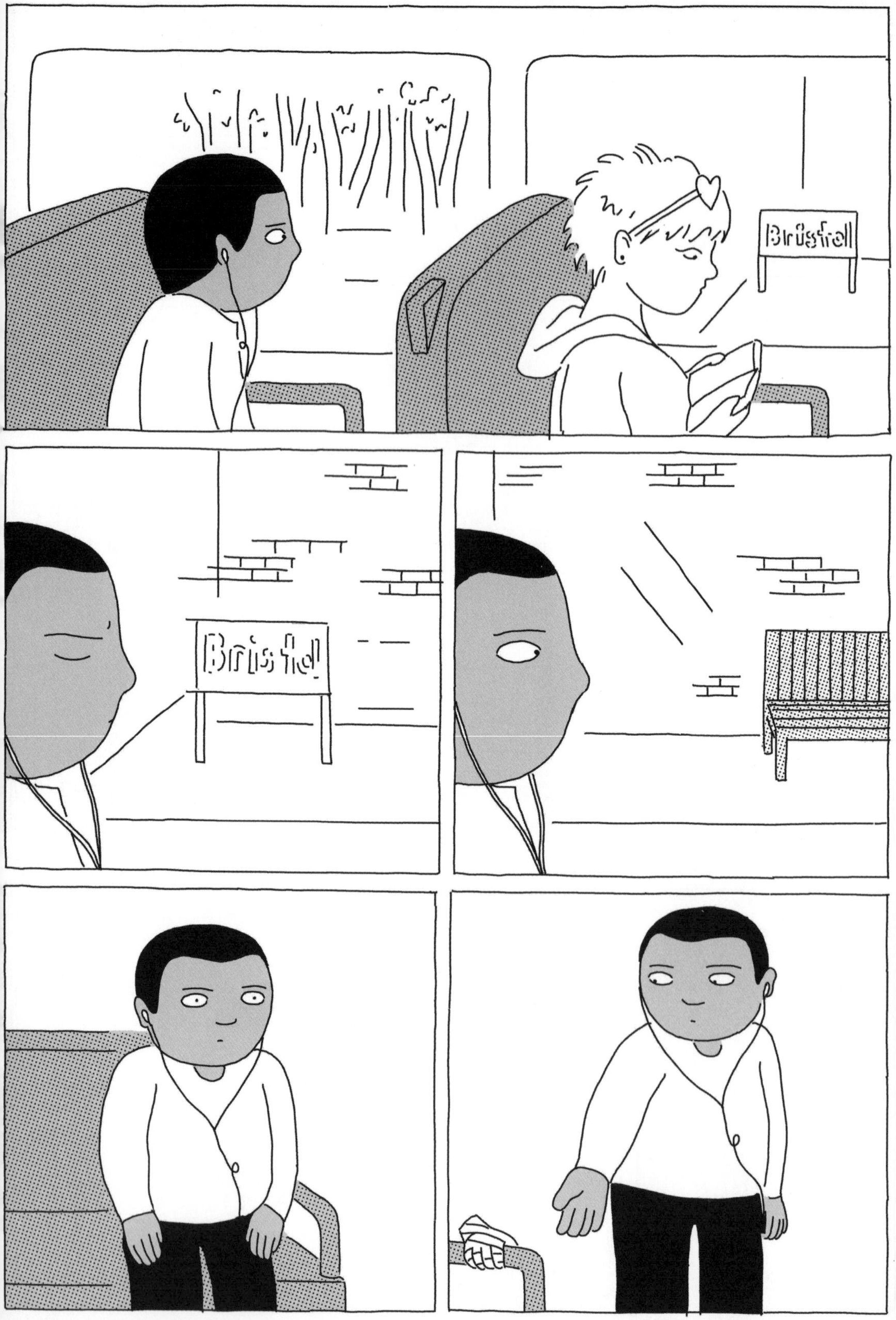
Bristol
Bristol

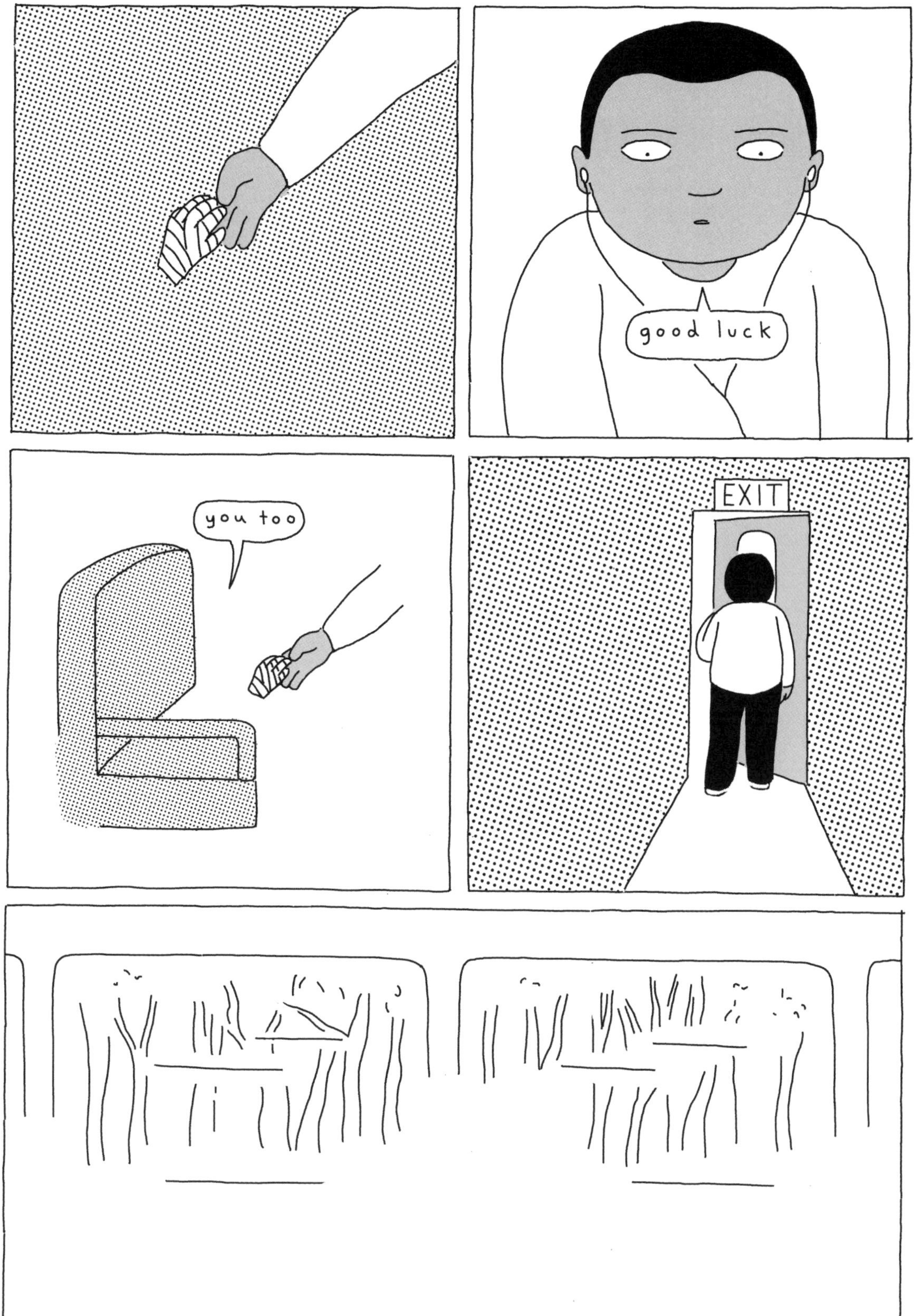
good luck
you too
EXIT

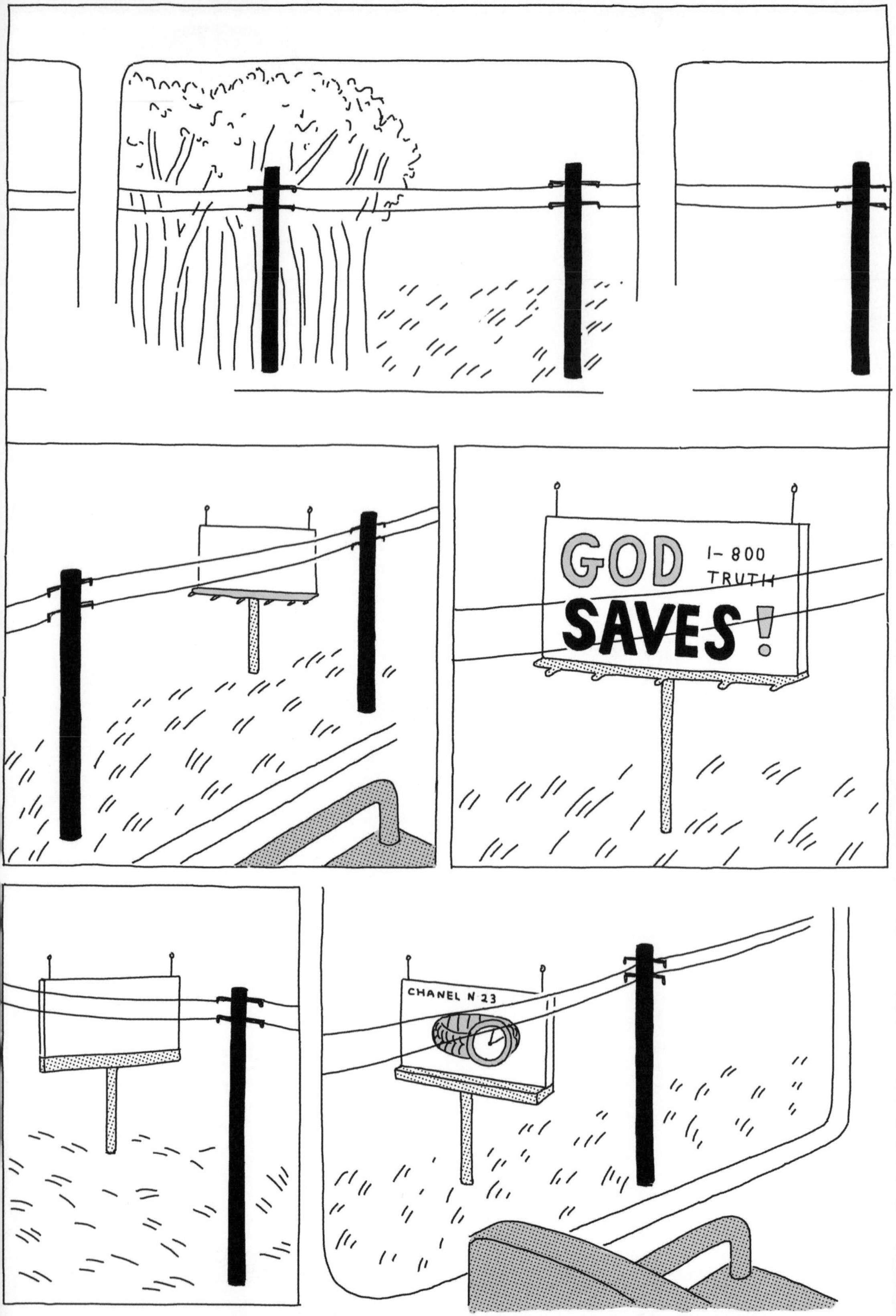
GOD
1-800
TRUTH
SAVES!
CHANEL N 23

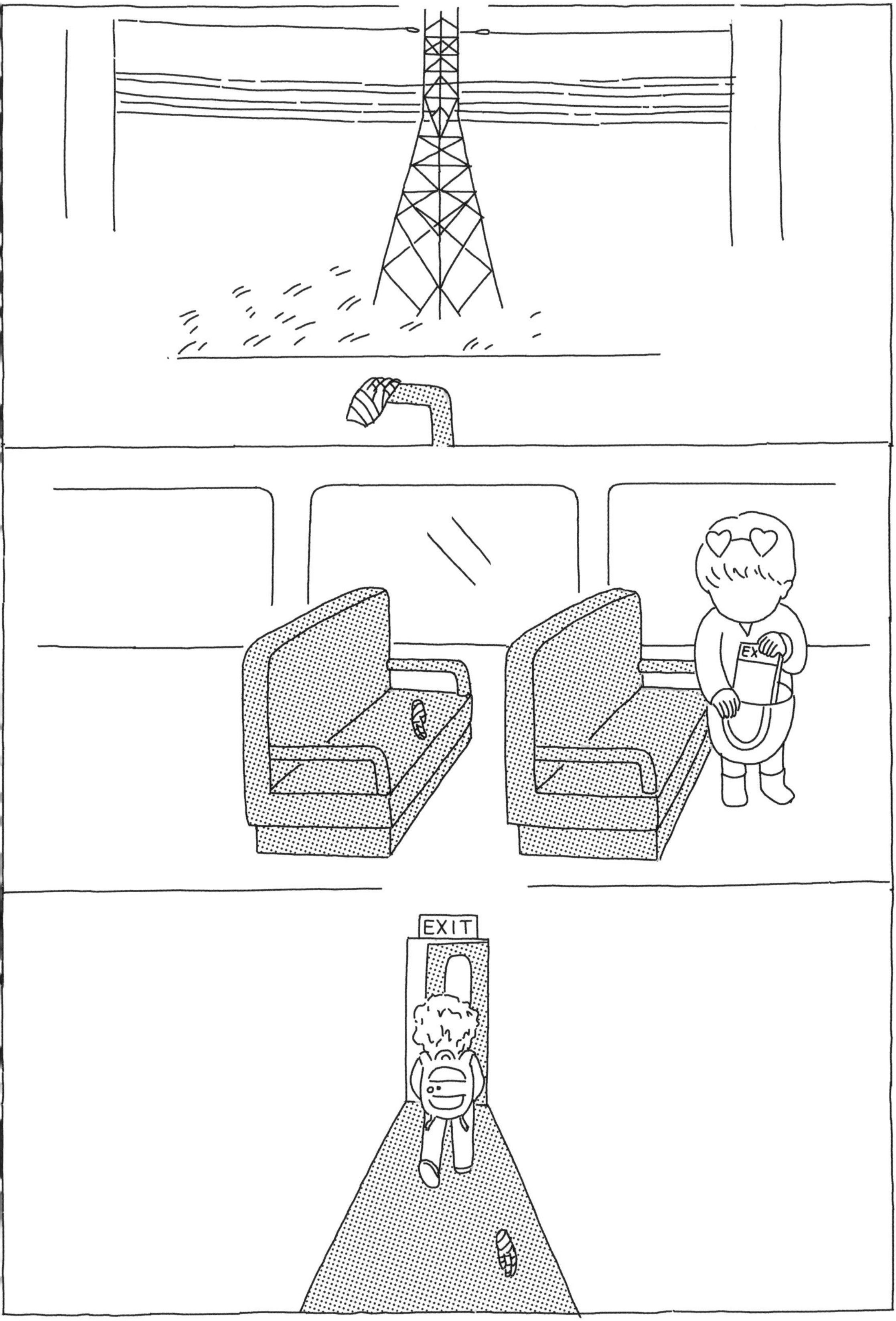
EX
EXIT

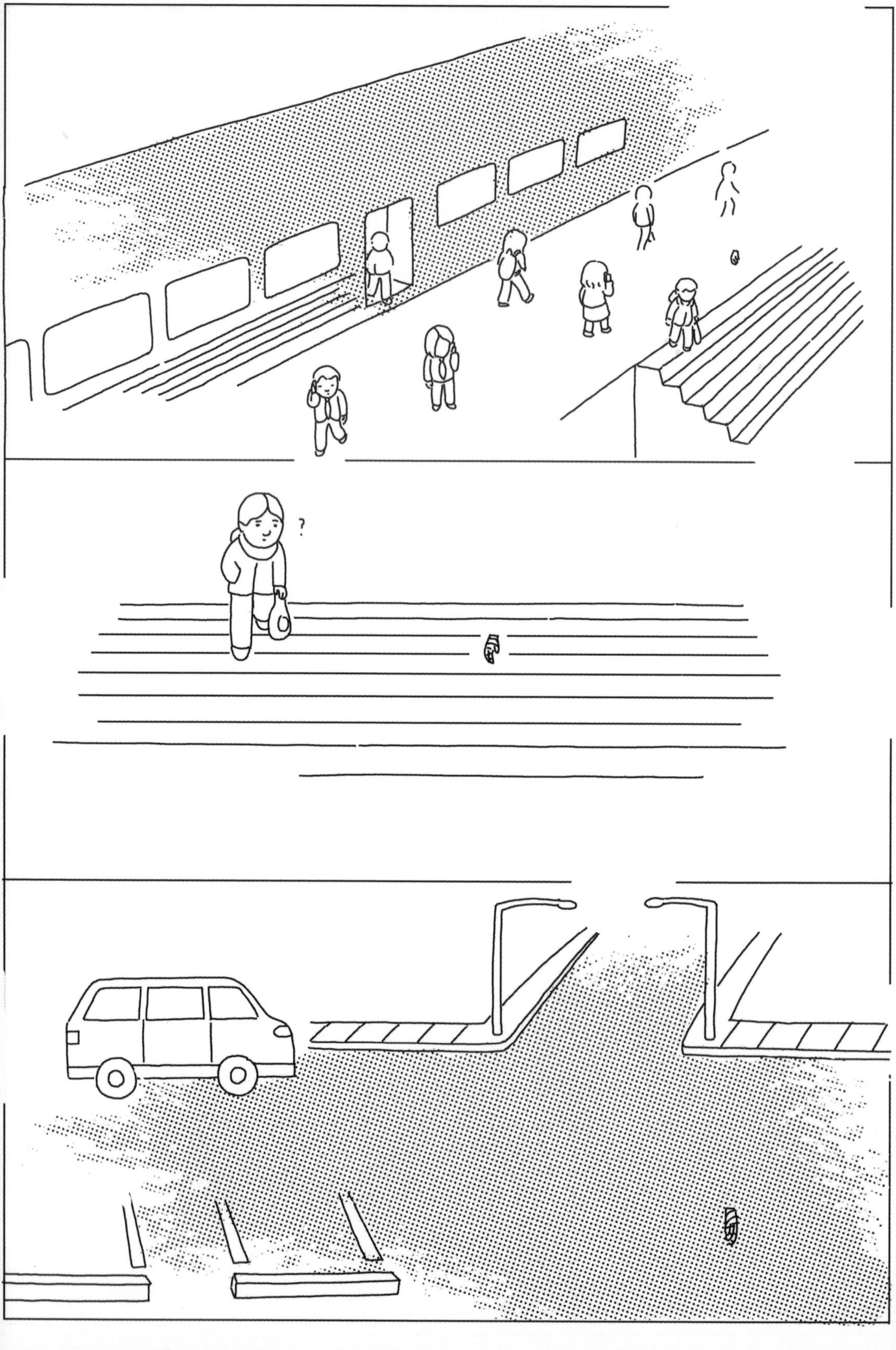
?

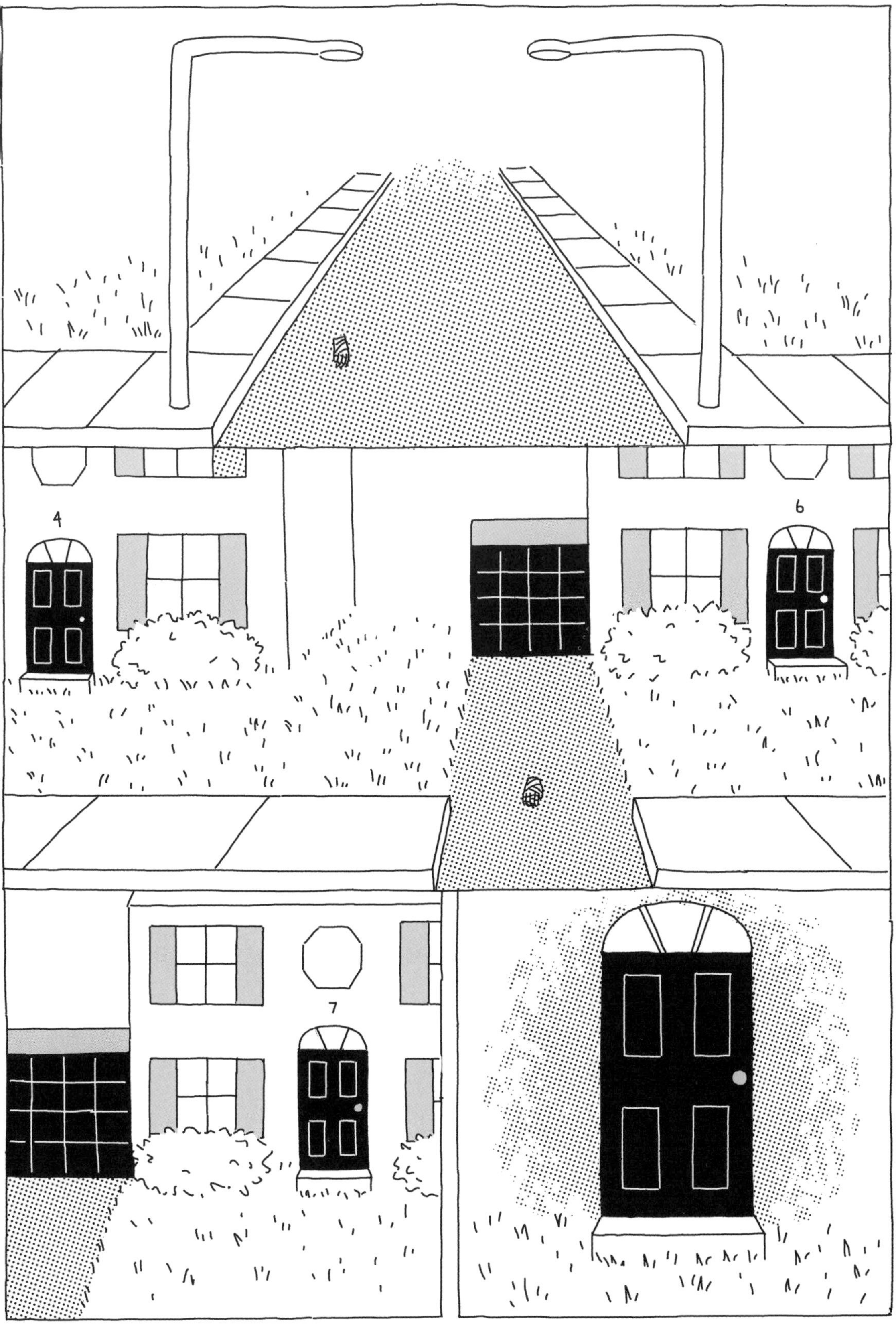
4
6
7

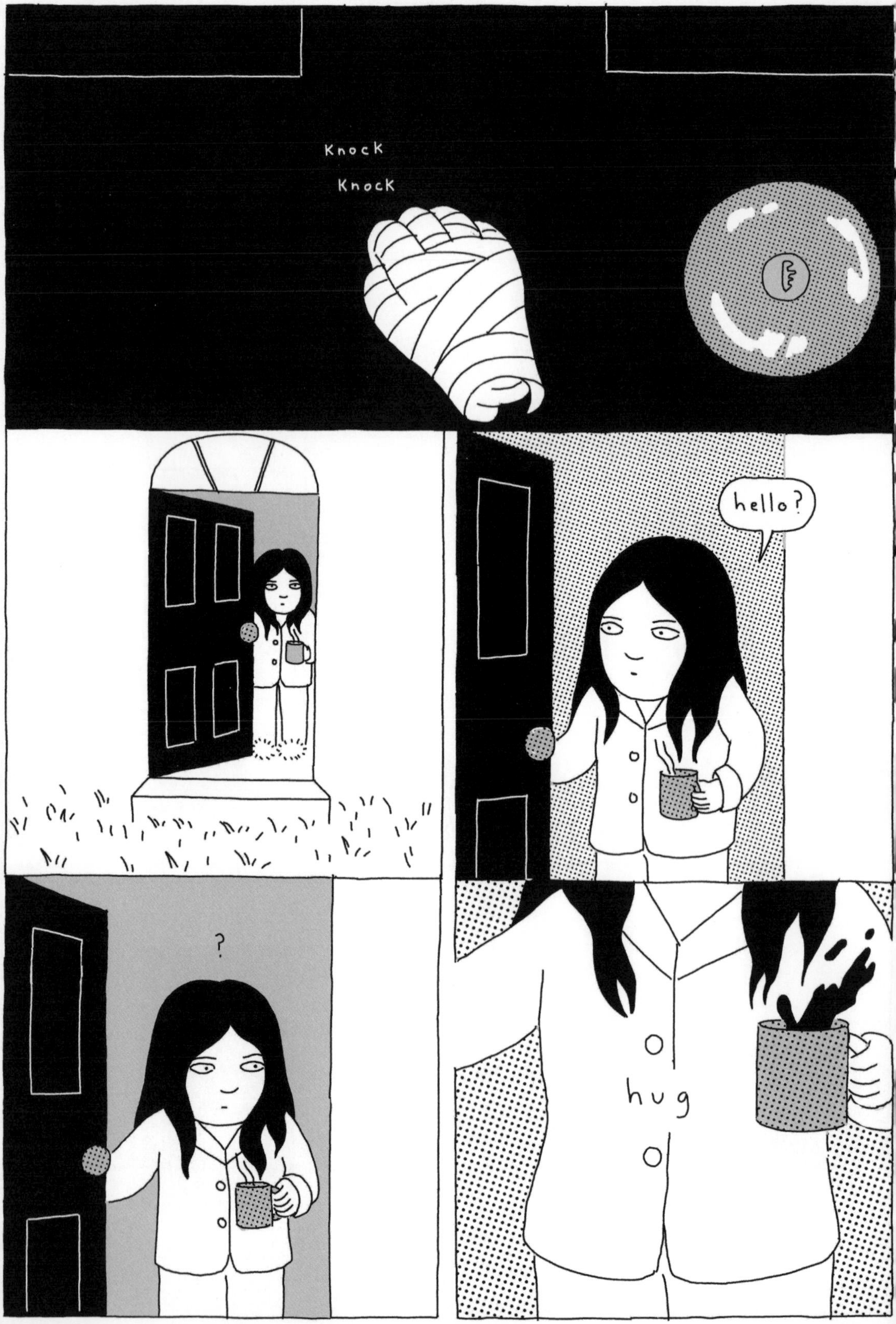
Knock
Knock
hello?
?
hug

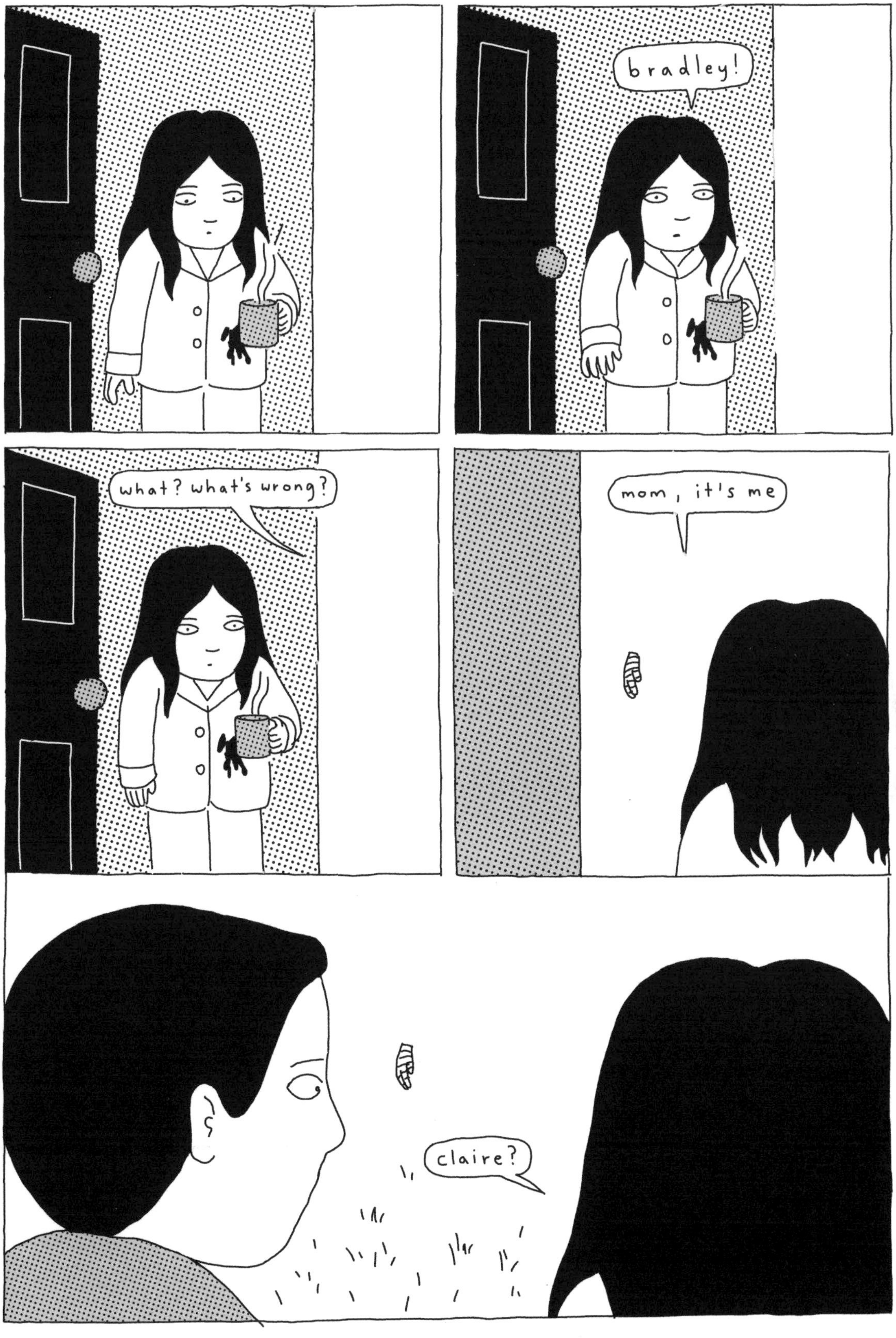
bradley!
what? what's wrong?
mom, it's me
claire?

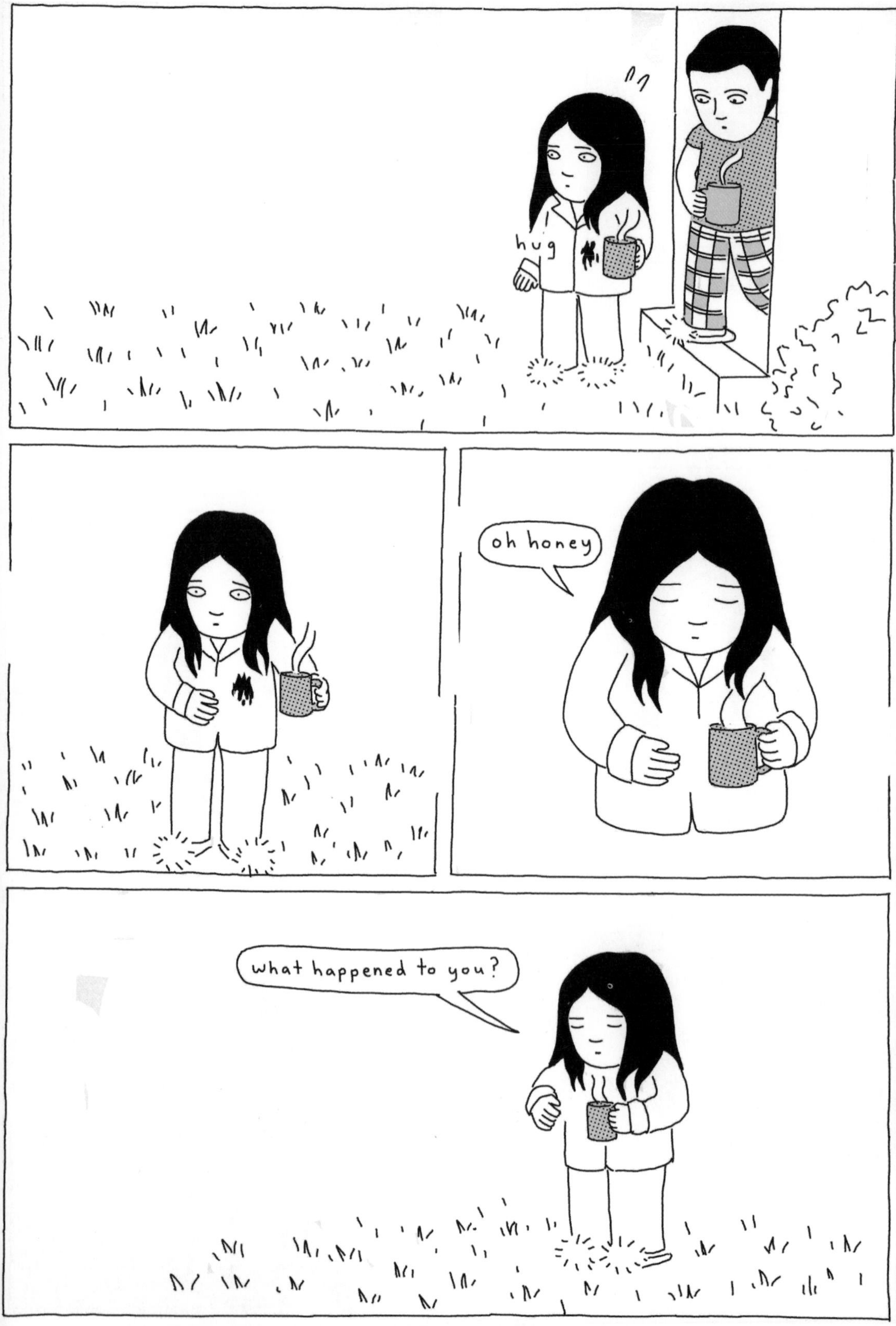
hug
oh honey
what happened to you?

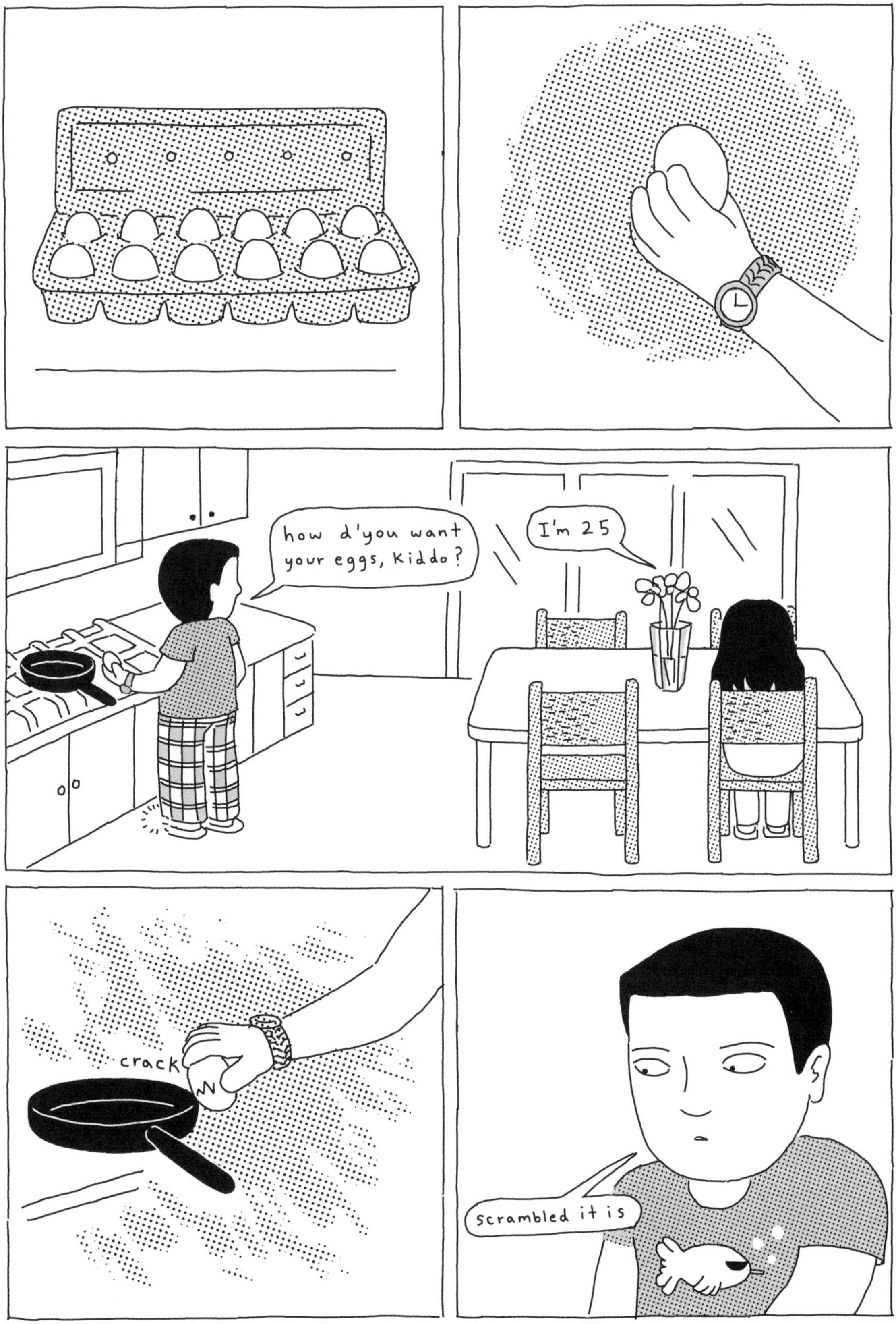
how d'you want your eggs, kiddo?
I'm 25
crack
scrambled it is

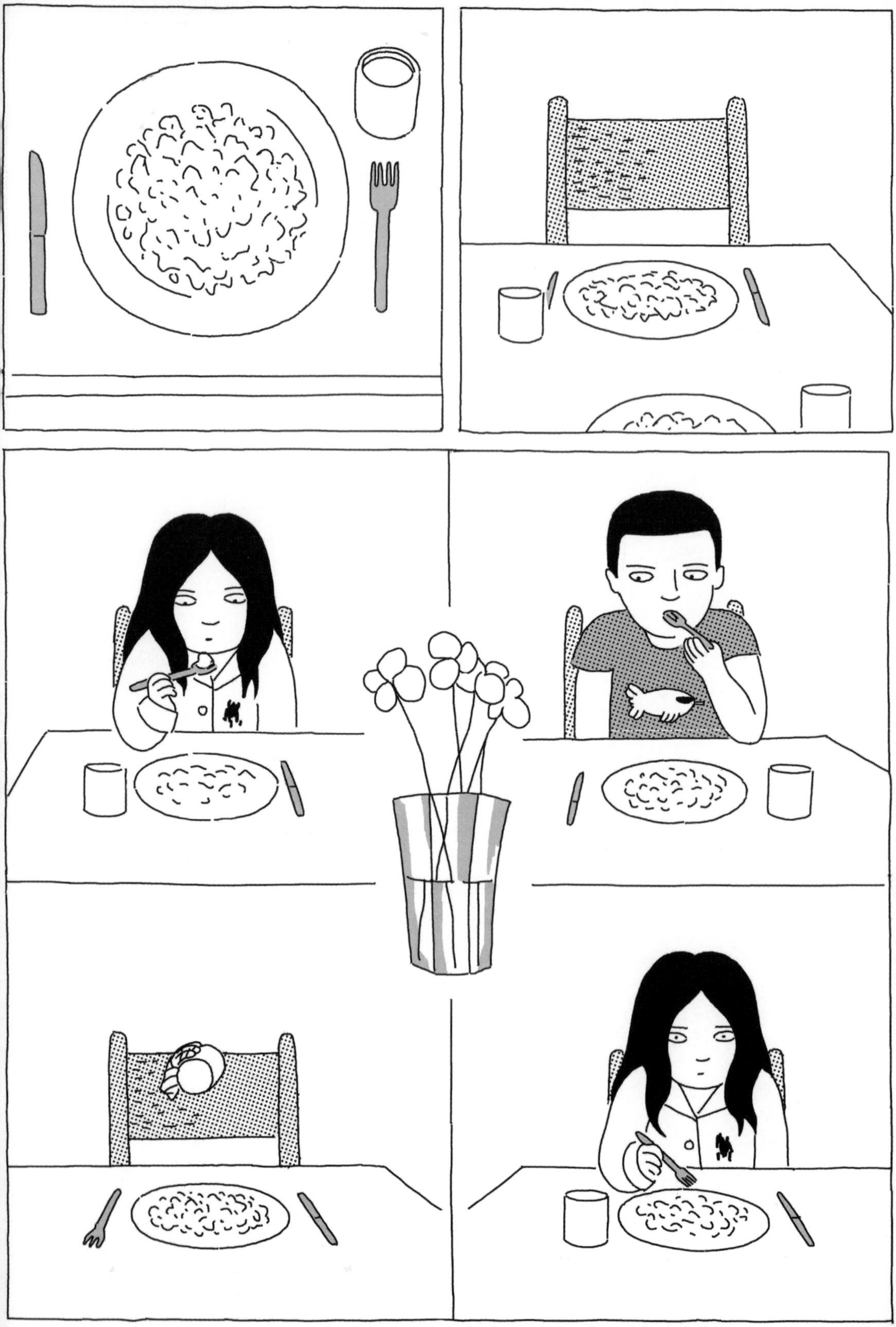

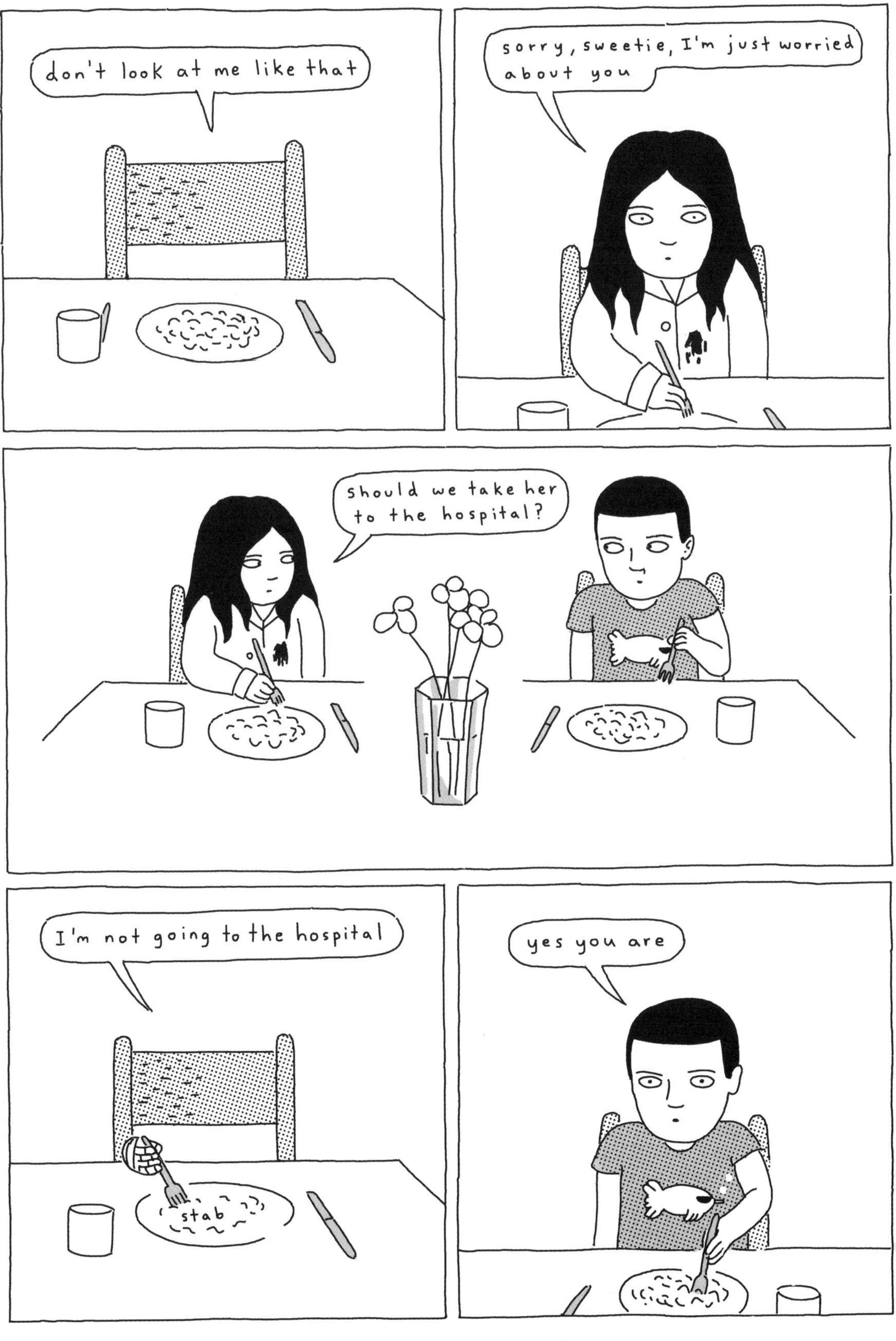
don't look at me like that
sorry, sweetie, I'm just worried about you
should we take her to the hospital?
I'm not going to the hospital
stab
yes you are

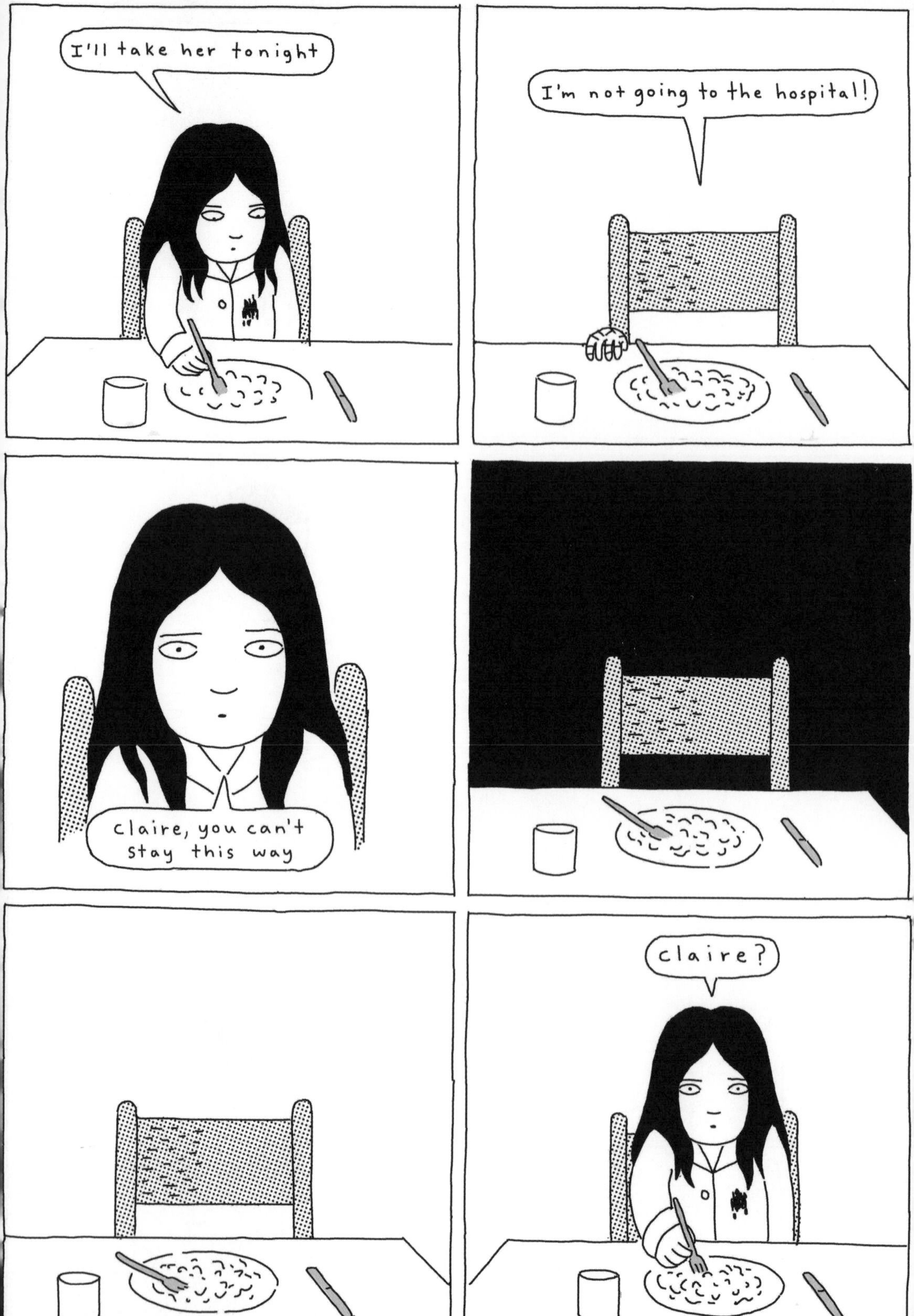
I'll take her tonight
I'm not going to the hospital!
claire, you can't stay this way
claire?

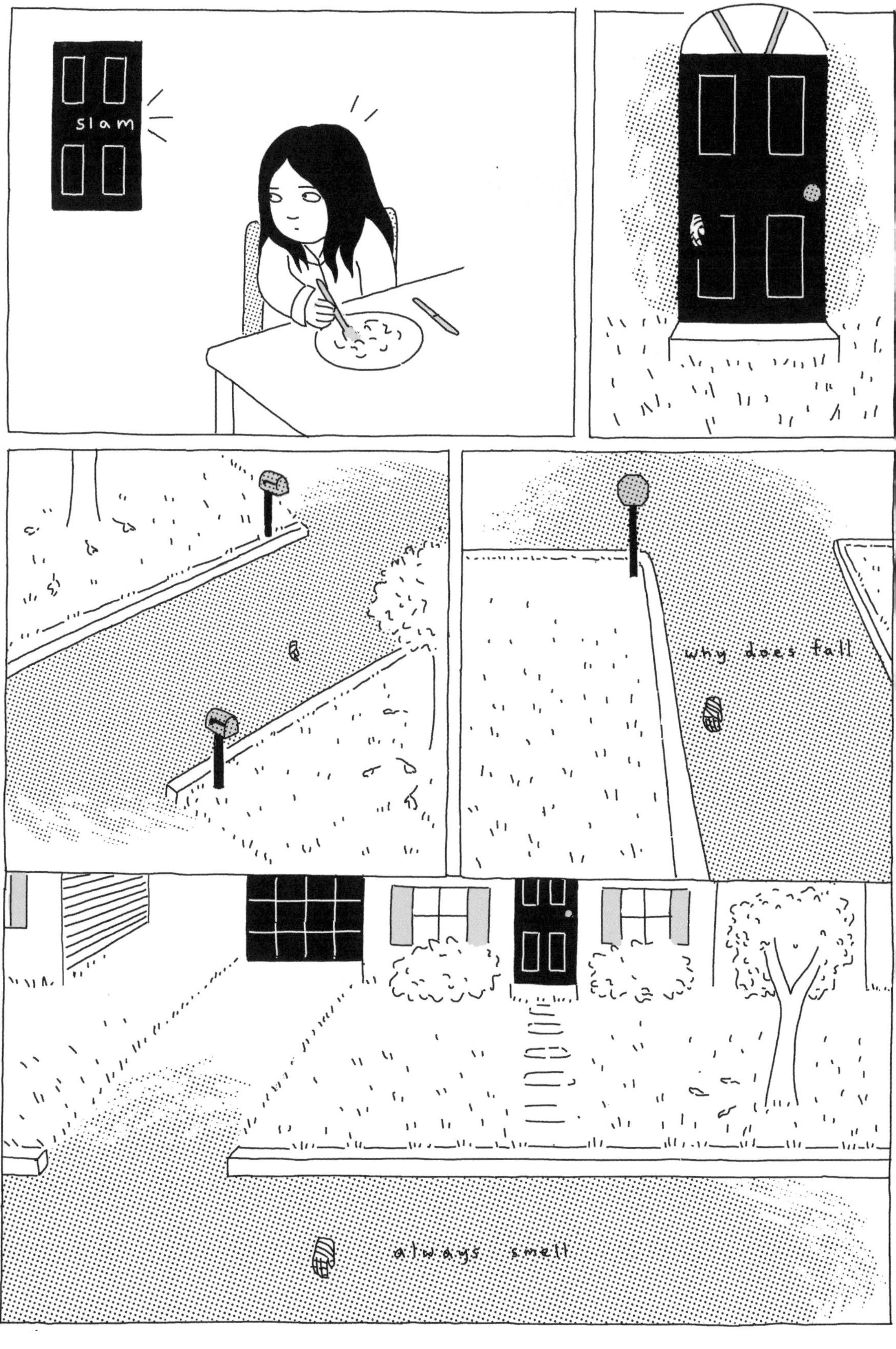
slam
why does fall
always smell

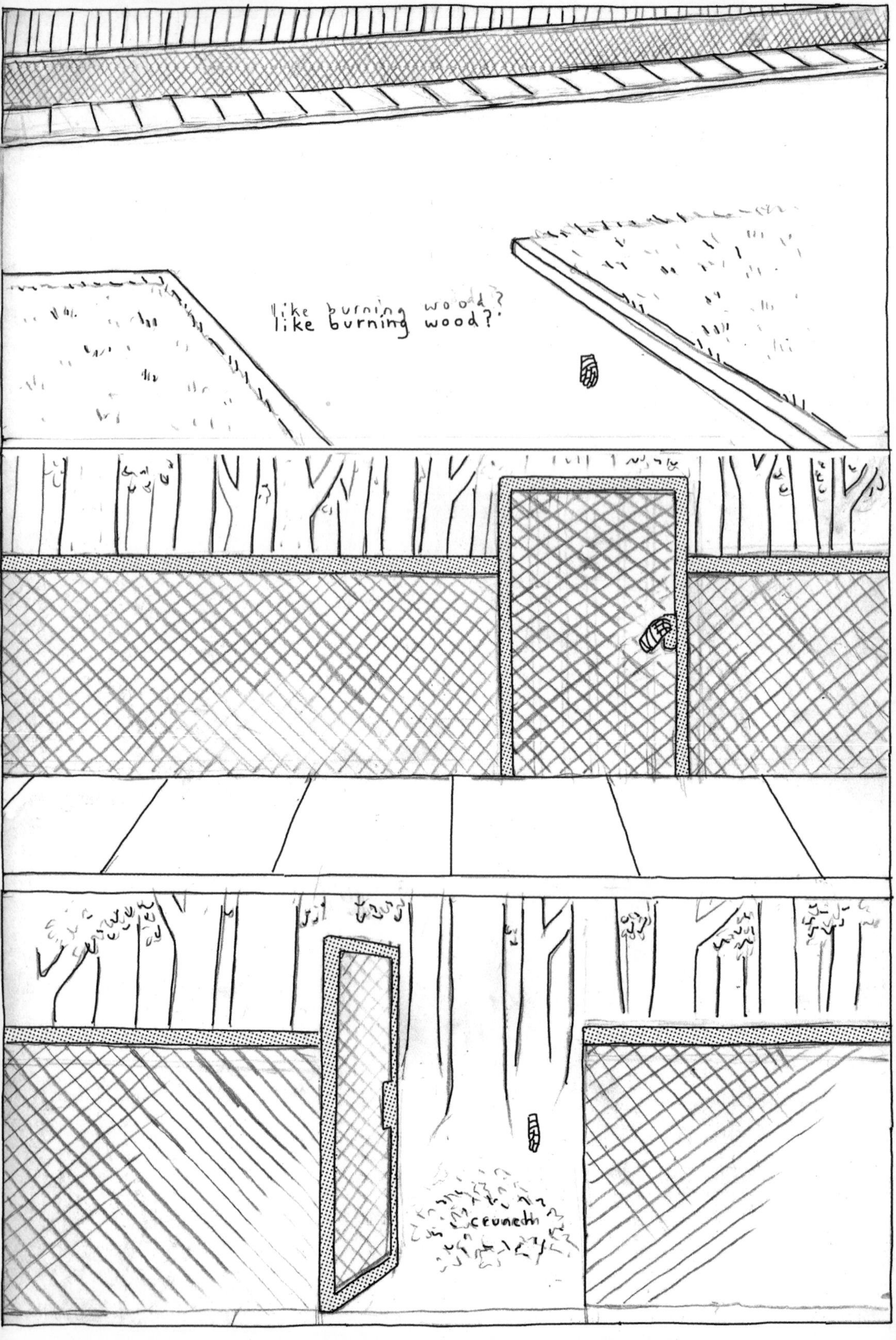
like burning woood?
like burning wood?
crunch

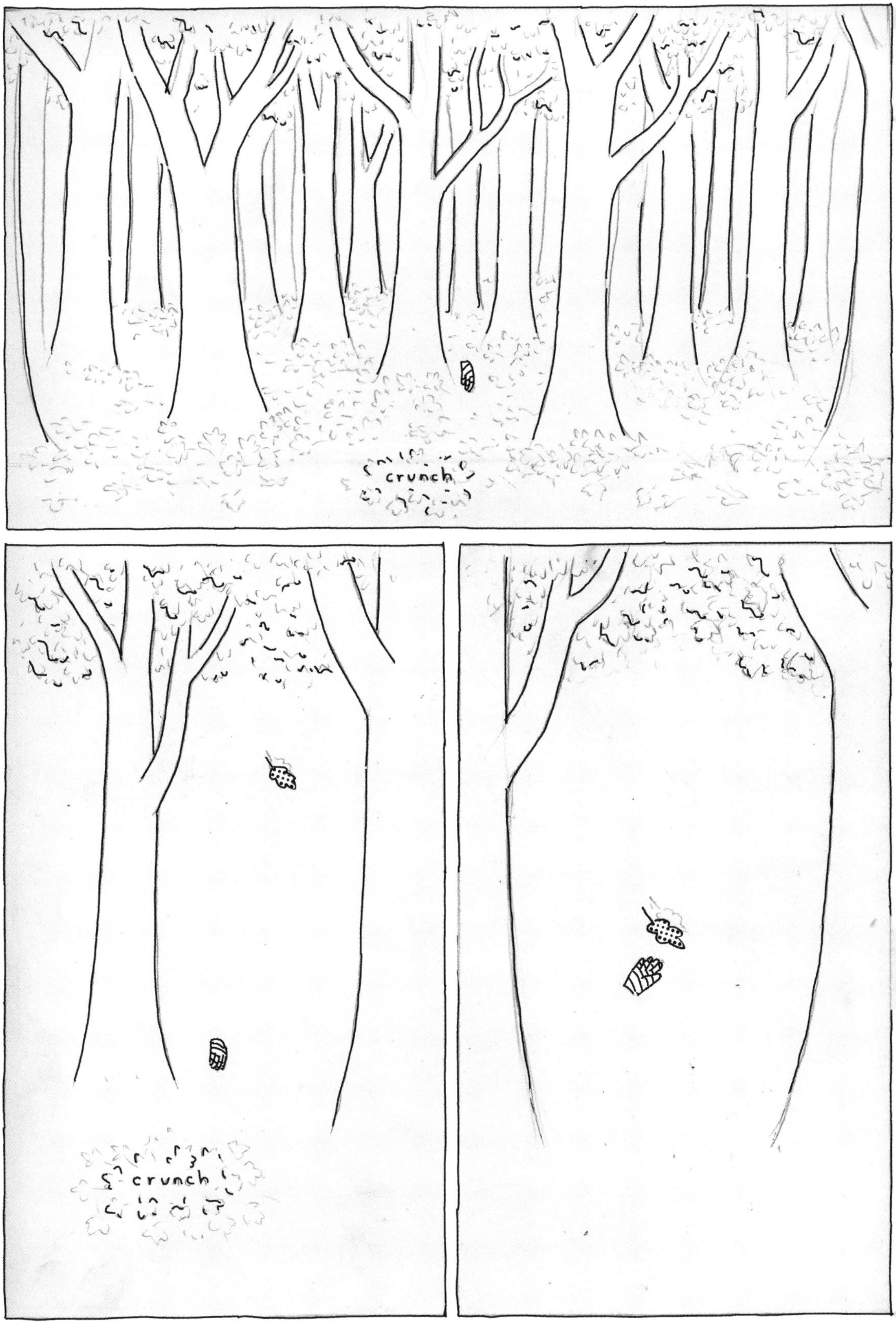
crunch
crunch

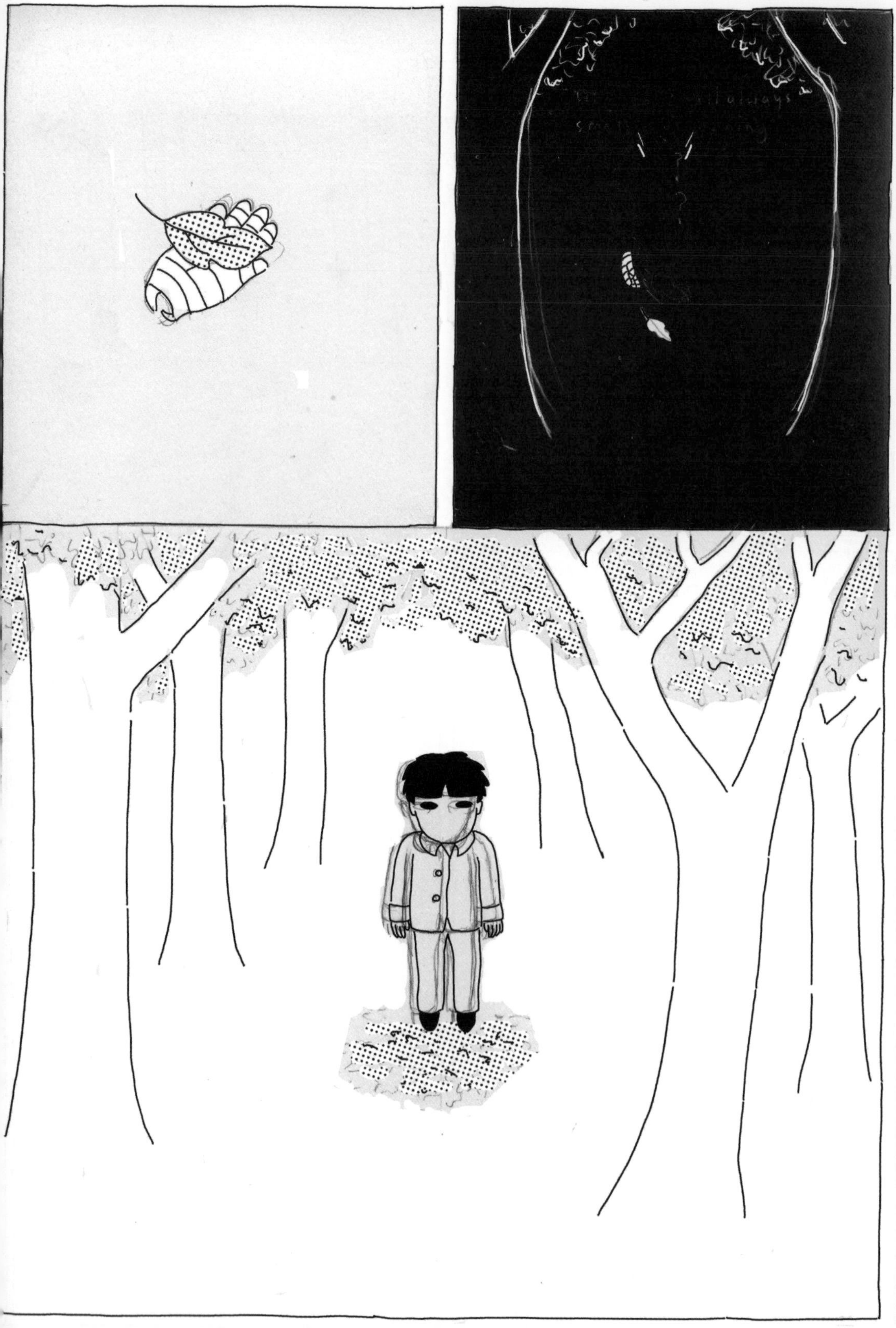

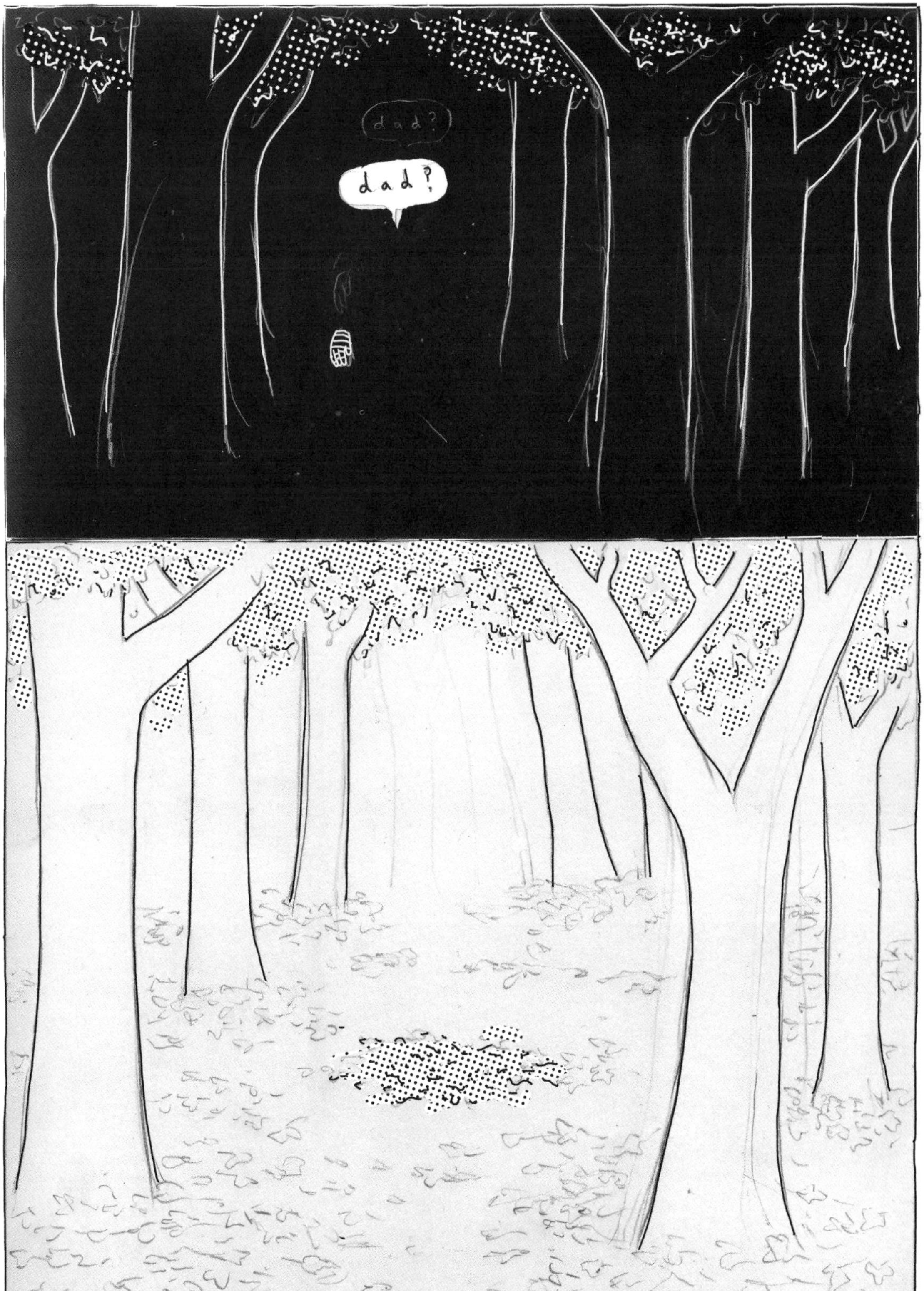
dad?
dad?

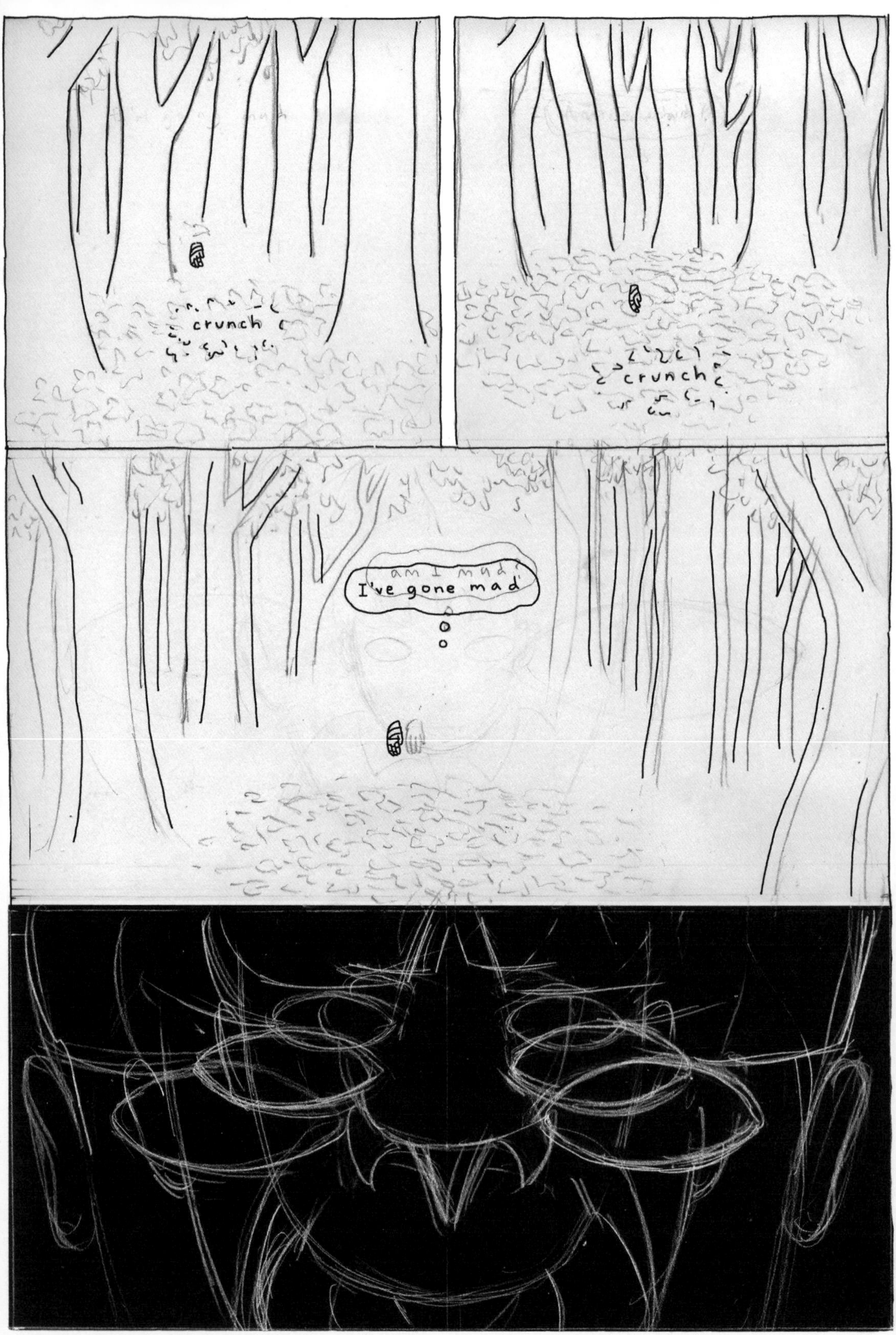
crunch
crunch
I've gone mad

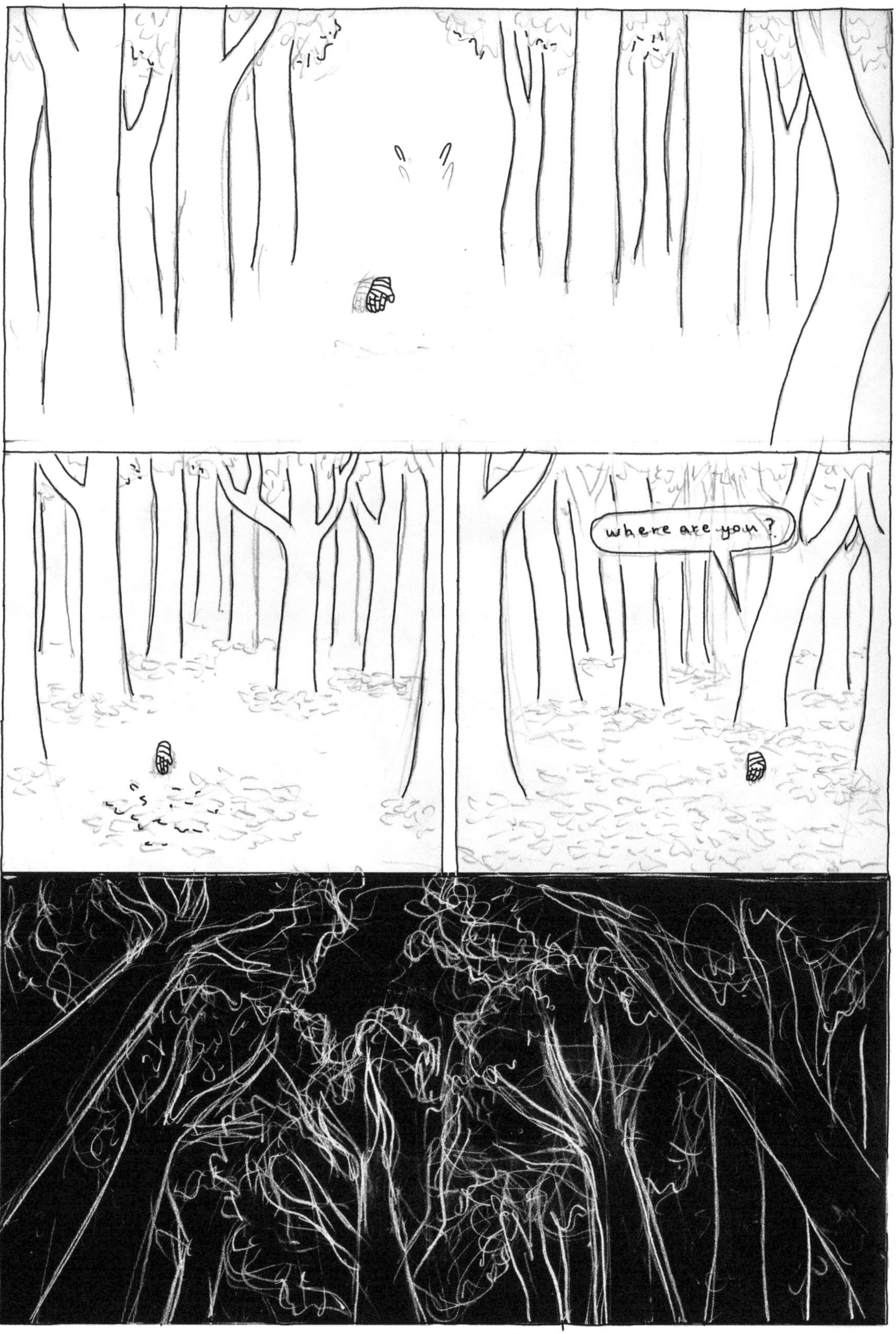
where are you?

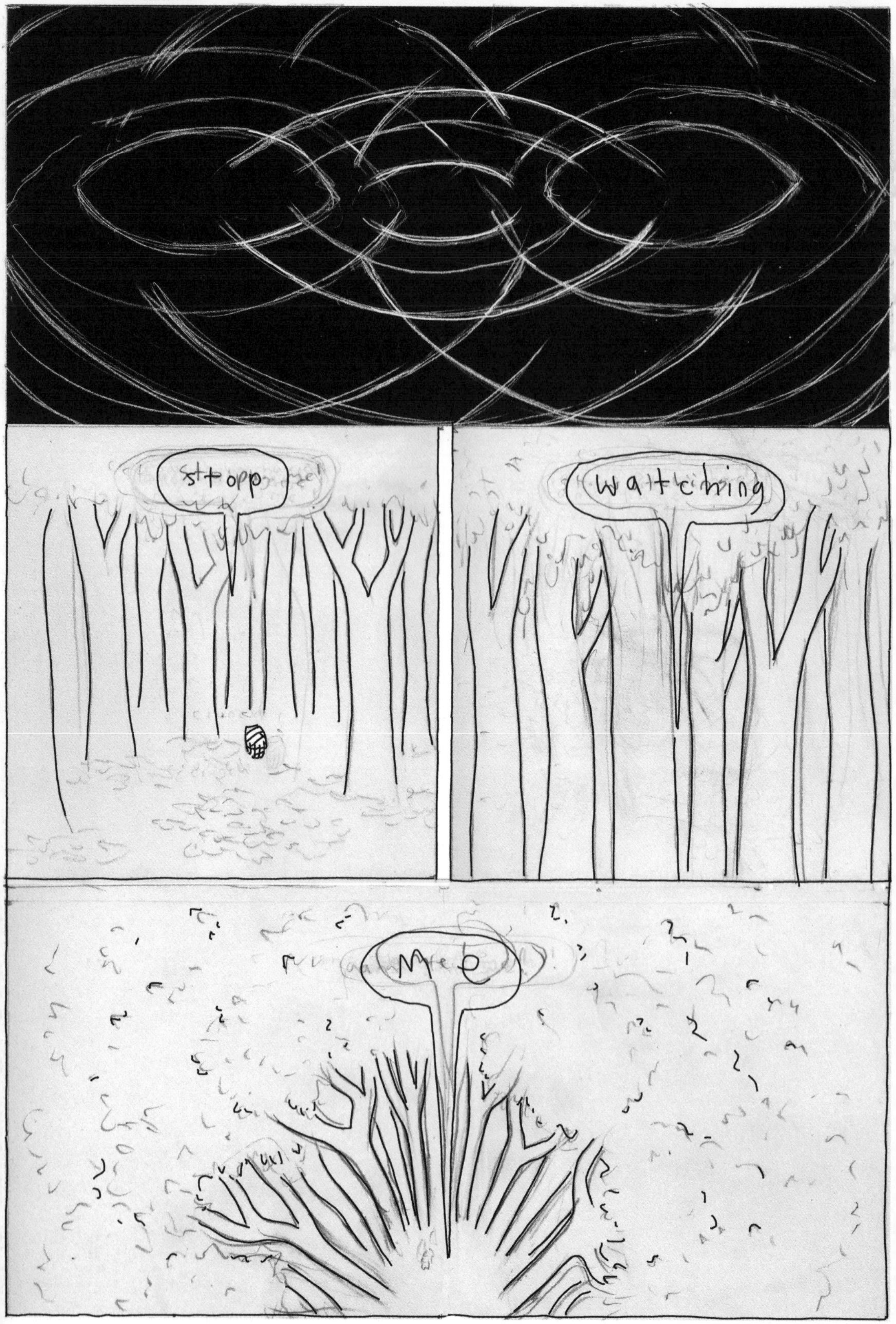
stopp
watching
me

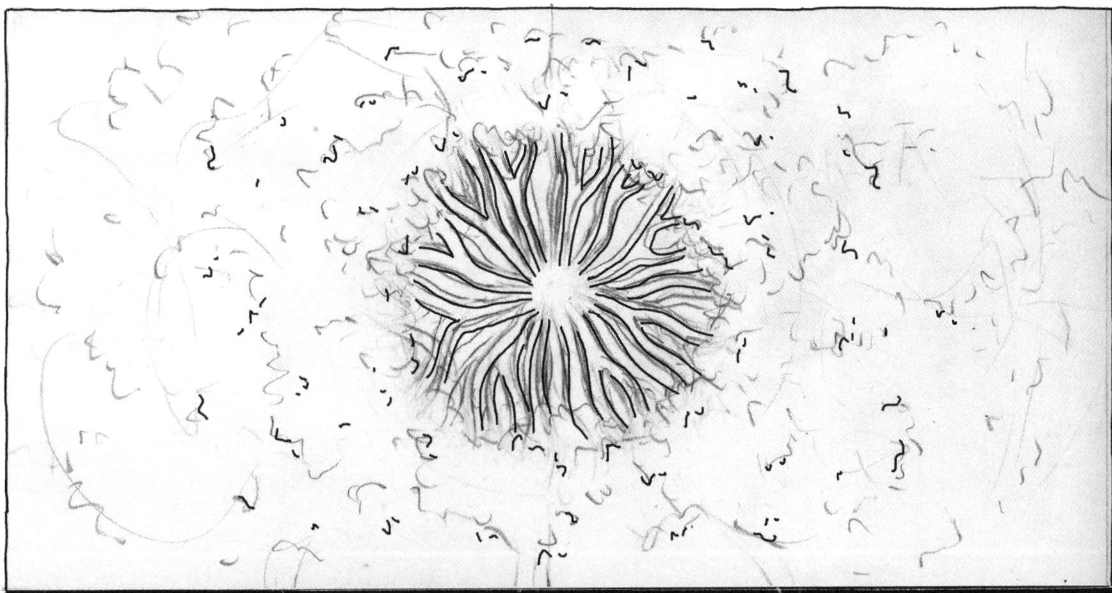

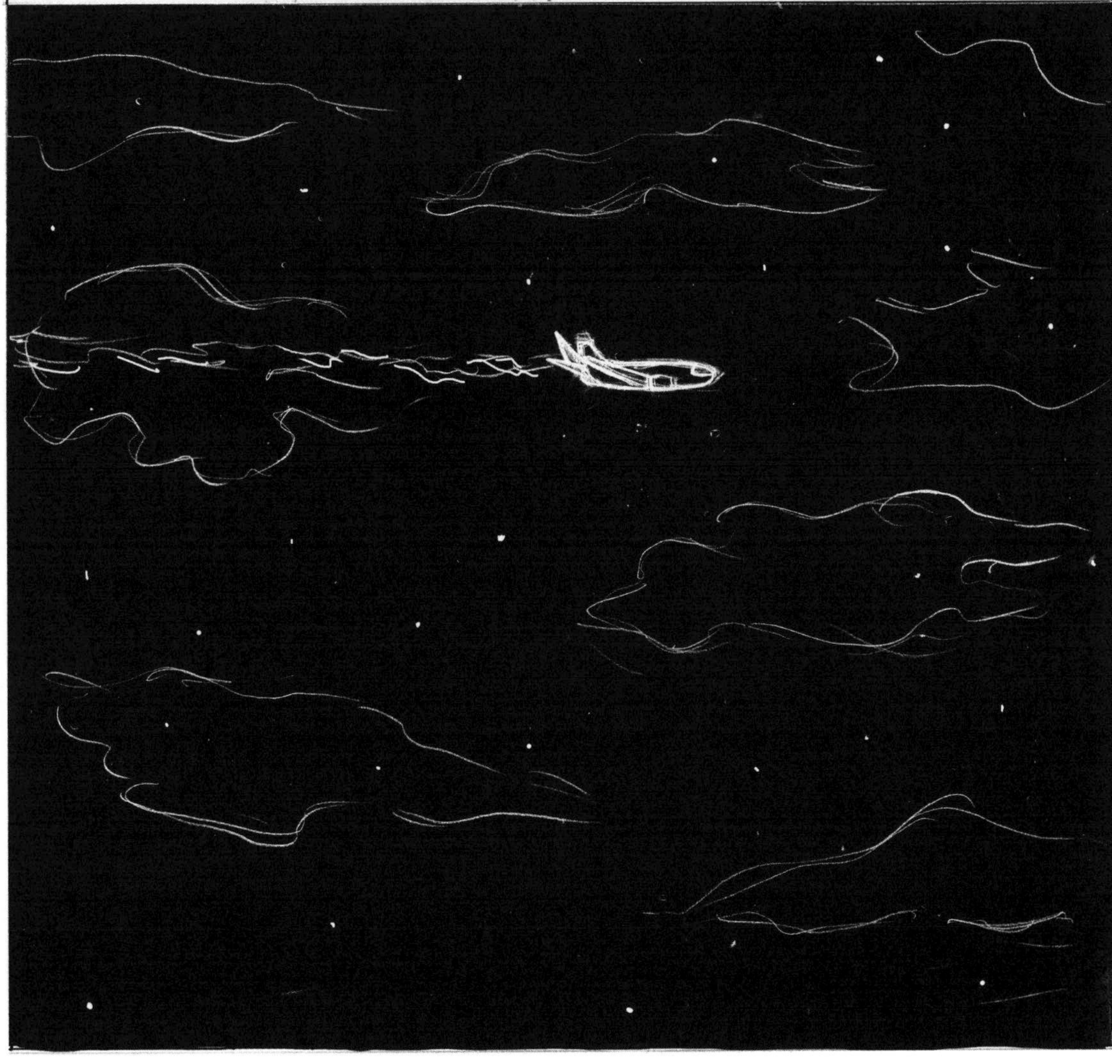

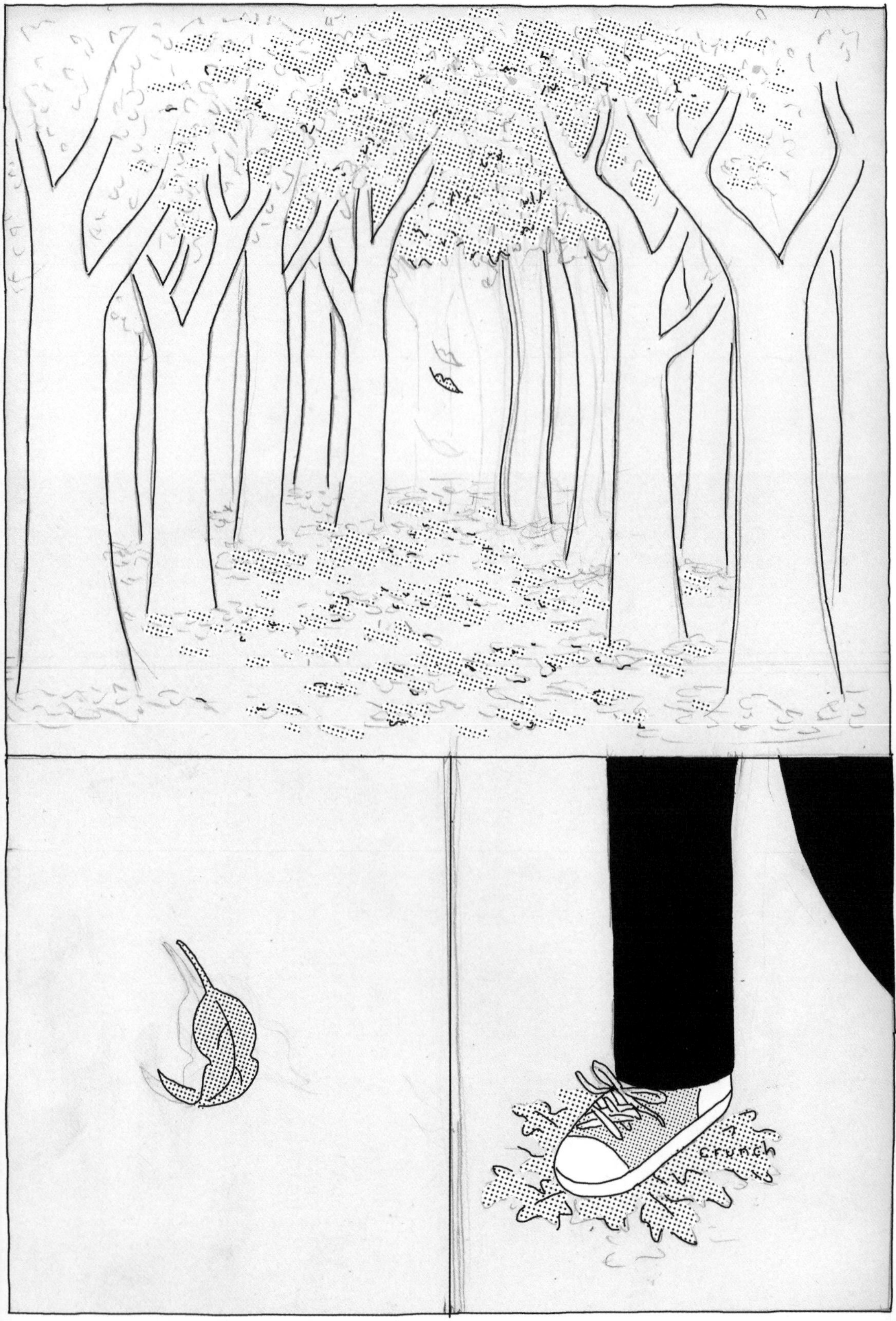
crunch

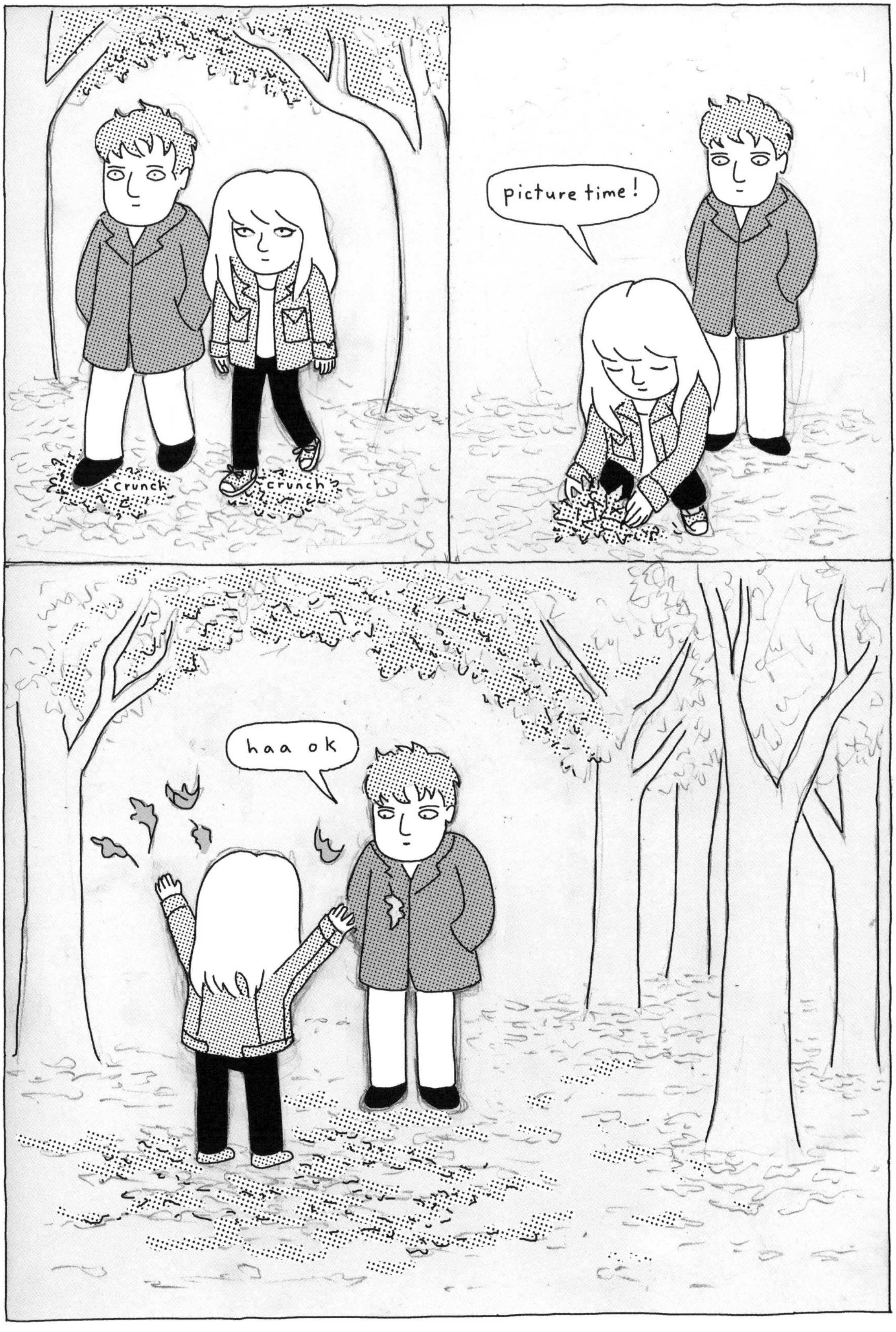
crunch
crunch
picture time!
haa ok

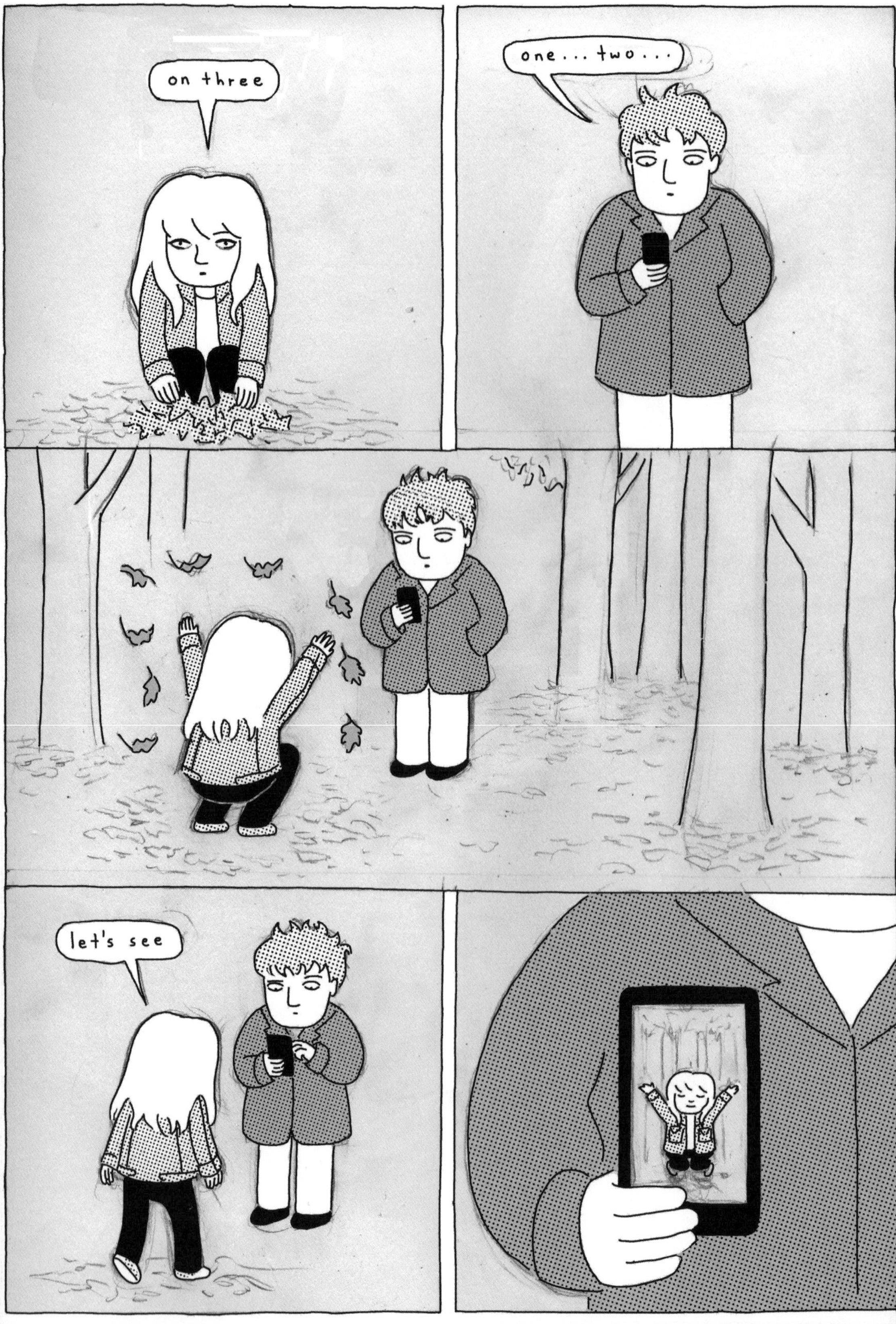
on three
one... two...
let's see

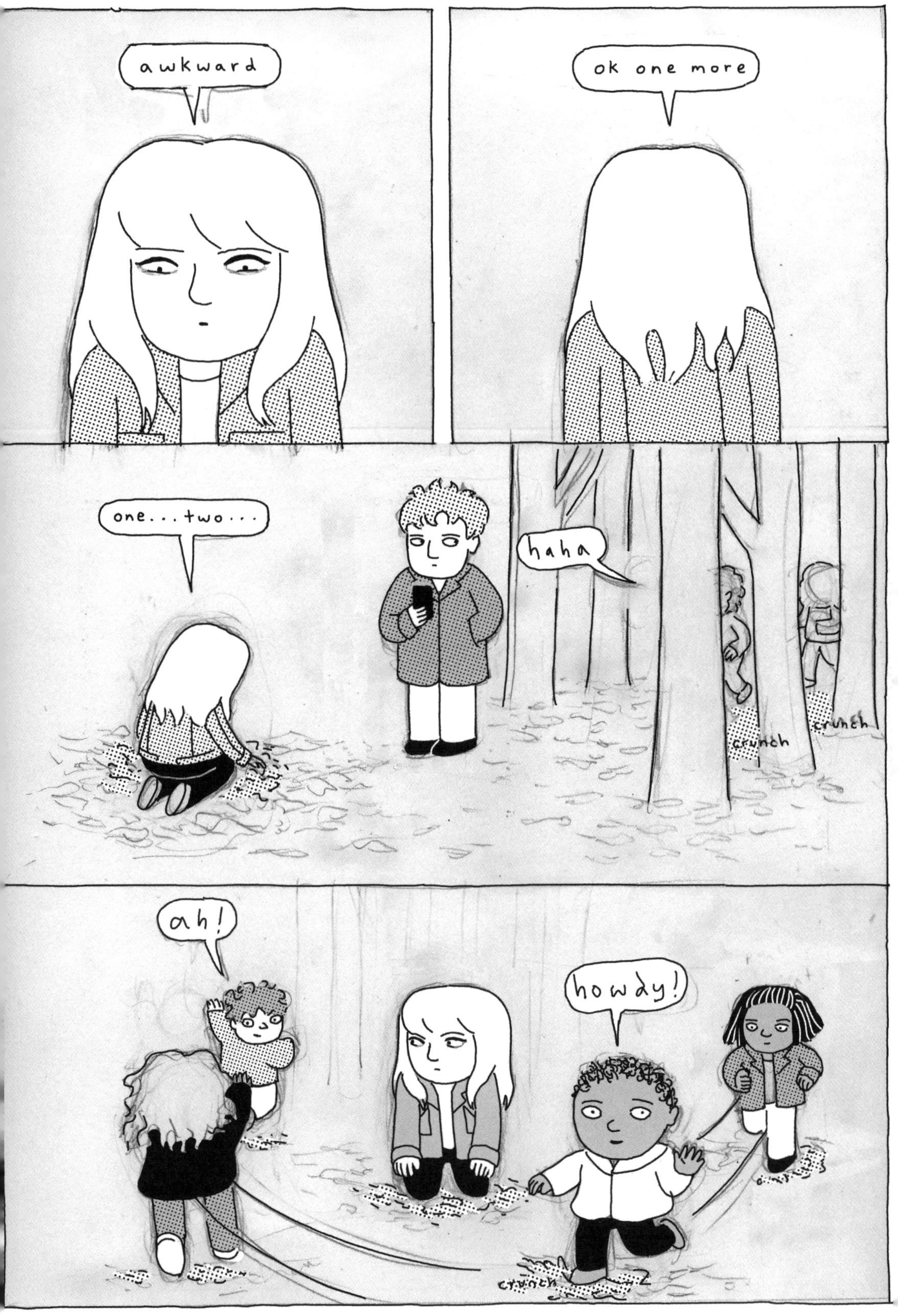
awkward
ok one more
one...two...
haha
crunch
crunch
ah!
howdy!
crunch

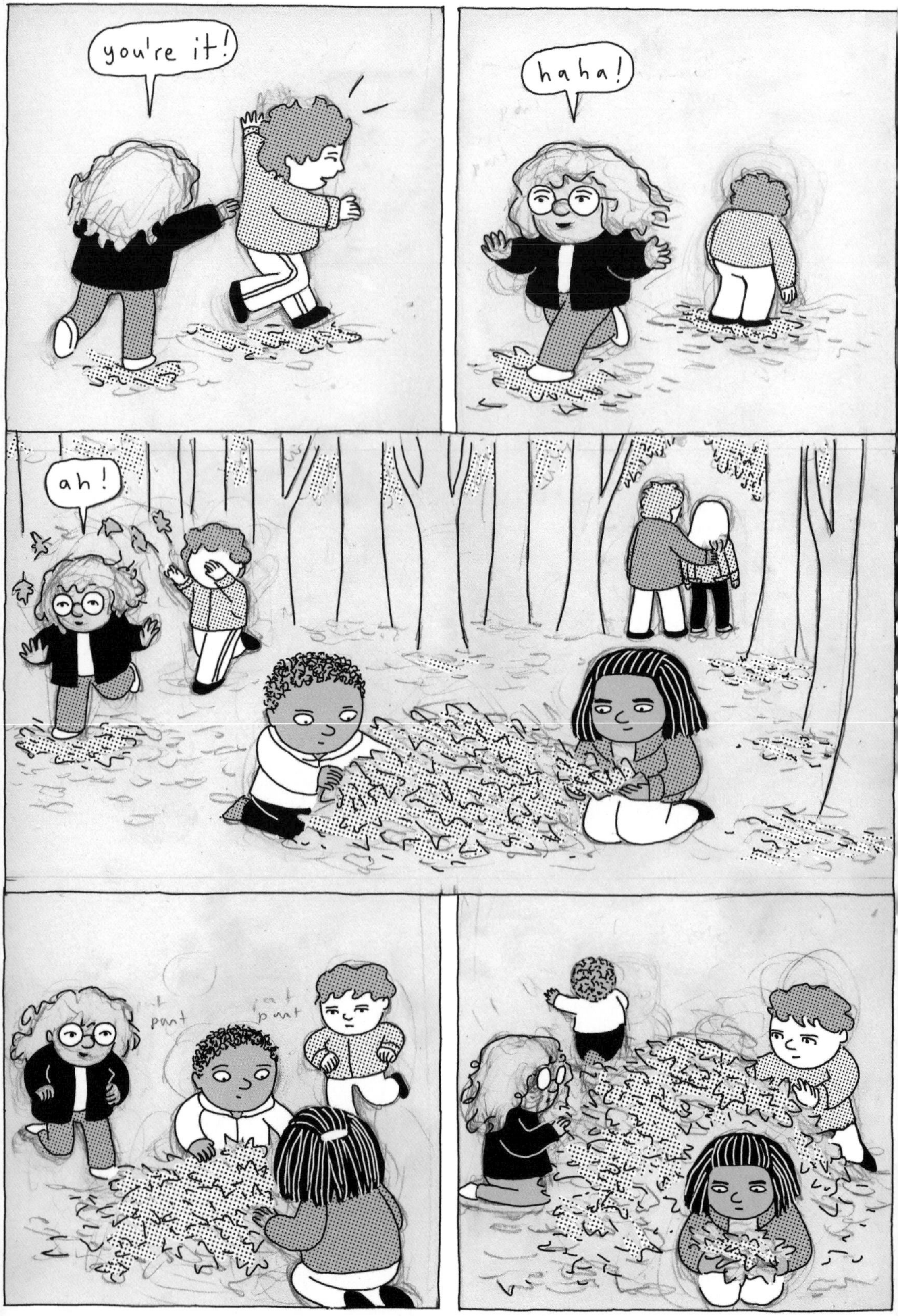
you're it!
haha!
ah!
pant
pant pant

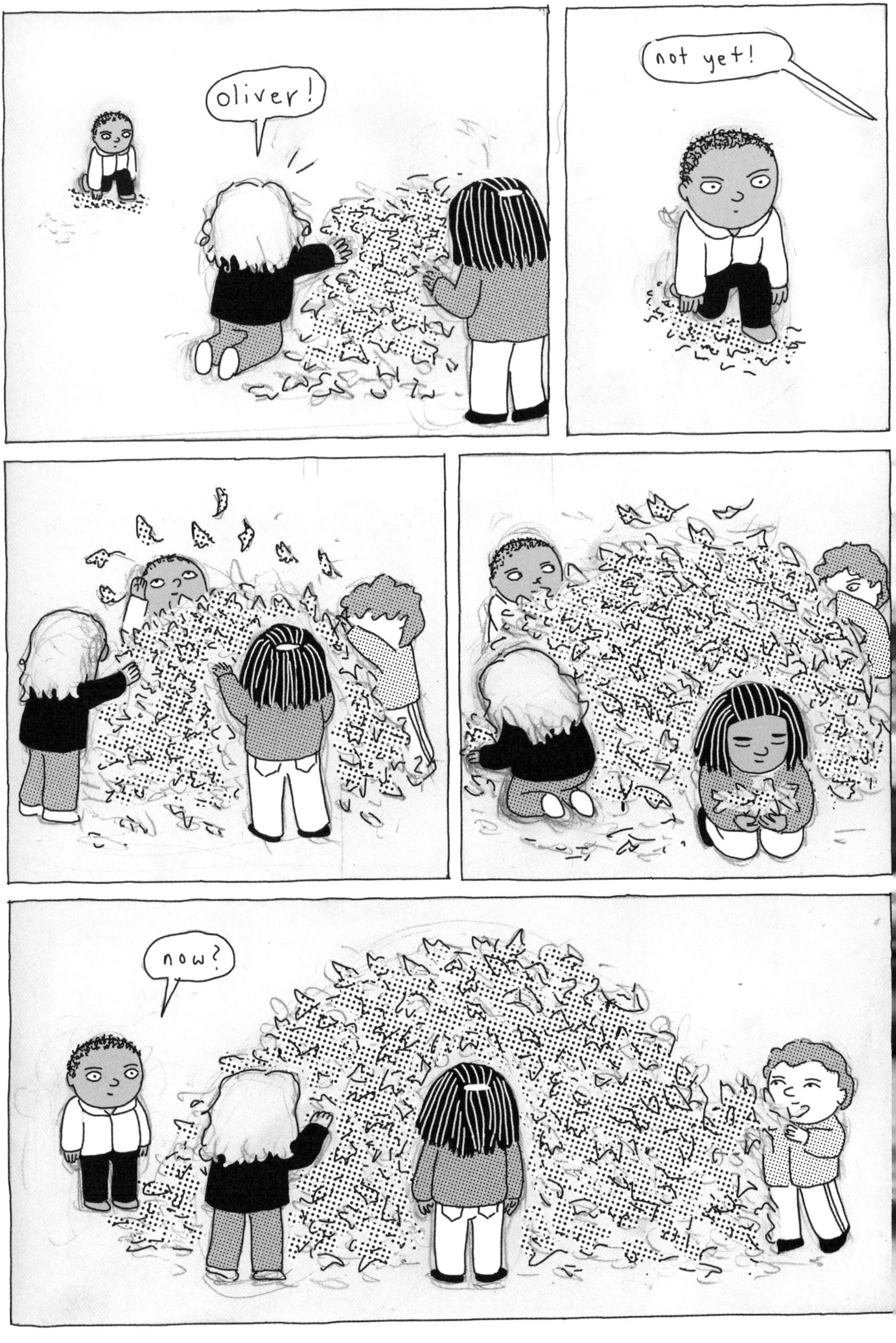
oliver!
not yet!
now?

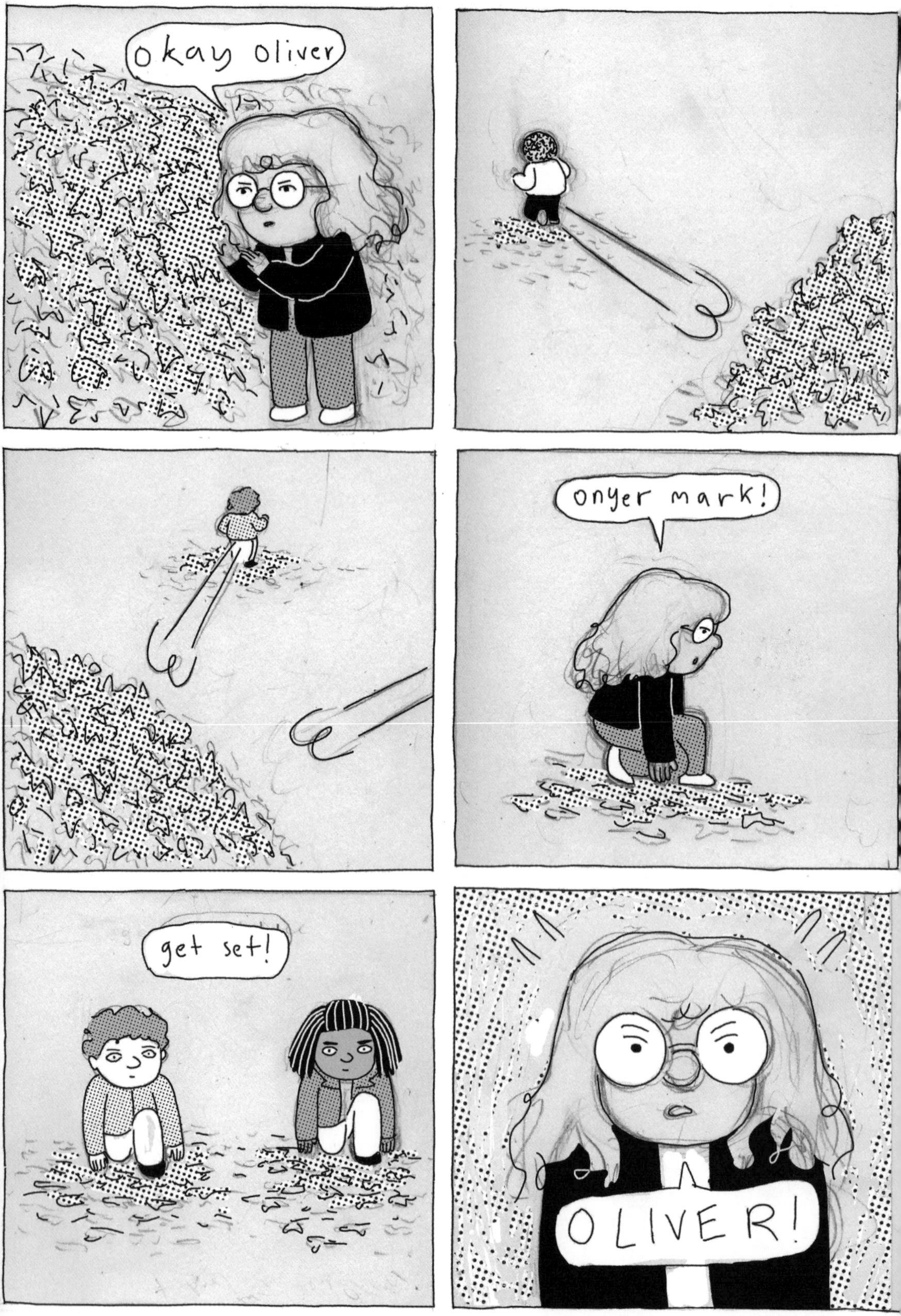
okay oliver
onyer mark!
get set!
OLIVER!

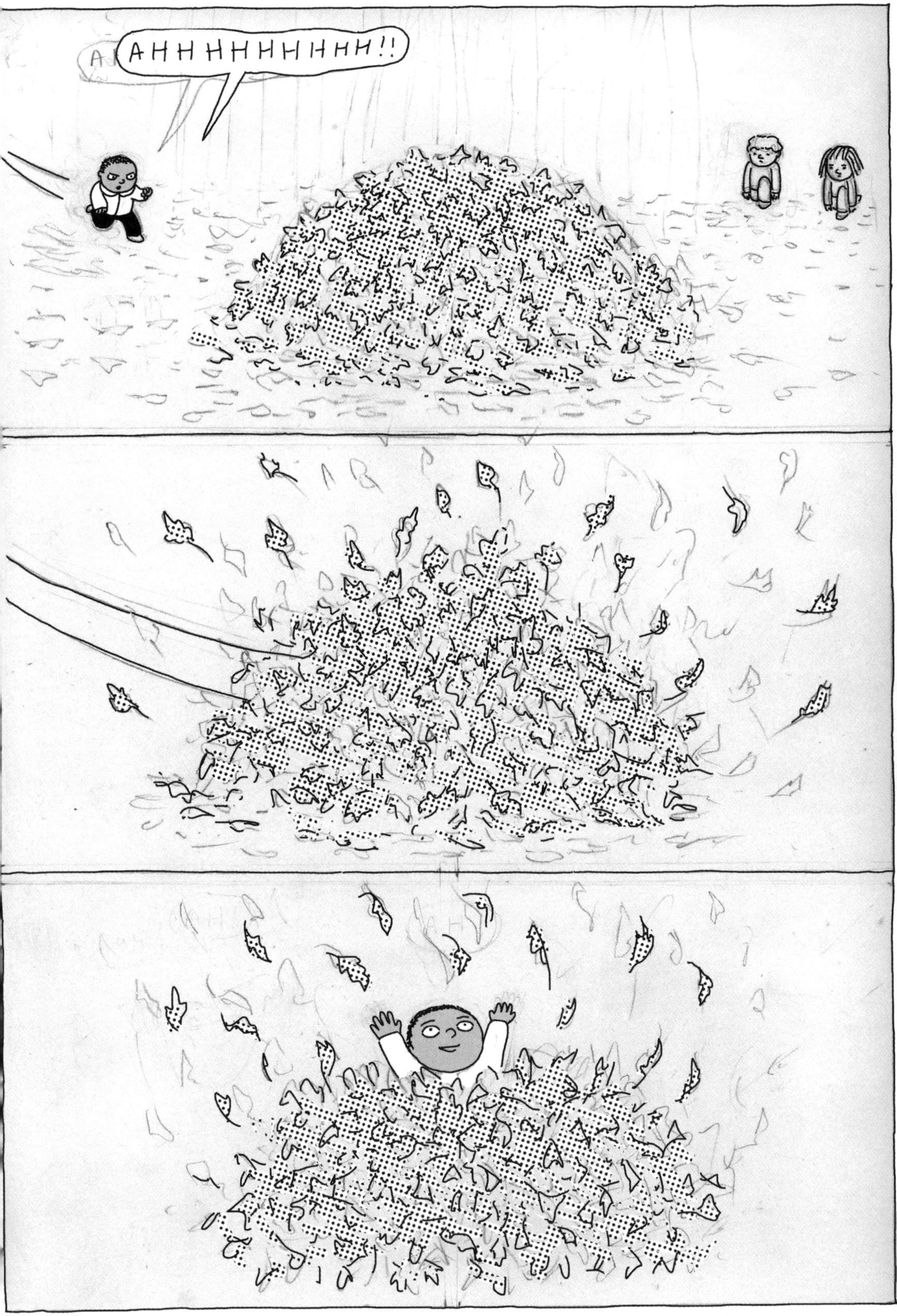
AHHHHHHHHHH!!

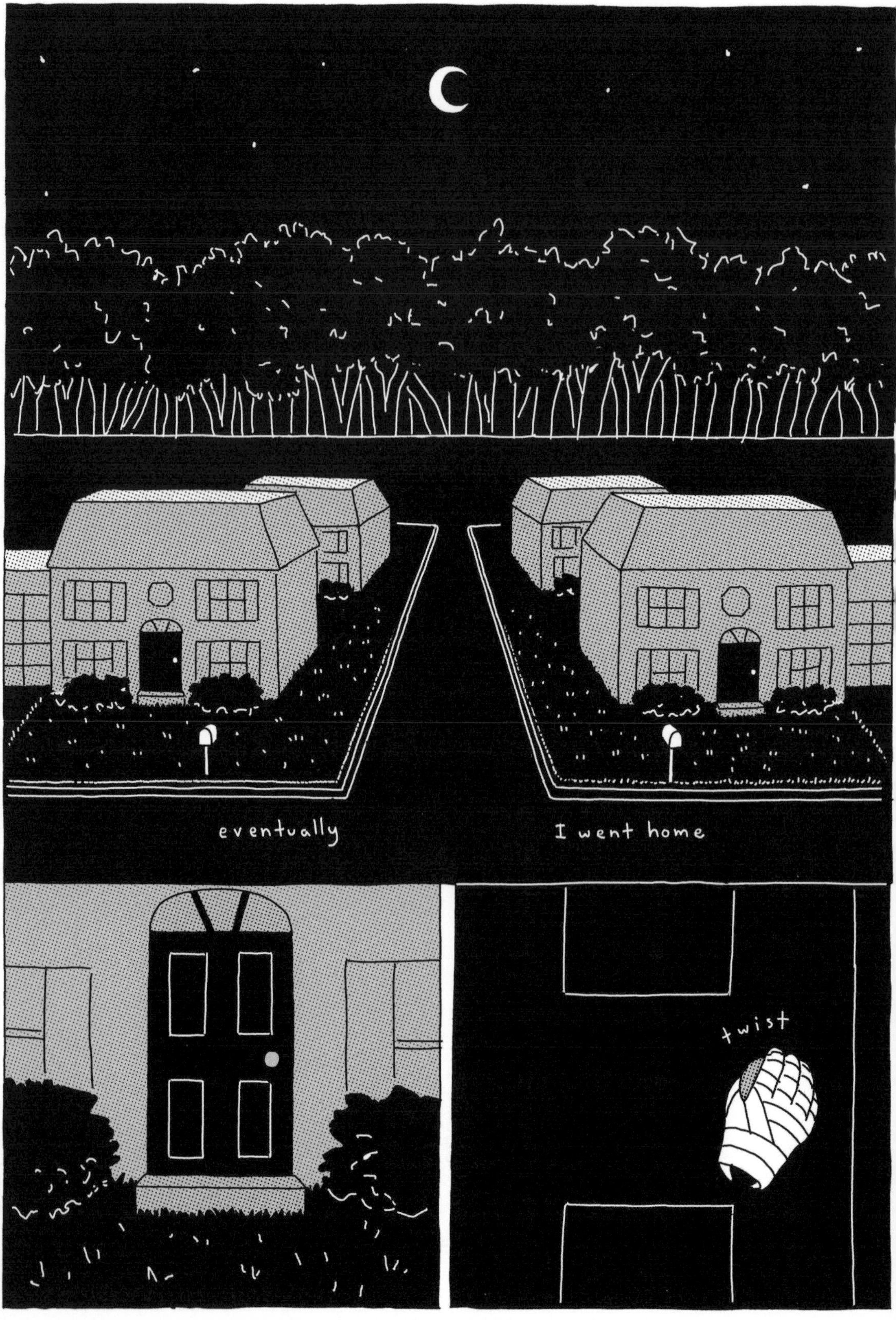
eventually
I went home
twist

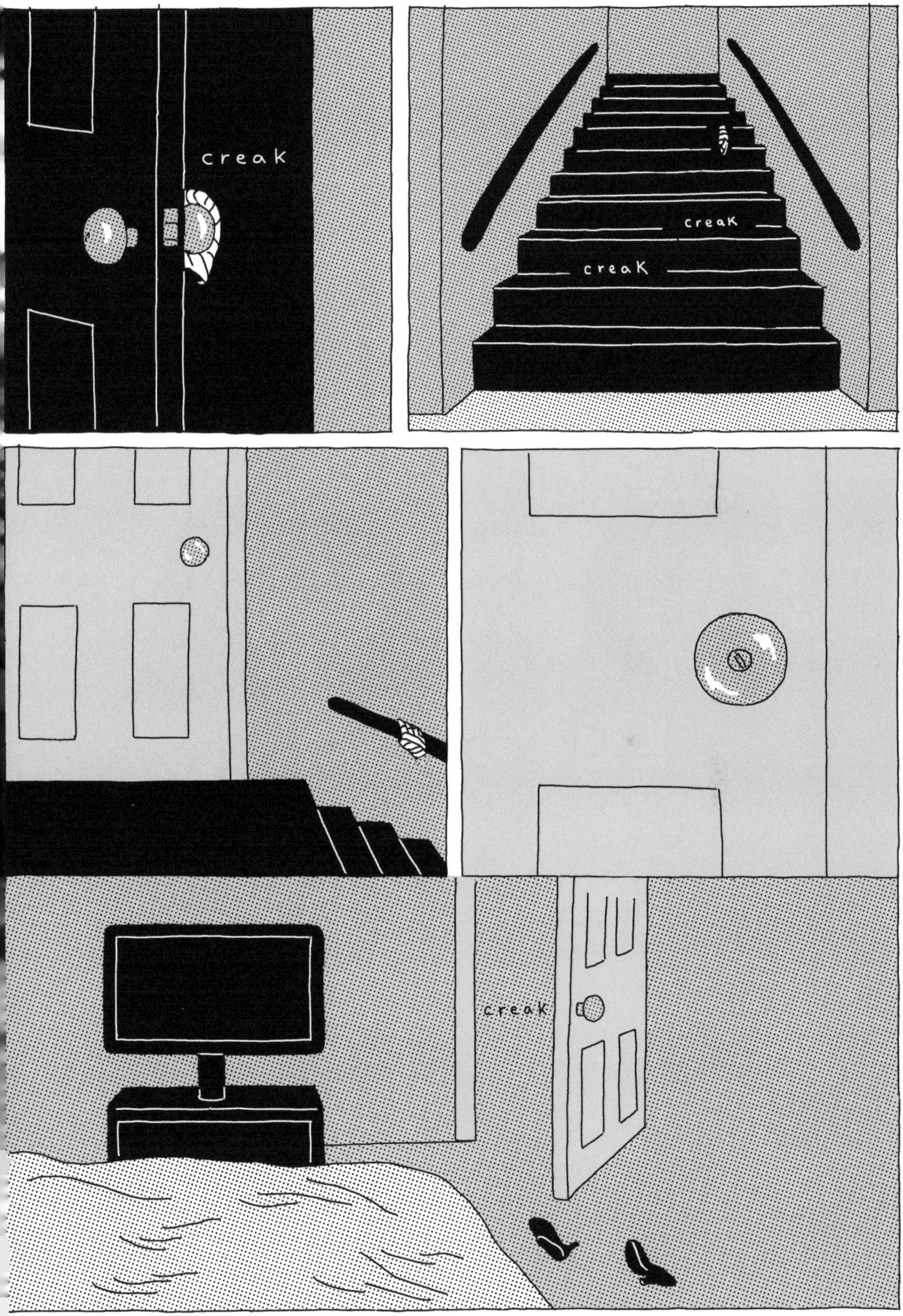
creak
creak
creak
creak

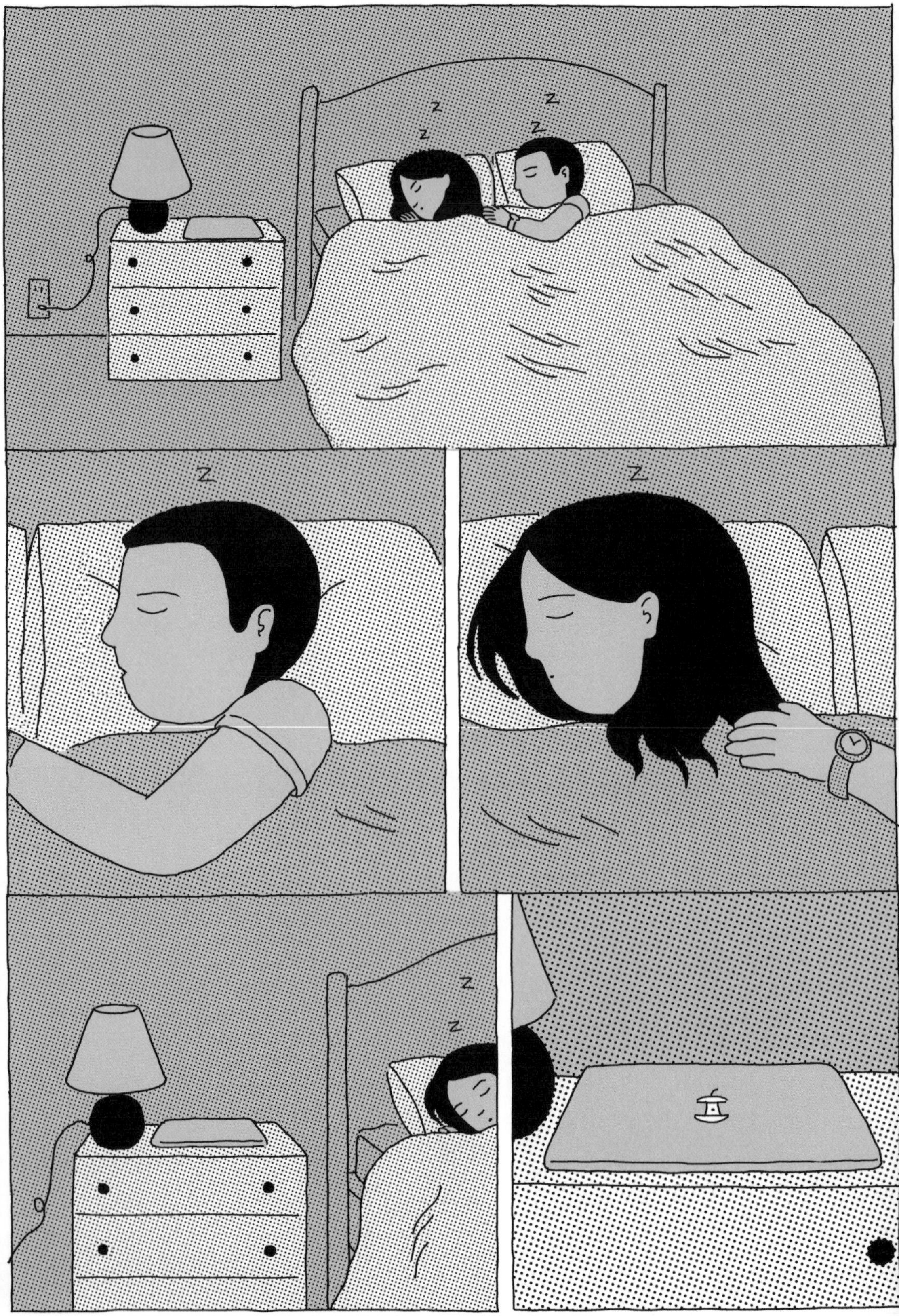
Z Z
Z Z
Z
Z
Z Z

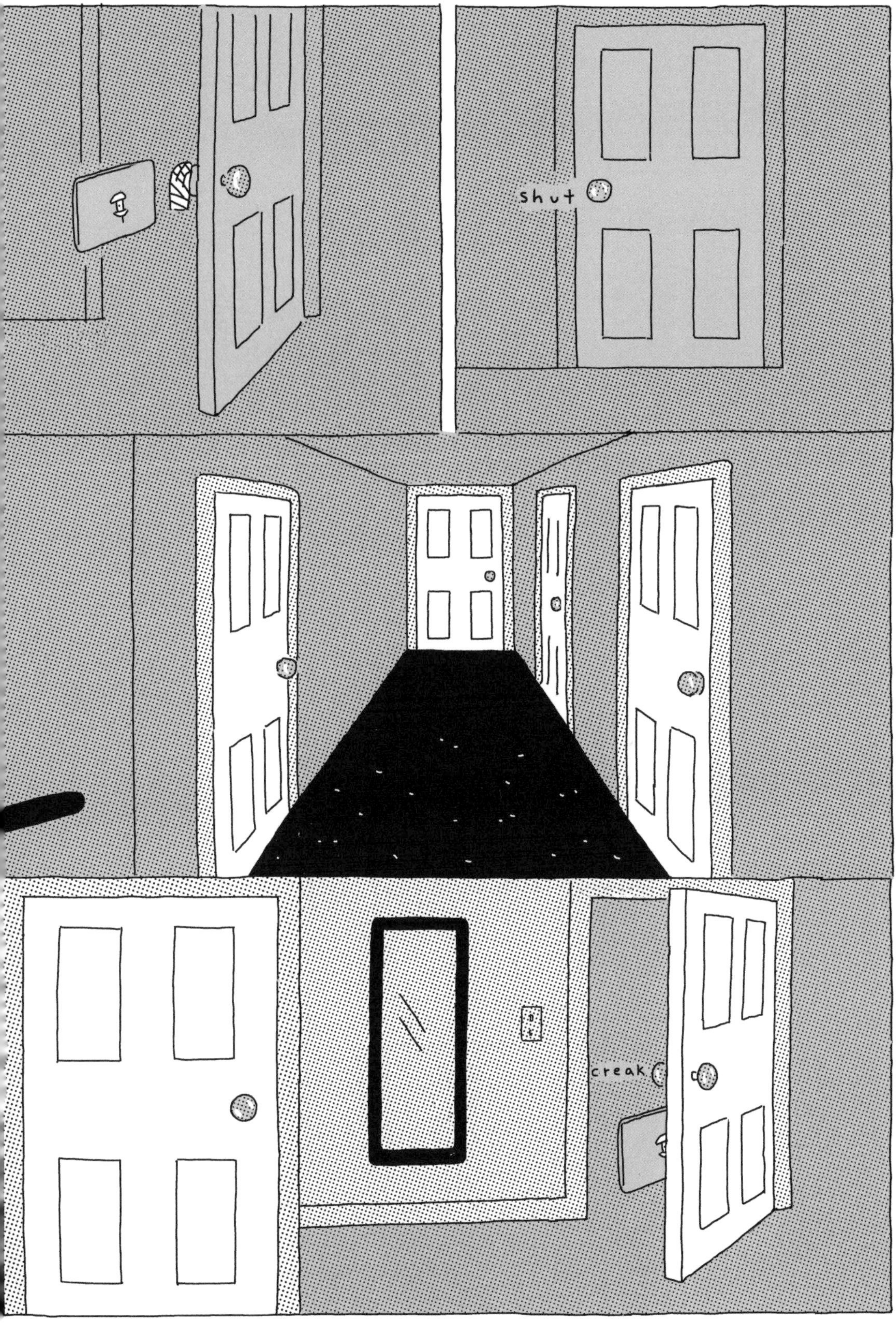
shut
creak

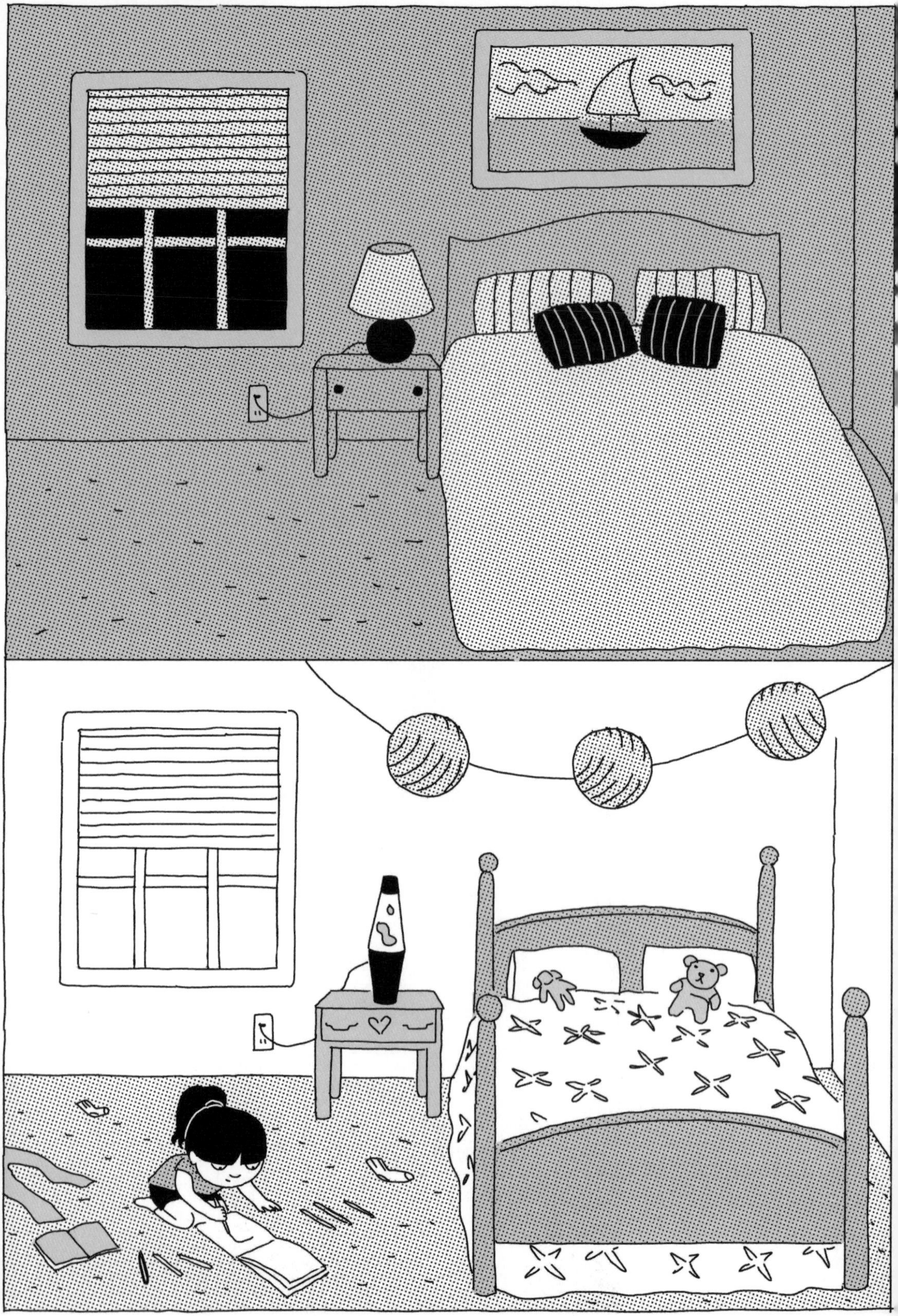

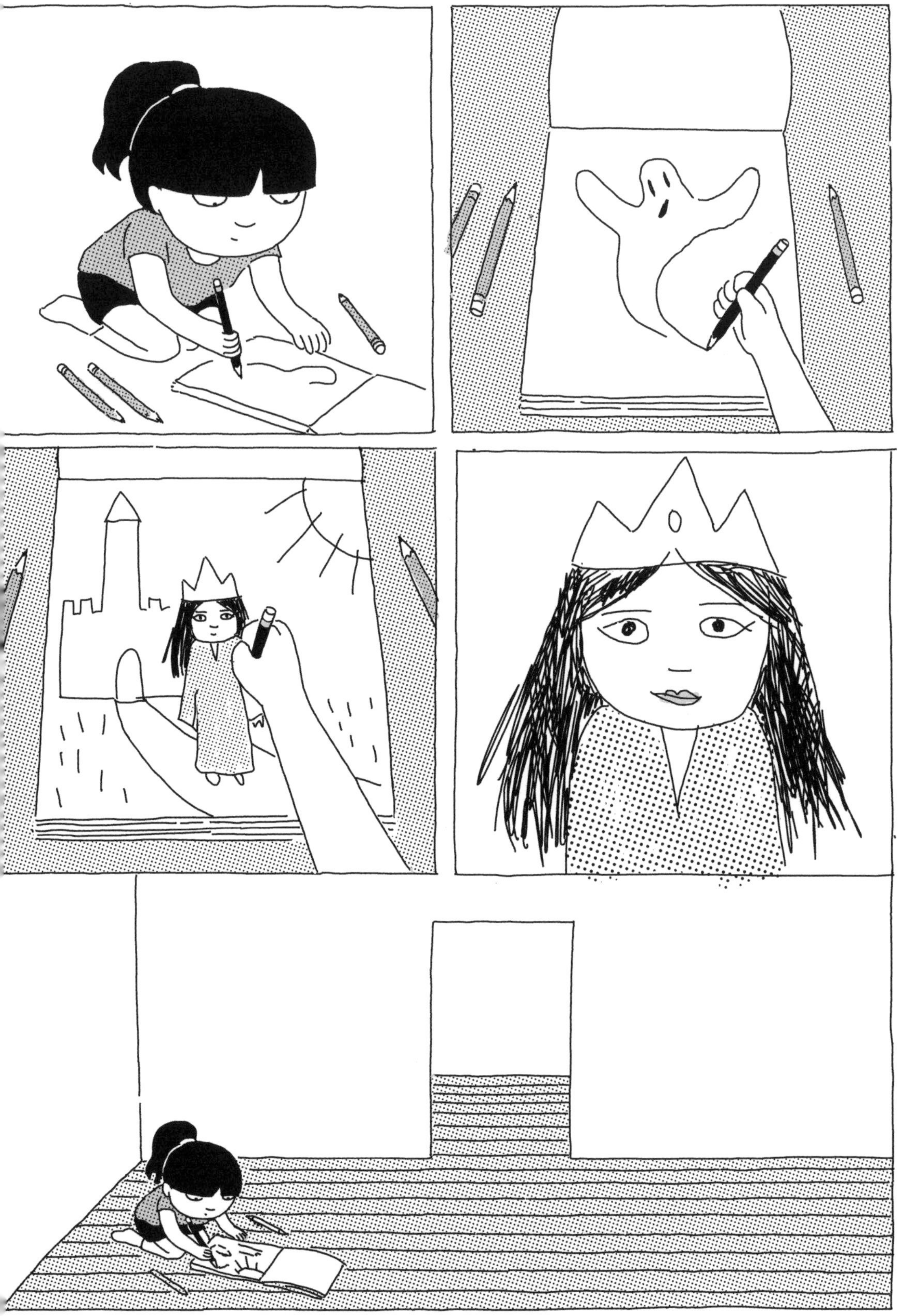

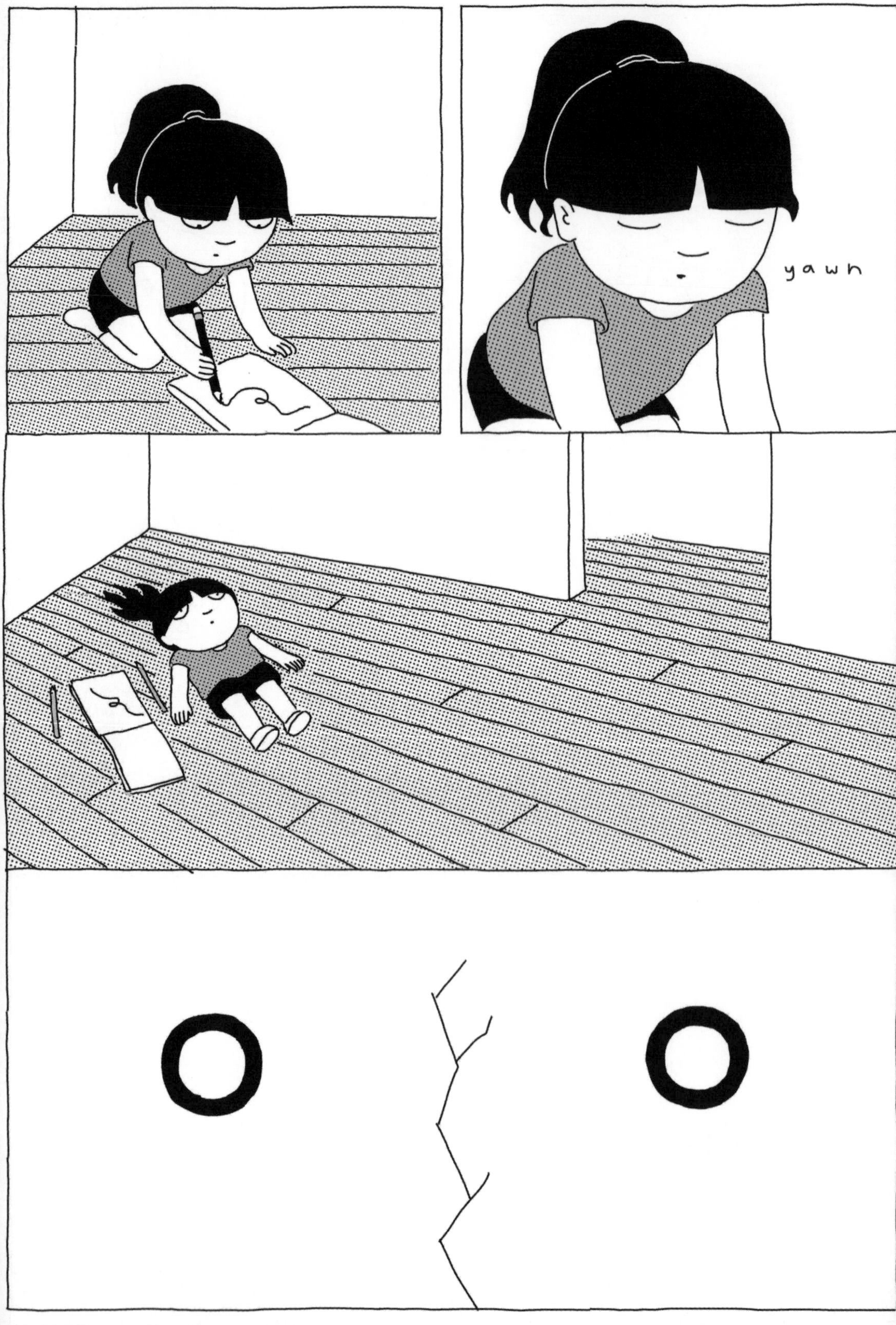
yawn

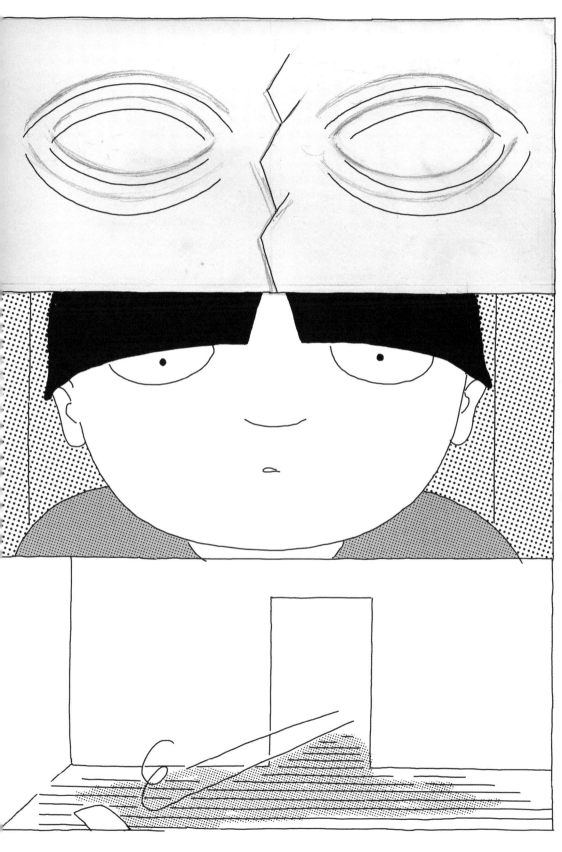

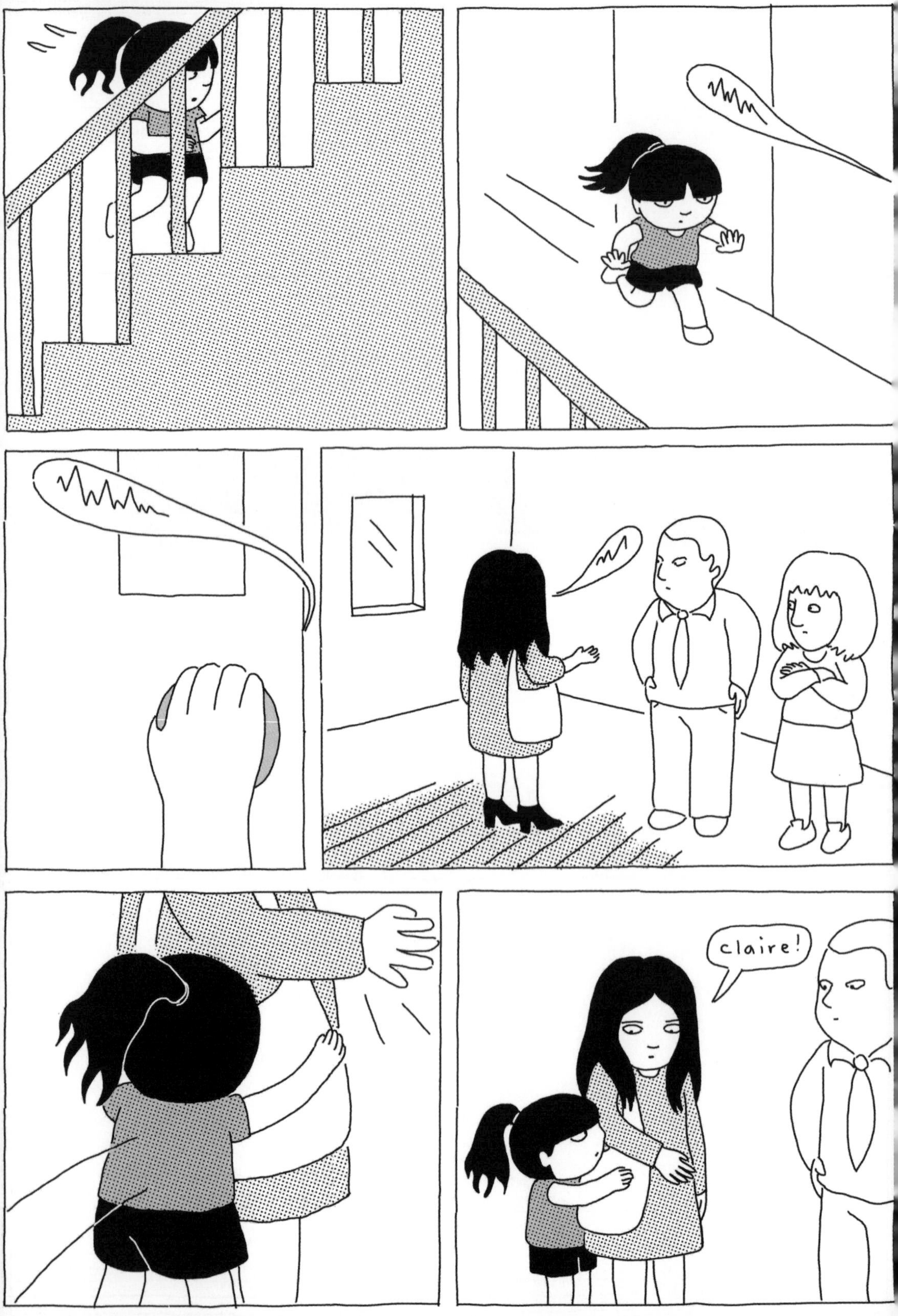
claire!

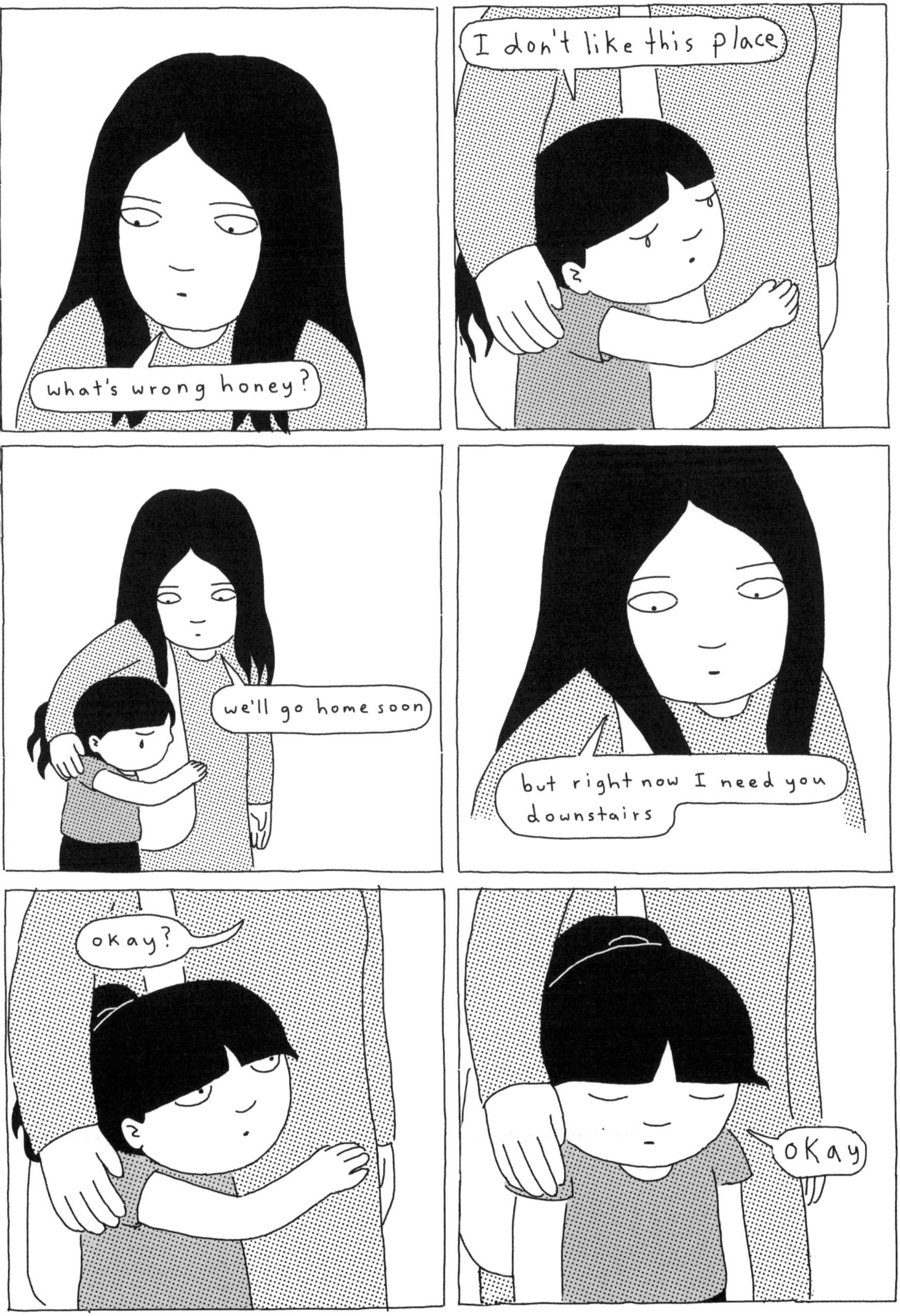
what's wrong honey?
I don't like this place
we'll go home soon
but right now I need you downstairs
okay?
OKay

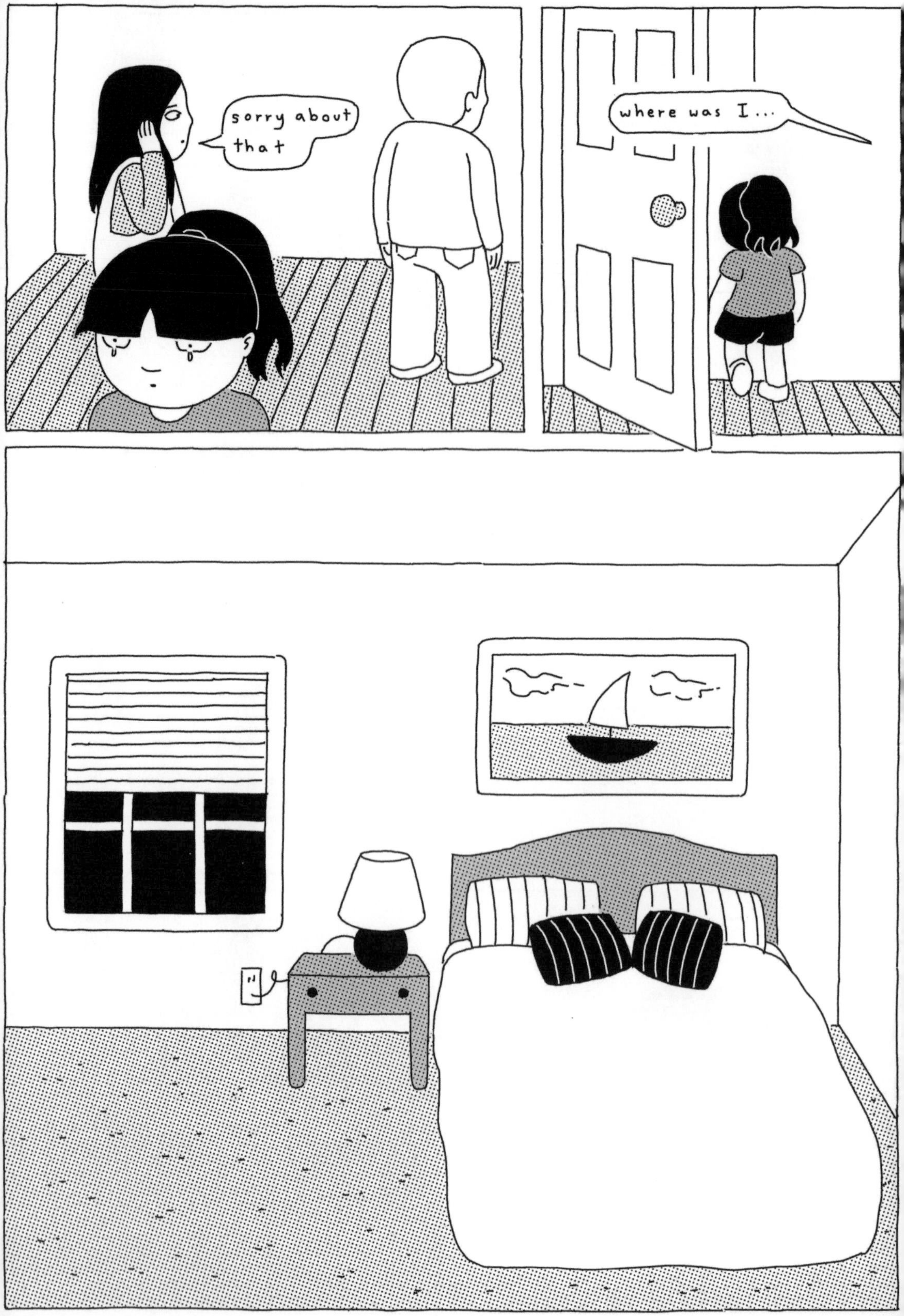
sorry about that
where was I...

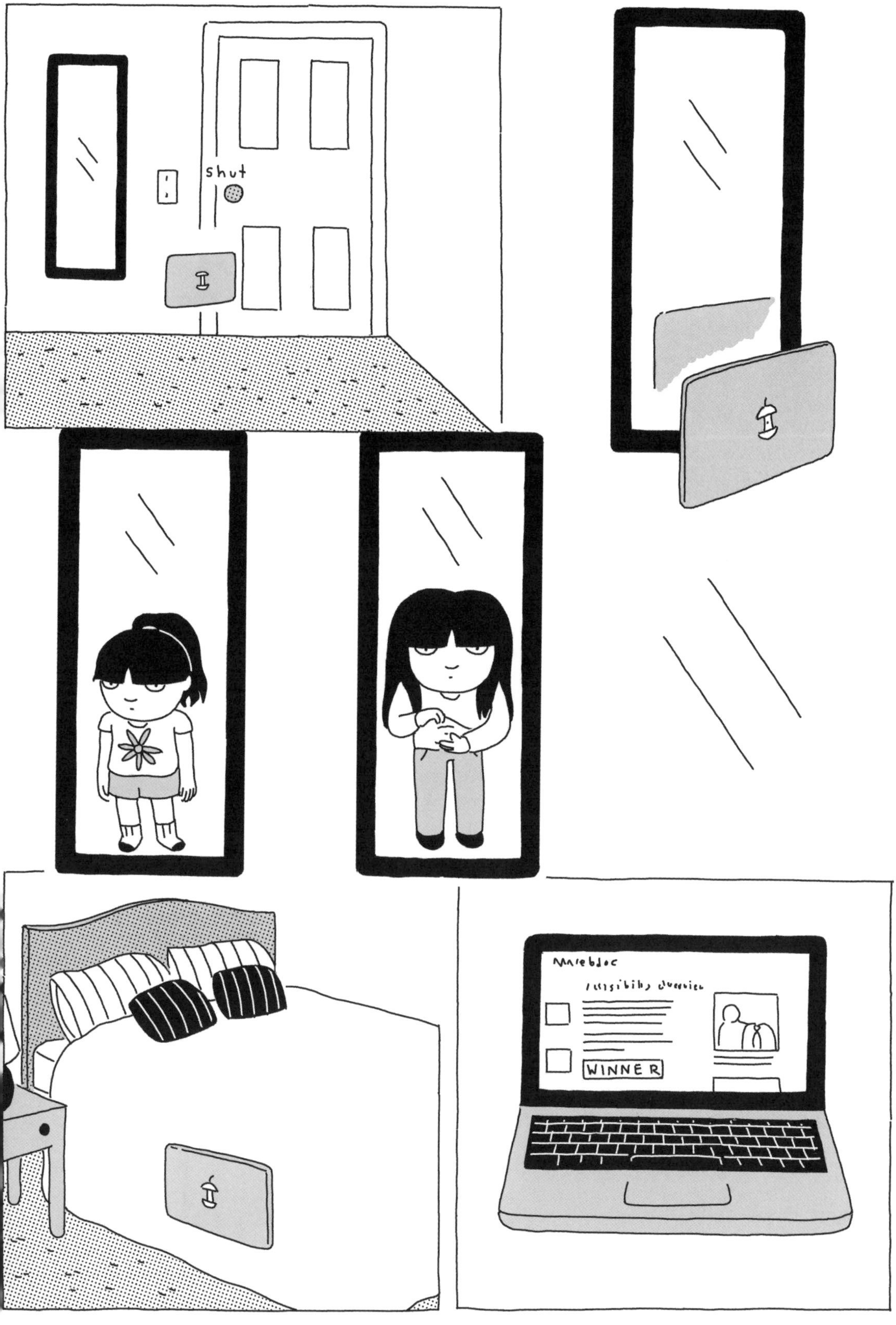
shut
WINNER

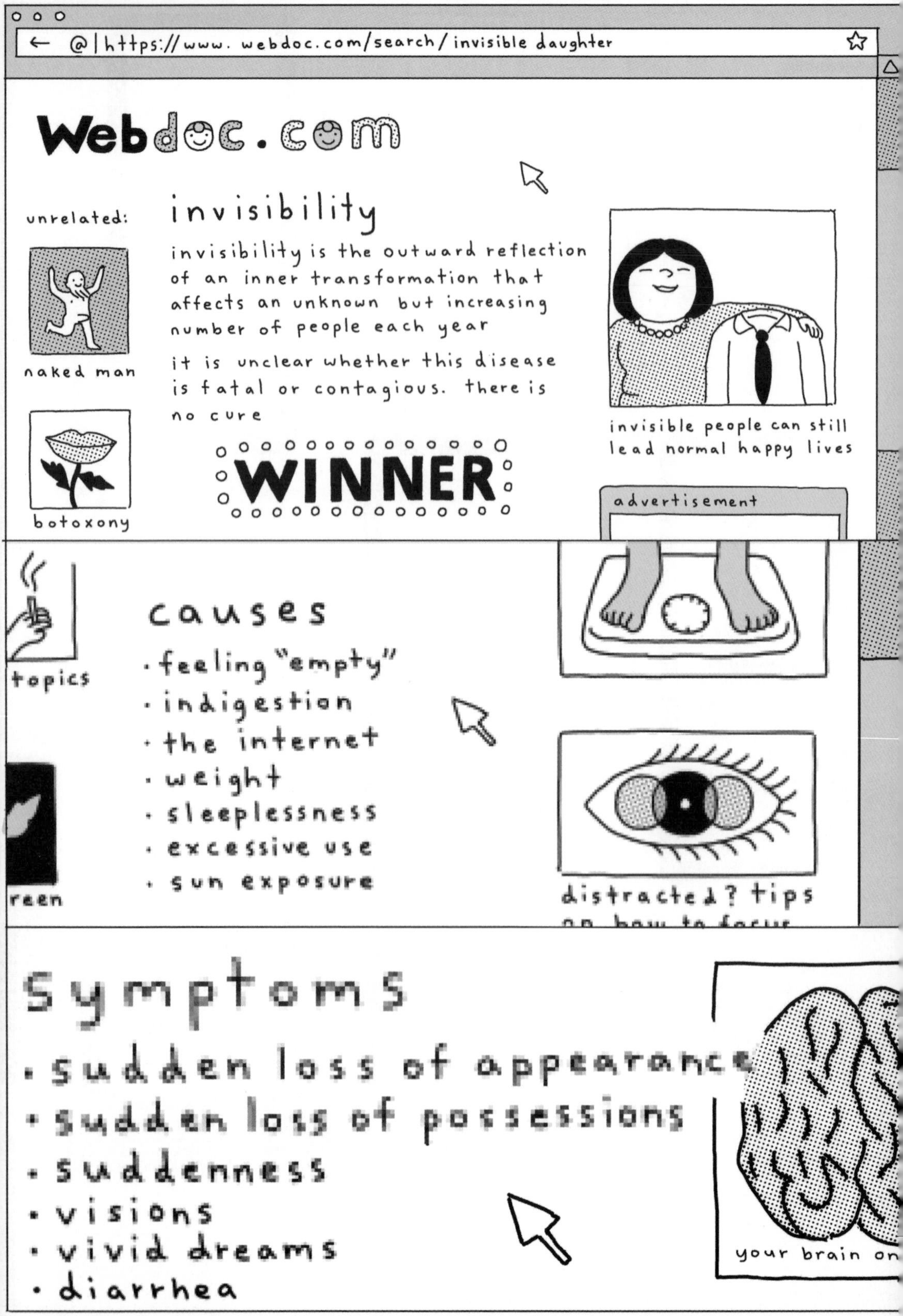

@|https://www.webdoc.com/search/invisible daughter
Webdoc.com
unrelated:
naked man
botoxony
invisibility
invisibility is the outward reflection of an inner transformation that affects an unknown but increasing number of people each year
it is unclear whether this disease is fatal or contagious. there is no cure
WINNER
invisible people can still lead normal happy lives
advertisement
topics
reen
causes
· feeling "empty"
· indigestion
· the internet
· weight
· sleeplessness
· excessive use
· sun exposure
distracted? tips
symptoms
· sudden loss of appearance
· sudden loss of possessions
· suddenness
· visions
· vivid dreams
· diarrhea
your brain on

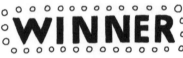

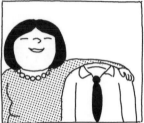

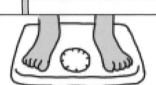

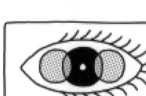

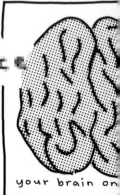

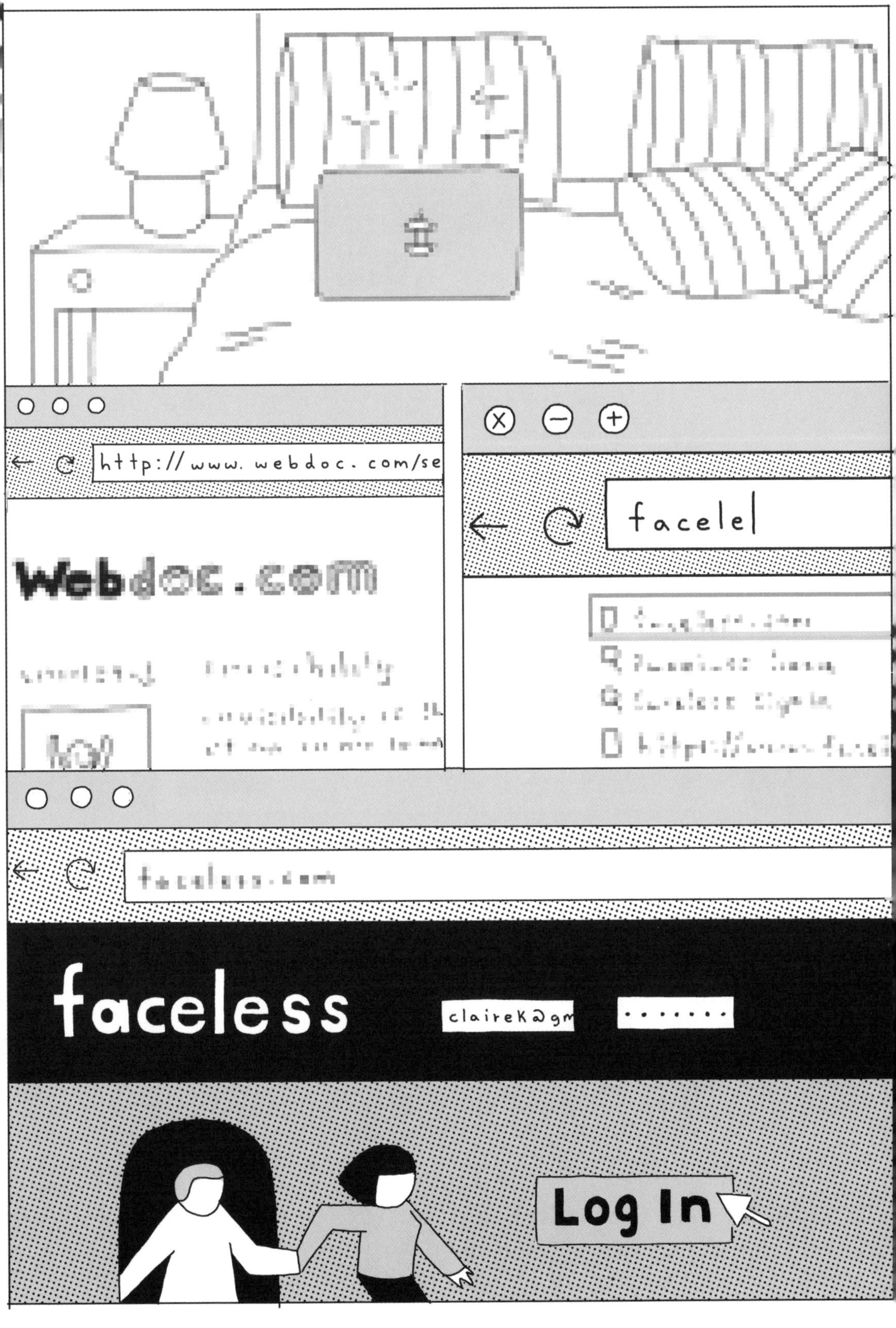
http://www.webdoc.com/se
facelel
Webdoc.com
faceless
claireK@gm
Log In

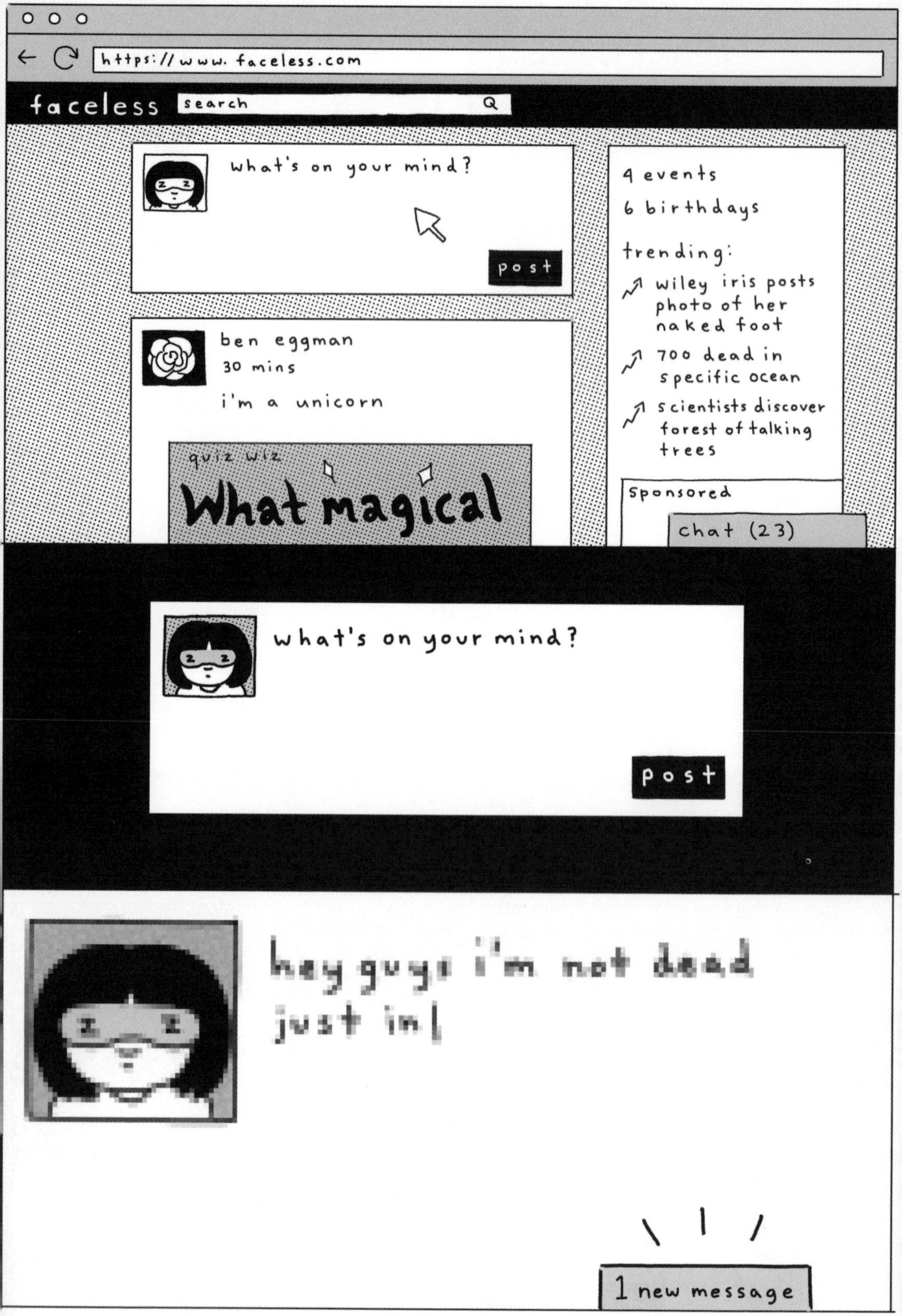
https://www.faceless.com
faceless
search
what's on your mind?
post
ben eggman
30 mins
i'm a unicorn
quiz wiz
What magical
4 events
6 birthdays
trending:
wiley iris posts photo of her naked foot
700 dead in specific ocean
scientists discover forest of talking trees
sponsored
chat (23)
what's on your mind?
post
hey guys i'm not dead
just in
1 new message

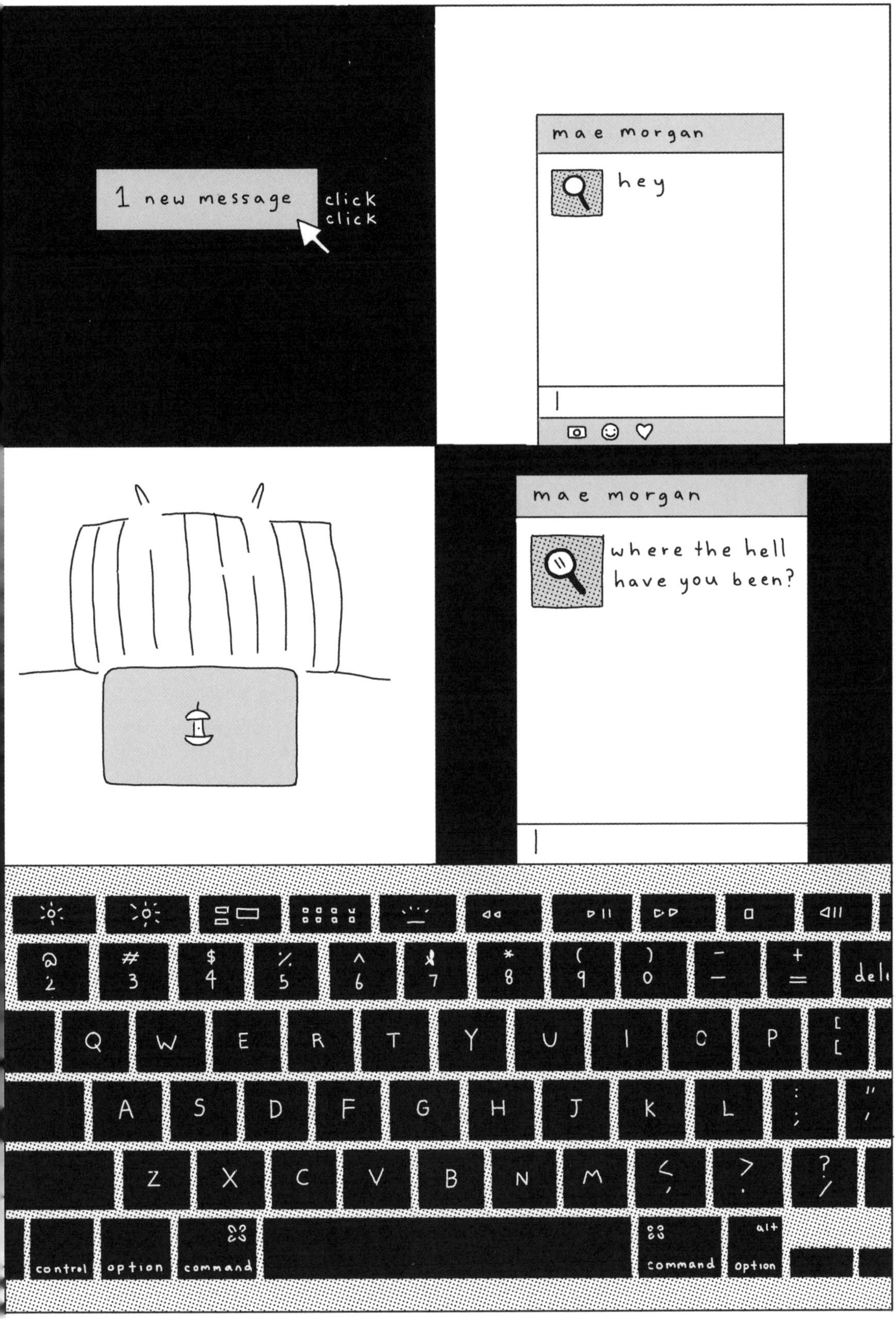
1 new message
click
click
mae morgan
hey
mae morgan
where the hell
have you been?
control
option
command
command
alt
option

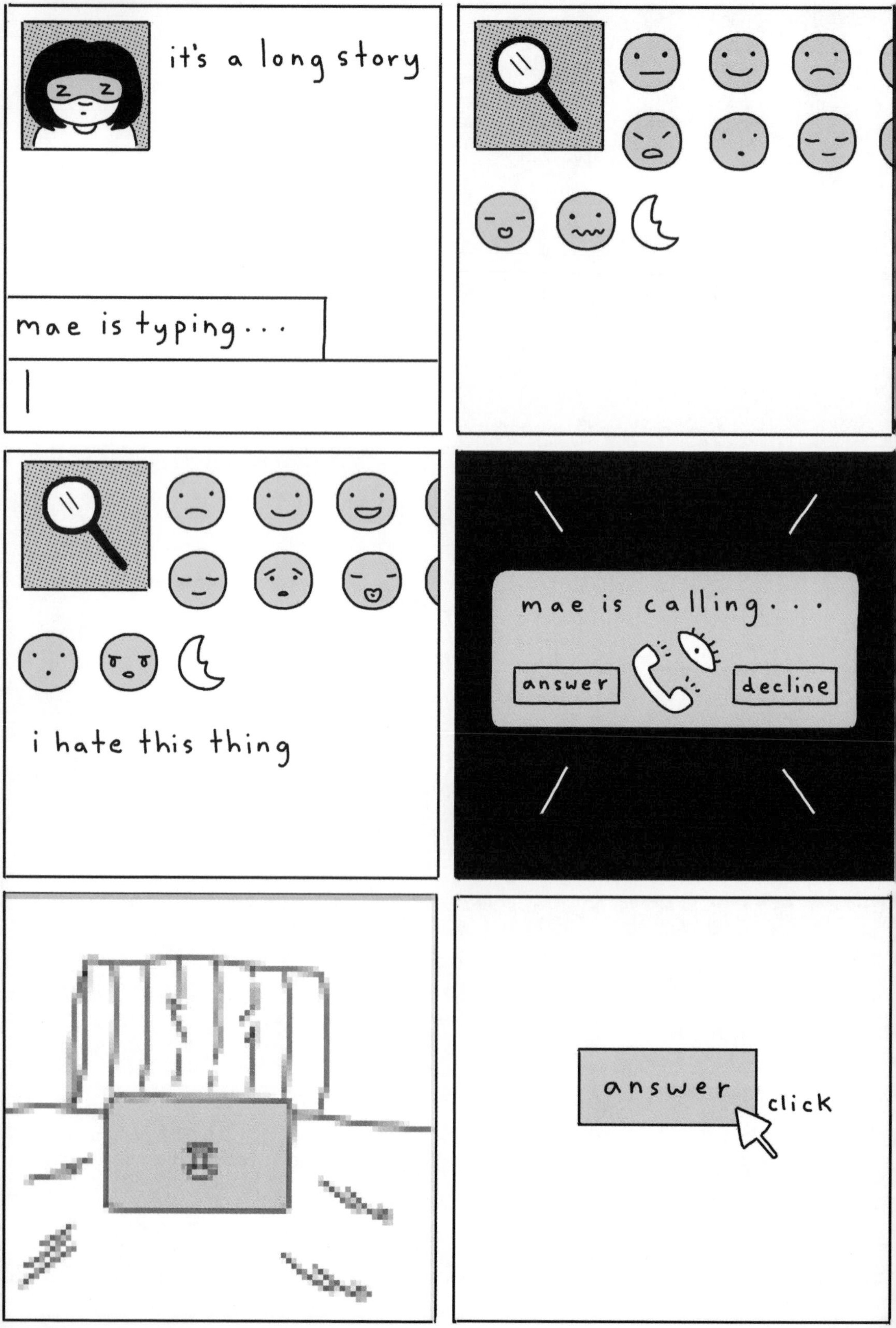

it's a long story
mae is typing...
i hate this thing
mae is calling...
answer
decline
answer
click

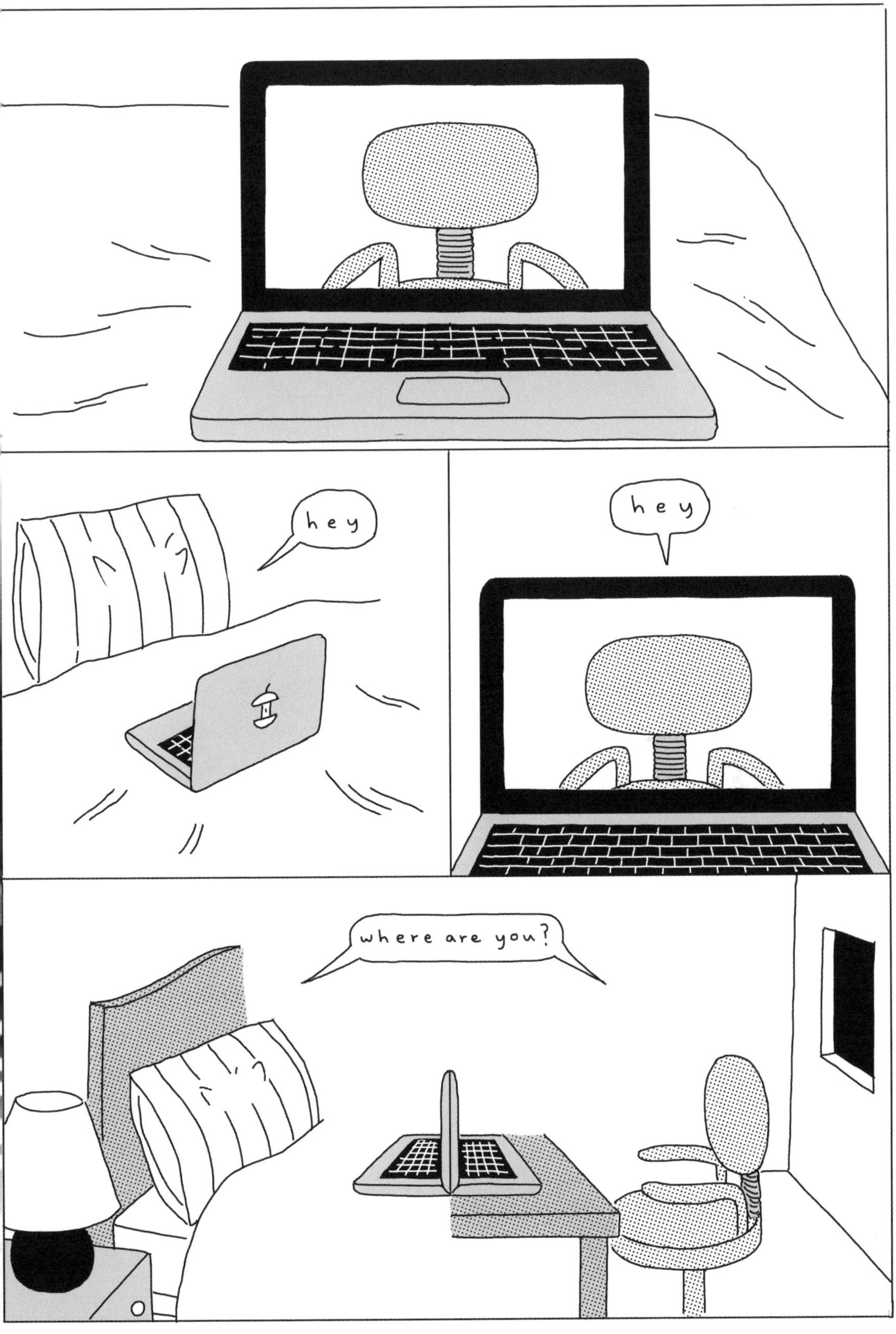
hey
hey
where are you?

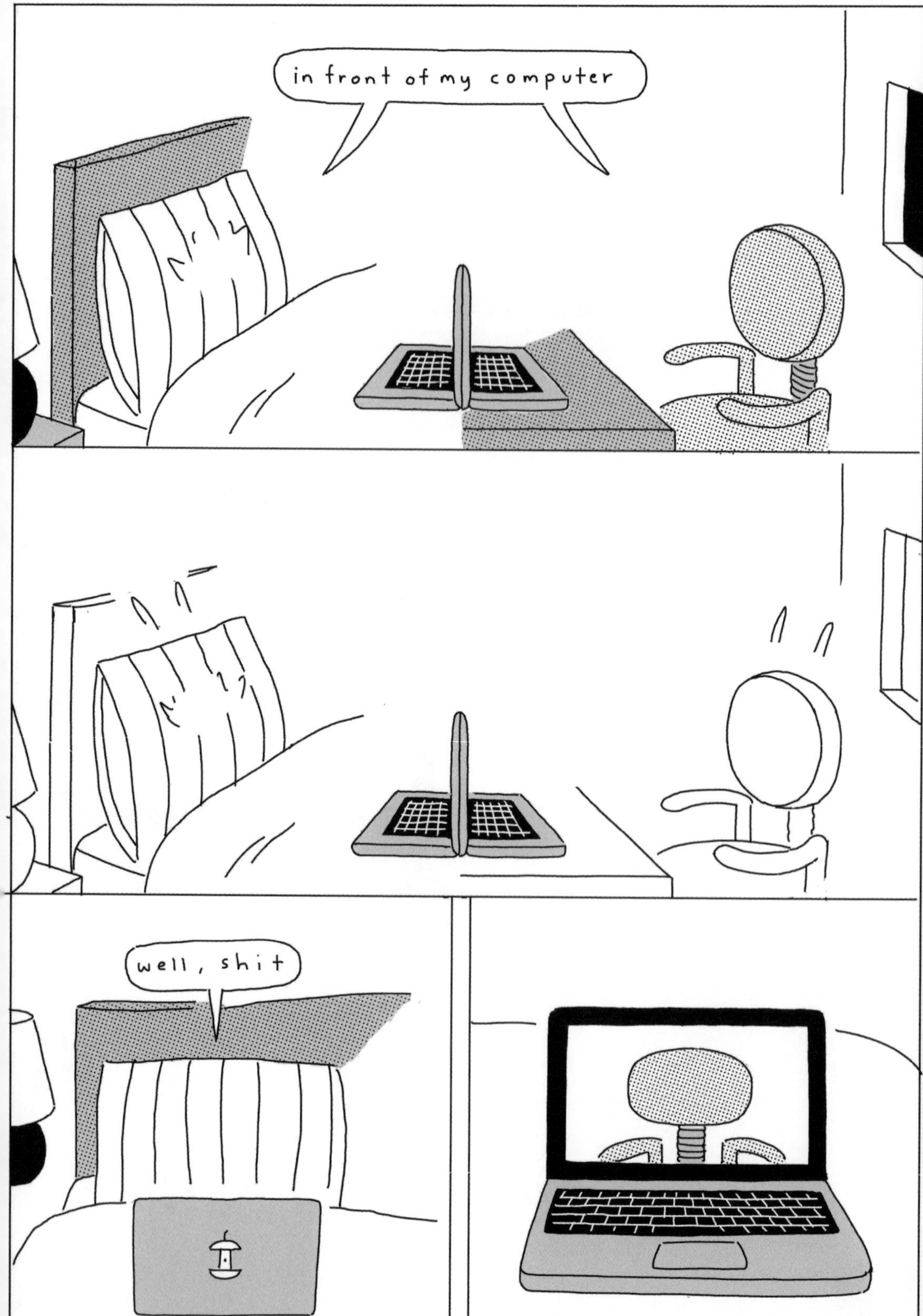
in front of my computer
well, shit

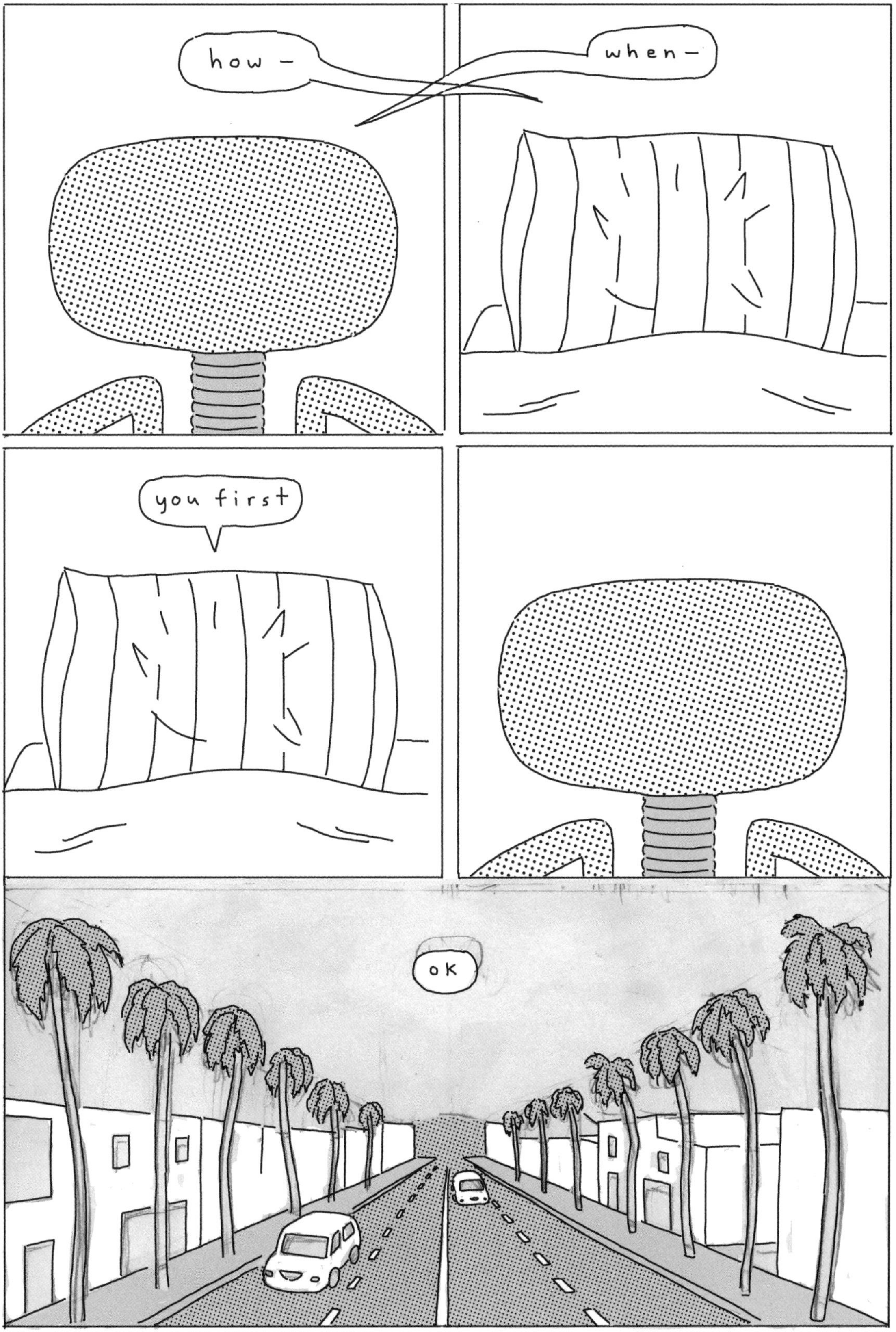
how -
when -
you first
ok

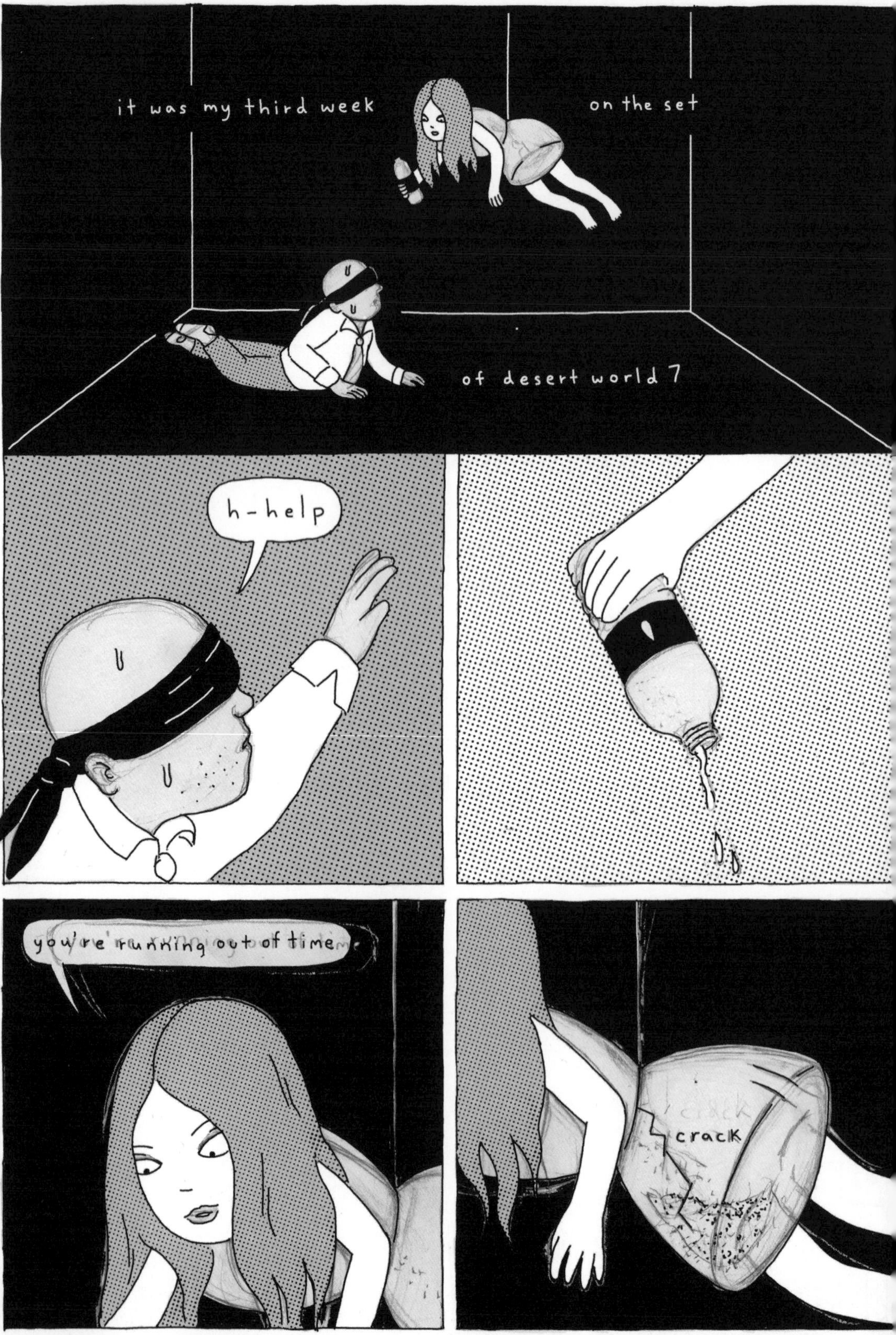
it was my third week
on the set
of desert world 7
h-help
you're running out of time
crack

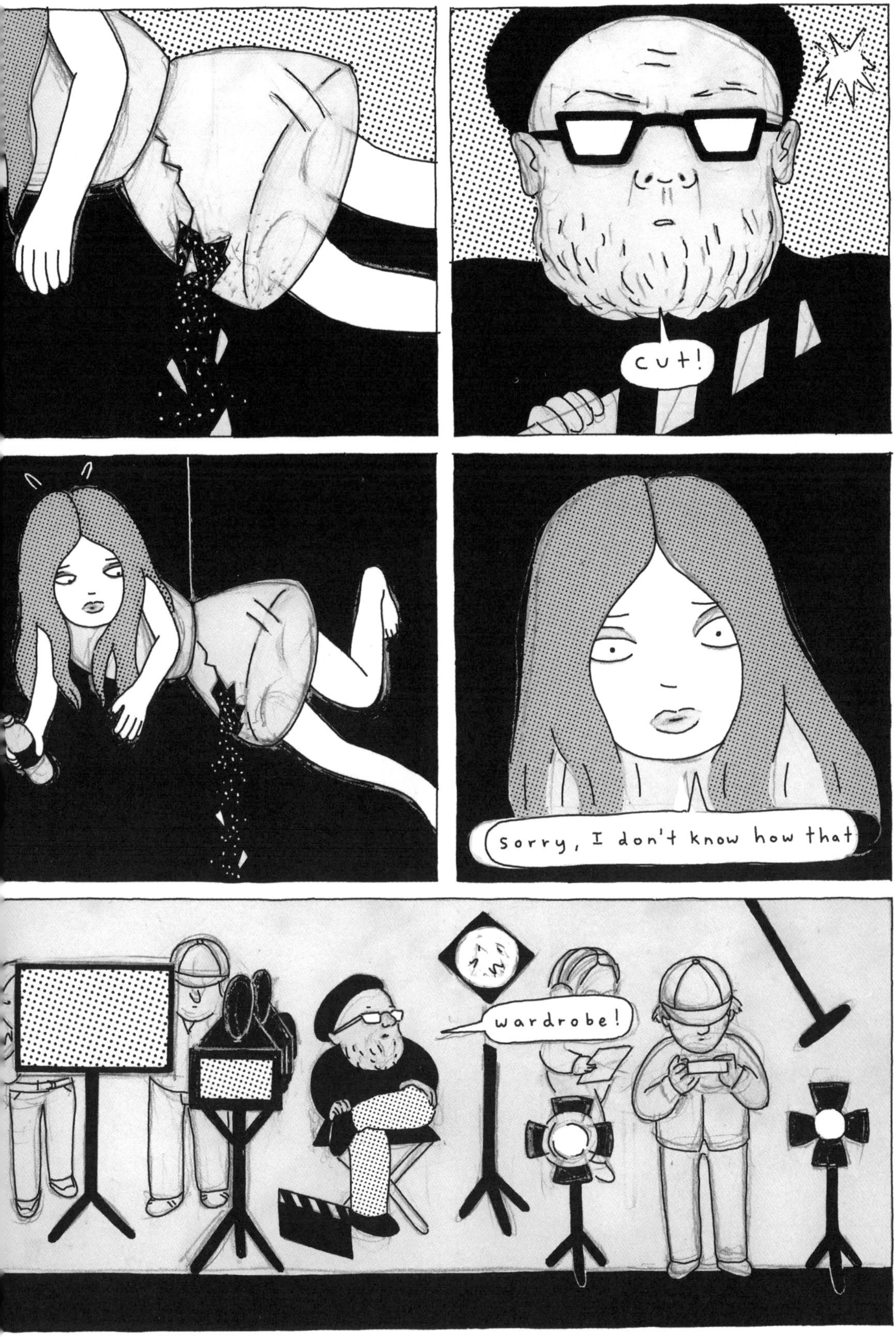
cut!
sorry, I don't know how that
wardrobe!

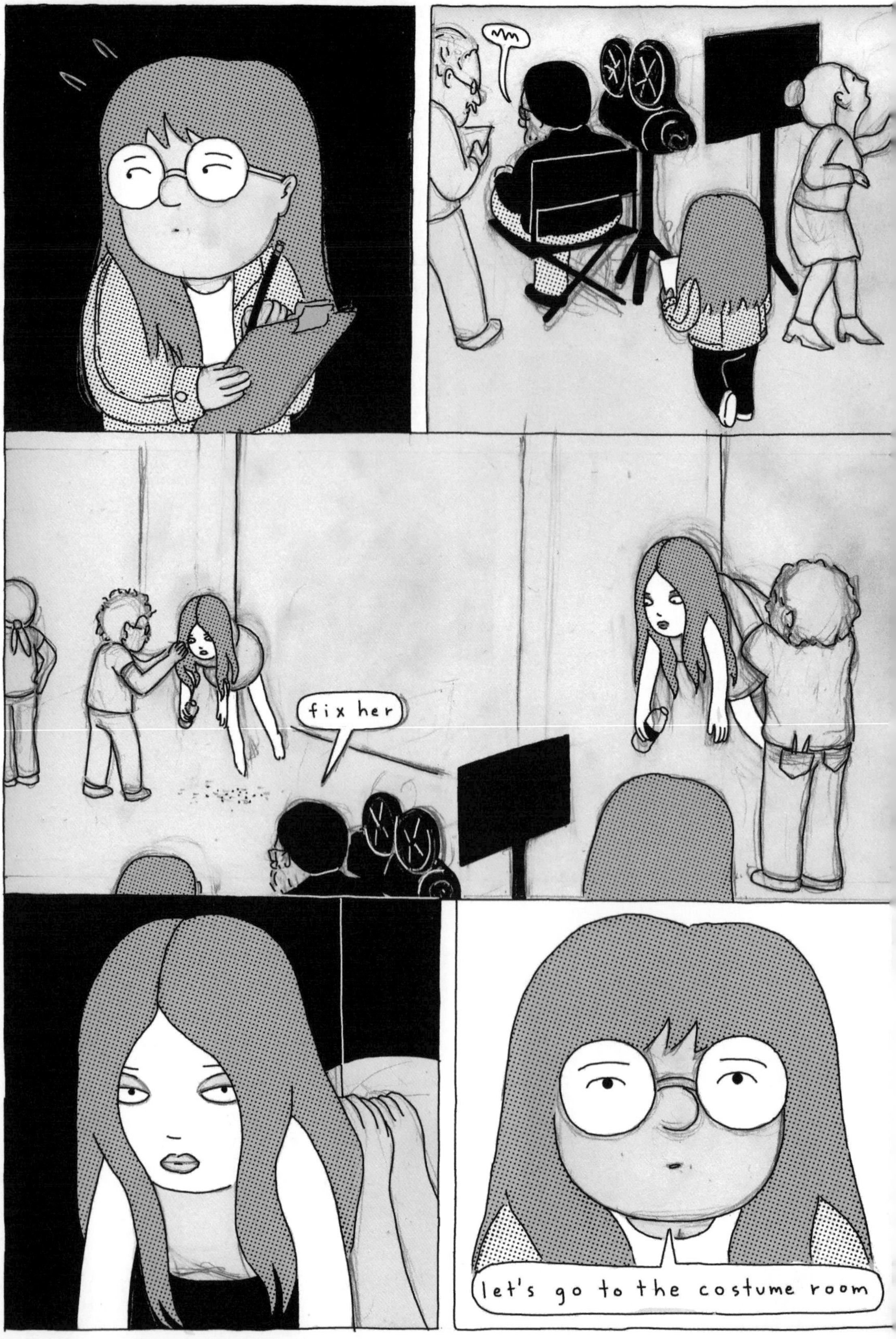
mm
fix her
let's go to the costume room

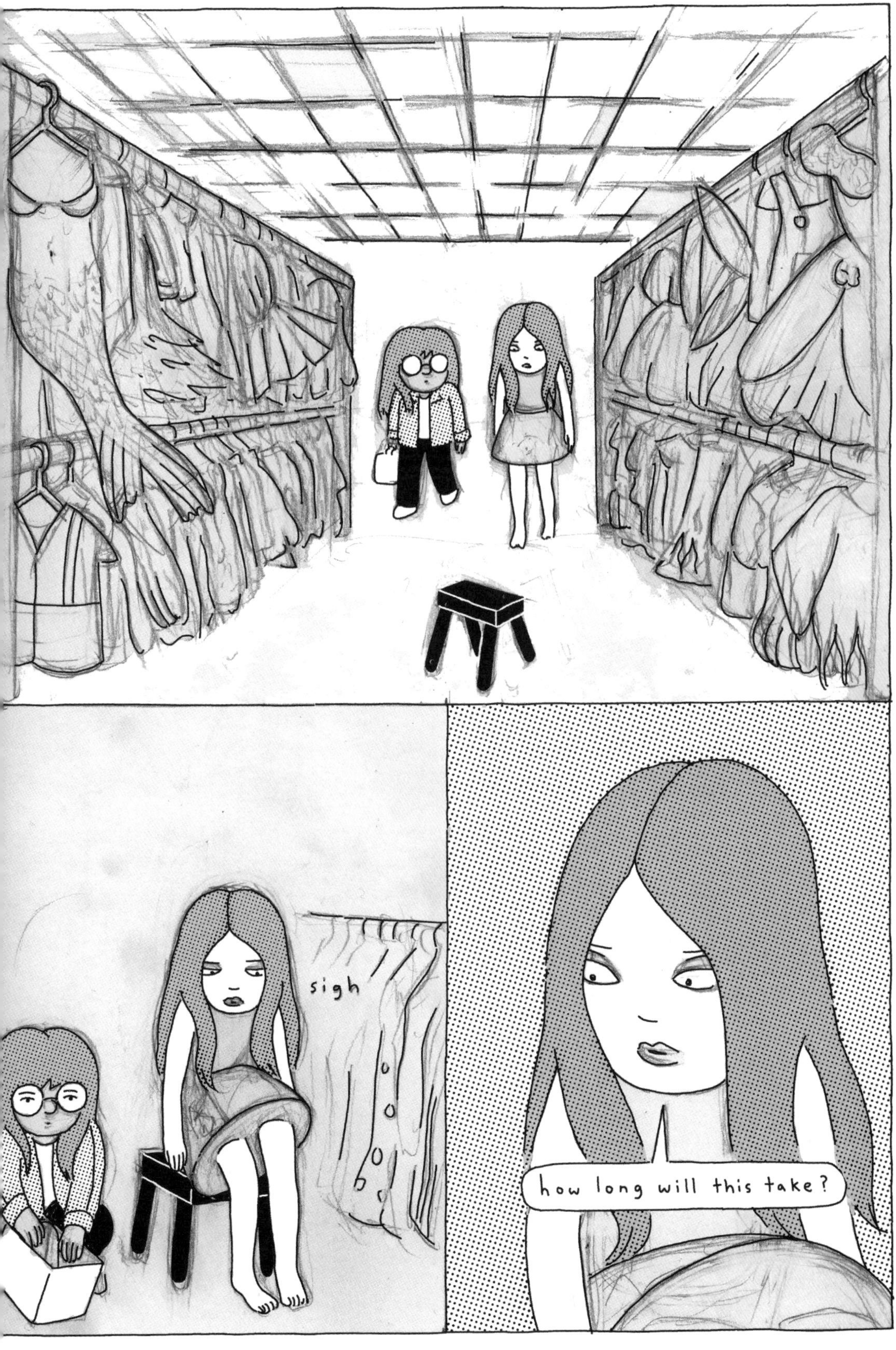
sigh
how long will this take?

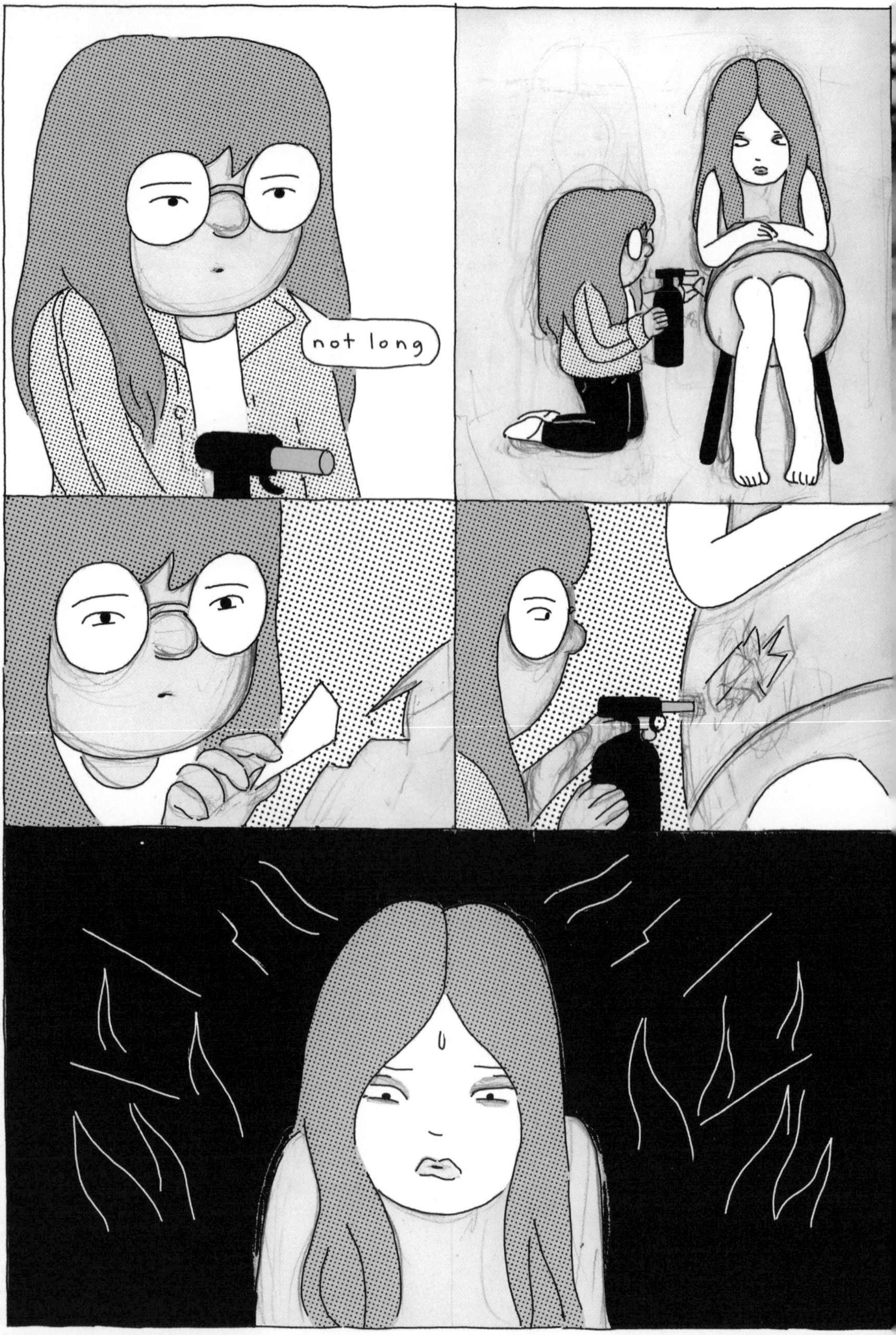
not long

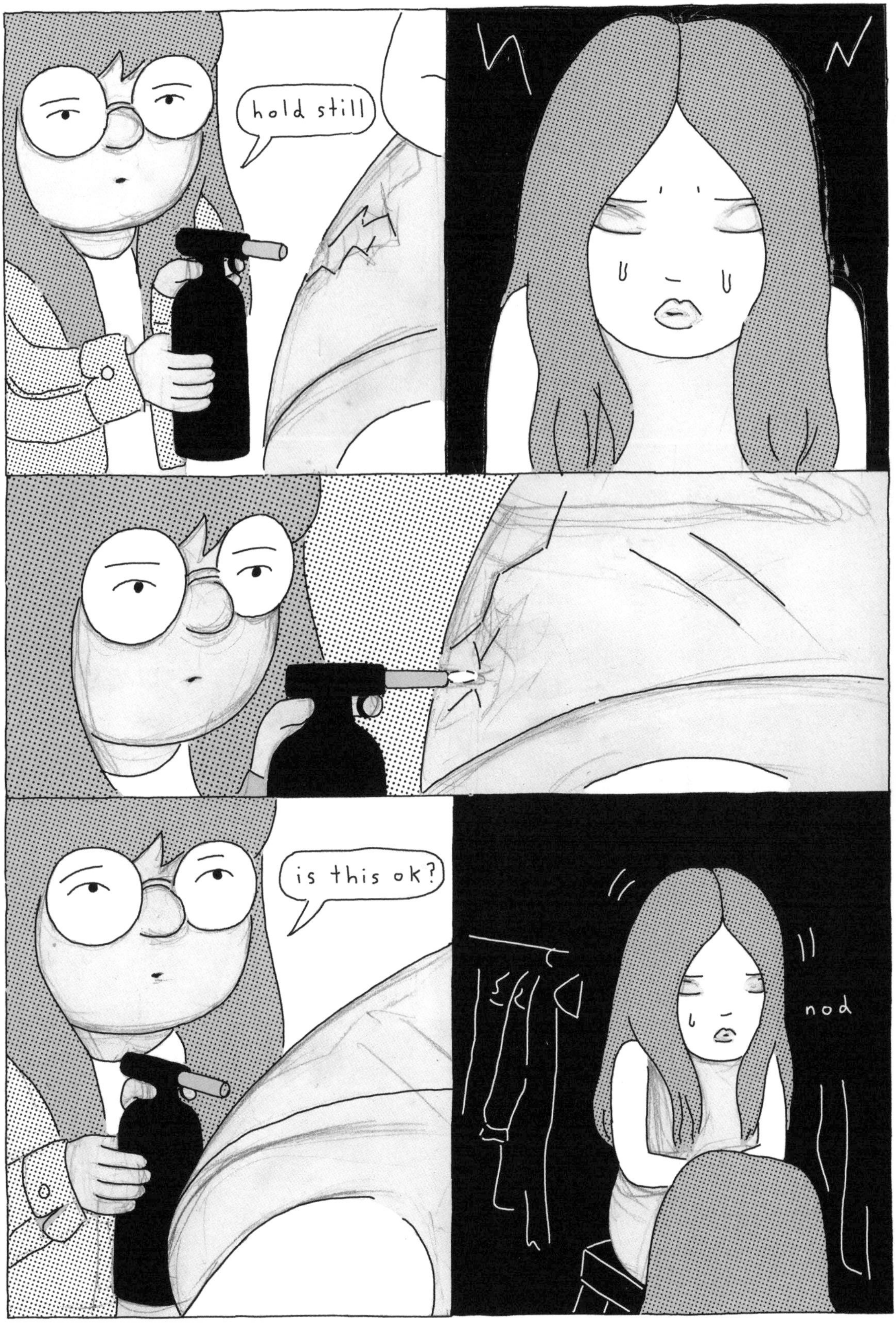
hold still
is this ok?
nod

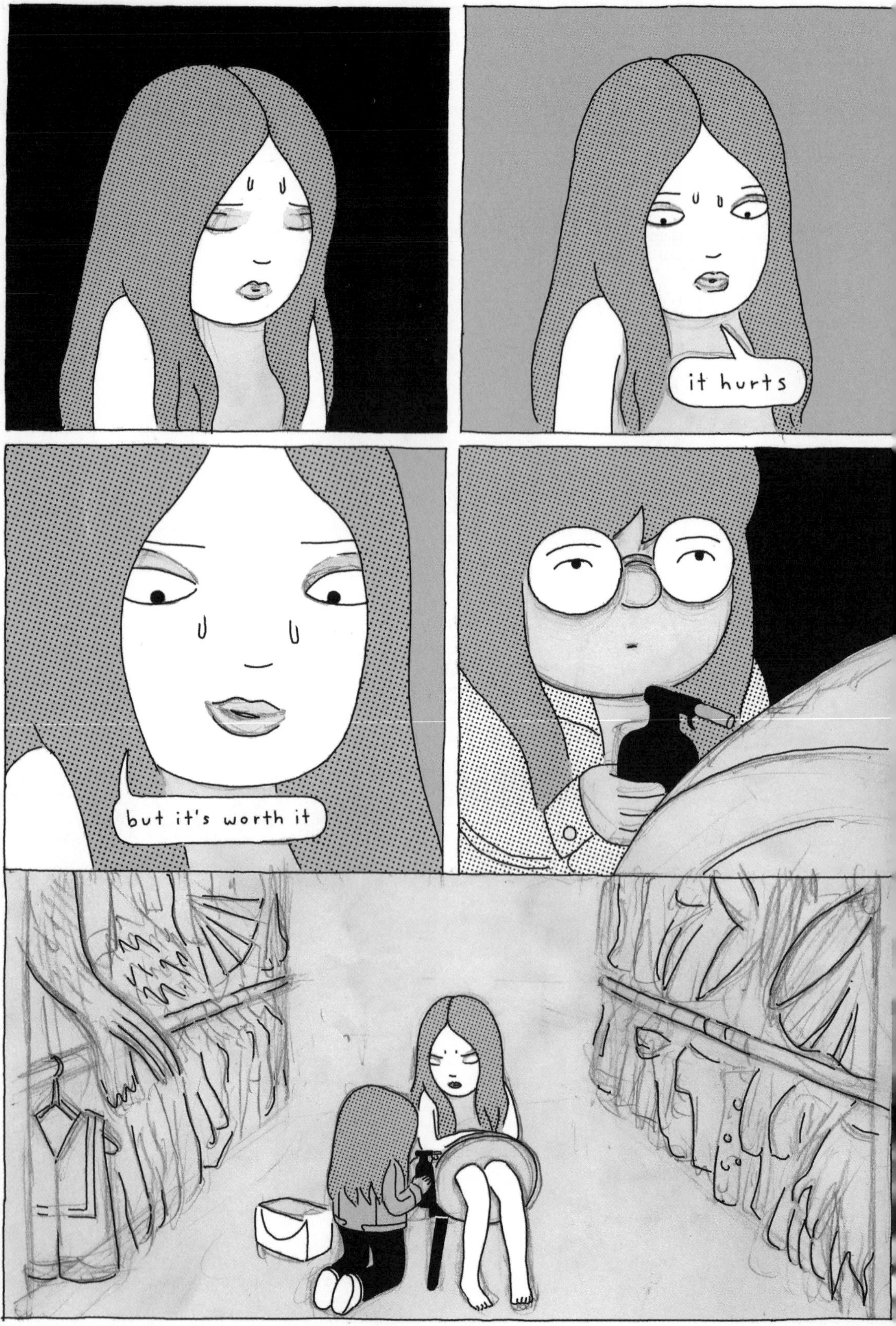
it hurts
but it's worth it

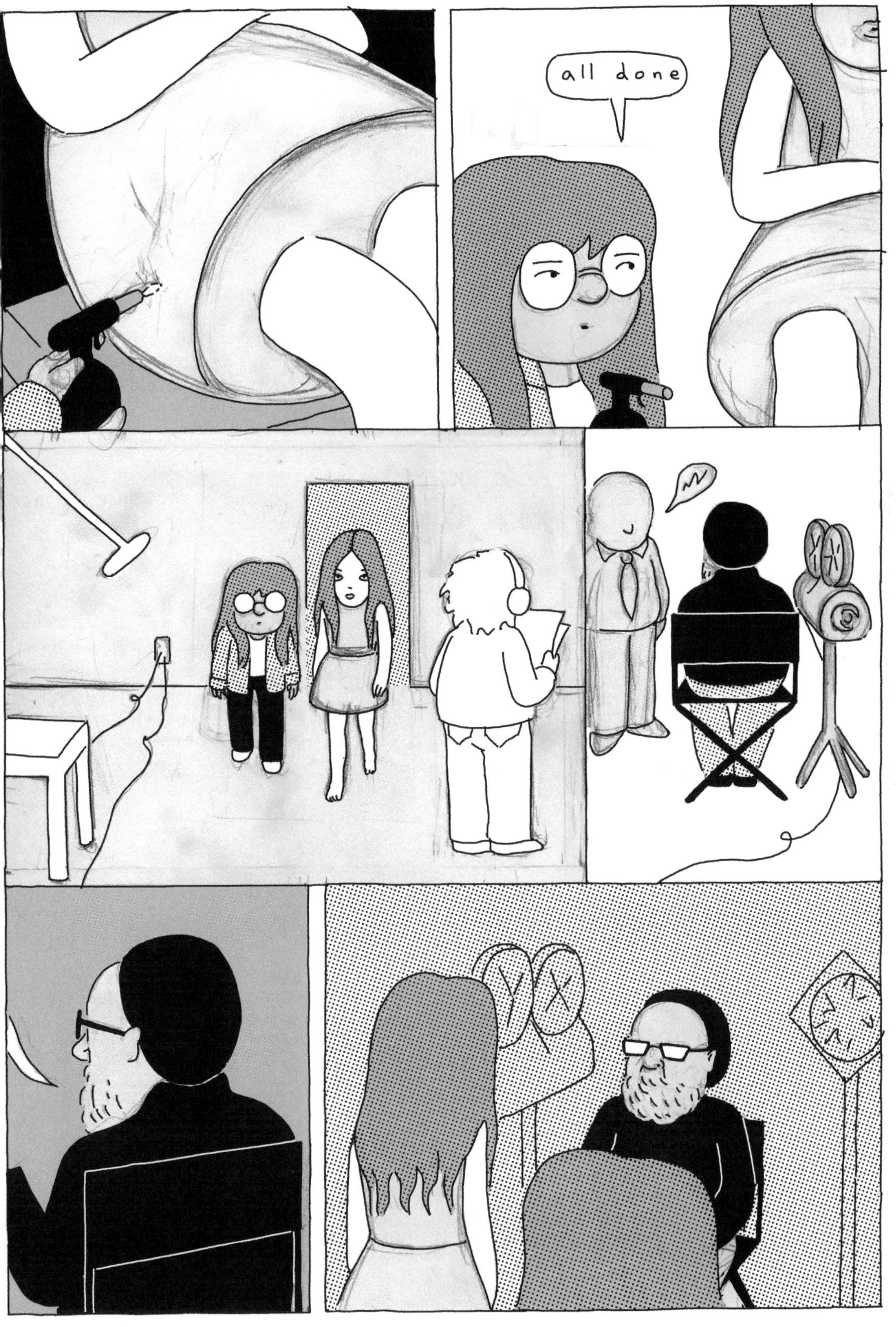
all done

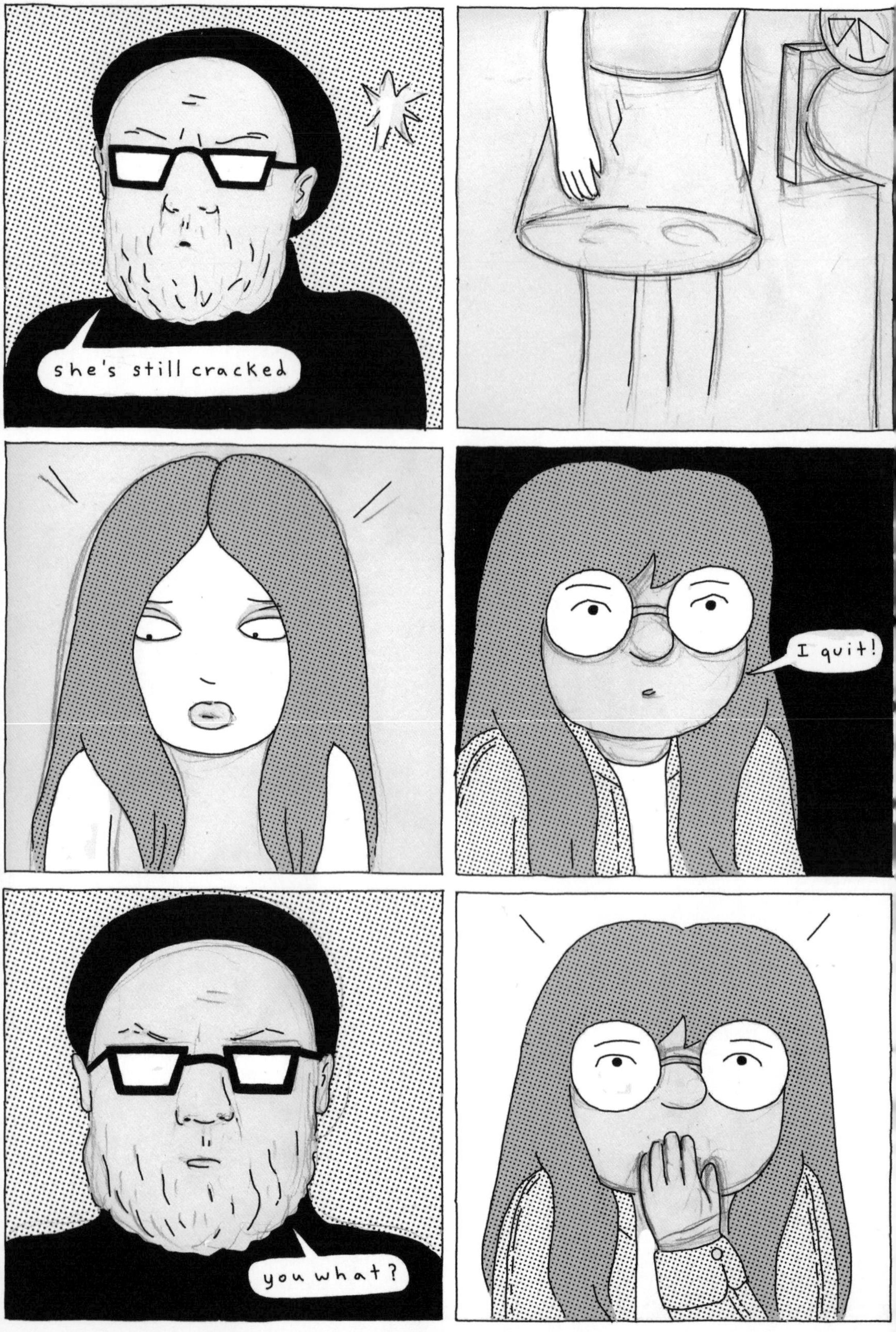
she's still cracked
I quit!
you what?

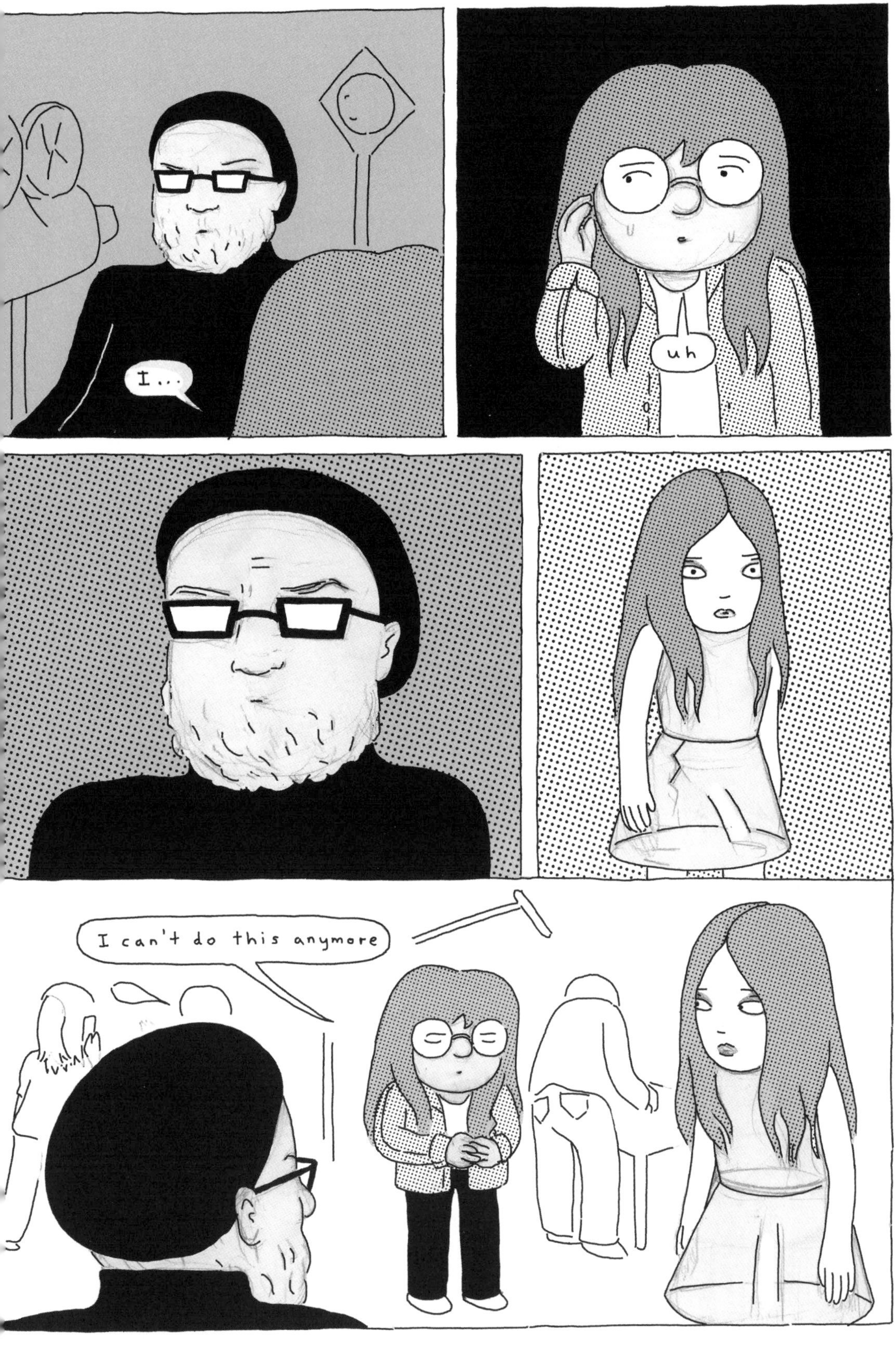
I...
uh
I can't do this anymore

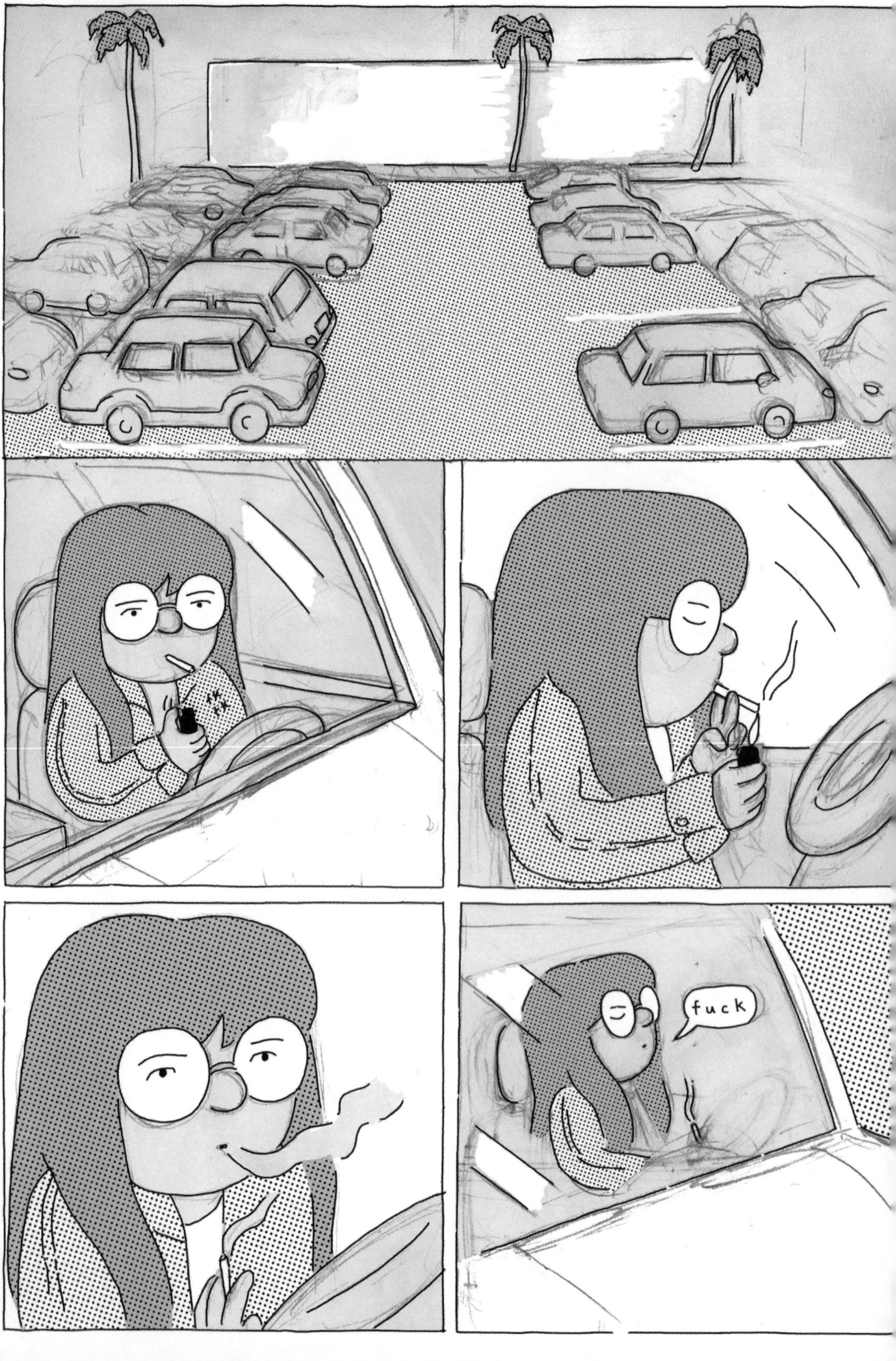
fuck

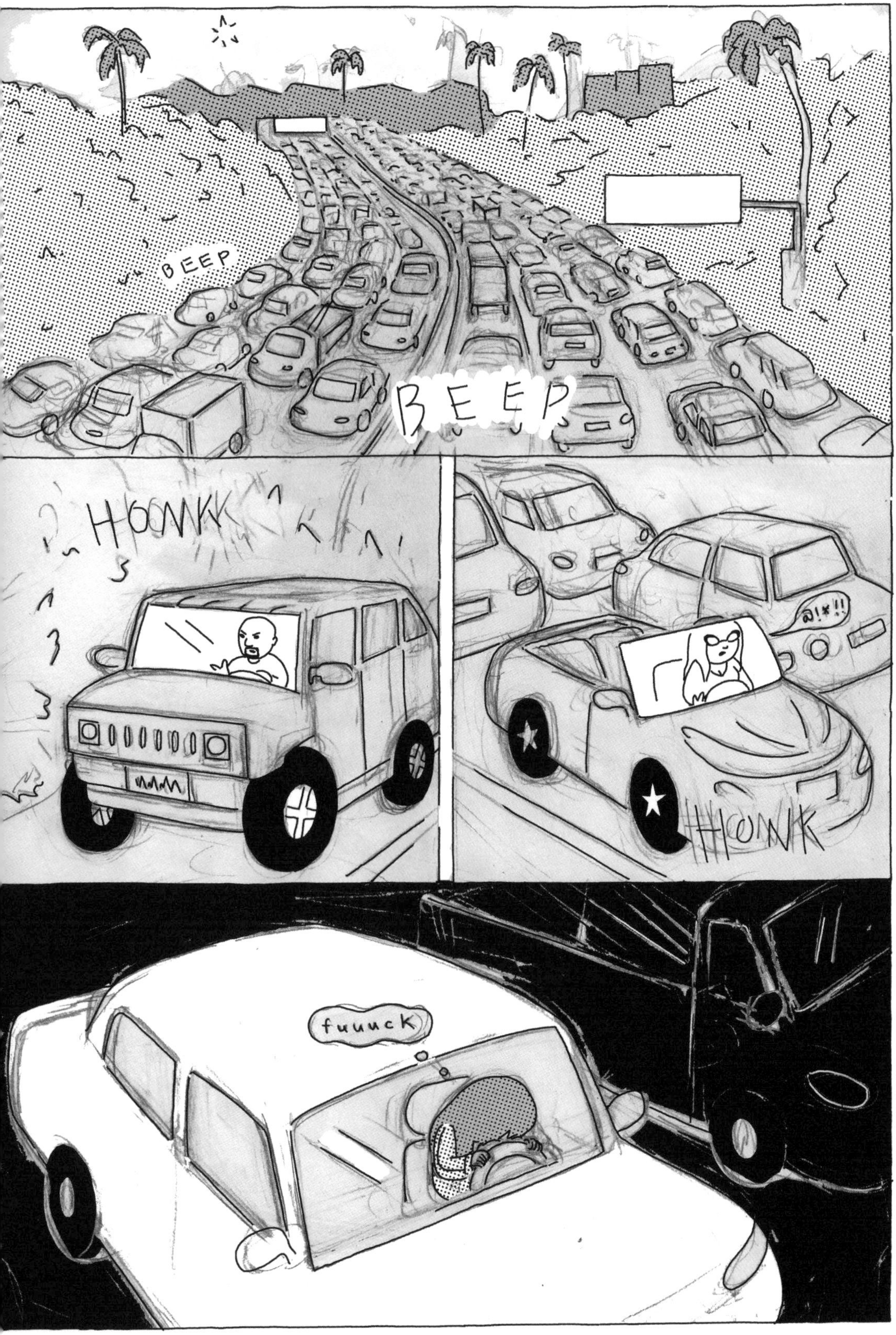
BEEP
BEEP
HONKK
@!*!!
HONK
fuuuck

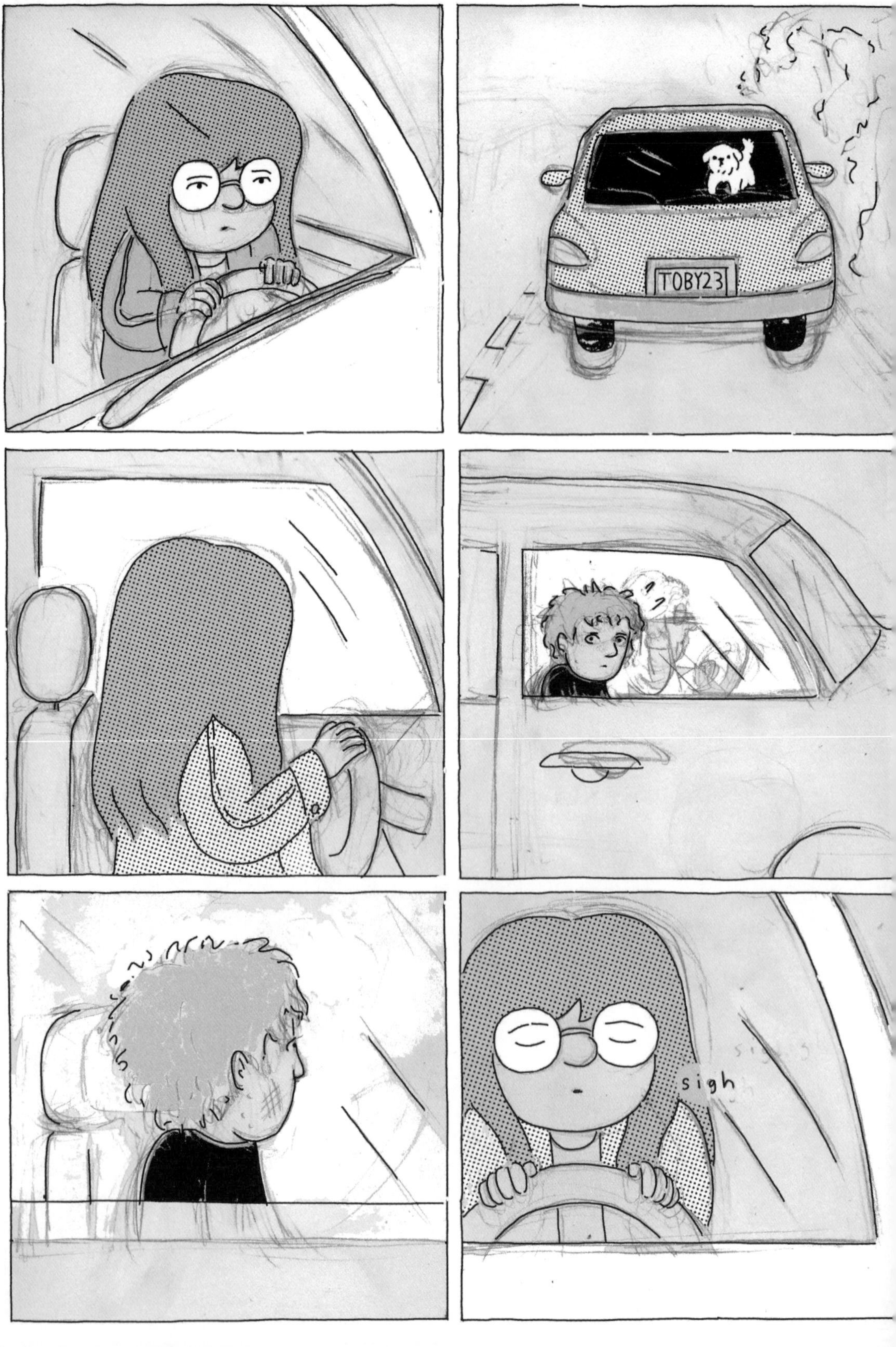
TOBY23
sigh

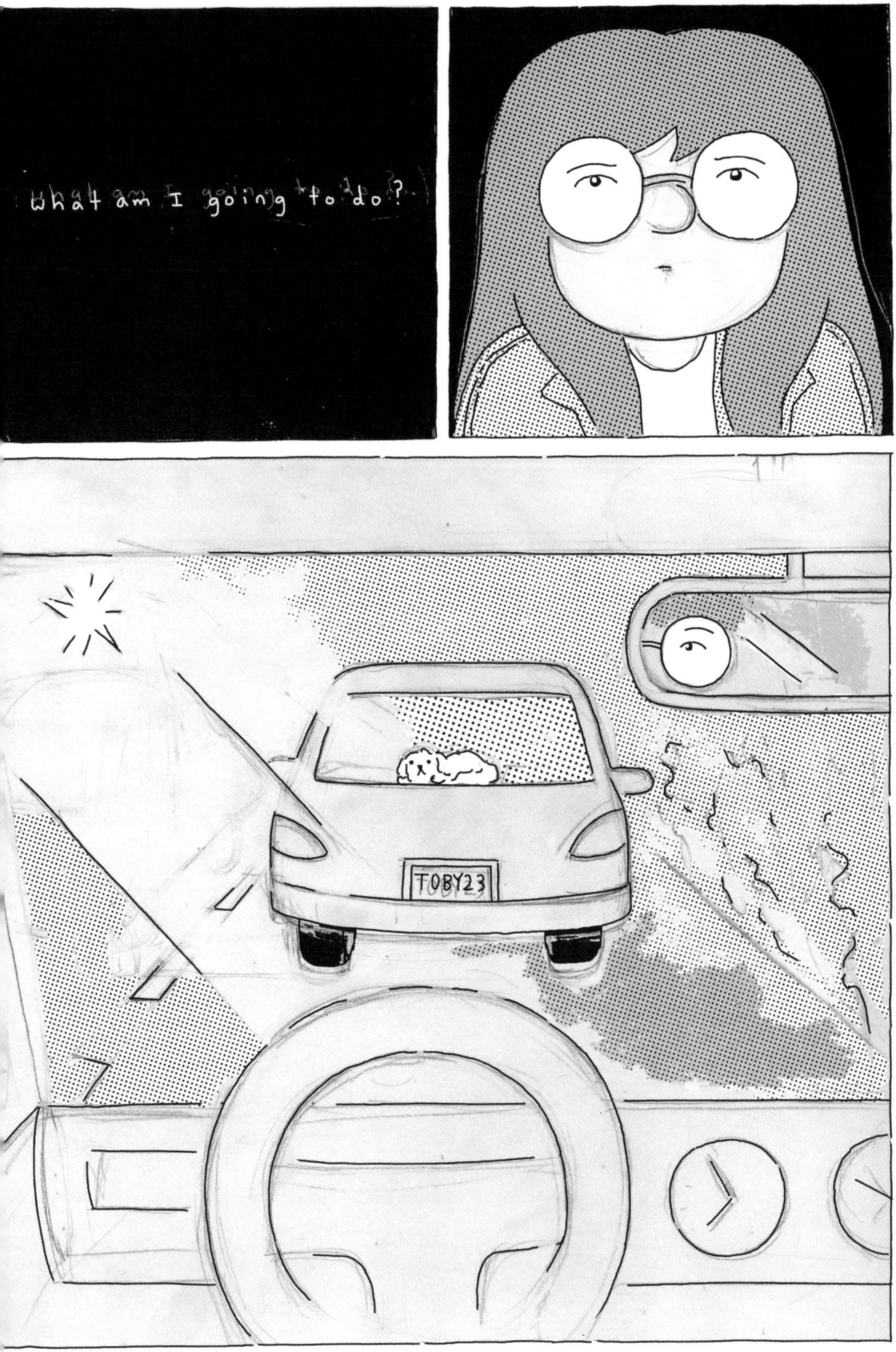
what am I going to do?
TOBY23

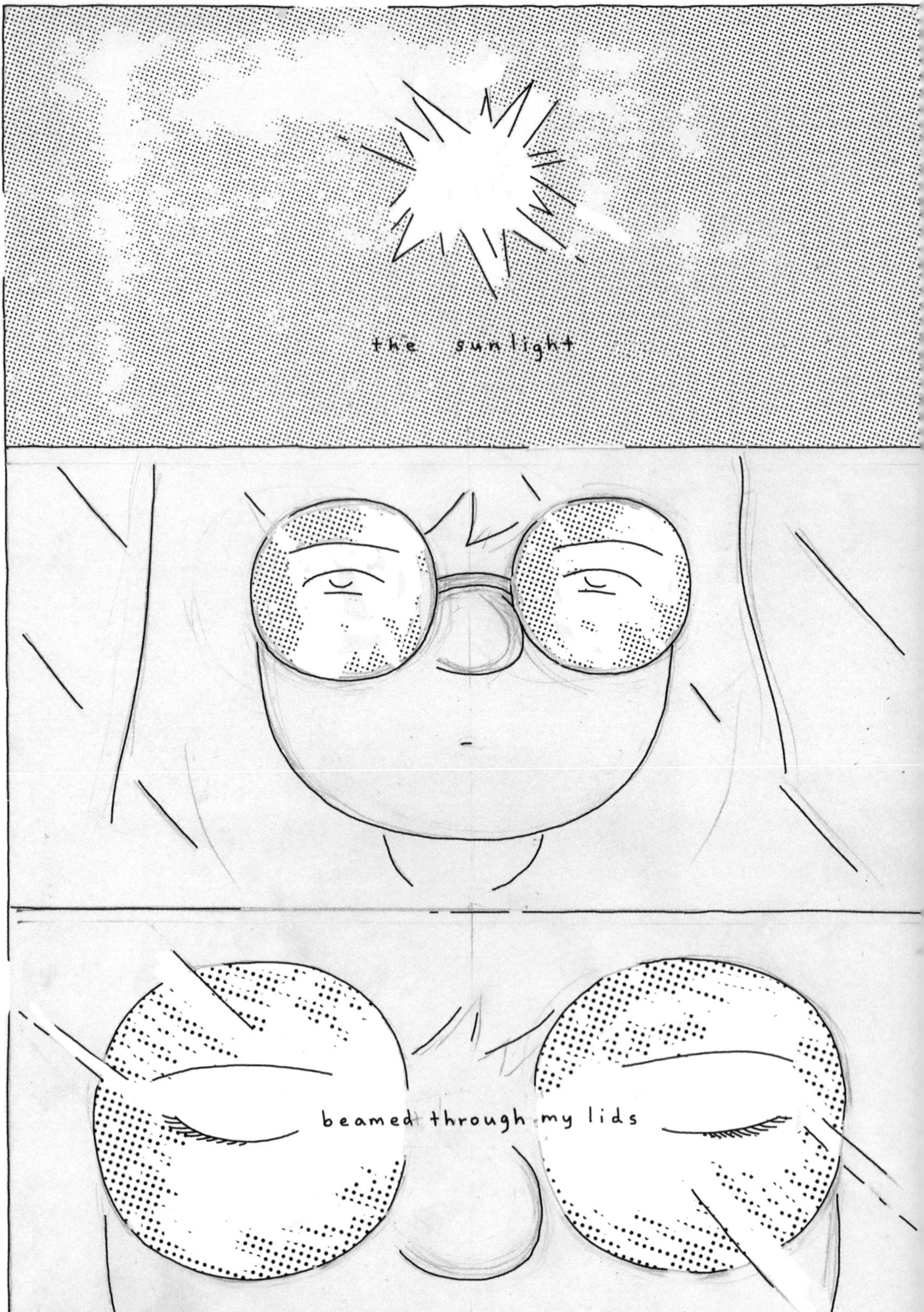
the sunlight
beamed through my lids

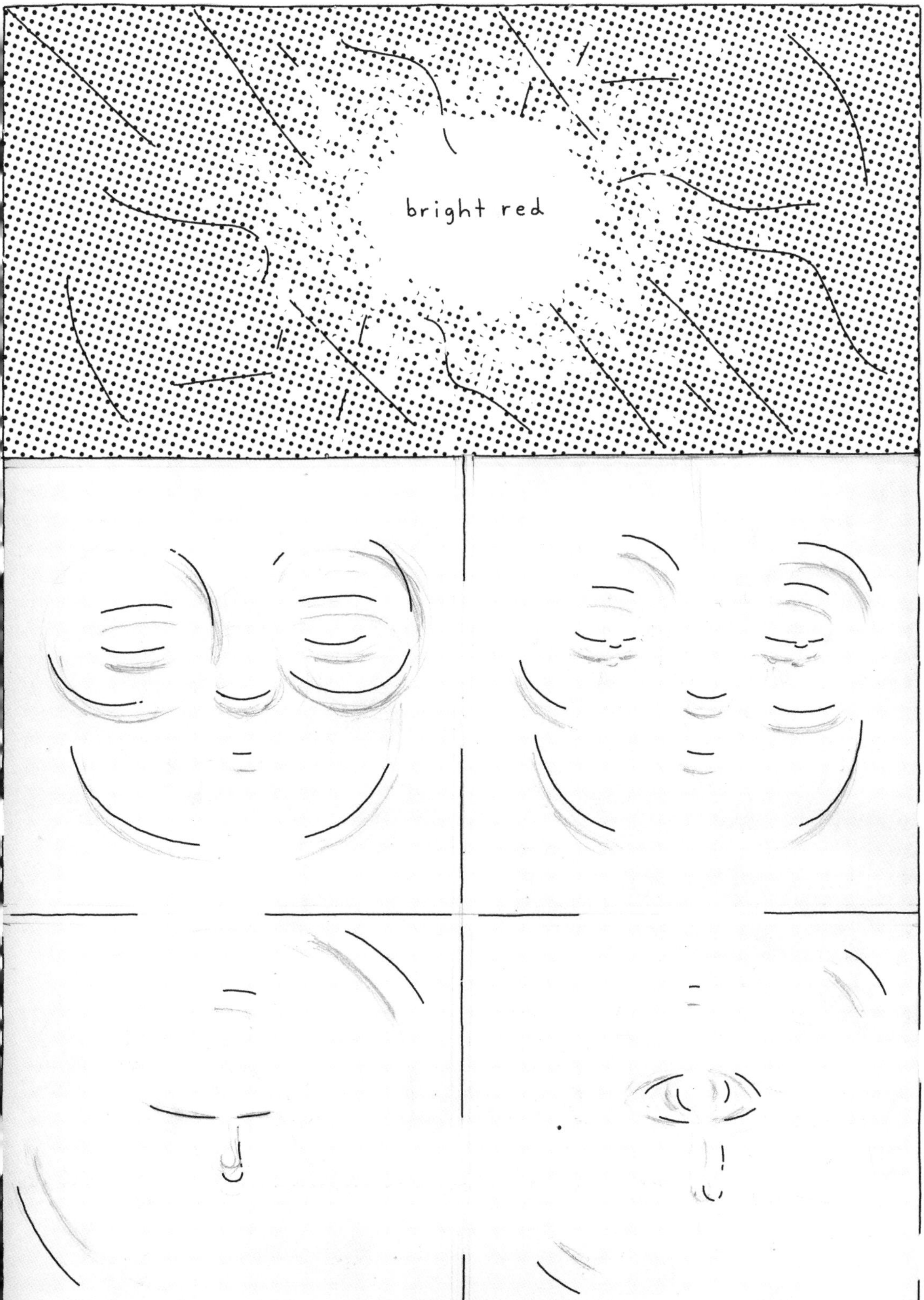
bright red

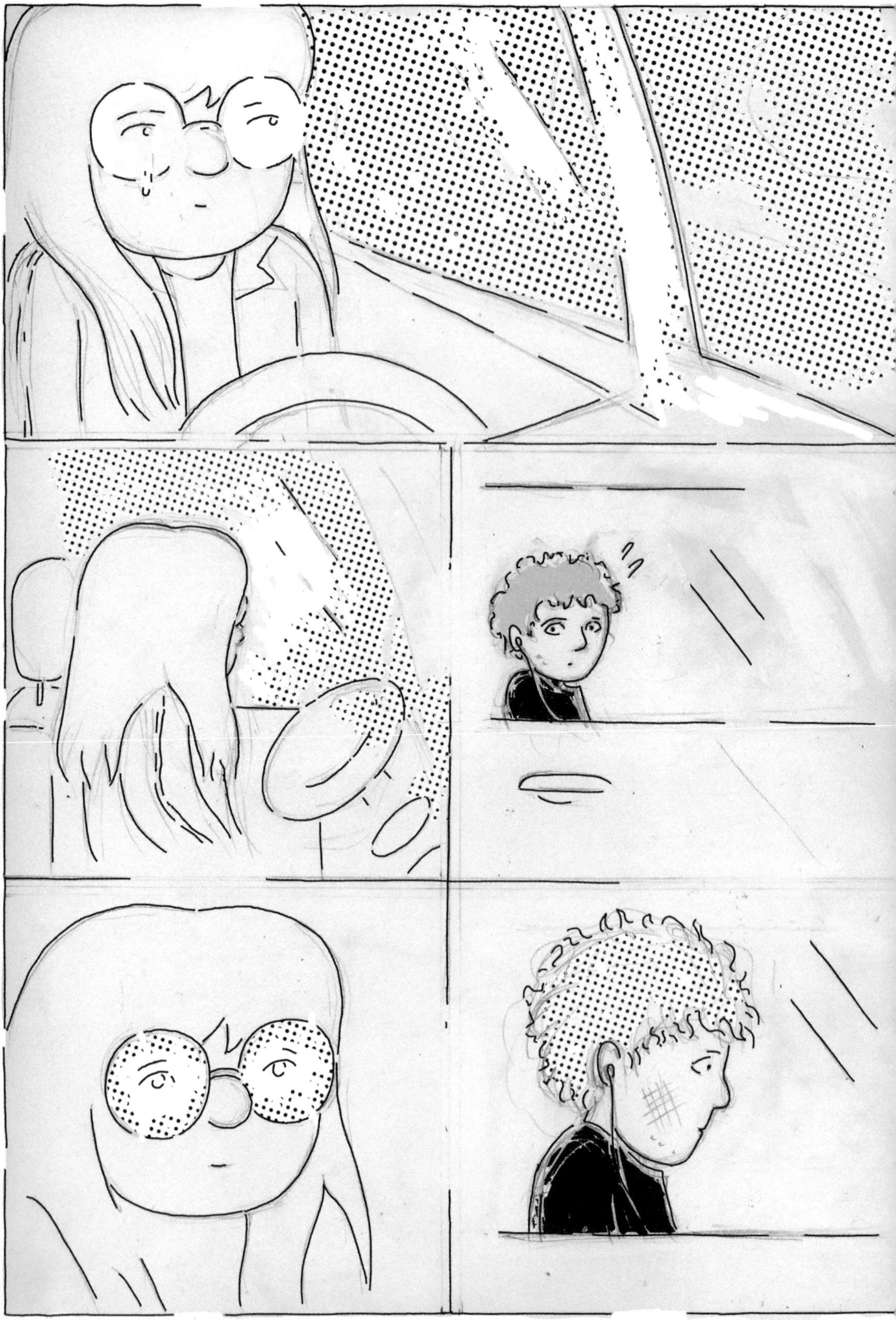

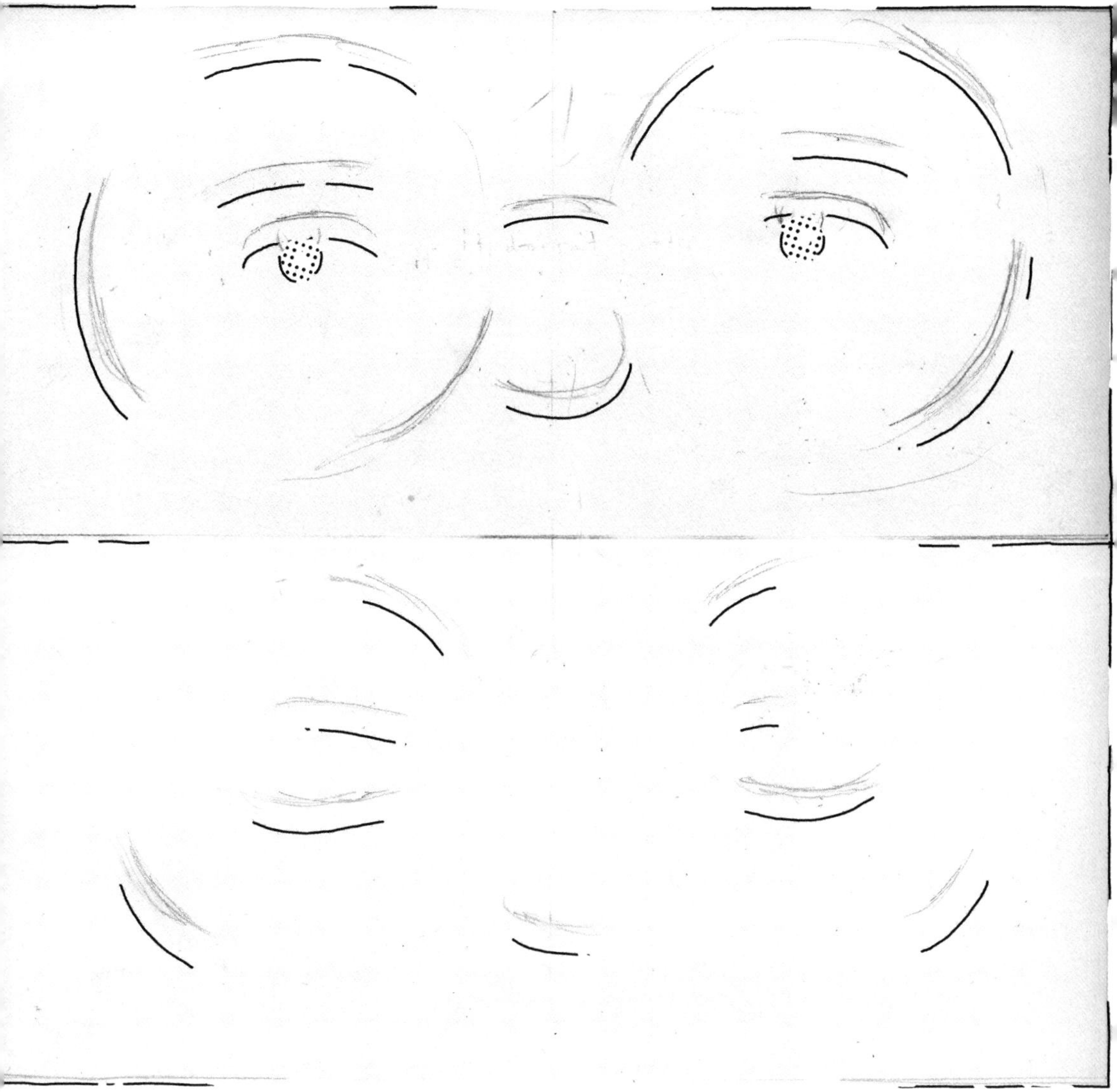

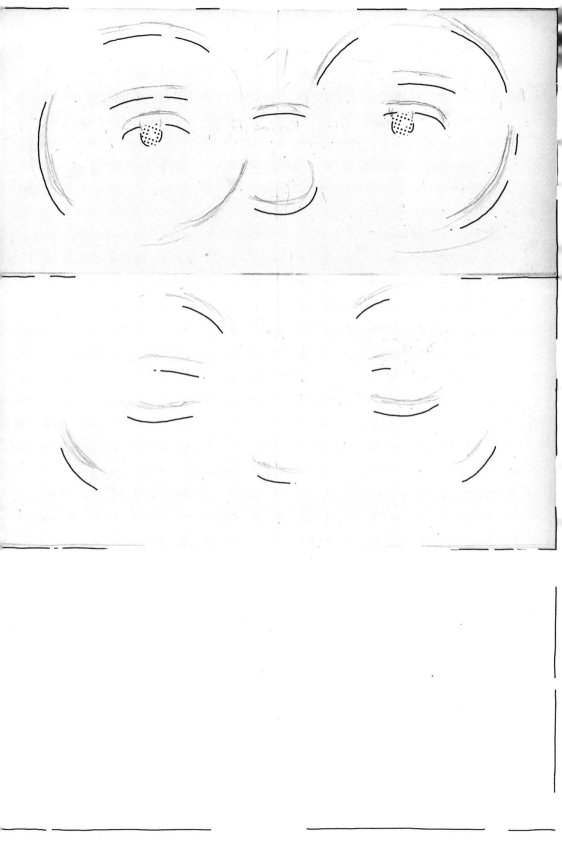

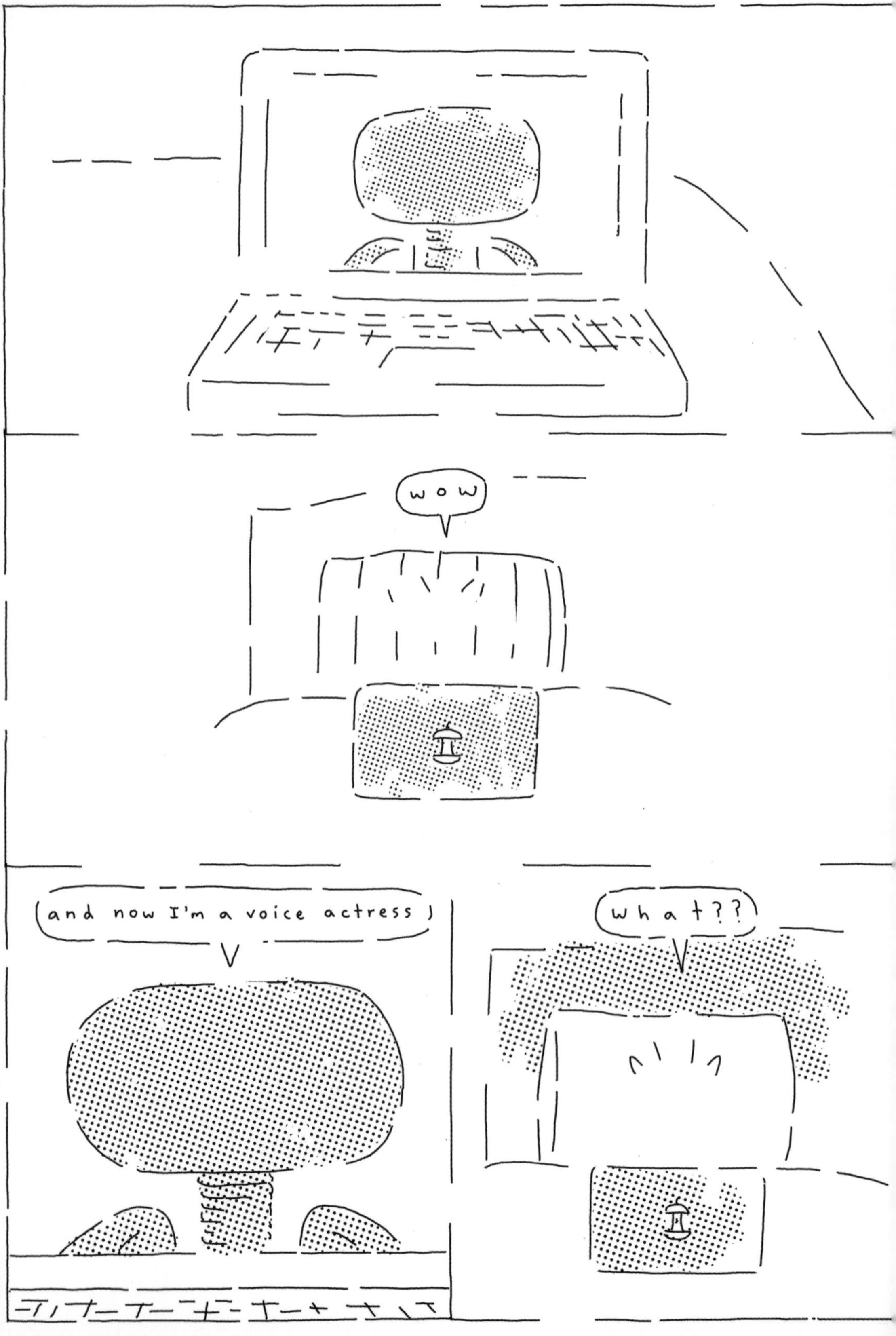
wow
and now I'm a voice actress
what??

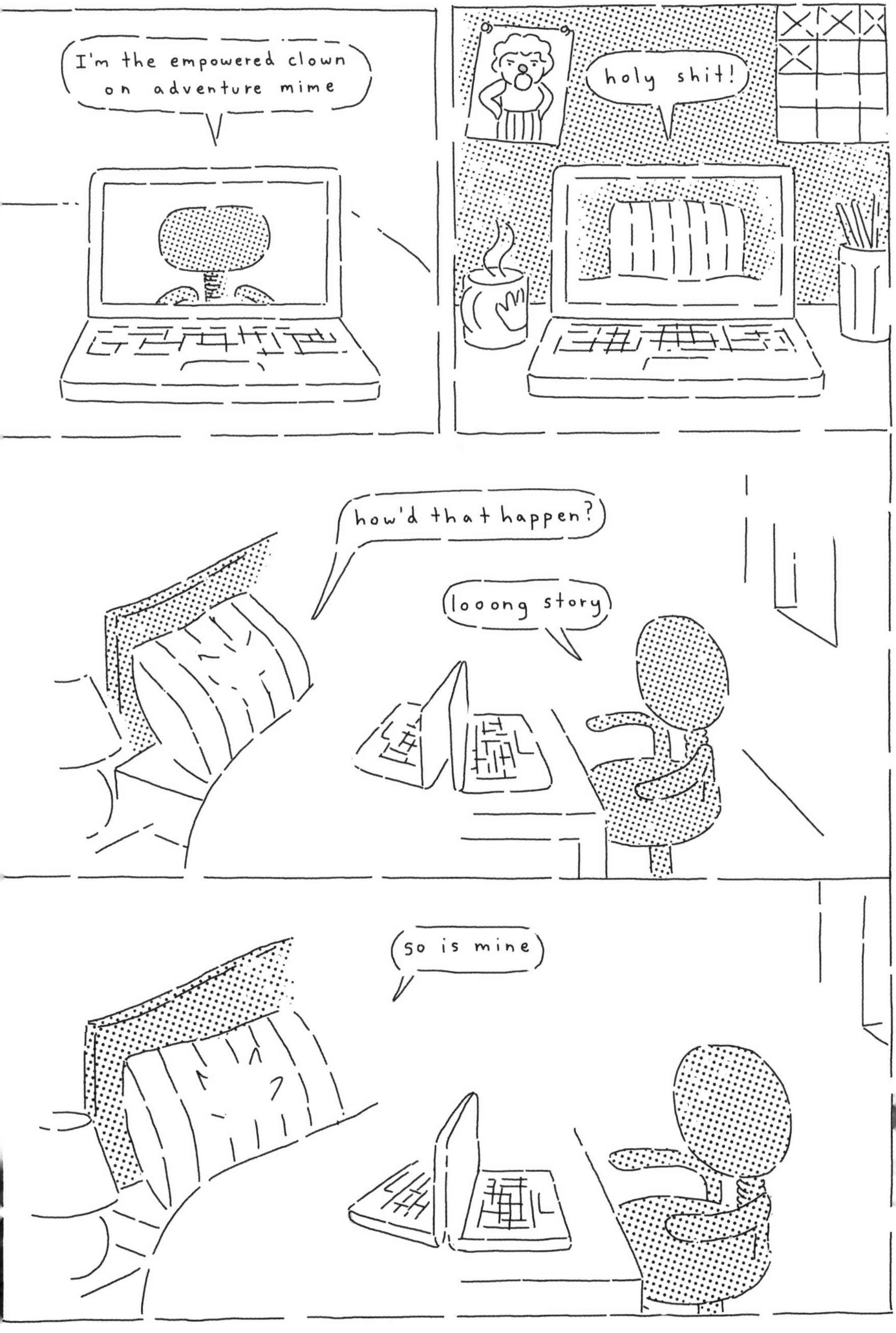
I'm the empowered clown on adventure mime
holy shit!
how'd that happen?
looong story
so is mine

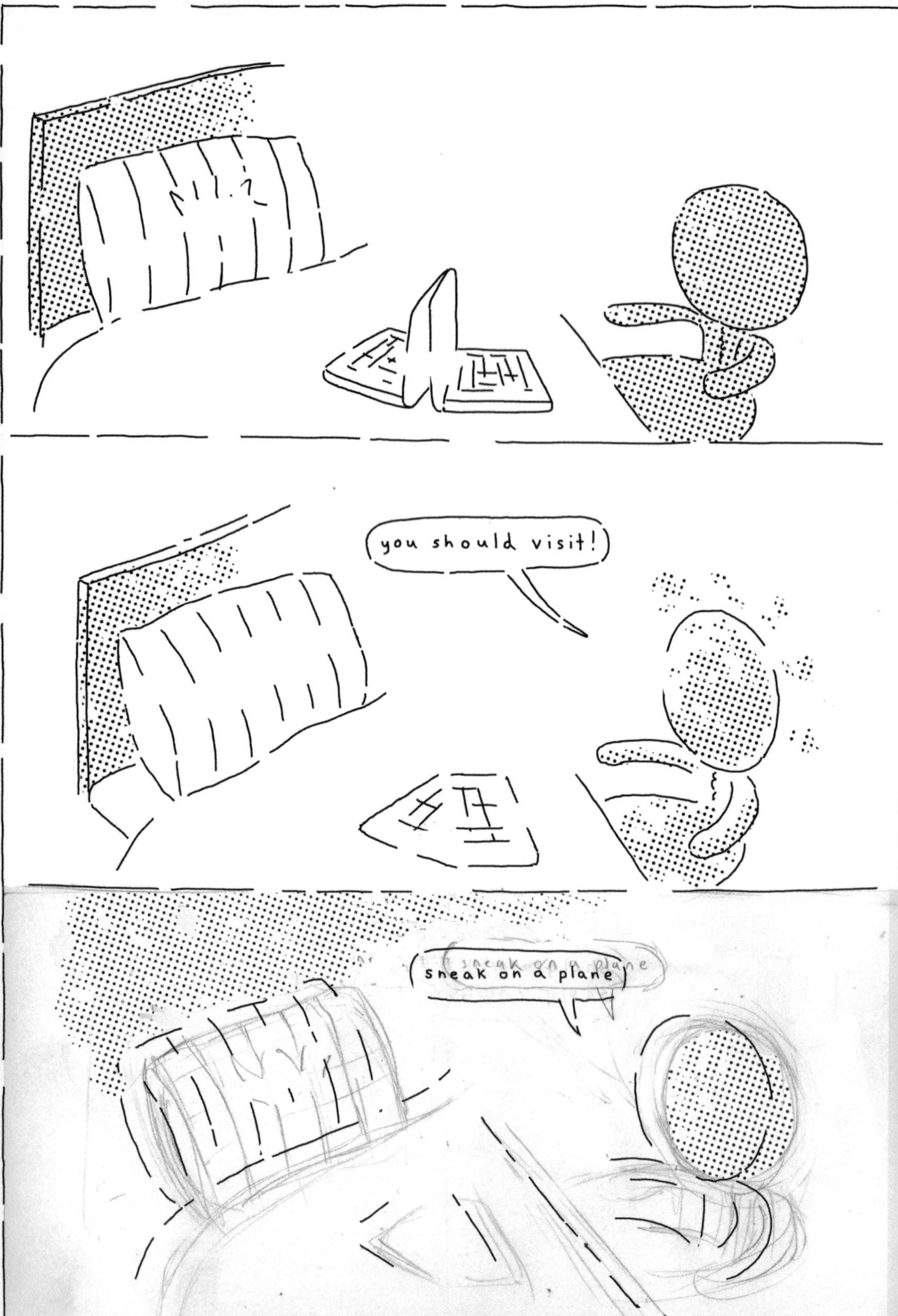
you should visit!
sneak on a plane

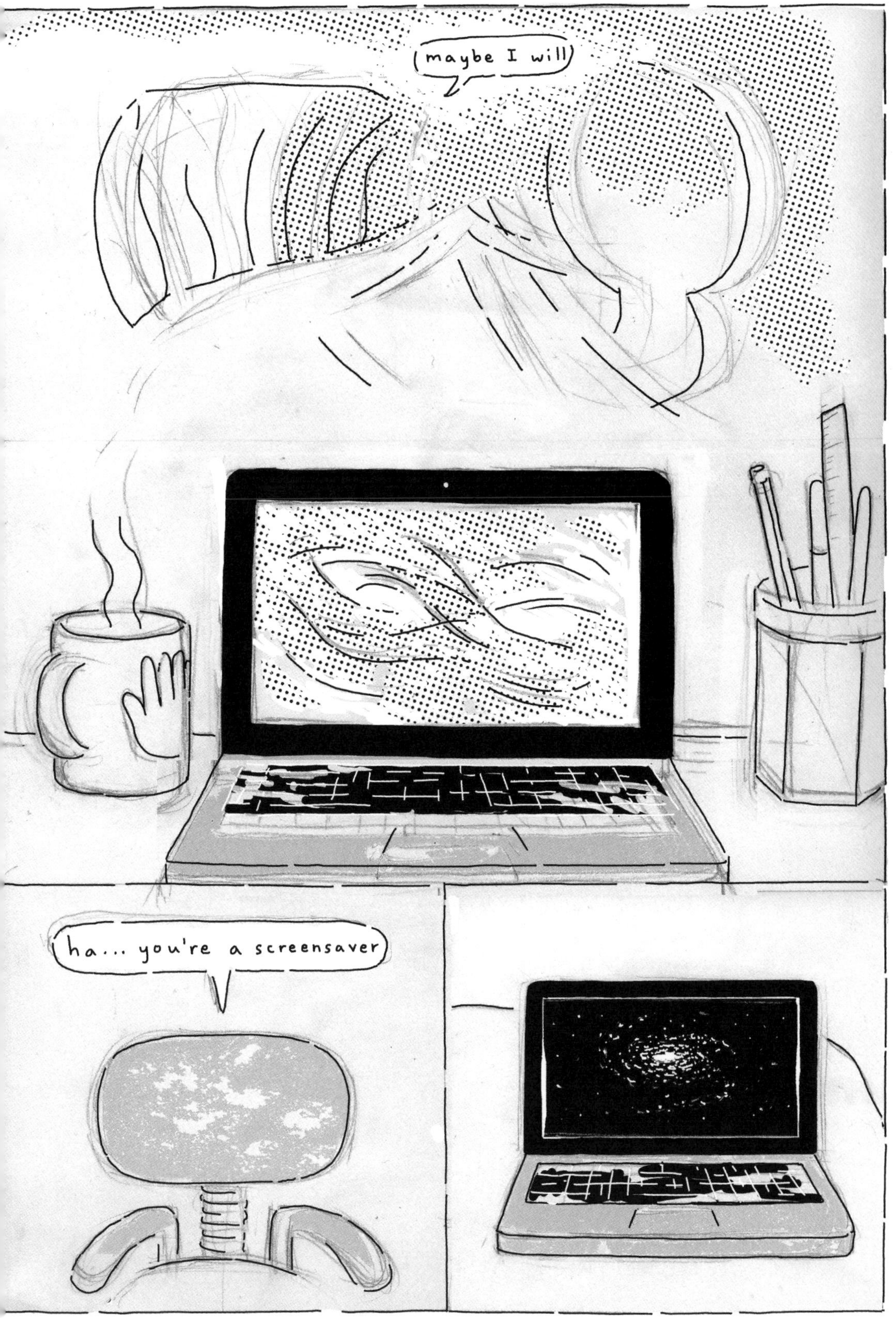
maybe I will
ha... you're a screensaver

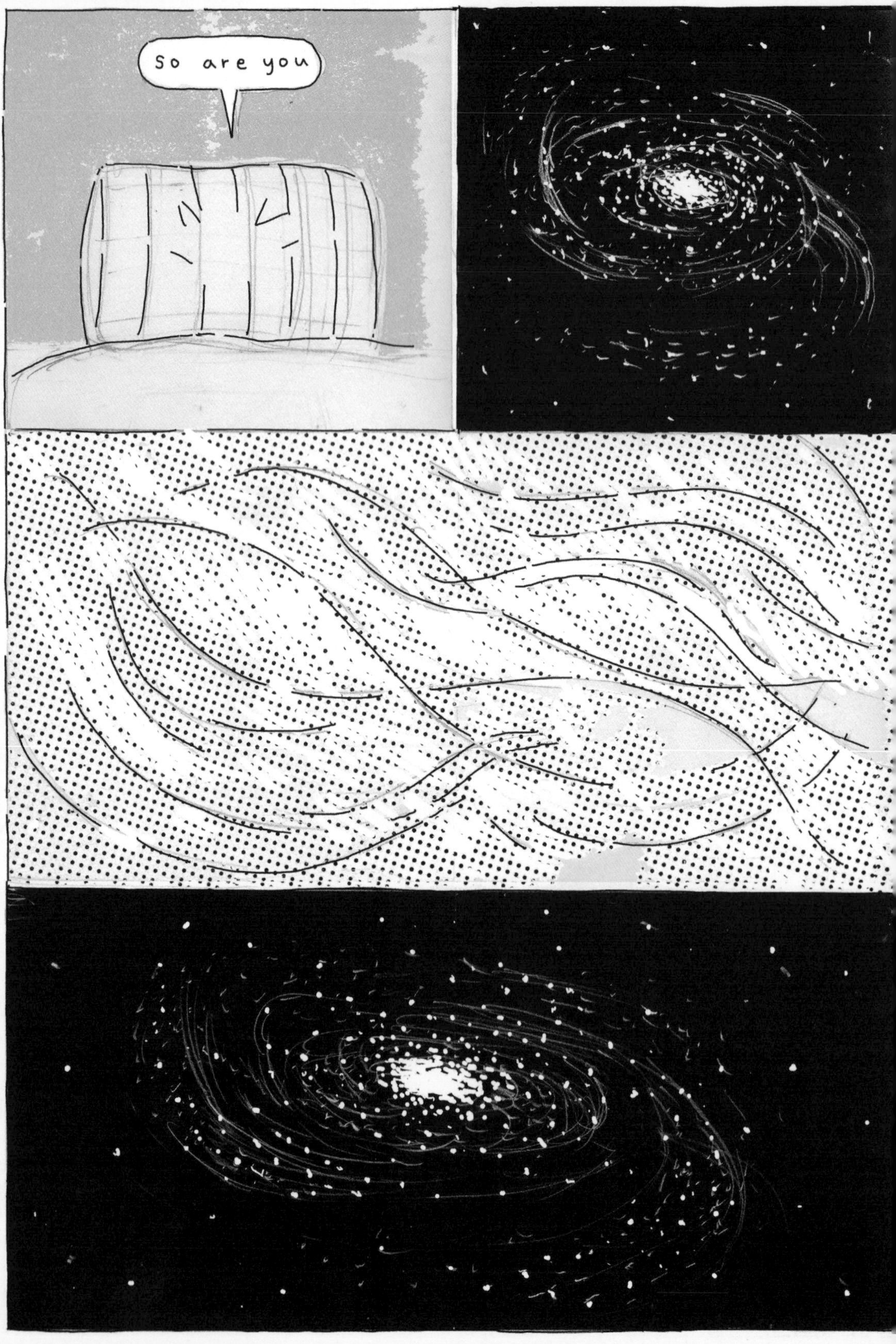
So are you

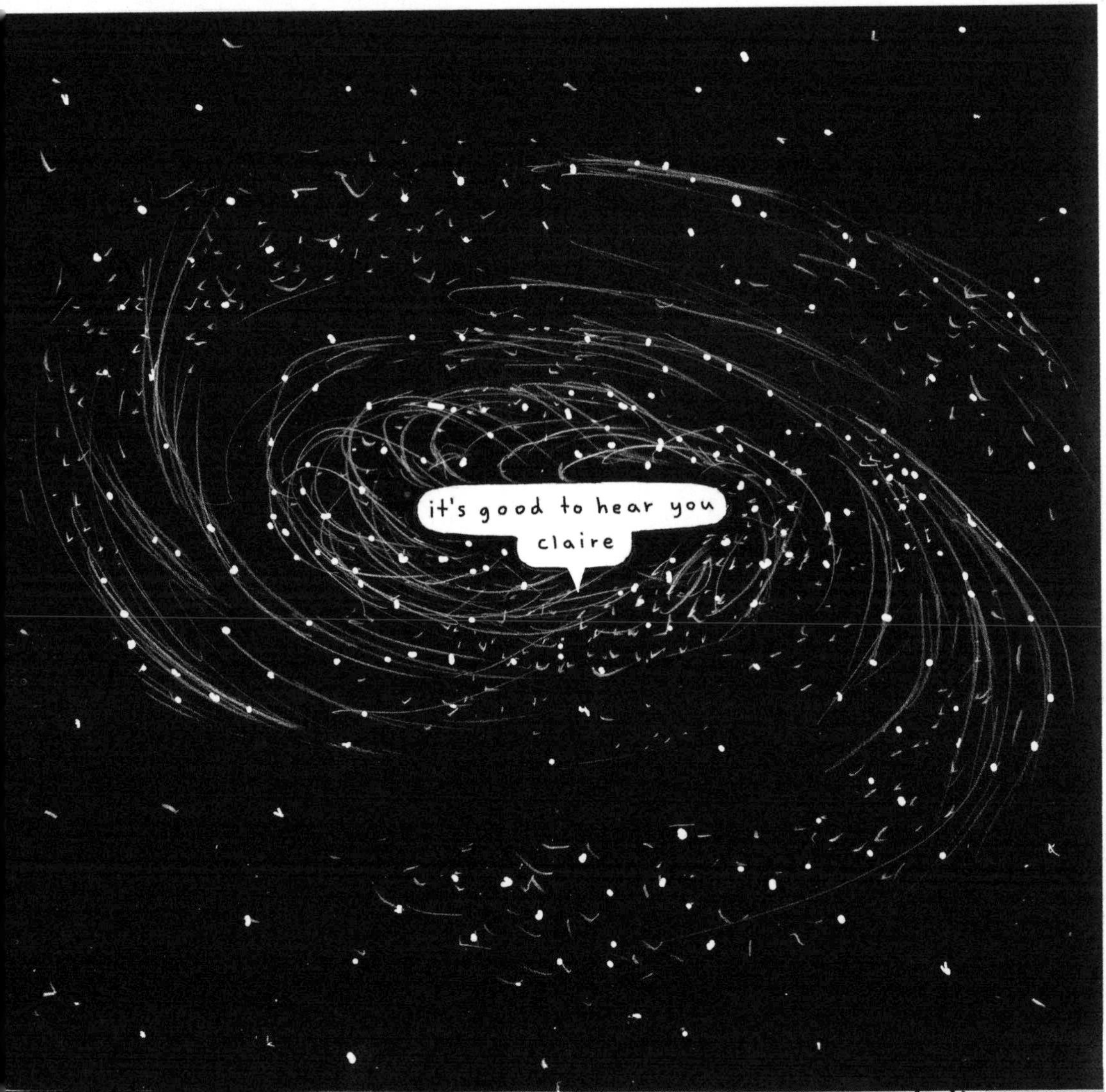
it's good to hear you claire

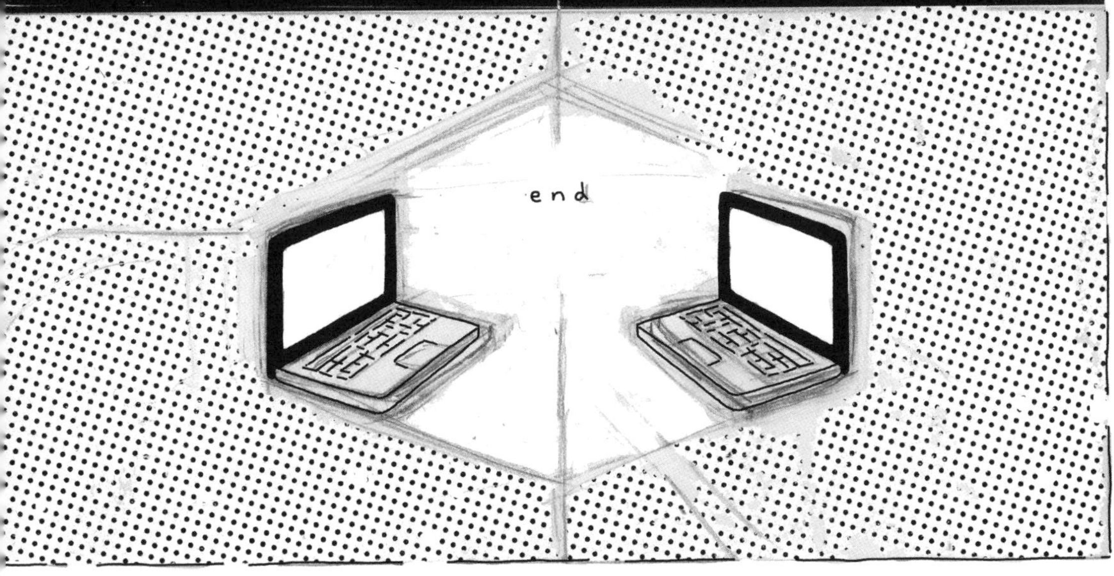
end

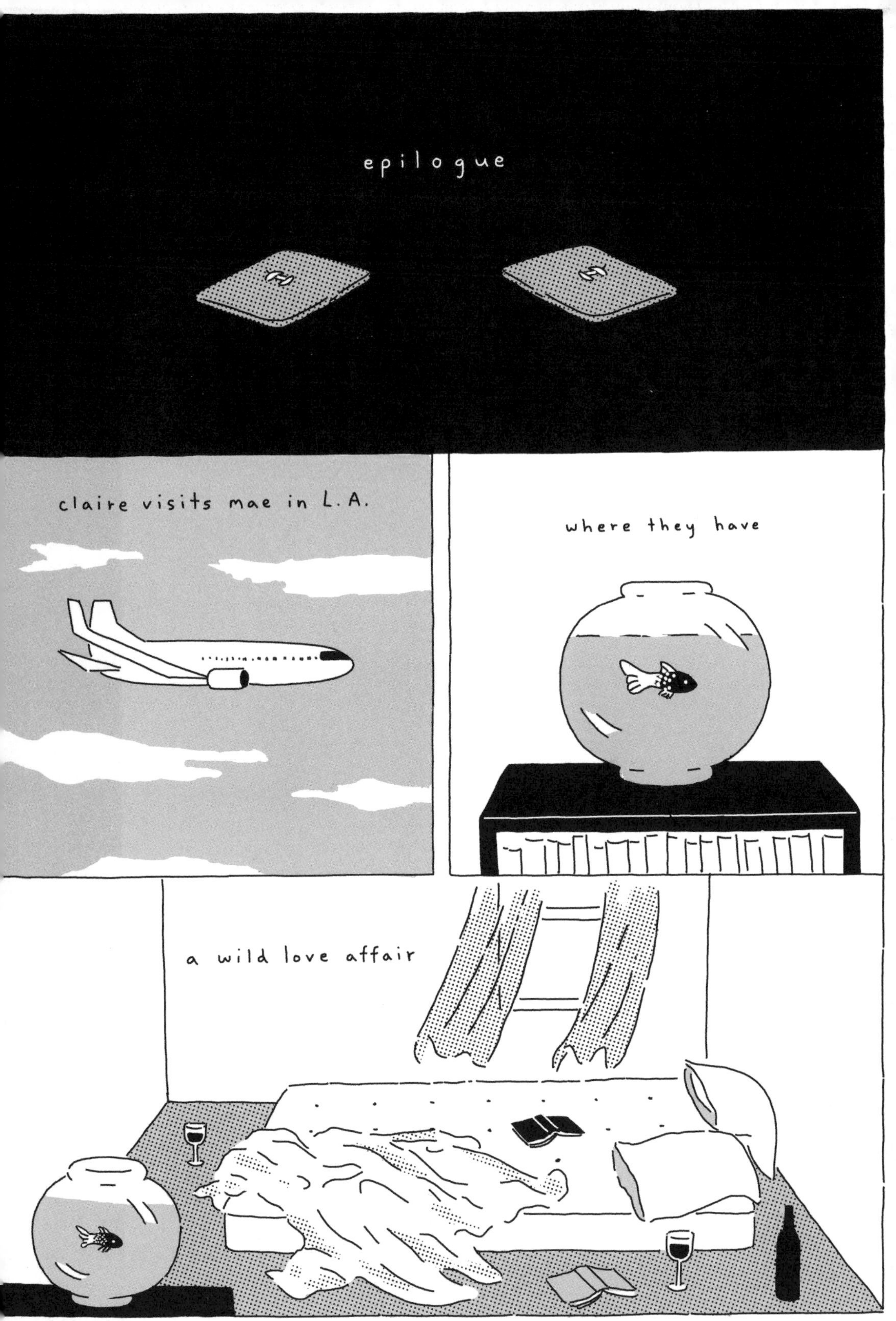
epilogue
claire visits mae in L.A.
where they have
a wild love affair

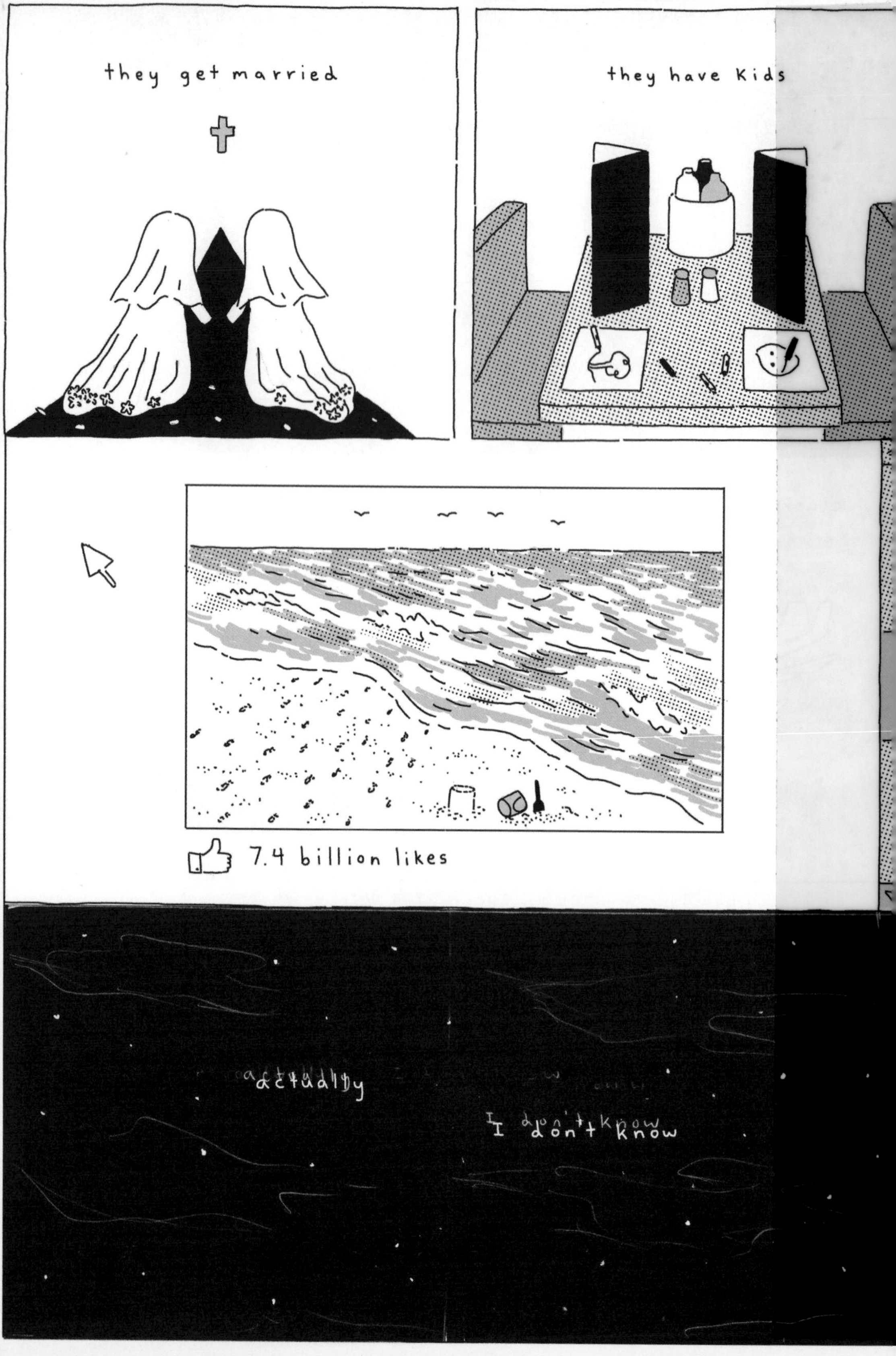
they get married
they have kids
7.4 billion likes
actually
I don't know

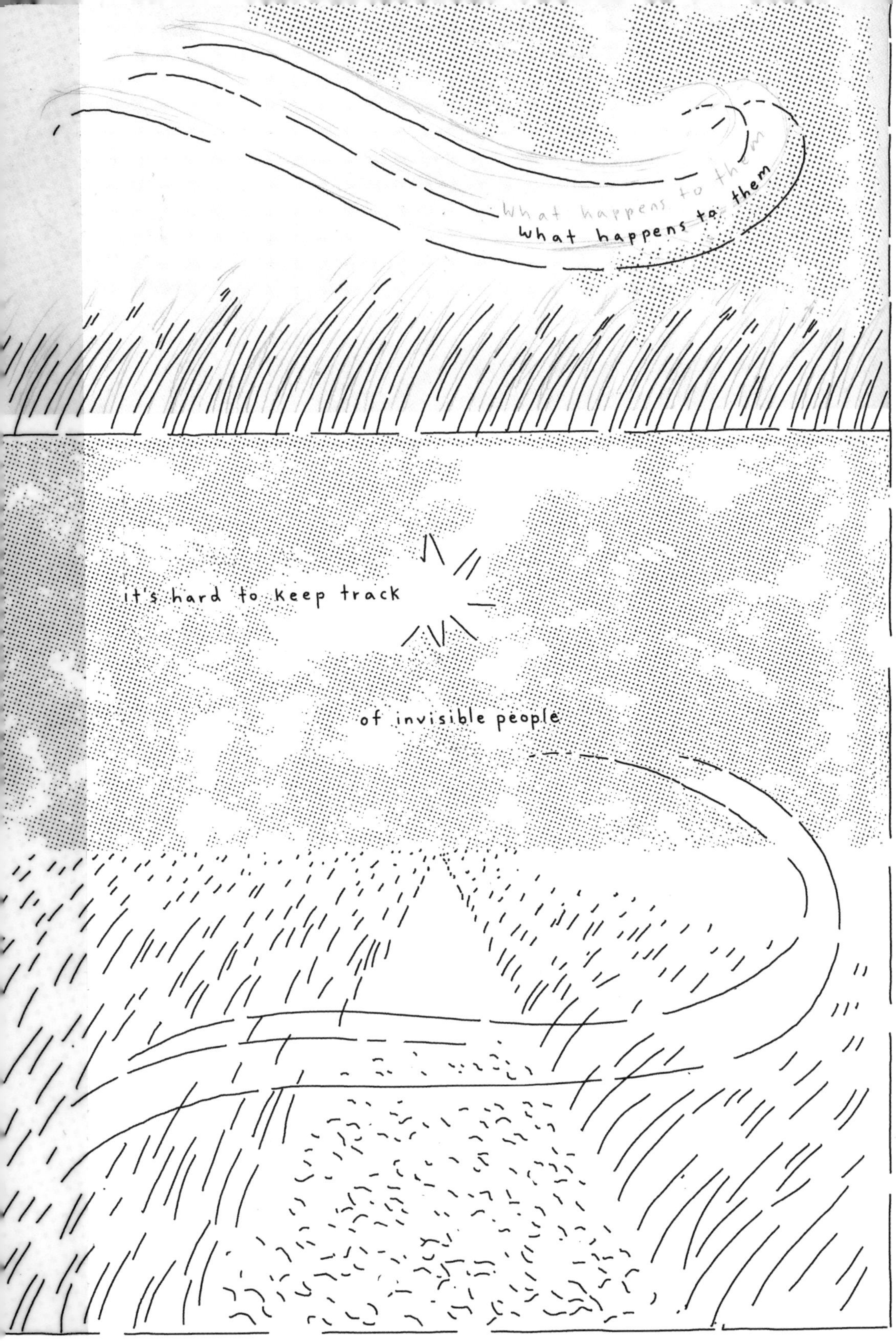
What happens to them
what happens to them
it's hard to keep track
of invisible people